FINANCIAL REGULATION IN CHINA

CRITICAL CONCEPTS IN FINANCE

Other titles in this series:

Entrepreneurial Finance
Edited and with a new introduction by Darek Klonowski
4 volume set

Finance in Asia
Edited and with a new introduction by Qiao Lin, Paul Lejot and Douglas Arner
4 volume set

Finance in Emerging Markets
Edited and with a new introduction by Vihang Errunza
4 volume set

Financial Derivatives
Edited and with a new introduction by David H. Goldenberg
4 volume set

The History of Financial Crises
Edited and with a new introduction by D'Maris Coffman and Larry Neal
4 volume set

Public Borrowing
Edited and with a new introduction by Tehreem Husain and D'Maris Coffman
4 volume set

Infrastructure Finance
Edited and with a new introduction by Roberto Cardinale, Tehreem Husain and D'Maris Coffman
4 volume set

FINANCIAL REGULATION IN CHINA

Critical Concepts in Finance

Edited by Jing Bian

Volume I
Financial Reform and Legal Development

Routledge
Taylor & Francis Group
LONDON AND NEW YORK

First published 2023
by Routledge
4 Park Square, Milton Park, Abingdon, Oxon OX14 4RN

and by Routledge
605 Third Avenue, New York, NY 10158

Routledge is an imprint of the Taylor & Francis Group, an informa business

British Library Cataloguing-in-Publication Data
A catalogue record for this book is available from the British Library

Library of Congress Cataloging-in-Publication Data
A catalog record for this book has been requested

ISBN: 978-1-138-80738-9 (set)
ISBN: 978-1-138-84536-7 (volume I)

Typeset in Times New Roman
by Apex CoVantage, LLC

Publisher's Note
References within each chapter are as they appear in the original complete work

To my late father

CONTENTS

VOLUME I FINANCIAL REFORM AND LEGAL DEVELOPMENT

VOLUME II BANKING SYSTEM: LAWS AND REGULATIONS

VOLUME III SECURITIES MARKET: LAWS AND REGULATIONS

ACKNOWLEDGMENTS

The publishers would like to thank the following for permission to reprint their material:

Taylor & Francis for permission to reprint Ling Chen and Barry Naughton, 'A Dynamic China Model: The Co-Evolution of Economics and Politics in China', *Journal of Contemporary China*, 2017, 26, 103, pp. 18–34.

The Chinese University of Hong Kong Press for permission to reprint Wei Shen and Casey G. Watters, 'Do All Roads Lead to China? Scholarship of Chinese Commercial Law in the Past Decade (Part 1)', *China Review*, 16, 2, 2016, pp. 165–196.

The Chinese University of Hong Kong Press for permission to reprint Wei Shen and Casey G. Watters, 'Do All Roads Lead to China? Scholarship of Chinese Commercial Law in the Past Decade (Part 2)', *China Review*, 16, 3, 2016, pp. 213–237.

ANU Press for permission to reprint Christine Wong, 'An Update on Fiscal Reform', in Ross Garnaut, Ligang Song and Cai Fang (eds.), *China's 40 Years of Reform and Development 1978–2018* (ANU Press, 2018).

The Chinese University of Hong Kong Press for permission to reprint Sanzhu Zhu, 'Implementing China's WTO Commitments in Chinese Financial Services Law', *China Review*, 6, 2, 2006, pp. 3–33.

Disclaimer

INTRODUCTION

The Development of the Chinese Financial Regulation

Jing Bian[1]

The Chinese financial system has gone through an amazing journey, from a mono-banking system to today's multilayered financial market. What are the legal institutions' functions? How do they facilitate the transformation of the financial system? Given today that China's position and influence have fundamental changes, what will China's financial laws and regulations look like in the future? And what are the key features of the legal reforms in the Chinese financial market?

This set of books is aimed at exploring these questions. It illustrates the gains and pains of this unique journey. Furthermore, it will seek to understand the foundation of the future reform of financial regulation in China, given China's global impacts are significantly different from before. Publications are selected based on the development process of financial regulation in China, with a particular focus on the significant events or phenomena in the financial system, as well as its subsequent legal reforms. Therefore, these papers are presented with the following structure: Volume I examines the key issues regarding the general financial reforms and legal development in China. Volume II focuses on the progress of the Chinese banking system. Volume III particularly addresses the issues within the Chinese securities and derivatives markets. Volume IV explores a broad range of topics, which reflect the special features or development of the legal institutions associated with the Chinese financial market.

These papers contained in the books are selected from published academic journal papers, book chapters, and, under special circumstances, policy papers or comments delivered by the financial regulators or partitioners, which related topics are presented together. A particular note to the readers is that, when examining and evaluating these publications, due attention shall be linked to the particular and actual development stages and time periods under which the relevant laws and regulations were set, as the reforms and changes in this field are with a very fast pace. Otherwise, there could be a mismatch with different periods.

Volume I: Financial Reform and Legal Development

Needless to say, the legal institutions to regulate the Chinese financial system cannot be developed without a suitable legal environment in general, in particular those with a focus on the economic aspects. However, a special feature of the Chinese legal system, after the establishment of the new People's Republic of China (hereafter PRC or China) in 1949, was that the previous legal regime established by the Nationalist was abolished while the new legal system was not fully established. There was a number of political campaigns during the first few decades since the establishment of the PRC, such as the Great Leap Forward and the Cultural Revolution, among others. There was also an embargo from some major economies, such as the United States.[2] Although there was a "honeymoon period" between China and the Union of Soviet Socialist Republics (USSR), this relationship was not without splits. Thus, the starting point of the new China was not easy; against this background, the development of an efficient financial system and a regulatory regime was hardly possible.

During this period, there was a mono-banking system. On 1 December 1948, the People's Bank of China (hereafter the PBOC) was established, which later was legally confirmed by the Law of the People's Republic of China on the People's Bank of China as the central bank of China.[3] The PBOC was formed on the consolidation of the Huabei Bank, the Beihai Bank, and the Xibei Farmer Bank.[4] It shall be noted that, under the centralized planned economy before 1978, the need to establish a comprehensive regulatory framework for the financial system was not most prominent. State-owned enterprises (hereafter the SOEs) were the major form of players in the market. Therefore, the financial laws and regulations mainly focused on facilitating the economic activities of the SOEs, as well as providing necessary assistance for the planned economy.

However, there were some attempts to address the deficiencies in the commercial law areas. In **The Establishment and Development of the Chinese Economic Legal System in the Past Sixty Years**, Chen Su reviews China's economic law within a highly centralized planned economic system from 1949 to 1978, the author goes further to examine the economic legal system in the early stage of the reform from 1978 to 1992, following this, a systemic study on the economic legal system under the socialist market system is presented.[5] As identified by the author, in the 1950s, several major economic regulations and rules were formulated, including the Decision on Unifying the State's Financial and Economic Work, Provisional Regulations on Budget and Final Account, Regulations on the Reform of the Financial Administration System, Key Principles of the National Tax Administration, and others.[6] Furthermore, a trial implementation of industrial and commercial tax was carried out in 1973.[7] It is beyond the scope of this Introduction to fully reflect and analyze this model; nonetheless, from the legal perspective, as described by Chen Su, "[o]verall, the economic legal system at this stage fluctuated significantly. It received much attention from 1949 to 1956, was ignored from 1957 to 1961, was on the verge of resumption from 1962 to 1964 and was then abolished from 1965 to 1978."[8]

After the economic reform started, given that economic activities have become more often and diverse, it was crucially important to have the respondent regulatory reforms in China, especially in the commercial law aspects. During this period, the world witnessed the development of the Chinese securities market, future market, bond market, insurance system, and how the mono-banking system evolved into a more comprehensive banking system. Nonetheless, it needs to be noted that, for China, there was a long period during which civil law was not fully established and property rights were not well defined. These had major impacts on the development of the financial market, as the debates around the protection of private rights, for their degree of protection and for their extent of protection, were always there. Therefore, how were the laws and regulations reformed? In **Do All Roads Lead to China? Chinese Commercial Law Scholarship in the Past Decade**, Wei Shen and Casey G. Watters systematically review the development of the scholars' perspectives on Chinese commercial law.[9] Among other issues, the banking and financial sectors' legal reforms are presented, which could provide very helpful guidance for the earlier question. One interesting observation from the authors is that

> Chinese scholars often took a nationalistic approach, primarily assessing laws on their impact on China, whereas non-Chinese scholars advocated the adoption of foreign laws or legal structures to create clear standards and provide certainty for investors, which in turn is believed to facilitate continued growth of the Chinese economy.[10]

From the development model of the Chinese financial system, as well as financial laws and regulations, one should notice the dynamic relationship among the economics, law, and politics in China. In **A Dynamic China Model: The Co-Evolution of Economics and Politics in China**, Ling Chen and Barry Naughton present a close examination on the relationship between economic and political development.[11] The authors have pointed out that China's evolution since 1978 has illustrated the interdependence and the co-evolvement between economic and political developments: "while the economic system has generally evolved toward greater marketization, and the political system towards greater rationality, neither of these developments was linear, nor can either be understood in isolation."[12] Chen and Naughton also have identified that the political and economic systems "each shapes and is shaped by the other."[13]

After understanding some of the key general features of the economic and commercial laws and institutions in China, some more technique topics are presented to the readers in Volume I. The development of corporate law has established a cornerstone for the Chinese financial system. Together with the other mechanisms, such as the confirmation of private property rights, reforming of commercial banking laws and regulations, the securities laws and regulations, and others, Chinese financial legal institutions are gradually formed. Corporate law in China, with an aim to modernize the practice of enterprises, has gone through a number of revisions and amendments. In **China Incorporated: The First Corporation Law of the People's Republic of China**, Robert C. Art and Minkang Gu have introduced the first national corporate law in China.[14] Having examined the relevant contents of this law, the authors have identified this law as a milestone in the development of Chinese ideology and policy, as it "establishes an organizational blueprint that offers great promise for solving China's chronic economic problems and, ultimately, for fully privatizing business."[15] However, the authors also argue that the success of this law would be dependent on the Chinese government's efforts on this regard beyond corporate law itself.[16]

It shall be noted that there were different revisions and amendments to the Chinese Company Law, for instance, a revision in 2005 and amendments in 2013 and 2018. Therefore, to understand Chinese financial laws and regulations, regular updating is required. For Volume I, the 2005 revision was chosen as an example to examine, as it conducted a thorough revision of the previous law. When the time came in 2005, more than a decade after the enactment of the first version of the Company Law, there were substantial changes to its contents to echo the significant shifts in the market's circumstances. In **Introduction to the New Company Law of the People's Republic of China**, Steven M. Dickinson analyses the new company law and its major impacts on doing business in China.[17] In detail the author examines the key changes, such as those on articles of association, capital requirements, limited liability companies, access to corporate information, piercing the corporate veil, third-party loans, legal remedies for improper actions, and more.

In **China's Financial System and the Law**, Franklin Allen and Jun 'QJ' Qian provide a review of China's financial system and the legal regime associated with it.[18] The authors have pointed out how financial markets and intermediaries contribute to the entire financial system and economy varies across countries. Based on this, the authors further examine what has worked and what has not within the two systems in China, as well as their impacts on the entire economy.[19]

One of the key aspects of the financial system reform is fiscal reform. In **An Update on Fiscal Reform**, Christine Wong has presented a review in this aspect, with a particular focus on the post-2014 reforms.[20] The author has pointed out that, during the past 40 years, China has had to entirely rebuild the public finance management (hereafter PFM) system and associated institutions, from the tax system to tax administration and budget management.[21] The author further argues that

> by far the most important step in the fiscal reform package was the rollout of the revised Budget Law in August 2014, which laid the legal foundation for improving the budget process, codifying many aspects of central – local government responsibilities and building a robust system of PFM.[22]

Volume I also presents an important step in the development of Chinese financial laws and institutions, the joining of the World Trade Organization (WTO). In **Implementing China's WTO Commitments in Chinese Financial Services Law**, Sanzhu Zhu examines the implementation of China's commitments to the WTO to further open up its banking, insurance, securities, and auto-financing markets, as well as the relevant reforms in the financial services laws and regulations.[23]

The author analyzes the economic influences that the changes in China's financial services laws and regulations have brought about in order to implement these commitments. In this article, Zhu also projects future changes in China's financial services laws and regulations.

The final paper contained in Volume I, **People's Republic of China Financial Sector Assessment Program Technical Note – Systemic Oversight of Financial Market Infrastructures**, drafted by the World Bank's Monetary and Capital Markets Department and Finance and Markets Global Practice illustrates a review of financial market infrastructures (FMIs) in China.[24] This paper identifies China's landscape for FMIs is "one of the largest and most complex in the world."[25] It further argues that the legal basis for FMIs supervision in China should be further strengthened as the current supervisory framework contains certain potential legal risks.[26]

Volume II: Banking System: Laws and Regulations

Volume II presents the legal development associated with the Chinese banking system. As pointed out earlier, the development of the Chinese banking system, from a mono-banking system to the current multilayered structure, represents the remarkable transformation of the Chinese financial system. This Volume will identify the key issues within this aspect.

In **Regulation of Foreign Bank Access in China**, Zhongfei Zhou addresses the issues associated with the foreign banks' access to China in the 1990s.[27] The author examines the question of how to reach a balance between granting market access/lowering regulatory barriers and the safety and soundness of the banking system. The author argues that

> regulation of foreign bank access with transparent entry standards, adoption of international rules and practice, restricted discretionary authority enjoyed by the PBOC and emphasizing international supervisory cooperation, may provide starting points for safe and sound operation of foreign banks and opportunities for fair competition for different applicants.[28]

As identified in Volume I, China has gone through a transition from a planned economy to a market economy. Despite its successes in many aspects, one issue that occurred in the development process of banking sector is the non-performance loan (hereafter the NPL) problem. In **China's Bank Non-Performing Loan Problem: Seriousness and Causes**, Jianbo Lou examines the seriousness and causes of the NPL problem in China, as well as its negative impacts on state-owned banks and the whole banking system, economic reform, and real economic growth. The author argues that, among other reasons, the failure of market discipline which "implies that lenders penalize excessive borrowing, first, by requiring a higher interest rate spread and, ultimately, by excluding the borrower from the market," has resulted in the huge amounts of NPLs on the balance sheets of Chinese state banks.[29]

In **China and WTO: Moving toward Liberalization in China's Banking Sector**, Wei J Lee addresses the impacts of China's banking industry's accession into the WTO.[30] Among other issues, this paper provides an overview of China's legal framework on banking at that time; in particular, the Central Banking Law and the Commercial Banking Law are examined. Furthermore, this paper discusses the ramifications of the banking laws on China's accession to the WTO. One particularly interesting issue has been raised by the author, as a question that remains is, "What role will legal practitioners have in post-WTO China?"[31] However, the article was published around 2003; today, the current status quo of the Chinese legal practitioners has already answered the question.

One feature of the development of the Chinese banking laws and regulations is incorporating international standards and best practices. However, this is not a simple process of passive incorporation or adaption; it has its Chinese specifics in the application. In **Banking Reform in China: International Standards and Chinese Specifics**, Zdenek Kudrna has reviewed the banking reforms in China from, among others, the implementation of international best practices in bank governance and regulation between 2002 and 2007.[32] Of course, the question as to how to best incorporate international standards and best practice, in order to suit the development of the Chinese banking system, still remains to be further examined, although the author has presented some interesting case studies for the period examined.

When the time entered the third decade of economic reform in China, the financial system had achieved substantial development. Given that this system was evolved from a mono-banking system, a crucial question about which operation model of the financial system China should adopt should be answered. In **Financial Conglomerates in China: Legality, Model and Concerns**, Li Guo has discussed this issue.[33] The author argues that China has gradually relaxed the segregation of financial business and supervision and explored the financial conglomerate operation, as the "recent amendments to the Commercial Bank Law and Securities Law seemed to open the door for financial conglomerate operations."[34] However, after examining the "universal bank" model and the "financial holding company" model, the author suggests that (at the time of the publication), neither of the two models should be embraced hastily in China without a critical review.[35]

Moving forward, the renminbi internationalization became one of the central concerns of the Chinese financial system. In **The Development of Offshore Renminbi**, Jing Bian discusses, at the early stage of the renminbi internationalization, how Chinese government and financial regulators have developed a series of rules and regulations in order to facilitate and supervise this process.[36] Among other issues, the author analyses the function of the PBOC, currency swaps, and offshore renminbi settlement, in this regard. For the further expansion of the renminbi internationalization, the author also argues that "a systemic and comprehensive regulatory regime is needed; in particular, targeted at the new concepts, the new business scope, the new risks and the new functions of the financial regulators."[37]

Another angle that cannot be ignored when examining the Chinese banking system is the shadow banking issue. What are the typical shadow banking activities in China? What is the scale of the shadow banking sector in China? How do the financial laws and regulations address these problems and challenges in this sector? In **Shadow Banking in China: Then and Now**, Chao Xi and Le Xia discuss China's booming shadow banking industry from a regulatory perspective.[38] The authors provide an overall assessment of the status quo of shadow banking; for instance, the forms of shadow banking transactions, the risks, and the regulatory framework. Furthermore, the authors analyze the impacts of the capital adequacy requirements and the liquidity rules on shadow banking activities.

The last two papers selected in Volume II focus on the customer/consumer protection regulation. There is a long discussion on the launch of deposit insurance in China, as since the gradually opening up the Chinese financial sector, the market is facing more risks. How to protect the banking customers effectively? In **Deposit Insurance and Banking Supervision in China: The Agenda Ahead**, Haibo Yan and Ying Huang propose the establishment of a supervisory function in China's deposit insurance.[39] The authors also suggest that "the supervisory responsibilities of the prospective deposit insurance agency in China are to some extent different from those of the existing banking regulatory institution," in order to avoid "overlap in regulation or overuse of regulatory resources."[40] According to the situation around the time when the paper was published, the authors propose that the design of such a system in China should be beyond "a simple 'pay-box,'" given there were different forms of banks in China, the status quo of regulation, risk exposures in bank operations, and the uncertainty of rescuing funds.[41]

Since the economic reform, the size of the retail financial market, as well as the number of the banking consumers, have significantly increased. However, as identified in Volume I, the regulatory regime is not fully established at the same time. So what has happened in the retail market? In **Banking Consumer Protection Regulation in China**, Shuying Wen identifies that China is "in the process of establishing a stricter regime of banking consumer protection."[42] The author further suggests that "an adequate legal framework and effective institutional structure are two inseparable components of effective financial consumer protection regulations."[43] The author also proposes reform suggestions; for instance, the mandate and function of the China Banking Regulatory Commission (hereafter the CBRC) on this aspect shall be made explicit, and the Banking Consumer Protection Department shall be given suitable independence on the selection and allocation of personnel, funds, and other resources, and a consistent regulatory treatment across the financial sector is important.[44]

Volume III: Securities Market: Laws and Regulations

Volume III is aimed at examining the significant issues and developments in the spectrum of Chinese securities laws and regulations. In this volume, readers will be able to enjoy the analysis and assessment of this aspect from a wide range of topics, which all reflect the development of the market itself, as well as the regulatory regime associated.

To examine the laws and regulations in the Chinese securities market, the first Securities Law cannot be overlooked. The operation of the Shanghai Stock Exchange in 1990 and the Shenzhen Stock Exchange in 1991 marks the establishment of the securities market in the PRC. Similar to the banking sector, the regulatory regime of the securities market has gone through a gradual reform as well. In The **First Securities Law of China: An Assessment**, Xian Chu Zhang reviews the early development of this regime and provides an analysis of the first Securities Law in detail.[45] Despite agreeing that this law will "mark the history of a market economy in China with a deep impact," the author also argues that this law is more appropriately considered "as a stepping-stone rather than a cornerstone," as the securities market in China and its regulatory regime "still have a long way to go to be integrated with the international market."[46]

With the development of the Chinese financial system, the derivatives markets have been progressively established. The next two papers collected in Volume III examine the laws and regulations in this aspect. In **Derivative Markets in China: Guest Editors' Introduction**, Berry F. C. Hsu, Lifen Pu, and Sanzhu Zhu review the regulatory framework for derivative markets prior to 2010, which consisted of legislation, rules, and regulations made by the CBRC, the China Securities Regulatory Commission (CSRC), and the guidelines of the Supreme People's Court (hereafter SPC).[47]

Following the lessons learned in the 2008–2009 global financial crisis, China revised the prudential regulation on the derivatives market. In **OTC Derivatives Regulation in China: How Far Across the River?** Mark Hsiao analyses how prudential regulation, supervision of conduct, and requirements to limit risk-taking are employed in the Chinese derivatives market.[48] Among other issues, the author further examines how domestic Chinese law, such as Contract Law 1999 and the Enterprise Bankruptcy Law 2006, could interact with the transplantation of the International Swaps and Derivatives Association (ISDA) Master Agreement 2002. The author also raises an interesting question for the future consideration, as to "how far Chinese authorities would be willing and prepared to cross the river on OTC regulation in order to converge with international practice."[49]

In **Market Solutions to the Information Challenge of China's Legal System: Overseas Listings of State-Owned Enterprises**, Ruoying Chen examines the impacts of a unique market solution, which to list China's SOEs in Hong Kong, and then offerings of securities by these companies in mainland China.[50] The author argues that "China has chosen a purely market-oriented transfer of human capital from entities in matured capital markets to those shaping and operating in China's legal system," which is differs to the "conventional methods" of "management training for legal professionals and officials."[51] The author further identifies the overseas listings have served as an example to illustrate "the existence of institutional competition and the market-oriented solution to the lag between legal developments and the commercial need for compatible and capable legal institutions."[52]

Similar to the banking sector, there have been different reforms in the regulatory regime on Chinese securities market. In **Legal Regulation of China's Securities Markets: Recent Improvements and Competing Advantages**, Tianshu Zhou discusses the reforms of the Securities Law and associated practices.[53] The author argues that there has been a "considerable improvement in the independence and expertise associated with China's judicial system."[54] The author also analyzes some of the key improvements on the formal legislation regulating China's securities market and concludes that it seems "that formal law is important in regulating China's securities markets," when compared with non-legal institutions that require the strong support from civil society.[55]

The reform of the Chinese securities laws and regulations continues. In 2019, a revision was made to the Securities Law, which came into force on 1 March 2020. In **Issuing New Securities in the China Market: Now Easier than Ever?** Xiaoyang Zhang reviews the new changes to this law.[56] The author introduces the newly implemented registration-based go-ahead system, for issuing shares or corporate bonds to the public at China's main stock exchanges. Furthermore, the author argues that "a new landscape is now emerging, heralding a possible escalation of further liberalization of China's financial markets in the near future, a chance to capture to all prospective securities issuers and traders (including foreign firms)."[57] However, this paper also recognizes that this method, namely, fully executing a manageable registration-based Initial Public Offering system, is "still at the stage of testing the water."[58]

The readers who are familiar with the Chinese securities market may have noticed the discussion on the topic of the creation of an international board. In **Reviewing Recent Developments in China's Capital Markets and Assessing the Relevance of the Proposed Shanghai International Board,** Ren-En Lim explores the rationale and progress of this proposal.[59] In reviewing China's plan to establish a multilayered capital market, the author argues that the then proposed Shanghai International Board (or a variation of it) "can be a prudent way to provide increased portfolio diversification options" for the investors and "improve corporate governance of the Chinese capital markets without jeopardizing China's control over capital flow."[60]

China has created the fastest developing venture capital (hereafter the VC) market. What are the key features of this Chinese VC market? How have laws and regulations facilitated the growth of this market? In **Engineering a Venture Capital Market: Lessons from China,** Lin Lin answers these questions, among other issues.[61] This author argues that the Chinese government has played an important role in facilitating the establishment and advancement of the VC market. Furthermore, the author identifies that one of the key features of the Chinese VC market is that it is "created and led by governments, both on central and local levels, through continuous law and policy reforms."[62] However, the author also presents the "various institutional impediments" that may prevent the sector from realizing its real potential.[63]

The final three papers in this volume address litigation and enforcement issues in the Chinese securities market. To echo the arguments presented in Volume II, the number of investors in the securities market has increased substantially; therefore, the channels to provide remedies for them shall be comprehensive, and a systemic disciplinary and punishment system for the wrongdoers shall be established. The three papers address issues in this aspect. In **Civil Litigation Arising from False Statements on China's Securities Market**, Sanzhu Zhu discusses the early development of the civil litigation mechanism against false statements from the securities market, with a particular focus on the three circulars issued by the SPC instructing local people's courts on how to handle civil compensation claims arising from securities market fraud.[64] Zhu identifies that these rules are the "first and important step towards the establishment of a civil litigation and compensation system to address securities fraud cases"; nevertheless, they "fail to surpass its predecessors and transcend their limitations."[65]

The next two papers focus on two different enforcement approaches of the Securities Law, namely, private enforcement and public enforcement. The different angles of discussion will present readers of this set of books with a comprehensive view. In **Private Enforcement of Securities Law in China: A Ten-Year Retrospective and Empirical Assessment**, Robin Hui Huang, based on an empirical study, examines whether private securities litigation has been effectively conducted during the first decade after it was formally permitted by the SPC in 2002.[66] Furthermore, a reform proposal is presented by the author with a focal point that the plaintiffs shall be given the option to "bring securities civil actions before the courts in the locality where the issuer company is listed."[67]

In **An Empirical Analysis of the Public Enforcement of Securities Law in China: Finding the Missing Piece to the Puzzle**, Wenming Xu, Jianwei Chen, and Guangdong Xu empirically investigate the public enforcement regime in China.[68] The authors argue that while the CSRC has limited resources at disposal compared to its counterparts in other jurisdictions; nonetheless, the public enforcers have significantly increased their outputs since 2011, after the CSRC delegated the authorities to issue administrative sanctions over minor cases to its regional offices.[69] However, the authors identifies that "the securities law is still taken as an ineffective weapon by harmed investors."

Volume IV: Special Topics

One amazing feature of the Chinese financial system is its creativity, such as the fintech sector. Furthermore, the fast evolution and the quick development of the various financial services can provide readers of the books with diverse subjects to examine. In Volume IV, topics cover the legal framework on insurance, trust, fintech, and sustainable finance, among others.

In line with the banking and capital market, the insurance sector in China has gained substantial development. In terms of the regulatory framework, a national Insurance Law was first enacted in 1995, and the Chinese Insurance Regulatory

Commission (hereafter the CIRC) was established in 1998 until its termination in 2018, which led to the creation of the China Banking and Insurance Regulatory Commission (hereafter the CBIRC).[70] The first two papers collected in Volume IV examine the issues, as well as laws and regulations in this sector. In **The Role and Powers of the Chinese Insurance Regulatory Commission in the Administration of Insurance Law in China**, Jeffrey E. Thomas analyses the role and powers of the then CIRC in the administration of the national Insurance Law of China.[71] This paper reviews the law and the CIRC's administrative powers, particularly under an appropriate legal and cultural context. The author also addresses the impacts of the accession to the WTO on China's insurance system.

Following this, a paper focusing on a unique angle to explore the insurance sector is collected in Volume IV, to present the readers with a detailed example. In **Insurance Plus Futures: Agricultural Commodity Price Reform in China,** Tristan Kenderdine examines the Insurance Plus Futures policy pilot in agriculture price reform and the relevant institutions.[72] The author identifies this policy pilot as "a leading indicator of reform in China's agricultural production and rural finance architecture."[73] Among other issues, this paper examines the government-mandated agricultural insurance as a mechanism "to cover the subsidy previously served by the minimum purchase price system" and evaluates "the prospects for institutional development of futures contracts, commodities exchanges and price formation institutions in China."[74]

Similar to some other non-Chinese legal traditions, the concept of trust has gained recognition in China, with the development of the economy. However, the development of the regulatory framework on trust has taken some time. The next two papers in this volume illustrate this evolvement process. In **Conceptualizing the Chinese Trust,** Rebecca Lee examines the initial and subsequent early development of the trust law in China.[75] The author also conducts a comparative analysis between the Chinese and English trust concepts. The author argues that, in the process of "transplanting the English trust institution to a civilian jurisdiction by the stroke of a legislative pen, China seems to have overlooked the technical difficulties of explaining the location of the trust property and the nature of the beneficiary's rights."[76]

In **Modernizing Chinese Trust Law,** Stephen Tensmeyer addresses the issue of how trust can be used to benefit small-scale civil matters.[77] The author presents an examination on the Chinese trust law and regulations, investigates the potential possibility of family and collective trusts for disabled beneficiaries, as the author argues that "the government has designed regulations for sophisticated financial institutions that provide investment funds known as 'trusts', and yet these regulations may apply to many other arrangements that fall under the name 'trust', or in Chinese, 信托 (xintuo)."[78] This paper also suggests future reforms for "at least three types of trusts that need to be distinguished and facilitated: commercial trusts, pooled civil trusts, and individual civil/family trusts."[79]

The next paper in Volume IV is aimed at exploring the Chinese financial leasing industry, which was launched during the 1980s. This sector has gained fast growth in China and serves as an important approach for raising capital. In **An Overview of the Development of the Financial Leasing Law in China,** Shiyuan Han and Wensheng Wang analyze the development of the financial leasing industry and provide an assessment of the laws and regulations in this regard, which include the transactional law, accounting law, tax law, and China's participation in UNIDROIT'S work on leasing, among others.[80] The authors also discuss the relevant cases in this field. The authors conclude that although "much has been achieved" in the financial leasing arena, "yet in practice there are still many shortcomings, both in terms of the rules themselves and of the relevant knowledge and know-how of dealers, judges and academia."[81]

Having read the previous Volumes, readers of this set of books shall be very familiar with the pilot approach employed by the Chinese regulatory framework. These pilot schemes, as the testing points within the different sectors of the Chinese financial system, have provided very valuable experiments and experiences for the subsequent development and reforms. In **Financial Reforms in Shanghai Free Trade Zone,** Liang Tao provides the readers with a detailed example.[82] The author explains the rationale behind the design of the Shanghai Free Trade Zone (hereafter the Shanghai FTZ), and identifies it as "a testing ground for future economic and financial reforms nationwide, especially in the fields of investment liberalization, financial reform, free trade in goods, and exchange rate reform."[83] The author introduces the governing rules in Shanghai FTZ and points out the key reforms, such as seasoning requirements for foreign-invested banks removed, capital requirements for certain financial leasing companies lifted, and wholly foreign-owned health insurer permitted, among others.[84]

One sector that demonstrates the creativity of the Chinese financial system is fintech. From a "cash economy" to today being one of the biggest fintech markets in the world, what is behind this amazing journey? How is this market regulated? In Volume IV, two papers are selected to reflect these points of view. In **The New Battle Field – An Analysis of the Payment Systems in China,** Jing Bian and Frank Marchione review the early development of the fintech payment systems and the associated regulatory framework in China.[85] The authors discuss the key infrastructure of the Chinese payment system, and present the growth of the non-financial-institution payment providers, including the key players in this market. Based on an analysis of the relevant law and regulatory approaches, the authors identify the key problems within this area and suggest some further reform proposals.

The second paper on Fintech collected in Volume IV examines the more recent regulatory approaches to the fintech industry. In **Legal Governance on Fintech Risks: Effects and Lessons from China**, Kang Yuan and Duoqi Xu identify risks associated with the fintech sector in China and explore the different regulatory measures.[86] The authors argue that "China's legal governance on fintech risks has been swinging between the paths of suppressive, indulging, and adaptive regulation."[87] The authors also suggest the vital importance of the fintech-risk law, the local resources, and exploring the intervening path "with more proactivity, foresight, and refined characteristics."[88]

In recent years, China has put great effort into promoting sustainable and green finance. The environmental, social, and governance consideration has become a key factor for the future sustainable development. Some significant progress has been made. In **Sustainable Finance & China's Green Credit Reforms: A Test Case for Bank Monitoring of Environmental Risk,** Virginia Harper Ho offers insight into the Chinese perspective of this issue.[89] Based on an analysis that uses data for 2012 through 2017 from the annual reports and sustainability reports of the 21 Chinese banks, as well as data from fieldwork conducted in 2016 and 2017, the author concludes that "the scale of green credit issued by China's largest banks has increased exponentially in recent years" and that "the green finance policies adopted by the CBIRC and other regulators are motivating top-tier financial institutions to implement environmental and social credit risk monitoring systems."[90] Furthermore, the author also points out the lessons learned from China, that the "real costs and capacity constraints can impede banks' ability to measure and monitor environmental risk," even under the Chinese context.[91]

The final paper of Volume IV, as well as the whole set, looks at the dispute resolution issue in the financial market. The Chinese financial system is moving toward a more sophisticated operational model. As a natural consequence, the level of complexity has been increased substantially. Therefore, an efficient dispute resolution mechanism is a must for the healthy development of the market. In **Financial Dispute Resolution in China: Arbitration or Court Litigation?** Shahla Ali and Hui Huang explore the possibility of the sound dispute resolution system.[92] The authors compare how the national arbitration commissions (such as the financial dispute-resolution mechanisms of the China International Economic and Trade Arbitration Commission (CIETAC) and specialized financial courts (such as the Shanghai Financial Trial Division) in China respond to the challenges resulting from the increase in the number of banking-related disputes.[93] The authors also suggest the long-term benefits of strengthening of national mechanisms such as CIETAC and self-regulatory financial dispute-resolution schemes, which "will provide additional avenues of recourse beyond the courts."[94]

Concluding Remarks

This set of books provides insight into how China developed its financial system and the associated legal institutions in the past few decades. As identified by the selected papers, challenges don't merely come from the economic and legal perspectives but also from the social and political aspects, don't merely come from the insufficient institutional supply to the classical financial operation model but also from the fast innovation of this financial industry, and don't merely come from internal but also from external.

Nonetheless, it is clear that the Chinese financial system cannot achieve its growth aim without a sound regulatory regime. And, the story of the legal reform continues.

Notes

1 Jing Bian would like to thank all the support from Routledge and the book editor, Mr. Simon Alexander. Jing Bian would like to thank all the experts, colleagues, friends, and family members who support the idea and the progress of the books. Special appreciation is also given to the European Institute for Chinese Studies, where I was a residential fellow.

2 Cain, F. America's trade embargo against China and the East in the Cold War Years. *J Transatl Stud* 18, 19–35 (2020). https://doi.org/10.1057/s42738-019-00037-7

3 See PBOC website, Purposes and Functions (pbc.gov.cn), last accessed: 11 July 2021. Law of the People's Republic of China on the People's Bank of China, promulgated date: 18 March 1995, effective date: 18 March 1995.

4 Ibid.

5 Chen Su, 'The Establishment and Development of the Chinese Economic Legal System in the Past Sixty Years'.

6 Ibid.

7 Ibid.

8 Ibid.

9 Wei Shen, Casey G. Watters, 'Do All Roads Lead to China? Chinese Commercial Law Scholarship in the Past Decade (Part 1)', *China Review* 16, 2, 2016, 165–196.

10 Ibid.

11 Ling Chen, Barry Naughton, 'A Dynamic China Model: the Co-Evolution of Economics and Politics in China', *Journal of Contemporary China* 26, 103, 2017, 18–34.

12 Ibid.

13 Ibid.

14 Robert C Art, Minkang Gu, 'China Incorporated: The First Corporation Law of the People's Republic of China', *Yale Journal of International* Law 20, 2, 1995, 273.

15 Ibid.

16 Ibid.

17 Steven M. Dickinson, 'Introduction to the New Company Law of the People's Republic of China', *Pacific Rim Law & Policy Journal* 16, 1, 2007, 1–12.

18 Franklin Allen, Jun 'QJ' Qian, 'China's Financial System and the Law', *Cornell International Law Journal* 47, 3, 2014, 499–554.

19 Ibid.

20 Christine Wong, 'An Update on Fiscal Reform', *China's 40 Years of Reform and Development 1978–2018*, 2018, 271.

21 Ibid. See also, Wong, C. and Bird, R. (2008), China's Fiscal System: A Work in Progress, in L. Brandt and T. Rawski (eds), China's Great Transformation: Origins, Mechanism and Consequences of the Post-Reform Economic Boom, New York: Cambridge University Press. Wong, C. (2013b), Reforming China's public finances for long-term growth, in R. Garnaut, C. Fang and L. Song (eds), China: A new model for growth and development, Canberra: ANU E Press. doi.org/10.22459/CNMGD.07.2013.10.

22 Ibid.

23 Sanzhu Zhu, 'Implementing China's WTO Commitments in Chinese Financial Services Law', China *Review* 6, 2, 2006, 3–33.

24 Monetary and Capital Markets Department, and Finance and Markets Global Practice, World Bank, 'People's Republic of China Financial Sector Assessment Program Technical Note Systemic Oversight of Financial Market Infrastructures', 2017.
25 Ibid.
26 Ibid.
27 Wei J Lee, 'China and WTO: Moving toward Liberalization in China's Banking Sector', *DePaul Business & Commercial Law Journal* 1, 3, 2003, 481–508.
28 Ibid.
29 Zhongfei Zhou, 'Regulation of Foreign Bank Access in China', *Yearbook of International Financial and Economic Law* 3, 1998, 431–504.
30 Ibid.
31 Jianbo Lou, 'China's Bank Non-Performing Loan Problem: Seriousness and Causes', *The International Lawyer* 34, 4, 2000, 1147–1192.
32 Zdenek Kudrna, 'Banking reform in China: International standards and Chinese specifics', *Acta* Oeconomica *58, 4*, 2008, 403–426.
33 Li Guo, 'Financial Conglomerates in China: Legality, Model and Concerns', *Peking University Journal of Legal Studies* 1, 2008, 255.
34 Ibid.
35 Ibid.
36 Jing Bian, 'The Development of Offshore Renminbi', *Journal of International Banking Law & Regulation* 30, 1, 2015, 13–22.
37 Ibid.
38 Chao Xi, Le Xia, 'Shadow Banking in China: Then and Now Part 2', *Journal of Banking and Finance Law and Practice* 28, 2017, 146–157.
39 Haibo Yan, Ying Huang, 'Deposit Insurance and Banking Supervision in China: The Agenda Ahead', The Geneva Papers, 33, 2008, 547–565.
40 Ibid.
41 Ibid.
42 Shuying Wen, 'Banking Consumer Protection Regulation in China', *Hong Kong Law Journal* 46, 2, 2016, 599–620.
43 Ibid.
44 Ibid.
45 Xian Chu Zhang, 'The First Securities Law of China: An Assessment', *Yearbook of International Financial and Economic Law* 3, 1998, 595–636.
46 Ibid.
47 Berry F. C. Hsu, Lifen Pu, Sanzhu Zhu, 'Derivative Markets in China: Guest Editors' Introduction', *Chinese Law and Government* 43, 4, 2010, 3–11.
48 Mark Hsiao, 'OTC Derivatives Regulation in China: How Far Across the River?', *Journal of Banking and Finance Law and Practice* 25, 1, 2014, 14–25.
49 Ibid.
50 Ruoying Chen, 'Market Solutions to the Information Challenge of China's Legal System: Overseas Listings of State-Owned Enterprises', Peking University Law Journal 1, no. 1, 2013: 133–162.
51 Ibid.
52 Ibid.
53 Tianshu Zhou, 'Legal Regulation of China's Securities Markets: Recent Improvements and Competing Advantages', *Economics and Regulation in China,* 2014, 63–84.
54 Ibid.
55 Ibid.
56 Xiaoyang Zhang, 'Issuing New Securities in the China Market: Now Easier than Ever?', *International Company and Commercial Law Review 31*, 10, 2020, 559–563.
57 Ibid.

58 Ibid.
59 Ren-En Lim, 'Reviewing Recent Developments in China's Capital Markets and Assessing the Relevance of the Proposed Shanghai International Board', *Capital Markets Law Journal* 12, 1, 2017, 78–93.
60 Ibid.
61 Lin Lin, 'Engineering a Venture Capital Market: Lessons from China', *Columbia Journal of Asian Law* 30, 2, 2017, 160–22.
62 Ibid.
63 Ibid.
64 Sanzhu Zhu, 'Civil Litigation Arising from False Statements on China's Securities Market', *North Carolina Journal of International Law and Commercial Regulation* 31, 2005, 377.
65 Ibid.
66 Robin Hui Huang, 'Private Enforcement of Securities Law in China: A Ten-Year Retrospective and Empirical Assessment', *The American Journal of Comparative Law* 61, 4, 2013, 757–798.
67 Ibid.
68 Wenming Xu, Jianwei Chen, Guangdong Xu, 'An Empirical Analysis of the Public Enforcement of Securities Law in China: Finding the Missing Piece to the Puzzle', *European Business Organization Law Review* 18, 2, 2017, 367–389.
69 Ibid.
70 National People's Congress, Decision of the First Session of the Thirteenth National People's Congress on the State Council Institutional Reform Proposal, date issued: 17 March 2018.
71 Jeffrey E. Thomas, 'The Role and Powers of the Chinese Insurance Regulatory Commission in the Administration of Insurance Law in China', *The Geneva Papers on Risk and Insurance* 27, 3, 2002, 413–434.
72 Tristan Kenderdine, 'Insurance Plus Futures: Agricultural Commodity Price Reform in China', Asia & the Pacific Policy Studies 5, 2, 2018, 331–346.
73 Ibid.
74 Ibid.
75 Rebecca Lee, 'Conceptualizing the Chinese Trust', *The International and Comparative Law Quarterly* 58, 3, 2009, 655–669.
76 Ibid.
77 Stephen Tensmeyer, 'Modernizing Chinese Trust Law', *New York University Law Review* 90, 2, 2015, 710–745.
78 Ibid.
79 Ibid.
80 Shiyuan Han, Wensheng Wang, 'An Overview of the Development of the Financial Leasing Law in China', *Uniform Law Review* 16, 2011, 241–270.
81 Ibid.
82 Liang Tao, 'Financial Reforms in Shanghai Free Trade Zone', *China's Foreign Trade, 2014.*
83 Ibid.
84 Ibid.
85 Jing Bian, Frank Marchione, 'The New Battle Field- An Analysis of the Payment Systems in China', *Journal of International Banking Law & Regulation* 29, 10, 2014, 641–649.
86 Kang Yuan, Duoqi Xu, 'Legal Governance on Fintech Risks: Effects and Lessons from China', *Asian Journal of Law and Society* 7, 2, 2020, 275–304.
87 Ibid.
88 Ibid.

89 Virginia Harper Ho, 'Sustainable Finance & China's Green Credit Reforms: A Test Case for Bank Monitoring of Environmental Risk', *Cornell International Law Journal* 51, 3, 2018, 609–682.
90 Ibid.
91 Ibid.
92 Shahla Ali, Hui Huang, 'Financial Dispute Resolution in China: Arbitration or Court Litigation?', *The Journal of the London Court of International Arbitration* 28, 1, 2012, 77–100.
93 Ibid.
94 Ibid.

1

THE ESTABLISHMENT AND DEVELOPMENT OF THE CHINESE ECONOMIC LEGAL SYSTEM IN THE PAST SIXTY YEARS

Chen Su
Translated by Xie Zengyi

Source: Columbia Journal of Asian Law, 23, 109, 2009–2010, pp. 110–136.

Since the establishment of the People's Republic of China (PRC) in 1949, the Chinese economic legal system has gone through multiple transformative stages, exhibiting different characteristics at each stage as a result of the interaction between the changing economic system and legal ideology of the time. Due to the differences between the prevailing economic systems and legal ideologies at different stages, the structural concepts, content, governing systems, implementation mechanisms and effects of the economic legal system vary significantly at each stage.

I. China's economic legal system within a highly centralized planned economic system (1949–1978)

Before the implementation of the Reform and Opening Up policy in 1978, China had a highly centralized planned economic system. Under the planned economic system, the formulation and implementation of state plans resembling administrative orders were the essence of the economy. "The essential feature of economic activities was state planning," which meant that "the economic activities were to be implemented according to the state plans."[1] Because economic activities were based on the plans formulated by government agencies, the enterprises carrying out specific business operations were actually affiliates of government agencies. As a result, laws were basically unnecessary in the governing of economic activities, and played little part throughout the formation, existence, and evolution of the planned economic system, which was initiated in the early 1950s, took shape in the late 1950s and declined by the mid- to late-1970s.

The laws, legal institutions and legal interpretation of the former government were abolished at the time of the establishment of the PRC.[2] In particular, the old civil laws were dismantled.[3] Thus, without inheriting any legal tradition from the past, the economic legal system of the PRC was reestablished over time in an inconsistent and unsystematic manner. In the early 1950s, several major economic regulations and rules were formulated, including the Decision on Unifying the State's Financial and Economic Work, the Provisional Regulations on Budget and Final Accounts, the Provisional Rules on Infrastructure Work, the Agrarian Reform Law, the Model Articles for Higher-Stage Agricultural Producers' Cooperatives, and the Provisional Regulations on Industrial Enterprises of Joint Public and Private Ownership. Meanwhile, economic legal institutions, such as the Economic Protection Tribunal, were also established.[4] However, very few economic laws were enacted in the following thirty years, and the ones which were enacted were vague and general in content, consisting mostly of administrative orders rather than laws passed by the legislature. With the exception of certain specific statutes, such as the Agrarian Reform Law, only a small number of these economic laws were consistently and effectively enforced.

The Common Program of the Chinese People's Political Consultative Conference adopted in 1949 effectively served as the interim Constitution for the country,[5] which stipulated that the state should coordinate and regulate the state-owned economy, the cooperative economy, the individual economy of peasants and manual laborers, the private capitalist economy and the state capitalist economy. In this way, all components of the social economy could, under the leadership of the state-owned economy, carry out division and coordination, and play their respective parts in promoting the development of the social economy as a whole.[6] Such provisions dealing with the basic Chinese economic system were further confirmed in the Constitution of 1954.[7] However, this policy was soon changed. From 1953 to 1956, China carried out a large-scale socialist transformation of the private economy, including the individual economy of peasants and manual laborers, private capitalist industry and commerce. This approach consisted mainly of directing individual agriculture and manual laborers towards cooperative economy, and to purchase capitalist industries and businesses.[8] This conversion from an individual agriculture to cooperative economy was implemented through the adoption of three economic institutions, namely, the mutual aid group, the lower-stage agricultural producers' cooperative and the higher-stage agricultural producers' cooperative.[9] The higher-stage agricultural producers' cooperatives were mostly established by the end of 1956, which marked the completion of the socialist transformation of rural areas and agriculture in China. The movement of people's communes was launched in September 1958, and communization was completed by the end of that year. The people's communes in the rural areas were a form of collective ownership economy,[10] an "integration of the administrative and the economic entity."[11] The collective economy in cities and towns formed gradually, starting from the 1950s,[12] and was formed mainly as a result of the cooperativization of individual manual laborers enterprises in urban districts.

The state-owned economy was the dominant economic system. All enterprises of national economic significance or wielding a controlling influence over people's livelihoods were under the centralized operation of the state.[13] However, there were no comprehensive legal regulations governing the organization of enterprises during this period. It was not until more than a decade after the end of this period that the Law of the People's Republic of China on Industrial Enterprises Owned by the Whole People (1988), the Regulation on Collective Ownership Enterprises in Rural Areas (1990), and the Regulation on Collective Ownership Enterprises in Urban Areas (1991) were enacted, though all these enterprises were then faced with the challenges posed by the new wave of reform.

The importance of the legal system in regulating economic activity diminished after China established a highly centralized planned economy based on state ownership. The contract law of economic transactions provides an example of this. The Finance and Economy Committee of the Government Administrative Council promulgated the Provisional Regulations on Concluding Contracts Between Government Agencies, State-Owned Enterprises and Cooperatives in 1950 (the first contract law in the PRC), and more than forty further regulations concerning contracts were adopted by relevant authorities by 1956. However, the contract system was abolished from the late 1950s until the early 1960s due to the prohibition on free production and exchange of goods. The contract system was reestablished temporarily from 1962 to 1966, but it was abandoned again at the start of the Cultural Revolution before ever being generally implemented.[14] In fact, the definition of "contract" during this period was fundamentally different from that under a market economy. Contracts in this period were executed and performed according to state plans, instead of being the product of the freedom of contract exercised by the relevant parties. Rather, they served as tools and mechanisms for the implementation of state plans. As late as 1978, policy makers saw breach of contract as prejudicing the socialist planned economy.[15] Since the economy during this period was basically limited to the state-owned economy, most production and consumption goods were assigned and distributed according to state plans. Trade credit was limited or abolished. After 1952, individuals could not write checks, and both promissory notes and bills of exchange were forbidden domestically. Bills of exchange could be used only for international trade.[16] Furthermore, free trade of goods that violated or evaded state plans (so-called "speculation") continued to be regarded as criminal offenses for a prolonged period of time, even after the commencement of reform and opening.[17]

There had long been a lack of a basic civil law system in China under the planned economy. Although the Standing Committee of the National People's Congress organized the drafting of the Civil Law in 1954 and finished a draft Civil Law in December 1956, the drafting process was suspended soon thereafter due to political unrest. The drafting process of the Civil Law resumed in 1962 when China attempted to develop the basis for the production and exchange of goods. A proposed draft was completed in July 1964, but the drafting process was suspended again due to the political movement that started in 1964.[18] Also, the property law in China during this period was underdeveloped. The Constitution of 1954 provided that the state should protect peasants' land ownership and the ownership of other means of production.[19] However, due to the socialist transformation and the movement for communization, peasants as well as other individuals had no ownership stakes in land or major means of production. The state only protected "the ownership of the labor income, savings, housing and other consumption goods."[20] Other types of property, such as shares, and intellectual property, were almost non-existent in economic life. China had not yet established an intellectual property legal system at this time. Although there were several regulations that could be categorized as laws relating to intellectual property, the content thereof was simple and not comprehensive. For instance, the trademark system was incomplete and the patent system essentially did not exist. Only four patents were granted from the adoption of the Provisional Regulations on Protecting the Right of Invention and Patents in July 1950 until its abandonment in November 1963.[21] The protection of copyrights mainly relied on certain administrative legal rules, which were general in content, such as the Rules on Combating the Copying of Books Without Authorization (1953), the Draft Provisional Rules on the Remuneration of Authors of Literature and Social Science Books.[22]

With regard to the financial and taxation system, the distribution of financial resources between central and local governments had long been the key to the reform of the financial system. The Regulations on the Reform of the Financial Administration System, adopted in 1957, stipulated the scope, allocation and type of financial revenue and expenditure for the central and local governments. The Key Principles of the National Tax Administration, promulgated in 1950, marked the unification of the Chinese tax administration and the establishment of a new tax system.[23] The Regulation on the Agricultural Tax, promulgated in 1958, set up a proportional tax system for agricultural taxation. The Regulations on the Consolidated Industrial and Commercial Tax, promulgated in 1958, was the second major reform of industrial and commercial tax.[24] In 1973, a trial implementation of industrial and commercial tax was carried out, marking the third major reform of industrial and commercial tax. Thereafter, only the industrial and commercial tax was levied on state-owned enterprises, while the industrial and commercial tax and the industrial-commercial income tax were levied on collective enterprises. The basic feature of tax reform at this stage was that the number of different taxes was reduced and the tax system was simplified.[25] China had also tried to increase financial revenue by issuing public debt. For instance, the Decision on Issuing People's Victory Parity Bonds in Kind, which approved the issuance of such bonds in 1950, was passed in December 1949.[26] To accelerate national economic development, China adopted specific regulations on the issuance of public debt for national economic development each year from 1954 to 1958. However, the issuance of public debt was suspended at the end of the 1950s, due to China's policy of having "neither international debt nor domestic debt."[27]

Overall, the economic legal system at this stage fluctuated significantly. It received much attention from 1949 to 1956, was ignored from 1957 to 1961, was on the verge of resumption from 1962 to 1964, and was then abolished from 1965 to 1978. The rise and fall of the economic legal system during this period can be attributed to several factors. First, from the standpoint of legal ideology, legal nihilism and legal instrumentalism gained popularity in turn, with legal nihilism prevailing.[28] Even though for a short period, considerable attention was paid to the economic legal system, this was merely a reflection of legal instrumentalism. Second, in connection with the social governance system, the "rule of man" prevailed over the rule of law. Often, leaders' words were regarded as law and thus the so-called law changed with leaders' pronouncements.[29] Third, with regard to economic administration policies, the political doctrines of "policy can replace law," "only policies, no laws" and "policy itself is law" were the dominant values.[30] Finally, in the economic system, the operational mechanism of the planned economy system left little room for the functioning of laws.

II. The economic legal system in the early stage after the policy of Reform and Opening (1978–1992)

Starting in 1978, China abandoned the political theme of "using class struggle as a principle" and decided instead to focus on economic development. It thus began to implement the Reform and Opening-Up Policy[31] that is still ongoing to date. Since the adoption of this new policy, with deepened knowledge obtained through experience and implementation, the economic system underwent a number of vital changes. In 1982, the economic system was described as a "planned economy supplemented by market mechanism"; in 1984, as a "planned commodity economy based on public ownership"; in 1987, the principle was that "the socialist planned commodity economy shall be the internal unification of the planned and market mechanisms"; in 1989, it was "the establishment of an economic system and operational mechanism that combines planned economy and market mechanisms, and capable of adapting to the socialist planned commodity economy"; and in 1992, China put forward a new aim for its economic system reform: the creation of a "socialist market economy."[32] Generally, the basic approach underpinning the Chinese Reform and Opening Up Policy consisted of three major themes: firstly, in terms of its foreign economic policy, attracting foreign capital and expanding exports; secondly, in terms of its domestic policy in rural areas, the key to reform was the policy of "a contract system with remuneration linked to output";[33] thirdly, in terms of its domestic policy in urban areas, the key was to increase the independence and vitality of enterprises and to adjust the relationship between the state and enterprises (most of which were state-owned).[34] The economic legal system at this stage was also based on the three policies above.

In order to expand international economic cooperation and technological exchange, China enacted the Law on Chinese-Foreign Equity Joint Ventures, allowing foreign companies, enterprises and other economic organizations or individuals to establish joint ventures with their counterparts in China.[35] This law established the legal status of Chinese-foreign joint ventures and the protection of their property. From a legal perspective, these are important landmarks of the Opening Up policy. In 1980 and 1981, China passed the Law on Income Tax on Chinese-Foreign Equity Joint Ventures and the Law on Income Tax on Foreign Enterprises respectively, which provided exemptions or other favorable tax treatment for foreign enterprises that needed encouragement and development. By the end of 1986, there were more than 3,000 Chinese-foreign equity joint ventures in China.[36] At the same time, to further improve the investment environment, protect the legitimate interests of foreign investors, and enrich the organizational forms of foreign enterprises as a means of attracting more foreign investment, China passed the Foreign-Invested Enterprise Law in 1986 and the Law on Chinese-Foreign Contractual Joint Ventures in 1988, and revised its Law on Chinese-Foreign Equity Joint Ventures in April 1990. By means of these laws, a comprehensive legal system regarding foreign enterprises was established.

In August 1980, the Fifteenth Session of the Fifth Standing Committee of the National People's Congress ratified the Regulation on Special Economic Zones in Guangdong Province, which set up three special economic zones in Shenzhen, Zhuhai and Shantou in Guangdong Province. In October of the same year, the State Council also granted approval to the city of Xiamen to set up its special economic zone. The legal basis for the special economic zones system with Chinese characteristics was thereby established. These special economic zones were designed with reference to the experiences of free trade zones and export processing zones in other countries, where more favorable policies, including exemption and reduction of taxes, were implemented in international economic activities."[37]

Beginning in the spring of 1979, different forms of the agricultural production responsibility system appeared in rural China and the "contract system with remuneration linked to output" eventually became the major form of agricultural production. Although there was considerable political controversy in the intervening period, 99.5%[38] of farmers' production teams[39] had adopted the "contract system with remuneration linked to output" by November 1982. The "contract system with remuneration linked to output" was not only a form of production – more importantly, it served as a framework for property rights and legal relationships. Based on this contractual system, individual peasants and their families would enjoy autonomy of agricultural production and property rights in their means of production. The implementation of the "contract system with remuneration linked to output" not only increased the income of peasants and promoted economic development in rural areas, but also made the people's communes redundant. The Constitution of 1982 changed the system of "integration of administrative and economic entities" into a system based on the separation of political and economic entities. While people's communes were solely preserved as economic organizations, local governments were established at the town level.[40] By the end of 1984, the people's communes that had existed in China for more than twenty years had disappeared.[41] However, it was not until the amendment of the Constitution of 1993 that the people's communes were abolished as a matter of law.[42] The establishment and expansion of the "contract system with remuneration linked to output" not only benefited rural China, but served as a pioneering example for the reform of urban China. In particular, the framework for property rights and obligations within that system helped to provide the conceptual foundation and practical experiences for creating further civil and commercial laws, which focused on property relationships. The development of agriculture was strongly influenced by national policy rather than law,[43] and so the rural reforms relating to major legal issues and property rights were also mostly determined by policy. Except for a handful of administrative rules, such as the Regulation on Collective Ownership Enterprises in Rural Areas, legislation concerning agriculture lagged behind.[44]

Serving as the focus of urban reform during this period, the reform of state-owned enterprises followed the basic principles of separating enterprises and government and expanding the autonomy of enterprises. In 1979, the State Council issued certain regulations including the Rules on the Expansion of the State-Owned Enterprises' Autonomy of Operation and Management and launched pilot projects in a few state-owned enterprises within the public transportation sector. To promote state-owned enterprise reform, several relevant regulations were issued, including the Provisional Regulation on Worker Representative Congresses in State-Owned Industrial Enterprises (1981), the Provisional Regulation on Factory Managers of State-Owned Enterprises (1982), the Regulation on Rewards and Penalties for Enterprise Employees (1982), and the Provisional Regulation on State-Owned Industrial Enterprises (1983). The Law on Industrial Enterprises Owned by the Whole People was enacted in 1998 based on practical experience gained from prior reforms, paying particular attention to the actual situation and the need for reform of the then more than 90,000 "industrial enterprises owned by the whole people" (which accounted for over 70% of the gross industrial domestic product).[45] This law abolished the relationship of non-separation between government and enterprises and recognized the autonomy of enterprises. It also gave them independent property rights through the separation of ownership rights and management rights. At the same time, the law overcame the disadvantages of enterprises "eating from the same pot"[46] as the state.[47]

During the process of state-owned enterprise reform, another important trend in the Chinese economy was gaining momentum: the emergence and development of private economy. At the time of the enactment of the Constitution of 1982, the only individual economy that was allowed was the individual economy of urban laborers.[48] However, a large number of private enterprises which owned assets and hired workers did emerge.[49] Under Article 1 of the Constitution as amended in 1988, "[t]he state permits the private sector of the economy to exist and develop within the limits prescribed by law. The private sector of the economy is a complement to the socialist public economy. The state protects the lawful rights and interests of the private sector of the economy, and exercises guidance, supervision and control over the private sector of the economy." Accordingly, the Provisional Regulation on Private Enterprises was passed in 1988 to stimulate and regulate private enterprises as well as to protect their legal interests.[50]

The country's Reform and Opening Up Policy led to the adoption of foreign-inspired mechanisms regarding production and the exchange of goods. As a result, the enactment of laws regarding property and transactions was placed on the agenda of the legislature. In November 1979, which marked the beginning of the Reform and Opening Up, a drafting group was set up to draft the Civil Law Code.[51] Considering the difficulties in enacting a comprehensive civil law code within a short period of time, the legislature adopted an approach of enacting separate, specific civil laws first, and then consolidating them in a comprehensive civil law code when conditions permitted.[52] The *General Principles of the Civil Law* passed in 1986 included nine chapters: Basic Principles (Chapter I), Citizens (Natural Persons) (Chapter II), Legal Persons (Chapter III), Civil Law Acts and Agency (Chapter IV), Civil Rights (Chapter V), Civil Liability (Chapter VI), Limitation of Action (Chapter VII), Choice of Law in Civil Relations with Foreigners (Chapter VIII), and Supplementary Provisions (Chapter IX). This law laid down the basic principles and institutions of civil law and served as the fundamental civil law in China before the Civil Law Code was enacted.[53]

Within civil law legislation, the evolution of land law was particularly notable. The forms of the ownership of land in China at the time included state ownership and collective ownership. Before the reform of the economic system, the law stipulated that no organization or individual may appropriate, buy, sell, or lease land or otherwise engage in the transfer of land by unlawful means.[54] But in reality, Article 5 of the Law on Chinese-Foreign Equity Joint Ventures (1979) provided that the "right to the use of a site" could be a form of contribution to joint ventures. The law did not specify whether the "right to the use of a site" contributed to a joint venture was a "contractual right" or a "property right." However, since the term of a joint venture was generally ten to thirty years, or even fifty years or more for special projects, this "right to the use of a site" could be regarded as an early form of "land use rights" in the nature of "property rights."[55] Due to the subsequent diversification and extension in the terms of the use of land, China adjusted its land law and created "land use rights" based on the idea of the separation of the ownership right in land and the right to use the land.[56] Such an arrangement laid the institutional foundation for the subsequent rapid development of the Chinese real estate market.

With the implementation of the policy of "revitalizing the domestic economy, and opening up to the outside world," the production and exchange of goods inevitably became important drivers of the economy. As a result, contract law gradually came to play a leading role in economic transactions. In 1981, the Economic Contract Law was enacted, which represented a significant development in the field of Chinese contract law. Thereafter, given the differences which existed between foreign-related contracts and domestic contracts, China passed its Foreign-Related Economic Contract Law in order to promote foreign trade. In 1987, to advance the development of science and technology and to control increasingly significant technological development, technology transfer, technology consulting and technology services, China passed the Law on

Technology Contracts. By then, China had essentially laid the foundations of its contract law.[57]

For the purpose of fair adjudication of economic disputes, the Chinese courts at all levels began to set up economic tribunals in the second half of 1979. All intermediate courts (with the exception of some courts in remote areas) and 93% of lower courts had set up economic tribunals by April 1985.[58]

The emergence of the Chinese securities market was another notable economic development during this period. Starting in 1981, China promulgated several Regulations on the Treasury Bonds of the People's Republic of China in consecutive years and issued treasury bonds to the public. The purpose of the treasury bond issuances was to cut the financial deficit and to maintain fiscal balance. The treasury bonds were not transferable. The issuances of treasury bonds marked the reappearance of securities in China after three decades, and marked also the emergence of the modern Chinese securities market. In November 1984, the Shanghai Feiyue Audio Company issued public shares, which was the first public offering in China since the initiation of the Reform and Opening Up Policy. In September 1986, the Shanghai Trust Investment Company, which was affiliated with the Industrial and Commercial Bank of China, began to operate the first stock exchange counter in China. In December 1990, the Shanghai Stock Exchange was established. Soon after that, the Shenzhen Stock Exchange was established in July 1991. The Chinese securities market developed rapidly thereafter.[59]

The establishment of the intellectual property system was initiated at the end of the 1970s and started to develop with the implementation of the Reform and Opening Up Policy.[60] In 1979, the registration of trademarks was resumed and approximately 26,000 trademarks were registered in 1980 alone.[61] In 1984, the *Patent Law* was enacted. By April 1, 1985, the day on which the *Patent Law* came into effect, a total of 3,455 applications had been received, setting a new world record in patent history at the time, according to the World Intellectual Property Organization (WIPO).[62] The General Principles of the Civil Law for the first time stipulated that "[c]itizens and legal persons shall enjoy rights of authorship (copyrights) and shall be entitled to sign their names as authors, issue and publish their works and obtain remuneration in accordance with the law."[63] In 1990, the Copyright Law was passed, and in 1991, the Regulation for the Protection of Computer Software was adopted. With the Reform and Opening Up Policy, the integration of the Chinese intellectual property system into the global system proceeded at an unprecedented pace. As early as 1980, China had submitted its application for membership to WIPO and became a member of the organization that same year. In 1984, China also submitted its application to join the Paris Convention for the Protection of Industrial Property and has been a member since 1985. In 1989, China submitted its application to WIPO to join the Madrid Agreement Concerning the International Registration of Marks, and has been a member since 1989. In July 1992, China submitted applications to WIPO and the United Nations Educational, Scientific and Cultural Organization to join the Berne Convention for the Protection of Literary and Artistic Works and the Universal Copyright Convention, respectively. In October of that year, China was accepted as a member of those two conventions.[64]

Before the reform of the economic system, China lacked a clear conception of modem environmental protection, as well as a system of environmental law.[65] However, contrary to common belief, China's approach was not one of "development first, environment later." Rather, it adopted a new environmental policy around the same time as the Reform and Opening Up Policy, and maintained a heavy emphasis on environmental legislation even as it developed its economy. Numerous laws and regulations in this field were enacted during this period, including the Environmental Protection Law (For Trial Implementation) (1979), the Marine Environment Protection Law (1982), the Provisional Regulation on Pollutant Discharge Fee Collection (1982), the Regulations of the People's Republic of China Concerning Environmental Protection in Offshore Oil Exploration and Exploitation (1983), the Regulations of the People's Republic of China on the Control over Prevention of Pollution by Vessels in Sea Waters (1983), the Law on Prevention and Control of Water Pollution (1984), and the Law on Prevention and Control of Atmospheric Pollution (1987). For all of this legislation, however, China's current environmental laws remain far from ideal, and these laws have not been enforced in a uniform and rigorous manner. These remain issues to be solved by Chinese environmental law.[66]

Generally, China made significant progress in the construction of its economic legal system during this stage. Firstly, the laws became integrated into the country's economy in all aspects. The legal system played an important role in protecting the rights of individuals in economic activities, maintaining economic order and promoting economic development. Secondly, legal ideology changed substantially during this period. The importance and necessity of the law in the economy was recognized and legal nihilism was abandoned. Thirdly, although certain economic laws remained general and incomplete, and their contents inconsistent with one another, the basic content and direction of the economic legal system were properly established. This foundation would promote the further development and reform of the Chinese economy.

III. The economic legal system under the socialist market economy system (1992–2009)

In 1992, China proposed the establishment of a socialist market economy system, which had long been a goal of the country's reform.[67] In 1993, Article 15 of the Constitution was amended. The Article had formerly stated that "the country will implement a planned economy on the basis of socialist public ownership," and this was now amended to state that "the country will implement a socialist market economy."[68] In order to develop the socialist market economy, China comprehensively strengthened the construction of its economic legal system, which went through a significant expansion during this period.[69] This development was marked by the following trends: firstly, the legislation and standards set by the economic legal system were designed to focus on practicality, in order to reflect the practices and inherent requirements of China's market economy.[70] Secondly, an emphasis was placed on the democratization of the economic legal system. Numerous measures were taken to increase democracy within the legislative process, particularly after 2000. In the creation of several major economic laws, such as the country's property law, labor contract law and social insurance law, actors in relevant sectors and fields were asked to comment on the draft laws. These drafts were also published in order to solicit opinions from the public.[71] Thirdly, the economic legal system focused on making systematic changes. In 2001, China proposed the development of a "socialist legal system with Chinese characteristics" to be completed by 2010, which would include seven bodies of law, namely, the Constitution and relevant laws, civil and commercial law, administrative law, economic law, social law, criminal law, litigation and non-litigation procedural law.[72] Fourthly, the economic legal system was built with a focus on globalization. In particular, emphasis was placed on making domestic laws conform with international rules in the period immediately preceding and following China's accession to the World Trade Organization (WTO). For example, in order to join the WTO, China adopted, revised and abolished a large number of laws, administrative regulations, rules and other legal documents that were not in accordance with WTO rules and various other international obligations that the country had undertaken.[73]

One distinctive feature during this period was that theoretical studies of law began to have a direct and significant impact on the economic legal system. For example, the Chinese Academy of Social Sciences Institute of Law first put forward the theory that "a socialist market economy is an economy that is under the rule of law" in 1993, stating that China should establish a socialist market economic legal system. The Institute also detailed the ideologies and basic structure that the socialist market economic legal system should adopt.[74] This work provided an important theoretical basis as well as policy suggestions for the development of the economic legal system that China subsequently undertook. In another example, legal scholars proposed in 1995 the legislation of a nationwide property law, while scholars in civil law also drafted proposals for a property law.[75] The country's Property Law was finally adopted in 2007, twelve years after these proposals were first made, with much effort and participation from academics.[76] As a third example, after China initiated the drafting of its Contract Law in 1993, scholars from twelve law schools around the country drafted proposals in 1995 which, after extensive discussion, served as the basis of the official draft prepared by the legislature and submitted to the Standing Committee of the National People's Congress.[77] Since then, the field of Chinese legal theory has continued to draw from numerous legal theories and the experiences of legal construction from different jurisdictions (including those from outside the country).[78] This absorption of various theories and experiences has served as one of the most powerful driving forces behind the development of the Chinese economic legal system.

During this period, China's public-owned economy continued to develop in accordance with the reform policy, but the traditional state-owned enterprise development policy of simply increasing the number and scale of enterprises was replaced by policies aimed at improving the quality of corporate governance and management. By the end of March 2009, there were 97,177,000 enterprises, of which 541,600 were state-owned enterprises.[79] State-owned enterprises accounted for only 5.57% of the total number of enterprises, but the operational mechanisms and corporate governance structures of such enterprises saw greater improvement during this stage than those of non-state-owned enterprises. In order to protect state assets and the state-owned economy's leading role in the national economy, and to promote the development of the socialist market economy, China adopted the State-Owned Assets Law in 2008. Along with the deepening of China's economic reform and the development of its market economy, the law increasingly warmed up towards the idea of a non-public ownership economy. With the Constitutional Amendment of 1999, the original provisions stipulating that "the private economy is a complement to the socialist public economy" were revised to state that "the non-public ownership economy is an important component of the socialist market economy."[80] The 2004 Constitutional Amendment also amended the original provision stating that "[t]he individual economy and private economy should be under guidance, supervision and management" to state that "the country encourages, supports and guides the development of the non-public ownership economy."[81] Abolishing or changing laws, regulations and policies limiting the development of the non-public economy became one of the key policies for stimulating the development of this sector.[82] With such welcoming laws and policies, China saw the rapid development of its private economy. By the end of March 2009, there were a total of approximately 6,642,700 private enterprises and 29,480,000 individual businesses.[83]

In the early stages of reform, there was a period of confusion in the area of Chinese enterprise legislation, but gradually two approaches to such legislation developed.[84] Under one approach, laws were enacted according to the different types of enterprise ownership. For example, in the cases of the Law on Industrial Enterprises Owned by the Whole People (1988), the Rural Collective Enterprises Regulation (1990), the Urban Collective Enterprises Regulation (1991), the Provisional Private Enterprises Regulation (1988), the Law on Chinese-Foreign Equity Joint Ventures (1979), the Foreign Enterprise Law (1986), the Law on Chinese-Foreign Contractual Joint Ventures (1988), all of these laws were formulated before the market economy policy.[85] Although they are still legally in force, the scope of application of these laws has been reduced.[86] Under the second approach, laws were created based on the legal forms of enterprises and investors' liability. Examples include the Company Law (1993), the Partnership Enterprise Law (1997), the Individually-Owned Enterprise Law (1999), and the Fanners Professional Cooperatives Law (2006). These laws were revised and improved along with the deepening of economic reform and an increased awareness of the function of enterprise laws.[87] They have since become the main legal norms governing the organization and operation of enterprises, and effectively promote the development of the economy and the flourishing of business.[88]

The enactment and revision of the Company Law is illustrative of the evolution in Chinese enterprise laws. After China's socialist economic transformation in 1956, the company as a corporate legal form disappeared for the following twenty-three years.[89] But after China enacted its Reform and Opening Up Policy, a large number of "companies" emerged within this freer economic environment, particularly after China adopted the socialist market economy policy. Companies spread rapidly across the country, with their numbers increasing from about 480,000 in 1992 to over 1,000,000 by the end of 1993.[90] In order to regulate the form of enterprises and to safeguard the economic order, China formulated the Company Law in December 1993. However, with the continued development of economic reform and the improvement of the market economy system, it became clear that the Company Law could not fully meet the needs of the new situation. Various problems began to emerge as a result of this inadequacy: for example, conditions that were too stringent on the incorporation of companies, inadequate corporate governance in some companies, insufficient protection mechanisms for shareholders (especially minority shareholders), and the lack of liabilities and fiduciary duties for company directors, supervisors and management.[91] Thus, in 2005, China enacted major changes to its Company Law.[92]

After the adoption of the market economy system, the development of a basic civil and commercial law, as well as economic law, became China's most pressing legislative task. With regards to transactional law, the formulation of contract law came as the first priority. Due to the existence of three separate contract laws, namely, the Economic Contract Law, the Foreign-Related Economic Contract Law and the Technology Contract Law, there were repeated, inconsistent and sometimes even contradictory provisions in these three laws, but no basic system governing all contracts, and no regulations for new and emerging forms of contract (such as the sale leaseback contract).[93] China therefore embarked on drawing up a new contract law in 1993, which underwent multiple drafts and revisions. In 1999, the Contract Law was promulgated, while the Economic Contract Law, the Foreign-Related Economic Contract Law and the Technology Contract Law were abolished.[94] The Contract Law provides a basic set of rules for contracts in its "General Provisions," and specific rules for fifteen types of commonly-seen contracts in its "Specific Provisions."[95] This law comprehensively and accurately reflects the essential requirements of the market economy, establishing a complete structure for a contracts system and advanced legislation techniques.[96] Some scholars believe that the Contract Law is one of the best examples of civil legislation in China.[97]

As the foundation of the country's market economy, China's property system also became one of the main focuses for legislative changes during this period. In order to regulate the utilization of land and to promote the development of real estate, China formulated the Urban Real Estate Administration Law in 1994, made revisions to the Land Administration Law in 1998, and adopted the Rural

Land Contracting Law in 2002. The system for the legal protection of personal property was consistently improved: in 2004, Article 13 of the Constitution was amended from stating that "the country protects the lawfully earned income, saving, housing and other property rights of citizens" to stating that "the property rights of citizens are inviolable."[98] The individual's legal right to private property is enshrined in the Constitution, and the property protected is no longer limited only to the materials necessary for subsistence, but also those needed for production. It became widely recognized in China that under the conditions of a socialist market economy, all market players should work together and operate on equal footing. They should all enjoy the same rights, observe the same rules and bear the same responsibilities.[99] Thus, as the country's basic property protection law, the Property Law established the principle of equal protection of property rights, stating that "[t]he state adopts a socialist market economy, and guarantees equal legal status and the right to develop to all market players," and that "[s]tate, collective and private property rights, as well as the property rights of other rights holders, are protected by law, which no unit or individual shall violate."[100] The principle confirmed in the Property Law that public and private properties are "both recognized and equally protected" was a milestone in China's legislative history.[101]

After the establishment of the market economy system, China further reinforced its intellectual property legislation, which had significant social and economic impact. For example, in 1993, the year that China made its first revisions to the Trademark Law, the number of trademark applications swelled to over 130,000.[102] Since 2002, the annual number of trademark applications has grown by almost 100,000 applications per year, making China the world leader in this respect for the past seven years.[103] According to the latest statistics released by the National Intellectual Property Bureau, by the end of July 2009, China had accepted 5,341,000 patent applications, of which approximately 4,457,000 were domestic applications, and 884,000 of which were foreign applications.[104] China also continues to actively participate in numerous international conventions relating to intellectual property rights; in 1994, the country joined the Patent Cooperation Treaty, and in 1995, it became a member of the Protocol on Madrid Agreement for International Registration of Trademarks. In 2001, China formally signed the Agreement on Trade Related Aspects of Intellectual Property Rights (TRIPS). In addition, China has continuously strengthened its efforts in the enforcement of intellectual property rights. For example, in the area of copyright protection, copyright administrative departments confiscated a total of 350,000,000 pirated copies of copyright-infringing materials between the years of 1995 to 2004. During that period, 51,368 tort cases were accepted for hearing by courts, of which 49,983 were decided.[105] To improve the quality of the trials in intellectual property rights cases, China has placed an emphasis on the consultation of intellectual property rights experts in particularly technical and difficult cases. By December 2006, there were sixty-two intermediate courts empowered to deal with patent disputes in the first instance, thirty-one courts for the patent disputes in the second instance, forty-three intermediate courts for integrated circuit layout and design cases in the first instance, and thirty-eight intermediate courts for new plant variety cases in the first instance.[106]

During this period, China paid heightened attention to the legal structures underpinning its market system, and in particular to legislation governing financial markets. In accordance with the development of financial market conditions, China successively enacted the People's Bank of China Law (1995), Commercial Bank Law (1995), Negotiable Instruments Law (1995), Insurance Law (1995), Securities Law (1998), and Trust Law (2001). The enactment of these laws provided basic rules for the maintenance of order and the effective regulation of the financial market. Existing financial laws continued to be frequently modified with the rapid development of China's financial markets, in order to adapt to ongoing changes.[107] As a result, the adoption and implementation of such laws protected and promoted the development of the financial markets. By the end of September 2006, there were 1396 listed companies in mainland China, with a security market value of over RMB 5.2 trillion. The number of accounts opened by investors totaled over 76 million, making China the third-largest securities market in Asia.[108]

Since 1992, China's financial regulatory system has undergone frequent changes. Following the State Council's Decision on Financial System Reform of 1993, China established an independent macro-control system for the People's Bank of China, as well as a financial institution system separating policy-oriented finance and commercial finance, where state-owned commercial banks coexist with multiple financial institutions. Prior to 1994, the People's Bank of China served as the sole regulatory body for financial institutions and financial markets (with the exception of the China Securities Regulatory Commission, which was partly in charge of securities market regulation).[109] In 1998, China made significant alterations to its finance regulatory system, one of which was to begin constructing separate sub-sector regulatory regimes. The People's Bank of China transferred its authority with regards to the securities market to the China Securities Regulatory Commission, and its supervision of the insurance market to the China Insurance Regulatory Commission, thus creating the basis for separate financial regulatory systems. In 2003, China reformed its financial system yet again by revising the Law on the People's Bank of China, which provides that the Bank's role is to ensure the formulation and implementation of national monetary policy, to establish and improve the Central Bank macro-control regulatory system, and to maintain financial stability.[110] At the same time, the government enacted the Banking Supervision Law, which clarified the authority of the banking regulatory body to monitor and regulate banking institutions and their business operations.[111]

The State Council's Decision on the Implementation of the Revenue-Sharing System of the Fiscal System was enacted in 1993 with regard to changes in China's taxation system. In accordance with the principle of combining financial revenue and financial expenditure, taxes were classified into three categories: central tax, local tax and shared tax. In addition, separate central and local taxation systems were established, with separate collection agencies for the two systems. Prior to the 2007 adoption of the new Enterprise Income Tax Law, estimates based on surveys of sources of corporate income tax showed that domestically funded enterprises had an average actual tax rate of approximately 25%, a figure which was 10% higher than foreign capital enterprises with a tax rate of approximately 15%. As such, there was high demand for a uniform tax rate in order to foster fair competition.[112] As a result of the enactment of the new Enterprise Income Tax Law in 2007, the enterprise income tax rate was uniformly set at 25% to advance equal treatment and fair competition. In addition, China revised the Tax Collection and Administration Law in 2001, which further improved the tax management system.

One legislative milestone during this phase was the enactment of the Anti-Monopoly Law. Before that, there were various rules prohibiting monopoly in the Anti-Unfair Competition Law (1993), the Price Law (1997), the Bidding Law (1999), and the Telecommunications Regulation (2000), but these rules proved insufficient in dealing with the changes in the socialist market economy and meeting the growing demands of international competition.[113] Although there were rules meant to curb monopolistic behavior dispersed throughout various laws and regulations, without a separate anti-monopoly law operating as a complete and uniform system of administrative sanctions, such scattered rules could not effectively combat anti-competitive behavior. These rules ultimately did not serve their purposes well, due to the lack of an independent and authoritative enforcement agency, amongst other reasons.[114] After over ten years of research and repeated rounds of revisions, China enacted the Anti-Monopoly Law in 2007, addressing issues such as monopoly agreements, abuses of dominant market positions, abuses of administrative power to eliminate or restrict competition, and the investigation of suspected monopolistic conduct. The enactment of the Anti-Monopoly Law had far-reaching importance in preventing and restraining monopolistic behavior, protecting fair competition in the market, enhancing economic efficiency, safeguarding the interests of consumers and the general public, and promoting the healthy development of the socialist market economy.

China has continued to pursue economic development while advancing the notion of building a harmonious society according to the principles of democracy and rule of law, fairness and justice, honesty and friendliness, dynamism, safety and good order, and coexistence between mankind and nature.[115] As such, China's economic legal system has placed a strong emphasis on promoting intrapersonal harmony, and on harmony between nature and mankind. Moreover, the government has taken into account the growing income disparity brought by the country's rapid economic growth. Thus, the government has attempted to balance the different interests of the people and deal adequately with potential social conflicts in drafting economic legislation. Statistics show that in the twelve years between 1995 and 2006, the number of labor dispute cases in China multiplied by approximately thirteen times; in particular, the figure for collective labor disputes grew fivefold.[116] Because emphasis has long been placed on the speed of economic growth, social legislation in China has lagged behind economic legislation for the past two decades.[117] However, since the notion of constructing a socialist harmonious society was first proposed in 2006,[118] China has reinforced legislation in the areas of labor relations and social security, by enacting and implementing the Labor Contract Law (2007), the Law on Employment Promotion (2007), the Law on Labor Dispute Mediation and Arbitration (2007), the Regulations on Paid Annual Leave of Workers (2007), and the Regulations on Labor Contact Law Enforcement (2008). These laws and regulations provide rules for the effective resolution of labor disputes. After the promulgation of the Labor Contract Law in 2008, the number of labor dispute cases submitted for arbitration increased by more than 98% compared with the number filed in 2007; these cases involved over 1.21 million workers.[119] In 2008, courts at all levels handled as many as 286,000 labor cases, 93.9% more than the number of cases handled in 2007.[120]

China has not neglected its efforts in environmental protection while developing its market economy, and has enacted a number of environmental laws and regulations such as the Law on the Prevention and Control of Atmospheric Pollution (as amended in 1995 and 2000), Law on Prevention of Environmental Pollution Caused by Solid Waste (as amended in 2004), Law on Prevention and Control of Environmental Noise Pollution (1996), Law on Anti-Desertification (2001), Law on Environmental Impact Assessment (2002), Law on the Promotion of Cleaner Production (2002), and the Law on Water Pollution Prevention and Control (as amended in 2008). Moreover, the country has established a relatively comprehensive legal system for environmental protection. With the latest scientific developments serving as a guide, China will seek to further balance the demands of both economic development and environmental protection, and strive to build an ecological and environment-friendly society.[121]

Despite all the ups and downs experienced over the past six decades in the construction of China's economic legal system, the overall trend is a positive one, pointing towards progress and prosperity.

Notes

1 王家福、谢怀栻等著, 合同法 [WANG JIAFU, XIE HUAISHI ET AL., CONTRACT LAW] 8 (中国社会 科学出版社 [China Social Science Press] 1986).

2 *See*中共中央关于废除国民党的六法全书与确定解放区的司法原则的指示 [Instruction of the Central Committee of the CPC Regarding the Repeal of "The Complete Book of Six Codes" of the Kuomintang and the Establishment of Judicial Principle in the Liberated Areas] (1949), *available at* www.dffy.com/sifashijian/jj/200809/20080921204129.htm (last visited Nov. 4, 2009).

3 *See* 中国法学四十年 [FORTY YEARS OF LEGAL STUDIES IN CHINA] 327 (张友渔 [Zhang Youyu] ed.,上海人民出版社[Shanghai People's Press] 1989).

4 *See* 经济法 [ECONOMIC LAW] 25 (王家福 [Wang Jiafu] ed.,中国经济出版社 [China Economic Press] 1988).

5 宪士学 [CONSTITUTIONAL LAW] 92 (吴家麟[Wu Jianlin] ed.,群众出版社 [Qunzhong Press] 1983).

6 中国人民政治协商会议共同纲领 [Common Program of the Chinese People's Political Consultative Conference] (1949) art. 26, *available at* http://china.flndlaw.en/fagui/gj/21/2.html (last visited Nov. 4, 2009).

7 1954 年宪法 [The Constitution of 1954] (promulgated by the Nat'l People's Cong., Sept. 20, 1954, effective Sept. 20，1954) Nat'l People's Cong. Gaz. (P.R.C.), art. 5.

8 *See* 张卓元，从百年积弱到经济大国的跨越 [Zhang Zhuoyuan, *Leap From a Century of Weakness to Economic Power*],光明日报 [Guangming Daily], Aug. 27，2009, at 11, *available at* www.gmw.cn/01gmrb/2009-08/27/content_970632.htm (last visited Nov. 4, 2009).

9 "Mutual aid groups" refers to the mutual assistance of farmers who owned the means of production; "lower-stage agricultural producers' cooperative" involves the unified operation of agriculture with private ownership of the means of production; "higher-stage agricultural producers' cooperative" means the unified operation of agriculture with public ownership of the means of production. *See* 农业合作化运动 [The Agricultural Cooperativization Movement], *available at* http://news.xinhuanet.com/ziliao/2003–01/20/content_697957.htm (last visited Nov. 4, 2009).

10 1975 年宪法 [The Constitution of 1975] (promulgated by the Nat'l People's Cong., Jan. 17, 1975, effective Sept. 20, 1954) Nat'l People's Cong. Gaz. (P.R.C.), art. 7.

11 The integration of the administrative and the economic entity means the combination of political power at the town level and at the level of economic organizations.

12 See 王兆国，在第十届全国人民代表大会第五次会议上的 《关于<中华人民共和国物权法(草 案)>的说明》[Wang Zhaoguo, Speech at the Fifth Session of the Tenth National People's Congress: Explanation on the Draft of the Property Law of the PRC] (2007), at section 3(4).

13 中国人民政治协商会议共同纲领 [Common Program of The Chinese People's Political Consultative Conference] (1949) art. 28.

14 *See* Wang Jiafu, Xie Huaishi et al, *supra* note 3, at 142–46.

15 *Id.* at 146.

16 *See* 射十不栻，票据法概论 [Xie Huaishi, The Law of Negotiable Bills of Exchange] 27 (法 律出版社 [Law Press] 1990).

17 刑法 [Criminal Law] (1979), 1979–1984 法律汇编 [Collected Laws] 98, *translated in* 1 P.R.C. Laws 87, arts. 117, 118.刑法 [Criminal Law] (1997), 1997 法律汇编 [Collected Laws] 87' *translated in* 9 P.R.C. Laws.

18 *See* 梁慧星，制定民法典的设想 [Liang Huixing, *Thoughts on the Making of Civil Law Code*], 现 代法学 [Modern Law Science], Vol. 2,2001, at 3.

19 The Constitution of 1954, *supra* note 7, art. 8.

20 *Id.* art. 9.

21 *See* 李顺德，知识产权法律基础 [Li Shunde, Fundamentals of Intellectual Property Law] 69 (知识产权出版社 [Intellectual Property Press] 2005).

22 知识产权法 [Intellectual Property Law] 64 (李明德 [Li Mingde] ed., 社会科学文献出版社 [Social Science Academic Press] 2007).

23 北京经济学院财政金融教研,新中国税制演变 [Finance Department of the Beijing Economy Academy, Reform of the Taxation System in China] 7 (天津人民出版社 [Tianjin People's Press] 1985).

24 *Id.* at 35.

25 *Id* at 51–53.

26 "In kind" means that the par value of the People's Victory Parity Bonds was calculated on the basis of the prices of daily necessities.

27 周恩来，在第四届全国人民代表大会上的《政府工作报告》[Zhou Enlai, Speech at the Fourth National People's Congress: Government Work Report] (1975), *translated in* Documents of the First Session of the Fourth National People's Congress of the People's Republic of China 45–65 (Foreign Languages Press 1975).

28 当代中国法学研究 [Contemporary Chinese Legal Research] 26–32 (陈甦 [Chen Su] ed., 中国社会科学出版社 [China Social Science Press] 2009).

29 邓小平文选第 2 卷 [Selected works of Deng Xiaoping Vol. 2] 146 (人民出版社 [People's Press] 1994).

30 *See* Forty Years of Legal Studies in China, *supra* note 3, at 90.

31 *See* 中共中央十－届三中全会决议 [Resolution of the Third Session of the Eleventh Central Committee of Chinese Communist Party] (1978).

32 江泽民，在第十四届全国人民代表大会上的《加快改革幵放和现代化建设步伐，夺取有 中国特色社会主义事业的更大胜利》谈话 [Jiang Zemin, Speech at the Fourteenth National People's Congress: Accelerate Opening Up Reform and the Pace of Modernization, Strive for the Success of Socialism with Chinese Characteristics] (1992), *available at* http://news.xinhuanet.com/ziliao/2003–01/20/content_697148.htm (last visited Oct. 18, 2009).

33 The "contract system with remuneration linked to output" was a form of production used in the Chinese rural collective economy, under which individuals or families contracted for the use of land or other means of production, and enjoyed autonomy in operation and management.

34 厉以宁，社会主义政治经济学 [Li Yining, Socialist Political Economics] 45 (商务印书馆 [Commercial Press] 1986).

35 中国合资经营企业法 [Law on Chinese-Foreign Equity Joint Ventures] (promulgated by the Standing Comm. Nat'l People's Cong., July 8, 1979, effective July 8, 1979) Standing Comm. Nat'l People's Cong. Gaz. (P.R.C.)' art. 1.

36 经济法要义 [Understanding Economic Law] 605 (王家福 [Wang Jiafu] ed.,中国财政经济出版社 [China Finance and Economy Press] 1988).

37 *Id* at 637–38.

38 The "farmer's production team" was the basic unit of rural production during the period of the movement for communization.

39 *See* 罗汉平，农村人民公社史 [Luo Hanping, The History of People's Communes in Rural China] 387–400 (福建人民出版社 [Fujian People's Press] 2003).

40 1982 年宪法 [Constitution of 1982] (promulgated by the Nat'l People's Cong., Dec. 4, 1982, effective Dec. 4, 1982) Nat'l People's Cong. Gaz. (P.R.C.), arts. 8, 95.

41 *See* LUO HANPING, *supra* note 39, at 413.

42 1993 年宪法修正案 [Amendment to the Constitution 1993] (promulgated by the Nat'l People's Cong., Mar. 29, 1993, effective Mar. 29, 1993) Nat'l People's Cong. Gaz. (P.R.C.), art. 6.

43 李成贵，中国农业政策一理论框架与用分析 [Li Chenggui, China's Agricultural Policy : Theoretical Framework and Analysis of Application] 3 (社会科学文献出版社 [Social Science Academic Press] 1999).

44 王存学、骆友生，中国农村经济法律基本问题 [Wang Cunxue & Luo Yousheng, Fundamental Legal Issues of the Chinese Rural Economy] 11 (法律出版社 [Law Press] 1998).

45 *See*吕东，在第七届全国人民代表大会第一次会议上的《关于<全民所有制工业企业法(草 案)>的说明》[Lu Dong, Speech at the Seventh Session of the First National People's Congress: Explanation on the "Draft Law on Industrial Enterprises Owned by The Whole People"] (1988), *available at* www.law-lib.com/fzdt/newshtml/20/20050721212402.htm (last visited Oct. 18, 2009).

46 "Eating from the same pot" is a metaphor for the extreme egalitarianism characteristic of the Chinese income system, wherein the people's income was not determined by the operation of enterprises or the performance of workers. This was considered analogous to a situation where each person shared the same amount of food from the same pot.

47 *See* Economic Law, *supra* note 6, at 34–36.

48 Constitution of 1982, *supra* note 40, art. 11.

49 According to statistics, in 1988 there were more than 90,000 private enterprises with about 1,640,000 employees, *see* 聚焦共和国第一个宪法修正案 [*Report on the First Amendment of the Constitution*], 检察日报 [PROSECUTION DAILY], Apr. 12, 2008.

50 私营企业暂行条例 [The Provisional Regulations on Private Enterprises] (promulgated by the St. Council, June 25, 1988, effective July 1, 1988) ST. COUNCIL GAZ. (P.R.C.), art. 1.

51 For example, on Dec. 23, 2002, the draft of the Civil Law Code was submitted to the Standing Committee of the National People's Congress for deliberation. There were nine chapters in this draft, namely, General Principles, Property Law, Contract Law, Personal Right Law, Marriage Law, Adoption Law, Inheritance Law, Torts Liabilities Law, and Choice of Law for Foreign-Related Civil Activities. 新华网 [XinhuaNet.com]，民法草案首次提请人大常委会审议 [The Draft of the Civil Law Code First Submitted for NPC Standing Committee's Review], *available at* http://news.xinhuanet.com/newscenter/2002-12/23/content_667932.htm (last visited Oct. 18, 2009).

52 梁慧星，民法总论 [LIANG HUIXING, FUNDAMENTALS OF CIVIL LAW] 19 (法律出版社 [Law Press] 1996).

53 梁慧星，民法 [LIANG HUIXING, CIVIL LAW] 10 (四川人民出版社 [Sichuan People's Press] 1998).

54 Constitution of 1982, *supra* note 40, art. 10.

55 中国物权法研究 [STUDIES IN CHINESE PROPERTY LAW] 599 (梁慧星 [Liang Huixing] ed., 法律 出版社 [Law Press] 1998).

56 城镇国有土地使用权出让和转让暂行条例 [The Interim Regulations Concerning the Assignment and Transfer of the Right to the Use of the State-Owned Land in the Urban Areas] (promulgated by the St. Council, May 19, 1990, effective May 19, 1990) St. COUNCIL Gaz. (P.R.C.), art. 1.

57 王利明、崔建远，合同法新论.总则 [WANG LIMING & CUI JIANYUAN, CONTRACT LAW: GENERAL PROVISIONS] 94–95 (中国政法大学出版社 [China University of Political Science and Law Press] 1996).

58 *See* UNDERSTANDING ECONOMIC LAW, *supra* note 36, at 731.

59 *See* 新证券法论 [SECURITIES LAW] 12–13 (周友苏 [Zhou Yousu] ed., 法律出版社 [Law Press] 2007).

60 *See* LI SHUNDE, *supra* note 21, at 69.

61 *See* 中国商标局 [Chinese Trademark Bureau], 历年商标注册申请及核准注册商标统计表 [*Statistics for Trademark Applications and Trademarks Approved in Force over Previous Years*], available at http://sbj.saic.gov.cn/tjxx/TJTableLNSBTJ.asp?BM=09 (last visited Nov. 5, 2009).

62 *See* 熊志云，浅谈令利档案及其管理 [Xiong Zhiyun, *Trademark Documents and Management*], 档案学研究 [RESEARCH IN ARCHIVAL SCIENCE], No. 1 1988, at 58.

63 民法通贝 [General Principles of Civil Law] (promulgated by the President of the People's Republic of China, Apr. 12, 1986, effective Jan. 1, 1987), art. 94.

64 *See* INTELLECTUAL PROPERTY LAW, *supra* note 22, at 511, 518, 532, 538.

65 马骧聪、蔡守秋，中国环境法制通论 [MA XIONGCONG & CAI SHOUQIU, GENERAL INTRODUCTION TO CHINESE ENVIRONMENTAL LAW] 42–43 (学苑出版社 [Xueyuan Press] 1990).

66 *See* 李恒远、常纪文，现状、问题与走向：中国环境法治 30 年之评析 [Li Henyuan & Chang Jiwen, *Current Situation, Problems and Future: Thirty Years of Chinese Environmental Law*], *in* 中 国环境法治 (2007 年卷) [CHINESE ENVIRONMENTAL LAW (2007)] 12–13 (法律出版社 [Law Press] 2008).

67 *See* JIANG ZEMIN, *supra* note 32.

68 Amendment to the Constitution 1993, *supra* note 42, art. 7.

69 By March 2008, China had 229 currently effective laws in total, nearly 600 administrative regulations, and more than 7,000 local regulations, among which economic

laws and regulations account for a large proportion. *See* 吴邦国，在第十一届全国人民代表大會第一次会议上的《常务委员会 工作报告》[Wu Bangguo, Standing Committee Work Report at the First Session of the Eleventh National People's Congress] (2008), *available at* www.jconline.cn/Contents/Channel_4095/2008/0321/74363/content_74363.htm.

70 *E.g.*, the "CPC Central Committee's Decision on the Establishment of a Socialist Market Economic System" (1993) pointed out that great importance should be attached to the legal system, and to laws and regulations incompatible with the establishment of a socialist market, which should be abolished or amended. 中知中央关于建立社会主义市场经济体制若干问题的决定 (1993) [CPC Central Committee Decision on the Establishment of a Socialist Market Economic System (1993)], *available at* www.china.com.cn/chinese/archive/131747.htm.

71 *E.g.*, in 2005, the fuil version of the Draft Property Law was published. From July 10th to August 20th, citizens sent in 11,543 opinions, in the form of both online and written letters. The Standing Committees in twenty-six provinces (including autonomous regions and cities with provincial status), as well as fifteen large cities, forty-seven governmental agencies, sixteen large companies, twenty-two legal teaching and research institutions also expressed their views on the draft. *See* 全国 人民代表大会法律委员会 [Nat'l People's Cong. Law Comm.], 关于物权法(草案)修改情况的汇报 *[Report on the Revision of the Draft Property Law]* (Oct. 22, 2005), *available at* www.cctv.com/news/china/20051002/100618.shtml.

72 *See* 李鹏，在第九届全国人民代表大会第四次会议上的《常务委员会工作报告》[Li Peng, Standing Committee Work Report at the Fourth Session of the Ninth National People's Congress] (2001).

73 By the end of 2001, China had formulated, revised and repealed about 1,150 laws in its process of legal reform. *See*新华网 [XinhuaNet]，履行入世承诺，我国清理法规 1150 余件 [Reviewing 1150 Regulations to Fulfil! Our Promise under WTO Laws], Dec. 28, 2001, *available at* http://news.xinhuanet.com/fortune/2991-12/28/content_216380.htm (last visited Oct. 18, 2009).

74 中国社会科学院法学研究所课题组，建立社会主义市场经济法律体系的理论思考和对策建议 [Chinese Academy of Social Sciences, Institute of Law Research Group, *Theories and Policy Proposals for the Construction of a Socialist Market Economy Legal System*], 法学研究 [Chinese Journal of Law], No. 6, 1993, at 3.

75 中国社会科学院法学研究所课题组，制定物权法的基本思路 [Chinese Academy of Social Sciences Institute of Law Research Group, *General Thinking on the Making of Property Law]*,法学研究 [Chinese Journal of Law], No. 3, 1995.

76 *See* 中国物权法草案建议稿 [Suggested Draft of Property Law of China] (梁慧星 [Liang Huixing] ed., 社会科学文献出版社 [Social Science Academic Press] 2000);中国物权法草案建议稿及说明 [Draft of Property Law of China and Explanation] (王利明 [Wang Liming] ed., 中国法制出版社 [China Legal Press] 2001).

77 *See* 合同法 [Contract Law] 10 (崔建远 [Cui Jianyuan], ed., 法律出版社 [Law Press] 2003).

78 The "Chinese Journal of Law" is China's most authoritative legal journal. Chang Peng'ao has compiled statistics on the citations of articles on civil law published in the "Chinese Journal of Law" in the thirty years from 1978 to 2007, which illustrate, to a certain extent, changes in Chinese legal research that reflect the influence of foreign theories. In civil law articles published in the "Chinese Journal of Law" between 1978–1986, a total of 127 citations were to the works of Marx and Engels, thirty-five to the works of Lenin, thirteen to Soviet sources, four to Yugoslav sources, eleven to Anglo-American legal sources, six to German sources, six to French sources, four to Japanese sources, fourteen to pre-1949 or Taiwan Province sources, and four to Roman legal literature. In the papers published in 1987–1999, 468 citations were to pre-1949 and Taiwan Province sources, 296 to Anglo-American law, 214 to Japanese

sources, sixty-four to German sources, thirty-five to the works of Marx and Engels, thirty to Roman law, twenty to French sources, and twenty-seven to Soviet sources. In 2000–2007, 595 citations referred to pre-1949 Chinese sources of Taiwan Province sources, 585 to German sources, 290 to Anglo-American law, 225 to Roman Law, 190 to Japanese law, fifty-nine to French sources, and 113 from other countries (including Italy, the Netherlands, Russia, and Argentina). *See* 常鹏紙《法学研究》三十每：民法学 [Chang Peng'ao, *Thirty Years of the "Chinese Journal of Law": Civil Law Studies]*, 法学研究 [Chinese Journal of Law], No. 3, 2008, at 19, 24, 31, 38.

79 *See* 国家工商总局 [State Admin. of Industry and Com.], 统计分析发布：2009年一季度全国市场主体发展情况报告 *[Statistical Analysis: Report on the Main Development of National Economic Organizations in the First Quarter of 2009]* (May 11, 2009*)*, *available at* www.saic.gov.cn/zwgk/tjzl/zhtj/bgt/200905/t2009051 1_47153.html (last visited at Oct. 18, 2009).

80 1999 年宪法修正案 [Amendment to the Constitution 1999] (promulgated by the Nat'l People's Cong., Mar. 15, 1999, effective Mar. 15, 1999) Nat'l People's Cong. Gaz. (P.R.C.), art. 16.

81 2004 年宪法修正案 [Amendment to the Constitution 2004] (promulgated by the Nat'l People's Cong. Mar. 14, 2004, effective Mar. 14, 2004) Nat'l People's Cong. Gaz. (P.R.C.), art. 21.

82 *See*中共中央关于完善市场经济体制若干问题的决定 [CPC Central Committee Decision on Improving the Market Economy System] (Oct. 14, 2003), *available at* www.china.com.cn/chinese/zhuanti/sljszqh/426675.htm#1 (last visited Oct. 18, 2009).

83 *See* State Admin, of Industry and Com., *supra* note 79.

84 *See* 赵旭东，企业与公司法纵论 [Zhao Xudong, Business and Company Law] 61–65 (法律 出版社 [Law Press] 2003).

85 *See* 经济法 [Economic Law] 162 (史际春[Shi Jichun], ed"中国人民大学出版社[China Renmin University Press] 2005).

86 *E.g.,* transforming state-owned enterprises into companies in order to establish a modern enterprise system has been the main thrust of state-owned enterprise reform after 1992. *See* CPC Central Committee Decision on the Establishment of a Socialist Market Economic System, *supra* note 70. If state-owned enterprises were reorganized into corporations, the *Company Law* would apply.

87 *E.g.*, the *Company Law* and *Partnership Enterprise Law* were modified significantly in 2005 and 2007, respectively.

88 As of the end of March 2009, there were 125,500 stock corporations, 6,336,700 limited liability companies, 123,100 partnership enterprises, 1,078,900 individual wholly-owned enterprises and 139,100 farmers' cooperatives. *See* State Admin. of Industry and Com., *supra* note 79.

89 *See* 王保树、崔勤之，中国公司法原理 [Wang Baoshu & Cui Qiuzhi, China's Company Law Theory] 10–15 (社会科学文献出版社 [Social Science Academic Press] 2000). In fact, the word "company" did exist at that time, but had no strict legal definitions. Often, it was used to name those commercial enterprises that could not be called "factories," such as department stores and public transport companies.

90 *See* 全国人民代'大会法律委员会 [Nat'l People's Cong. Law Comm.], 《关于<公司法*(草案)*> 审议结果的报告》 [*Report on the Result of Deliberation on the Draft Company Law*] (Dec. 20, 1993).

91 *See* 曹康泰，在第十届全国人民代表大会第十四次会议上的《关于<公司法(修订草案)>的说 明》[Cao Kangtai, Speech at the Fourteenth Session of the Tenth National People's Congress: Explanation on the Draft of the Revision of *Company Law]* (2005), *available at* www.5izy.cn/ articles/h000/h01/l 143710658dl 198.html (last visited Oct. 18, 2009).

92 There were 230 articles in the *Company Law* at its adoption in 1993. In the National People's Congress amendment to the law in 2005, forty-six of the original articles

in the law were deleted, forty-one new articles were inserted, and 137 articles were revised. *See* 周友苏，新公百J法论 [Zhou Yousu, New Survey on Corporation Law] 3 (法律出版社 [Law Press] 2006).

93 *See* Contract Law, *supra* note 77, at 10.

94 合同法 [Contract Law] (promulgated by the Nat'l People's Cong., Mar. 15, 1999, effective Oct. 1, 1999) Nat'l People's Cong. Gaz. (P.R.C.), art. 428.

95 *See* Contract Law, *supra* note 77, at 10–11.

96 韩世远，合同法总论 [Han Shiyuan, Contract Law] 27 (法律出版社 [Law Press] 2008).

97 Amendment to the Constitution 2004, *supra* note 81, art. 24.

98 Amendment to the Constitution 2004, *supra* note 81, art. 24.

99 王兆国，在第十届全国人民代表大会第五次会议上的关于《关于<中华人民共和国物权法 (草案) >的说明》[Wang Zhaoguo, Speech at the Fifth Session of the Tenth National People's Congress: Explanation on the Draft of the Property Law of the PRC] (Mar. 8, 2007), at section 3(4), *available at* www.gov.cn/20071h/content_545775.htm (last visited Oct. 18, 2008).

100 物权法[Property Law] (promulgated by the Nat'l People's Cong., Mar. 16, 2007, effective Oct. 1, 2007), arts. 3,4.

101 孙宪忠，中国物权法总论 [Sun Xianzhong, Chinese Property Law] 15–17 (法律出版社 [Law Press] 2009).

102 *See*曹中强、黄晖，中国商标报告（第四卷）[Cao Zhongqiang & Huang Hui, China Trademark Report Vol. iv] 300 (中信出版社 [Citic Press] 2005).

103 *See* 中国商标局[Chinese Trademark Bureau], 商标申请与注册概况表 [*Table of Trademark Applications and Registration*], *available at* http://sbj.saic.gov.cn/tjxx/tjxx.asp (last visited Oct. 18, 2009).

104 *See* statistics on the website of 国家知识产权局 [State Intellectual Property Office], www.sipo.gov.cn/sipo2008/tjxx (last visited Oct. 18, 2009).

105 *See*国务院新闻办公室，中国知识产权的新进展（白皮书）[State Council Info. Office, White Paper on New Progress in China's Intellectual Property] (2005).

106 *See* 中国知识产权保护体系改革研究 [China's IPR Protection System Reform] 227–28 (中国社会科学院知识产权中心 [Chinese Academy of Social Sciences Intellectual Property Center] ed.,知识产权出版社 [Intellectual Property Press] 2008).

107 *See, e.g.,*证券法[Securities Law] (2005); 保险法 [Insurance Law] (2002); 保险法 [Insurance Law] (2009);中国人民银行法 [Law on the People's Bank of China] (2003); and 商业银行法 [Commercial Bank Law] (2003), which all underwent substantial changes.

108 陈洁，证券法 [Chen Jie, Securities Law] 25 (社会科学文献出版社 [Social Science Academic Press] 2006).

109 中国金融法治报告 (2009) [Chinese Financial Law Report 2009] 5 (胡滨、全先银[Hu Bin, Quan Xianyin] eds" 社会科学文献出版社 [Social Science Academic Press] 2009).

110 中国人民银行法 [Law on the People's Bank of China] (promulgated by the Nat'l People's Cong., Mar. 18, 1995, effective Mar. 18, 1995) Nat'l People's Cong. Gaz. (P.R.C.), art. 1.

111 中华人民共和国银行业监督管理法 [Banking Supervision Law] (promulgated by the Standing Comm. Nat'l People's Cong., Dec. 27, 2003, effective Feb. 1, 2004) Standing Comm. Nat'l People's Cong. Gaz. (P.R.C.), art. 1.

112 金人庆，在第十届全国人民代表大会第五次会议上的《关于<中华人民共和国企业所得税 法（草案)>的说明》[Jin Renqing, Speech at the Fifth Session of the Tenth National People's Congress: Explanation on the Draft Enterprise Income Tax Law] (2007), § 1, *available at* www.law-lib.com/fzdt/newshtml/20/20070308112435.htm (last visited Nov. 4, 2009).

113 曹康泰，在第十届全国人民代表大会常务委员会第二十二次会议上做的《〈反垄断法（草 案）>说明》[Cao Kangtai, Speech at the Standing Committee of the

Tenth National People's Congress: Explanation on the Draft Anti-Monopoly Law] (2006), *available at* www.npc.gov .cn/wxzl/gongbao/2007–10/09/content_5374671 .htm (last visited Nov. 4, 2009).

114 *See*王晓晔，竞争法学 [WANG XIAOYE, COMPETITION LAW] 195–97 (社会科学文献出版社 [Social Science Academic Press] 2007).

115 *See*中国共产党中央委员会，中共中央关于构建社会主义和谐社会若干重大问题的决定 [CPC CENT. COMM., DECISION ON ESTABLISHING A SOCIALIST HARMONIOUS SOCIETY] (2006), *available at* http://news.xinhuanet.com/politics/2006-10/18/content一5218639.htm (last visited Nov. 4, 2009).

116 全国人大法律委员会主任委员，解读劳动合同法 [Chairman of the Law Comm, of the Nat'l People's Cong., INTERPRETATION OF THE LABOR CONTRACT LAW] (2007), *available at* www.xinhuanet.com/zhibo/20070723/wz.htm (last visited Nov. 4, 2009).

117 史探径，社会法学 [SHI TANJING, SOCIAL Law] 35 (中国社会保障出版社 [China Labor and Social Security Press] 2007).

118 *See* CPC CENT. COMM., *supra* note 115.

119 人力资源社会保障部、国家统计局，2008年人力资源和社会保障失业发展统计公报 (DEPT. OF HUM. RES. AND SOC. SEC. & NAT'L BUREAU OF STAT., STATISTICAL BULLETIN OF THE DEVELOPMENT OF HUMAN RESOURCES AND SOCIAL SECURITY IN 2008) (May 19, 2009*)*, *available at* www.stats.gov.cn/tjgb/qttjgb/qgqttjgb/t20090519_402559984.htm (last visited Oct. 18, 2009).

120 王胜俊，2008年最高人民法院工作报告 [WANG SHENGJUN, SUPREME PEOPLE'S COURT WORK REPORT 2008] (2009).

121 *See* 蔡守秋、王欢欢，论加强环境法治文化建设的重要性和迫切性 [Cai Shouqiu & Wang Huanhuan, *The Importance and Urgency of Strengthening the Foundations of Environmental Law], in* 中国环境法治（2007 年卷）[CHINESE ENVIRONMENTAL LAW (2007)] 27–33 (法律出版社 [Law Press] 2008).

2

DO ALL ROADS LEAD TO CHINA?

Chinese Commercial Law Scholarship in the Past Decade (Part 1)

Wei Shen and Casey G. Watters

Source: The China Review, 16, 2, 2016, pp. 165–196.

Abstract

China's recent development of a modern legal system coupled with unparalleled economic growth have drawn substantial attention from commercial law scholars. This review summarizes Chinese- and English-language commercial law academic literature from the past decade contributed by both Chinese and non-Chinese scholars while discussing their different focuses, approaches, and methodologies. China's use of vague laws that rely upon implementation rules resulted in a substantial proportion of articles focusing on policy discussions and comparison to foreign approaches. Subsequently, a common theme in both Chinese and English literature was transplantation of foreign law. Chinese scholars often took a nationalistic approach, primarily assessing laws on their impact on China, whereas non-Chinese scholars advocated the adoption of foreign laws or legal structures to create clear standards and provide certainty for investors, which in turn is believed to facilitate continued growth of the Chinese economy. The literature is grouped into subject categories, allowing for discussion of important works and representative articles from leaders in their respective fields.

> And do as adversaries do in law, strive mightily, and eat and drink as friends.
>
> – William Shakespeare, *The Taming of the Shrew*

1. Introduction

China's unprecedented economic growth has spurred substantial debate regarding the role of law in China, the impact of existing law, and the need for legal reforms. The academic literature focused on commercial and economic reforms includes a wide assortment of topics due to the speed of legal reforms and economic growth China has implemented in recent years. This review summarizes the recent Chinese- and English-language academic literature contributed by both Chinese and non-Chinese scholars. Major works are grouped into subject categories, allowing for discussion of important works and representative articles from leaders in their respective fields.

By utilizing vague laws that rely on implementation rules and local interpretations and enforcement, the nature of the Chinese legal system lends itself to broader policy discussions than foreign commercial law literature. The policy analysis trend is exasperated in the foreign literature both due to the limited number of cases and interpretations available in English and because non-Chinese scholars are more inclined to engage in a longer and extensive analysis critical of Chinese policy. Chinese scholars were not only less critical, but often advocated laws and legal interpretation based on the benefit to China from a pluralistic perspective, whereas foreign scholars advocated certainty and fair treatment under the law in a stricter legalistic sense. In this regard, Chinese scholars appear more invested in the outcome with due appreciation of domestic discourse and conditions in lifting rule of law standards, while foreign scholars are comparative law oriented and ideologically objective—an understandable dynamic as Chinese commercial law most significantly impacts Chinese society and citizens.

There is a strong connection between foreign investment into China and academic publications on commercial law, as demonstrated in Table 2.1, which indicates the evolution of research focus on a variety of commercial law fields in the past three decades. China's entrance into the World Trade Organization (WTO) in 2001 sparked a series of reforms opening the Chinese market to foreign investment. In response to the reforms and increased foreign investment, publications focused on commercial law increased substantially, more than tripling in the commercial law areas represented in Table 2.1 below. The level of investment increased during the early 2000s with publications peaking in the 2005 to 2009 period. In 2008, China responded to the global financial crisis with economic reforms aimed at transitioning from an export-based economy to a domestically driven economy in order to counteract decreased demand for products prompted by the diminished spending capacity of Western consumers. Increased Chinese wages and lowered incentives for foreign investment, which was concentrated primarily in factories and export-based business, slowed the rate of foreign investment into China and subsequently the number of publications focused on investment decreased, as demonstrated in Table 2.1, during the previous five-year period.

Classifying law is a largely academic endeavor and commercial law, defined as "the body of law applicable to the rights, intercourse, and relations of persons engaged in commerce, trade, or mercantile pursuits,"[1] encompasses a wide range of laws and legal issues.[2] This article is structured into sections that present a general overview while balancing the competing objectives of scope and depth of analysis. Table 2.1 presents the number of articles published in English sources relating to selected topics of commercial law to illustrate trends in commercial law literature over 25 years.[3]

Across a wide range of commercial law topics, scholars regularly advocated the Chinese adoption of foreign laws or legal structures to facilitate the growth

Table 2.1 Publication Trends by Year and Type from Google Scholar (1990–2014)

	1990–1994	*1995–1999*	*2000–2004*	*2005–2009*	*2010–2014*
Banking	24	92	222	463	354
Securities	29	54	139	245	150
Company law	6	10	12	41	27
Bankruptcy	2	9	18	52	32
Property rights	29	95	165	327	247
WTO	3	136	1,550	540	282
Investment	270	697	1,350	2,450	2,040
Total	363	1,093	3,456	4,118	3,132

Note: A Google Scholar search was conducted on 23 July 2015 for publications containing the specified terms and the word "China" in the title. It should be noted that Google provides a rounded estimation. The growth of the Chinese economy spurred an increase in the number of publications focused on Chinese commercial law; however, the numbers may exaggerate this trend because earlier publications are less likely to be available digitally and are therefore less likely to appear in the Google Scholar database.

of the Chinese economy and provide certainty for investors. Although advocating this approach is more prevalent among non-Chinese academics, it is nonetheless widespread. Certainly, China can learn from the laws and experiences of other countries, as can any nation. However, China's government, culture, and legal system are unique in the economically developed world and the economic change and legal reform are unprecedented. It is naïve to think China can simply adopt, by legal transplants, comprehensive commercial law statutes from other jurisdictions and receive the same results.

After an overview of Chinese commercial law and the Chinese legal environment in section 2, this article is broken into five general sections that allow for the discussion of a majority of the commercial law literature while grouping articles into sections with similar broad themes.[4] Section 3 examines Chinese banking and corporate law and its developments as the Chinese economy matures and attempts to adjust from an export driven economy. Section 4 examines the real property rights, an important consideration for development and commercial land use because real and personal property rights are fundamental to commerce. Sections 5 and 6, respectively, discusses China's trade policy and investment treaties, including domestic policy impacting trade and the impact of the WTO and bilateral investment treaties on Chinese business law and practice in a cross-border context. A review of the literature regarding the enforceability business agreements in China is the focus of section 7, which reviews the importance of arbitration and the role of courts and judicial reform in China's business activities. This is an area normally not associated with commercial law but that requires addressing in a Chinese context as the enforceability in commercial agreements is a central focus of Chinese business law. A conclusion follows at the end.

2. Chinese commercial law framework

In the Chinese context, commercial law is always intertwined with civil law. The explanation for this state of affairs may be historical—in a civil law jurisdiction, commercial law is often viewed as part of the civil law even though some legal systems have a commercial code specifically designed and intended to meet the particular needs of the mercantile community.[5] China is now in a process of codifying a civil code, a fact confirmed in the Chinese Communist Party's communique for the fourth plenary session of the 18th Central Committee. In this legislative process, Chinese scholars can be generally divided into two groups. One group advocates a so-called uniform model combining civil law and commercial law together while the other group of scholars prefers to separate them in a "parallel model."[6] There are many arguments and counterarguments on both sides to support their schools of thoughts. For instance, the uniform model school contends, among others, that the uniform model is a legislative trend,[7] which fits the reality in a modern society where civil and commercial relationships should be governed similarly in a market economy due to the fact that both are horizontal in nature.[8] By contrast, the proponents for the parallel model argue that both branches of law have different focuses, targets, principles, and rules, as well as protect different interests.[9] Apart from this dichotomy, there is bound to be some controversy over the precise contents covered by the brand of commercial law. It appears that no two commercial law books are the same. However, the task in deciding which areas of the subject to include, and which to exclude, is made easier thanks to the customary view in Chinese legal academic circles.

A 2007 special issue of *China Quarterly* focused on trends in the Chinese legal system and serves as a good, although somewhat dated, overview of Chinese legal development. The articles cover a wide array of topics; however, the issue is nevertheless useful in illuminating the legal structure to provide context for the commercial law analysis. The same year, Donald Clarke published "China: Creating a Legal System for a Market Economy." While already nine years old, the article provides a skillful analysis of the Chinese legal environment while arguing that China needs to relax the top-down model and allow market-driven solutions to commercial legal problems.[10] The key question here, as with much academic literature, is what laws and institutions are necessary for a market economy. Within the context of a discussion of China's reforms directed at becoming a market economy, it is worth noting that Chinese law and literature regularly refers to the system as a "socialist" market economy. Somewhat contradictory, China regularly places provisions in treatise requiring nations to recognize, and subsequently treat, China as a market economy—a more beneficial status in regards to international trade. Regardless of labels, the Chinese legal system operates in a top-down manner and the state is resistant to bottom-up approaches to legal problems.[11] During the 1980s there was a period of decentralization; however, "from the vantage point of today it is hard not to be impressed by the staying power of the Chinese state."[12]

Whereas most legal scholars merely assume a developed market economy requires an advanced legal system, Clarke addresses the connection between the law and economic growth, reviewing among other arguments, that "economic growth requires a legal order offering stable and predictable rights of property and contract because absence of such rights discourages investment and specialization. Without the security of expectation offered by such a legal order, according to the Rights Hypothesis, the risks of a great number of otherwise beneficial transactions far outweigh their expected return, and as a result such transactions simply do not occur."[13] There are a variety of other theories expounded by academics, and while most scholars assume the Chinese legal system requires reform to sustain development, the current growth in China and other developing countries show that a certain degree of economic success and commercial activity can be sustained without an advanced legal system. Standing in contrast to the Rights Hypothesis expounded above, the size of the Chinese market creates opportunities for wealth that will entice many investors, foreign and domestic, to enter into commercial deals and stimulate the market. Nonetheless, conventional business wisdom and business theory dictate that increased certainty adds to investment and development. In this regard, not only clarity of the law and a dependable legal system but also access to information are necessary.

The lack of transparency in the Chinese legal system and government agencies has received substantial academic attention because it creates risk for foreign and domestic investors through increased uncertainty. Aside from local "open government" regulations, China's first major attempt at increasing transparency, the Regulation of the People's Republic of China on Open Government Information, was adopted by the State Council in 2007 largely for economic reasons in an effort to provide information necessary for economic development.[14] In 2014, the State Council General Office issued a set of annual priorities regarding disclosure which emphasized disclosure of regulatory decisions.[15] The approach, supporting those who advocate transplanting foreign legal regimes, was similar to President Obama's 2011 Presidential Memorandum on Regulatory Compliance.[16] It nonetheless operates within the Chinese system and local governments, utilizing the provision's requirement a party have "special need" for information regarding a penalized party, have been reluctant to disclose requested information.[17]

Driven in part by the lack of cases and empirical data, publications tend to respond to particular developments in the law that allow policy arguments and increased conjecture. Therefore, implementation and interpretations of key commercial statutes—the company law, contract law, enterprise bankruptcy law, and securities law, to name a few—are followed by publications explaining or criticizing the development. However, one area that is comparatively overlooked is the area of non-corporate company entities. While partnerships and one-person companies are common for Chinese nationals,[18] perhaps for ease or lack of understanding regarding limited liability protection, foreign investors are required to engage in an approval process with the Ministry of Commerce to form a business in China, making the additional steps to incorporate either necessary or comparatively less inconvenient. Foreigners' lack of utilization on partnerships likely contributes to the limited literature on the subject. Nonetheless, some limited works exist, and Nicholas Howson provides a great overview of the history of Chinese partnership law springing from the Qing dynasty in 1904 and culminating in the Enterprise Partnership Law (2006).[19] While non-corporate business entities are less important for foreign investors and lawyers, they are important in understanding the Chinese market. People engaged in business outside the legal framework under the planned economy and the establishment of formal non-corporate business entities legitimize small business and bring it under the framework of the legal system—a necessary step for a regulated market economy. To this end, alternative business forms deserve greater attention than they are receiving.

The primary focus of business law discourse, corporations, centers articles largely on the application of foreign legal principles to Chinese law. Commonly addressed elements of business law include agency and director duties,[20] including the business judgment rule,[21] and other issues of corporate governance and liability such as piercing the corporate veil[22] and derivative suits.[23] Derivative suits, a largely American element of corporate law that is rarely used in other countries, serves as an example of how foreign laws are often incompatible with the Chinese system.[24] Although admittedly the Chinese previsions authorizing derivative suits offer limited guidance to courts, this is true for much of Chinese law where vague laws are left to local governments to implement and interpret as necessary—a key problem for advocates of the Rights Hypothesis. Even adoption of foreign law that is viewed as identical, like the Chinese adoption of the doctrine of good faith in the contract law, takes on its unique Chinese flavor when implemented.[25] While conceptually identical, the United States and China have "a striking difference in attitude with respect to the doctrine of good faith," with US courts applying the doctrine in a substantially more limited manner.[26] The different approaches of the United States and China reflect the countries' "profound cultural, political, and legal difference."[27]

Irrespective of the area of substantive commercial law, the focus is disputes. This includes creating a clear body of law that provides notice and reasonable certainty of outcome for business entities and a dispute resolutions system that is fair and predictable. A number of works focus on the Chinese judiciary and, to a large extent, the independence of the judiciary.[28] "China is still far from the complete rule of law state with seamless protection of property rights and expectations."[29] However, the development and application of corporate law "has spurred the nation's formal legal institutions to develop real competence, substantial autonomy, and hints of political independence in application of the kind of law so important for growth."[30] Nevertheless, foreign parties must recognize the unique Chinese culture and legal tradition and not expect laws to be applied in the same manner. As mentioned above, the predictability is necessary for an advanced legal system and sustained economic growth. However, the adoption of foreign law without adaptation to the Chinese legal system does not guarantee identical outcomes or necessarily produce the same level of predictability until the Chinese legal system is fully matured. Countries all have traditions, each developed "in its own way, each solving the problems in a way understood and accepted within its own frame of reference."[31] Transplanting law is not always a workable option because "[n]o one party has a monopoly on the correct way to resolve disputes, nor the correct version of the Rule of Law."[32]

3. Banking and corporate law

Foreign investment into China prompted attention on banking, investment, and securities law, especially as China attempts to make Shanghai a international financial center and strengthen ties with Hong Kong. While some attention has been paid to the traditional investment and retail banking sectors, most banks take the form of state-owned enterprises (SOEs), creating a virtual government monopoly and limiting the need for discussion regarding the legal regime for Chinese banking. Although no categories perfectly represent reality, the Chinese financial sector can generally be broken down into banking, primarily concerned with lending, and investment tools with their accompanying regulations, such as insider trading and reporting requirement. As Chinese companies expand abroad, acquiring foreign enterprises, and foreign companies enter the Chinese market through local acquisition, the latter will grow in importance and likely experience an increase in academic discourse. Mergers and acquisitions are also a relatively under-researched area of Chinese law, with Google Scholar reporting only 77 articles for the five-year 2010 to 2014 period. Securities investment and banks compose the two main mechanisms for generating capital and therefore play vital roles in a developed economy.

a. Banking law

The state-owned banking sector remains the main target of academic research, with a number of empirical studies highlighting the negative economic impacts of state-owned banks.[33] For example, SOEs often receive substantial preference in the borrowing process by receiving high-risk loans and low interest rates—a phenomenon resulting in an abundance of nonperforming loans.[34] Private firms, on the other hand, are more likely to face political discrimination and tend to gain their competitive edges by bonding with commercial banks through holding significant ownership.[35] Bonding helps relax the financing constraints and allows the private firm similar benefits as SOEs such as lower interest rates and easier access to short-term loans when the government monetary policy is tight.[36] Minority foreign ownership is an instrument to improve the efficiency of Chinese banks.[37] Empirical findings show minority foreign ownership in the Big Four significantly improved performance and illustrated the value of ownership diversification, thereby providing a foundation for further banking reform through increased foreign minority ownership.

The number of banking-related articles published decreased in the past five-year period; however, the following year will presumably see a wave of publications as China's 2014 easing of restrictions on foreign banks, a largely symbolic act, was followed by opening the Chinese market to foreign credit card clearing services in June 2015 and a recent announcement was made that China will allow repos for a limited number of offshore lenders.[38] The latest financial crisis has generated renewed interest in how the institutional and regulatory environment influence bank risk taking and performance. Stronger law enforcement and greater bank risk taking have proved to have a correlative relationship,[39] which has a strong policy implication on the banking reform. Listing banks in domestic or overseas stock exchanges is one way of improving the enforcement mechanism by providing an additional level of regulatory oversight.[40] The banking sector's liberalization by allowing foreign ownership is the other route for further reform. Foreign ownership will most notably benefit the private sector, where it may break the monopolist dominance enjoyed by SOEs.[41] Foreign ownership, independent from local political pressure, will make interest rate decisions based on perceived risk and eliminate the power of state-owned banks to offset the expense of low-interest loans to local SOEs with high interest rate private loans. The end result may be a more efficient banking sector with a higher percentage of performing loans, an outcome both politically and economically desirable.

Apart from ownership and market stability, the most obvious side of the banking sector is loans, which are important on both the commercial level and for consumers seeking residential property. "To a substantial degree, residential units have become a commodity, serving as one the few investment vehicles available to the person on the street seeking a place to park some money and watch it grow."[42] Therefore, lending has become a highly regulated industry with the government setting down payment requirements to control the residential property markets.[43]

Somewhat counter-intuitively, the literature on banking calls simultaneously for deregulation,[44] in an effort to open the field to foreign institutions and domestic privately held corporations, and calls for greater regulatory enforcement in a fair and predictable manner. While the concurrent calls for increased and decreased regulation focus primarily on the lending market and investment tools, many touch on other areas or attempt to examine broader social implications. One largely interconnected area is property rights, with commercial land rights being of particular importance. But the latest financial crisis changed the landscape.

The global financial crisis and the resulting domestic reform to the commercial and retail banking sectors is a key area of recent academic research. While China has remained somewhat insulated from the global crisis,[45] experiencing slowed growth rates instead of recession, the domestic financial regulatory structure needs to be reformed to avoid or better weather the next financial crisis and economic slowdown. Stability also incentivizes China to implement international standards by aligning its laws with the Basel III Accord.[46] There are two schools of thought with respect to why China should adopt international banking standards, one looking inward at the domestic market and the other externally at China's increasing role in offshore finance. First, China is assuming an increasing active role in shaping international banking regulation in the aftermath of the financial crisis,[47] not the least of which is evidenced by the establishment of the International Development Bank. This changing assertiveness is evidenced by China's institutional build-up efforts as well as its willingness to accept and implement Basel-based banking regulatory norms.[48] Second, China's domestic financial regulatory structure merits some improvements, if not a complete overhaul, and Australia's Twin Peak model is a preferred direction for reform.[49]

With the banking sector controlled by SOEs, private businesses and individuals face difficulty securing loans, and the resulting shadow banking industry has becoming an increasingly popular subject among academics in the aftermath of the financial crisis.[50] Although China escaped the recessions experienced in many developed countries, the extent of Chinese shadow banking grew substantially, which may increase risk in China's banking and financial sectors.[51] While scholars agree regarding the risks associated with the shadow banking sector, the size[52] and causes[53] of the shadow banking sector are a point of academic debate, as are possible solutions. A leading argument is that structural imbalancing is the key cause of shadow banking in China: excessive dominance of the state sector in the marketplace, misallocation of credit and financial resources, policy propensity toward state-owned banks, and disregard of financial consumers in policy making.[54] Designing sensible policies to bring shadow banking into the light however is not that straightforward. While the need for deeper financial reform enjoys a widespread consensus, the medicine prescribed by academics is different. Further efforts are imperative in order to develop moderate and appropriate regulation and draw clearer legal boundaries.[55] Moving a sector-based regulatory model to a Twin-Peak model, though attractive, involves switching costs.[56] More troublesome for policy makers is the lack of analytical theories to support such a design. As such, it is advisable to employ a cautious approach to structural reforms to ensure risk is not merely displaced. The other is a market-oriented approach calling for a change to the dominant role played by the SOEs and state-owned banks and reforms leading to more robust capital markets and through increased availability of funding subsequently reduces the demand for illegal lending practices.[57]

Related to the financing is hybrid financing such as private equity and venture capital. Conventional corporate literature in China rarely touches upon corporate finance; however, private equity[58] and venture capital[59] have recently drawn attention from the academic circle. The key question is whether the Silicon Valley-originated financing instrument fits the Chinese market structure and Chinese company law and how the Company Law influences private equity transactions in China.[60] Apparently, no Chinese legislative document, judicial interpretation, or court ruling has provided explicit guidance on how a company could issue multiple classes of shares to different classes of shareholders. More preferential rights often granted by the founding shareholders to preferred shareholders including the anti-dilution provision remain vague under Chinese company law without a secure legal foundation, even though these rights have been negotiated and adopted into private equity transactions. A lack of a secure legal foundation for these preferential rights casts considerable doubt on the enforceability of private equity agreements and may dissuade venture capitalist for investing in China.[61]

Limited research has been conducted on the interplay between these investors' preferential rights under private equity agreements and the Company Law, and the possible mitigating strategies or causes of actions to minimize the uncertainty of enforcing preferential rights in China.[62] In attracting private equity investors and circumventing the clumsy Chinese Company Law, these innovative transactional models have been invented in the market. Along with this line of thinking, the rarely explored regulatory competition framework has also been utilized to investigate if there is a race to the top phenomenon in a centralized jurisdiction in which regulatory competition is not supposed to exist.[63] These angles are fresh but constructive in the Chinese context.

b. Chinese exchanges and cross-listing

The two stock exchanges in Mainland China, the Shanghai and Shenzhen Stock Exchanges, "do not yet play a very important role in the finance of the Chinese economy. The finance of the Chinese economy continues to be dominated, on large scale projects, primarily by bank finance and direct and indirect government support and, on entrepreneurial finance level, primarily by foreign direct investment and a range of less formal arrangements."[64] The majority of foreign securities markets formed over time in a bottom-up manner as businesses sought to use the market to attain additional capital and businessmen pursued investment opportunities. However, the Chinese stock exchanges were formed over a much shorter time by the government in a top-down manner serving as a source of revenue primarily for SOEs.[65] As a result, the stock exchanges principally serve state purposes and exist as a funding mechanism for the state-controlled sector of the economy.[66] The role of the changes and regulatory framework have discouraged the listing of foreign companies, leaving large international companies to list in the Hong Kong, Tokyo, or established Western stock exchanges, and the limited involvement of foreign companies[67] and investors explains the lack of attention by non-Chinese scholars.

Foreign scholars predominately advocate for reforms that would bring the Chinese exchanges more in line with exchanges in other global financial centers. Such arguments, however, rely on a Chinese desire to reform to a market economy beyond what might be rightfully considered a socialist market economy, and assume the market and the entrepreneurial benefits of a bottom-up approach to funding business is the ideal system to stimulate the Chinese economy. While this assumption is perhaps accurate, the role of SOEs makes the Chinese market and political system interconnected, albeit in a complicated and often inexplicit manner. The government has been central in establishing the current markets, and while deregulation is an option to reform Chinese exchanges, it is naive to assume government action can forcefully create exchanges that mirror those in more mature economies with a history of free market activity.[68]

Reformative measures advocated in academic literature have a three-pronged approach. First, the reform should be implemented within the public enforcement regime.[69] To this end, administrative law needs to be strengthened to empower regulators to ensure compliance with trade regulation and regulators must utilize their legal authority. Insider trading prohibitions, for instance, are currently enforced through nonlegal and nonregulatory guidance, which itself is a violation of law.[70] Second, the private enforcement regime is investigated through the study of the nature and extent of private securities litigation.[71] The number of civil securities cases was trivial in the decade following China's statutory adoption of derivative actions, which suggests an ineffectiveness of wholesale transplantation of foreign law and the low possibility of success in transplanting the legal norm of class actions from the United States.[72] Third, scholars examine a semi-enforcement regime focusing on the role of the stock exchanges as regulators and sources of information.[73] The stock exchanges in China are empowered to monitor the market through publicizing public criticism of listed companies. An event study together with extensive interviews of market actors demonstrated the significant impact public criticisms had on listed companies and their executives.[74] The reputational sanctions, if effective as claimed, may match the relational finance that is popular in China. This may help technically fill the vacuum left in the LLSV doctrine and explain the mystery of China's economic growth without a strong legal infrastructure.

Traditional logic dictates that reforms are necessary to attract investors and increase the standing of the two exchanges;[75] however, the Chinese growth model has repeatedly transcended traditional logic. Even without reforms, the Chinese stock exchanges are becoming increasingly attractive to foreign investors and China experiences a higher economic growth rate than developed economies while investors seek access to the Chinese consumer market numbering 1.3 billion. China is even positioned to allow cross-listing of foreign enterprises on Chinese markets.[76]

Cross-listing is also an effective corporate governance tool on which Chinese firms can rely to improve their corporate governance and corporate performance.[77] The underlying logic is that by "piggybacking" on an exchange in a jurisdiction with more stringent financial regulations and more effective oversight, Chinese firms through overseas listing can strengthen their corporate governance regime by making use of a more vibrant capital market and rights-oriented corporate law regime overseas.[78] Overseas listings creates a bonding effect, which helps a large number of Chinese firms to implement more stringent accounting rules, higher disclosure standards, and more user-friendly minority shareholder protection rules or mechanisms.[79]

Businesses domiciled in developed countries cross-listing in China or other emerging markets runs contrary to the "legal bonding" hypothesis, which states that listing in the United States or jurisdictions with higher regulatory standards reassures investors and allows listed companies to demand a higher premium for shares.[80] In fact, when US companies list on foreign exchanges, the shares "exhibit negative abnormal returns."[81] This phenomenon, dubbed "Reverse Cross-listing" and explained with a consumer-commercial markets bonding (CCMB) theory by Howson and Khanna, is nonetheless taking place, albeit still on a limited scale.[82] Under CCMB, the listed company is willing to forgo the premium price benefits of its jurisdiction for a greater connection with the target country. Benefits may include a local corporate identity, establishing a commitment to the local market, as well as a "tipping of the hat" to Chinese regulators.[83] The last benefit may be significant considering the role of relationship *guanxi* in Chinese business and the degree of discretion afforded Chinese regulators.[84]

Even with a top-down model, China can attract greater investment through increased transparency and targeting corruption.[85] Ultimately, the important reforms center on corporate governance and accountability of corporate officers and directors.[86] Unless investors are confident in government oversight, enforcement of anticorruption provisions and the ability of the government to address the agency problem, reform will be necessary to empower shareholders. These include mechanisms like derivative[87] or direct[88] suits that will reassure investors that management will behave responsibly and in the investors' best interests.

Insider trading is another issue that threatens investment and is a key concern of the Chinese market, prompting various calls for reform-most commonly calls for fair and uniform enforcement.[89] Insider trading is prohibited under the Chine Criminal Law; however, the law fails to prescribe details on what constitutes insider trading. The PRC Securities Law, passed in 2006, not only disallows insider trading under civil law but has no scienter requirement or affirmative defenses for corporate leaders, or shareholders attaining a 5 percent threshold, who profit from stock held less than six months.[90] The vague provisions of the law allow the government to virtually enforce and interpret insider trading provisions in any way they deem fit,[91] a structure that flies in the face of reforms moving towards the rule of law but something arguably necessary for investors to gain confidence in the China market. In China, where insider trading is accepted by many as pervasive, limitations on the government's ability to prevent insider trading would shake confidence in the exchanges and undercut a fundamental objective of "rule of law" reforms—to promote investor confidence in the Chinese market. While the Chinese law is currently modeled after the US insider trading provisions, adoption of the same system as that used in the United States, as advocated by some Western scholars, may be against the best interests of China in the short term.

Hostile takeovers are yet to be a common phenomenon in China's capital markets even after the end of the equity-division reform at the end of 2006.[92] However, scholars predict that China will experience a rise of the number of hostile takeovers in the near future.[93] Research has been conducted through the lens of the multi-factor model. The law needs to be amended to add a shareholder ratification mechanism for the adoption of pre-tender-offer anti-takeover measures by target-company management. Before this gap is filled, the China Securities Regulatory Commission can be in a position to exercise its authority to review the legitimacy of pre-tender-offer anti-takeover measures as an interim approach.[94] However, it should be noted that the adoption of these market reforms requires changing fundamental economic and political settings. The over-concentrated shareholding structure of listed companies may not constrain the conglomerate operation of listed companies, thereby effectively blocking China's hostile takeover market.

c. *Roles of SOEs and sovereign wealth funds*

More vibrant capital markets often possess a self-enforcing (or private enforcement) model, which has led some Chinese scholars to prefer the adoption of a similar model.[95] While a self-enforcing model is likely to be more cost-effective,[96] the efficacy of this model, which relies on independent courts and a diffused market structure, is doubtful in China due to the overconcentrated ownership structure of listed companies and strong influence by regulators.[97] Majority shareholders are dominant players in the capital markets and most of them are SOEs, which have natural political connections with the courts and are less willing to rely on derivative actions to protect their rights in the courts.[98] The limited number of derivative actions filed in China demonstrates the reluctance of minority shareholders to challenge the political and economic privilege of SOEs, either because minority shareholders believe they cannot win or because the costs exceed the benefits of litigations.[99] In addition, investor confidence in the courts is low due to perceived corruption, inefficiency, and the inexperience of Chinese judges in commercial litigation. The robustness of the capital markets is unlikely to be supported and facilitated by the current legal infrastructure.

For Chinese companies, operating as a conglomerate generally decreases profitability and efficiency while providing increased risk.[100] Nevertheless, there has been a revival of academic interest in Chinese SOEs. There are several possible reasons for this. First, there is a rosy picture of China's SOEs in the aftermath of the financial crisis.[101] In particular, the Big Four became four of the top five commercial lenders worldwide and performed far better than their counterparts in the United States or Europe. A decade ago, these Western commercial lenders were invited to rescue Chinese banks, which were almost on the edge of technical insolvency.[102] Ten years later, the Big Four, together with other Chinese commercial banks, became the cash box for their Western counterparts to polish their balance sheets. Second, China became the second largest country in terms of the number of *Fortune* Global 500 companies, right after the United States. Most of these Chinese companies included in the *Fortune* Global 500 are SOEs, which may leave an impression to the world that SOEs in China are profitable and efficient. Irrespective of the cause, the recent success of SOEs has attracted tremendous interests in the academic circle.

SOEs continue to be the foundation of the Chinese economy but are the source of inefficiency and unbalancing.[103] The study of SOEs has not been included in the mainstream research of corporate law. Instead, it is a key topic in the economic law scholarship with a focus on the government's regulation of economic activity.[104] Outsiders connect a strong state sector with state capitalism and try to rationalize SOEs' surprising success in the past decade.[105] The attempt is thus made to unpack the black box of "state capitalism" in China through the examination of business group ownership structure within the national SOEs. The organizational structure and its organic links to the party-state are said to be one of the most important feature of SOEs in China.[106] This institutional feature, that is, a strong connection between the national champions and the organs of the party-state, forms a solid foundation for SOEs' survival and revival. In this context, the conventional agency problem is no longer the core doctrinal framework connecting all the moving pieces in corporate law. Rather, the network of firms embedded in the SOE group fits and advances the key objectives a party-state-driven economic growth model is supposed to achieve. This can be a stepping stone for further in-depth research on SOEs and their dynamic relationship with China's growing economy.

Special attention has been paid to the China Investment Corporation.[107] The concern is about not only its status as a sovereign wealth fund with US$500 billion capital but also its potential to gain control of other countries' key assets thereby influencing the host countries' politics. While major Western countries also have their own sovereign wealth funds possessing some strategic assets such as oil and mining, China's sovereign wealth fund is alarming to some foreign scholars due to its size and its unconventional way of handling fundamental international law issues such as state immunity.[108] The latest Congo case again confirms China's unconventional stance on state immunity.[109] The literature has focused on the function and role of the China Investment Corporation in facilitating China's domestic and global strategies. The findings have shown that the giant China Investment Corporation has been deployed not only to advance China's domestic objectives, that is, diversifying its massive foreign exchange reserves and supporting its pillar industries, but also to enhance its natural resource security and build international partnerships.[110]

The other angle to look into the China Investment Corporation and China's Central Huijin Investment Limited is a lens of financial regulation.[111] They are characterized as bank holding companies under US financial law and granted some conditional exemptions such as nonbanking restrictions. However, regulatory principles such as the systemwide supervisory approach and the source of strength doctrine may apply to the entities. Improving transparency in using the national foreign exchange reserve as a special form of the central government's debt financing and joining the global effort to govern and streamline the sovereign wealth fund should be two pillars for China to remove the widespread misgivings that the international community embraces against China's sovereign wealth funds.[112] This financial regulation perspective again stresses the need to improve the corporate governance regime of the sovereign wealth funds.

Transformation of financial conglomerates is a prevalent topic in Chinese commercial law.[113] The segregation of financial conglomerates appears beneficial to the real economy by injecting liquidity into the market and boosting the private sector. However, Chinese banks are moving toward a universal banking model, opposite to the market expectation and trend of deregulation that was experienced prior to the most recent financial crisis. As discussed above, administrative monopoly and market failure may help explain this averse phenomenon. Policies that deepen market economy reform and liberalizing foreign investment laws to further diversify equity ownership of listed companies should be the key instruments to restructure the financial market.[114]

The basic fabric of SOEs is a political logic, which is not in line with the shareholder primary doctrine or the profit maximization goal.[115] SOEs in China are still tasked with contributing to the national welfare, maintaining a harmonious society, and ensuring sustainable economic development. These goals together with state control shape, but distort, corporate governance.[116] SOEs' improving corporate performance does not fundamentally change the basic fabric of the dual-goal model of corporate governance.[117] It is a natural outcome to see SOE reform trapped in a deadlock without substantial breakthroughs.

This also explains why transplanting some corporate governance instruments into China does not guarantee sensible outcomes. The corporate governance tool of appointing independent directors onto the listed firms' board of directors has long been incorporated into China's corporate law and listing rules. However, this corporate governance system is derived from a defused market structure to address the agency problem in a market composed of businesses with, practically speaking, the sole purpose of attaining profit while owing a fiduciary duty to shareholders independent of any political goals. To be successful, the system requires independent courts equipped to address issues of corporate governance and sophisticated independent directors. While the law reflects a similar stated goal in China, in practice independent directors do not function as a monitoring mechanism in listed firms due to the lack of independence and effectiveness.[118] Recruiting an independent director is a near insurmountable obstacle for minority shareholders as one qualified and familiar with the industry would necessarily be connected with government or related SOEs.[119] In addition, the lack of other supplementary institutions or mechanisms leads to the dysfunction of independent directors in reality.[120]

(To be continued in the next issue)

Notes

* The authors thank the two reviewers for their constructive comments on previous drafts of this article and acknowledge Yu Tao's research assistance in completing citations of Chinese-language materials.

1 Alan M. Fisch, "Seeking the Intersection of Two Legal Sets: A Review of the Commercial Law of Intellectual Property," *Columbia-VLA Journal of Law & the Arts,*

Vol. 19 (Spring/Summer 1995), p. 307, quoting *Black's Law Dictionary,* 6th ed. (St. Paul, MN: West, 1990).

2 The *Wex Legal Dictionary and Encyclopedia* provided by Cornell Law School list 11 bodies of law under the broader title of commercial law: banking, bankruptcy, consumer credit, contracts, debtor and creditor law, landlord-tenant, mortgages, negotiable instruments, real estate translations, sales, secured transactions. See *Commercial Law: An Overview,* available at www.law.cornell.edu/wex/commerciallaw.

3 The chart, while not exhaustive, attempts to include a range of commercial law subjects, as discussed in note 2. However, terms were selected based on common usage, and many were excluded if a substantial portion of articles employing the term fell outside the scope of commercial law.

4 After reviewing articles with the higher citation rates or more relevance in each of the major categories of commercial law, as discussed in note 2, and articles by leaders in their respective fields, the articles included here were selected either because they are highly representative of the academic literature on point or because the articles presented a unique and impactful argument (something generally accompanied by a high citation rate).

5 L. S. Sealy and R. J. A. Hooley, *Commercial Law: Text, Cases and Materials,* 2nd ed. (London: Butterworths, 1999), preface.

6 Wang Liming, "Minshang heyi tili xia woguo minfadian zongze de zhiding" (Enactment of a Chinese Civil Code Under the Civil-Commercial Combination System), *Fashang yanjiu* (Studies in Law and Business), No. 4 (2015), p. 3; Wang Meili, "Tongze shang de minshang heyi yu ge shangshi danxingfa duli bingxing-Zhongguo shangshi lifa moshi de xuanze" (Civil-Commercial Combination as a General Rule Runs Parallel with Commercial Specific Regulation: China's Choice of Commercial Legislation Mode), *Zhengzhi yu falii* (Political Science and Law), No. 3 (2006), p. 119; Zhao Wanyi, "Lun minfa de shangfahua yu shangfa de minfahua-Jiantan woguo minfadian bianzuan de jiben linian he silu" (On Commercial Law of Civil Law and Civil Law of Commercial Law-Current Discussion about the Basic Ideal and of the Thinking of Codification of Our Civil Code), *Faxue luntan* (Legal Forum), No. 4 (2005), p. 128; Zhao Wanyi, "Lun minshangfa jiazhi quxiang de yitong jiqi dui woguo minshang lifa de yingxiang" (A Study on Trends in Valuation of Civil and Commercial Law and the Influence of Legislation Regarding China8 Civil Legal System), *Faxue luntan* (Legal Forum), No. 6 (2003), pp. 12–21.

7 Ma Junju, "Minfadian: jianshe shehuizhuyi fazhi guojia de jichu-Zhuanjia xuezhe tan zhongguo minfadian de zhiding" (A Civil Code: The Foundation of Building a Socialist Country under the Rule of Law—Scholars' Discussion on Codification of Civil Law), *Falü kexue* (Law Science), No. 3 (1998), p. 6; Liang Huixing, "Zhiding minfadian de shexiang" (Observations on Drafting a Civil Code in China), *Xiandai faxue* (Modern Law Science), No. 4 (2001), pp. 3–6.

8 Ma Junju and Mei Xiaying, "Woguo weilai minfadian zhong shezhi caichanquan zongzebian de liyou he jiben gouxiang" (A Proposition for Setting up General Rules of Property Rights in the Future Civil Law Code and Its Logic), *Zhongguo faxue* (Chinese Legal Science), No. 4 (2004), p. 31.

9 Wang Liming, "Zhongguo minfadian de tixi" (The System of China's Civil Code), *Xiandai faxue* (Modern Law Science), No. 4 (2001), pp. 45–54; Xu Xuelu, "Minshang fenli shi woguo shichang jingji lifa moshi de zuijia xuanze" (To Separate Civil Law and Commercial Law Is the Best Choice for China's Market-Oriented Economy), *Xiandai faxue* (Modern Law Science), No. 2 (1993), pp. 18–23.

10 Donald C. Clarke, "China: Creating a Legal System for a Market Economy," Asian Development Bank/GWU Law School Public Law Research Paper No. 396 (2007), available at http://papers.ssrn.com/sol3/papers.cfm?abstract_id=1097587.

11 See Donald C. Clarke, "The Chinese Legal System since 1995: Steady Development, Striking Continuities," *China Quarterly,* Vol. 191 (2007).
12 Ibid., p. 556.
13 Clarke, "China," p. 2.
14 Jamie P. Horsley, "China Adopts First Nationwide Open Government Information Regulations" (2007), available at www.law.yale.edu/documents/pdf/intellectual_life/cl-ogi-china_adopts_jph-english.pdf.
15 Jamie P. Horsley, "China Deepens Its Disclosure Regime" (4 April 2014), available at www.law.yale.edu/images/IntellectualLife/Freedom_Info.pdf.
16 Ibid.
17 Ibid.
18 A large percentage of Chinese small businesses remain unregistered.
19 Nicholas Calcina Howson, "Return of the Prodigal Form?—Partnerships and Partnership Law in the People's Republic of China," in *Research Handbook on Partnerships, LLCs and Alternative Forms of Business Organizations,* edited by Robert W. Hillman and Mark J. Loewenstein (Northampton: Edward Elgar, 2015) pp. 4–32.
20 Wei Yuwa, "Directors' Duties under Chinese Law: A Comparative Review," *University of New England Law Journal,* Vol. 3, No. 1 (2006), pp. 31–56.
21 Charlie Xiao-chuan Weng, "Assessing the Applicability of the Business Judgment Rule and the 'Defensive' Business Judgment Rule in the Chinese Judiciary: A Perspective on Takeover Dispute Adjudication," *Fordham International Law Journal,* Vol. 34 (2010), p. 124.
22 Shen Wei and Casey Watters, "Is China Creating a New Business Order? Rationalizing China's Extraterritorial Attempt to Expand the Veil-Piercing Doctrine," *Northwestern Journal of International Law & Business,* Vol. 35, No. 3 (2015), pp. 469–556.
23 Hui Huang, "The Statutory Derivative Action in China: Critical Analysis and Recommendations for Reform," *Berkeley Business Law Journal,* Vol. 4 (2007); Donald C. Clarke, "Pathway to Minority Shareholder Protection: Derivative Actions in the People's Republic of China," GW Law Faculty Publications & Other Works Paper 1064 (2011), available at http://scholarship.law.gwu.edu/faculty_publications/1064.
24 Casey Watters, "Chinese Derivative Suits: An Incompatible Adoption of Foreign Law" (paper, Conference on Interdisciplinary Business Studies, Bangkok, 2014).
25 Chulin Leonhard, "A Legal Chameleon: An Examination of the Doctrine of Good Faith in Chinese and American Contract Law," *Connecticut Journal of International Law,* Vol. 25 (2010), p. 305.
26 Ibid., pp. 307–308.
27 Ibid., p. 308.
28 Nicholas C. Howson, "Judicial Independence and the Company Law in the Shanghai Courts," in *Judicial Independence in China: Lessons for Global Rule of Law Promotion,* edited by Randall Reerenboom (Cambridge: Cambridge University Press, 2009), pp. 134–153.
29 Ibid., p. 152.
30 Ibid., p. 153.
31 Benedict Sheehy, "Fundamentally Conflicting Views of the Rule of Law in China and the West & Implications for Commercial Disputes," *Northwestern Journal of International Law & Business,* Vol. 26 (2006), p. 265.
32 Ibid., p. 266.
33 Cui Jianjun, "Guoyou shangye yinhang xindai jizhong de fumian yingxiang jiqi jiaozheng" (The Negative Impact of Loan Centralization of State-Owned Commercial Banks and Its Rectification), *Henan jinrong guanli ganbu xueyuan xuebao* (Journal of the Henan Institute of Financial Management), No. 5 (2004), p. 13.
34 He Xianjie, Zhu Hongjun, and Chen Xinyuan, "Zhengfu de duochong liyi qudong yu yinhang de xindai xingwei" (Multiple Benefits Drive Government and Bank's

Lending Behavior), *Jinrong yanjiu* (Journal of Financial Research), No. 6 (2008), p. 18.

35 Li Cuangzi and Liu Li, "Zhaiwu rongzi chengben yu minying xindai qishi" (Debt Financing Costs and Credit Discrimination on Private Firms), *Jinrong yanjiu* (Journal of Financial Research), No. 12 (2009), p. 149.

36 Zhengfei Lu, Jigao Zhu, and Weining Zhang, "Bank Discrimination, Holding Bank Ownership, and Economic Consequences: Evidence from China," *Journal of Banking and Finance,* Vol. 36 (2012), pp. 341–354.

37 Ai Hongde and Zhang Yu, "Waizi yinjin zhanlue yu zhongguo yinhangye gaige: Xiaolv yu wending de quanheng" (The Strategy of Foreign Capital and the Reform of the Chinese Banking Industry: The Trade-off of Efficiency and Stabilization), *Guangdong jinrong xueyuan xuebao* (Journal of Guangdong University of Finance), No. 4 (2006), p. 7.

38 Bloomberg, "China Opens Repo Market to Overseas Banks in Push on Yuan Usage," *Bloomberg Business,* 3 June 2015, available at www.bloomberg.com/news/articles/2015–06–03/china-s-pboc-opens-interbank-repo-operations-to-banks-overseas.

39 Jianhua Zhang, Peng Wang, and Baozhi Qu, "Bank Risk Taking, Efficiency, and Law Enforcement: Evidence from Chinese City Commercial Banks," *China Economic Review,* Vol. 23 (2012), pp. 284–295; Zhou Wen, "Yingxiang yinhang maoxian xingwei de yinsu-Laizi woguo yinhangye de shizheng jianyan" (Factors Affecting Bank Risk Taking: Evidence from China), *Caijing lilun yu shijian* (The Theory and Practice of Finance and Economics), No. 149 (2007), p. 43.

40 Ma Jing, Huang Fuguang, and Tian Yao, "Guquan duoyuanhua he woguo shangshi yinhang de zonghe jixiao" (Ownership Diversification and the Comprehensive Performance of China's Listed Banks), *Nankai jingji yanjiu* (Nankai Economic Studies), No. 3 (2014), pp. 123–124.

41 Xiong Zhengde and Hou Lijuan, "Waizi rugu dui shangye yinghang xiaolv de yingxiang: Jiyu mianban shuju de fenxi" (The Efficiency Effects of Introducing Minority Foreign Ownership into China's Commercial Banks: Based on the Panel Data), *Caijing lilun yu shijian* (The Theory and Practice of Finance and Economics), No. 159 (2009), p. 22.

42 Gregory M. Stein, "Commercial Leasing in China: An Overview," *Cornell Real Estate Law,* Vol. 8 (2010), pp. 26–33.

43 Guo Ye, "Zhengce tiaokong, gangganlv yu quyu fangdichan jiage" (Policy Adjustment Leverage and Property Prices across Regions), *Xia'men daxue xuebao* (Journal of Xiainen University [Arts & Social Sciences]), No. 4 (2011), p. 50.

44 Jiao Haitao, "Yinhang baoli de falii kongzhi: Fangsong guanzhi er'fei fanlongduan" (Legal Control on Huge Profits for Banks: Deregulation Instead of Anti-Monopoly), *Huadong zhengfa daxue xuebao* (Journal of the East China University of Political Science and Law), No. 2 (2013), p. 42.

45 Chen Siqing, "Dui 2008 nian jinrong weiji de zairenshi" (Recognition of the Financial Crisis in 2008), *Guoji jinrong* (International Finance), No. 4 (2013), p. 10.

46 Hui Huang, "China's Legal Response to the Global Financial Crisis: From Domestic Reform to International Engagement," *Australian Journal of Asian Law,* Vol. 12, No. 2 (2010), p. 157.

47 Wan Tailei, Li Songliang, and Huang Xin, "Guoji jinrong jianguan hezuo ji zhongguo canyu lujing" (International Cooperation and China's Participation in Financial Supervision), *Guoji jingji pinglun* (International Economic Review), No. 3 (2014), pp. 127–129.

48 Chao Xi, "Domestic Politics as International Norms: China's Changing Roles in International Banking Regulation," *Banking and Finance Law Review,* Vol. 30 (2014), pp. 69–88.

49 Hui Huang, "Institutional Structure of Financial Regulation in China: Lessons from the Global Financial Crisis," *Journal of Corporate Law Studies,* Vol. 10, No. 1 (2010), pp. 219–254.

50 Wang Jing, "Zhongguoshi yingzi yinghang fanchou ji jianguan jinzhan" (Scope and Supervision Progress of Chinese Shadow Banking), *Guanli xiandaihua* (Modernization of Management), No. 2 (2014), p. 2.

51 Dong Tao and Weishen Deng, "China: Shadow Banking-Road to Heightened Risks," Credit Suisse Economics Research Paper (2013), available at www.credit-suissee.com/researchandanalytics (accessed 15 August 2015).

52 Wang Boli and Li Jianjun, "Zhongguo yingzi yinhang de guimo, fengxian pinggu yu jianguan duice" (The Size of Chinese Shadow Banking, Risk Assessment and Supervision Countermeasures), *Zhongyang caijing daxue xuebao* (Journal of Central University of Finance & Economics), No. 5 (2013), p. 22; Pei Pin and Yin Wen, "Zhongguo yingzi yinhang de xinyong chuangzao jiqi guimo cesuan" (Credit Creation from Chinese Shadow Banking and the Scale Estimation), *Jingji guanli* (Economic Management Journal), No. 3 (2014), pp. 103–105; Zhan Yi and Wang Long, "Zhongguo yingzi yinhang xindai guimo ji dui yinhang tixi wendingxing de yingxiang fenxi" (Analysis of the Scale of Chinese Shadow Banking and Its Influence on the Stability of the Banking System), *Shijie jingji yu zhengzhi luntan* (Forum of World Economics & Politics), No. 5 (2014), pp. 68–69; Sun Guofeng and Jia Junyi, "Zhongguo yingzi yinhang jieding jiqi guimo cesuan-Jiyu xinyong huobi chuangzao de shijiao" (Defining China's Shadow Banking and Assessing Its Scale—Seen in Terms of the Creation of Credit Money), *Zhongguo shehui kexue* (Social Sciences in China), No. 11 (2015), pp. 104–108.

53 Zhao Yingwei, "Woguo 'yingzi yinhang' de xinyong fengxian juji-Jiyu lici jinrong weiji de fengxi" (A Comparison of 'Shadow Banking' Credit Risk: Aggregation from the Global Major Financial Crisis), *Caijing kexue* (Finance & Economics), No. 11 (2013), pp. 27–28; Shen Wei, "Zhongguo yingzi yinhang fengxian jiqi guizhi gongju xuanze" (Risks of Chinese Shadow Banking and Choice of Regulatory Tools), *Zhongguo faxue* (China Legal Science), No. 4 (2014), pp. 164–166; Xie Fengmin, He Lingyun, and Zhou Yingying, "Zhongguo yingzi yinhang fazhan chengyin shizheng fenxi-Jiyu 2002–2012 nian yuedu shuju" (An Empirical Analysis of the Cause of the Development of China's Shadow Banking Based on the Monthly Data from 2002 to 2012), *Lilun yu shijian* (The Theory and Practice of Finance and Economics), No. 187 (2014), p. 25.

54 Shen Wei, "Shadow Banking System in China—Origin, Uniqueness and Governmental Responses," *Journal of International Banking Law and Regulations,* Vol. 28, No. 1 (2013), pp. 20–26.

55 Li Guo and Daile Xia, "In Search of a Place in the Sun: The Shadow Banking System with Chinese Characteristics," *European Business Organization Law Review,* Vol. 15 (2014), pp. 387–418.

56 Hui Huang, "The Regulation of Shadow Banking in China: International and Comparative Perspectives," *Banking and Finance Law Review,* Vol. 30, (2015), p. 481.

57 Shen Wei, "Shadow Banking System in China."

58 Dai Yiyi, Pan Yue and Liu Xinyu, "Shehui ziben, zhengzhi guanxi yu woguo simu guquan jijin tourongzi xingwei" (Social Capital, Political Connections and PE's Investment and Financing Behavior in China), *Nankai guanli pinglun* (Nankai Business Review), No. 4 (2014), pp. 88–97; Liang Qinghua, "Lun woguo simu xinxi pilu zhidu de wanshan" (On the Perfection of Our Country's Information Disclosure Requirement), *Zhongguo faxue* (China Legal Science), No. 5 (2014), pp. 149–159; Liu Ming, "Lun simu guquan gongkai zhongchou zhong gongkai xuanchuan guize de tiaozheng lujing-Jianping 'simu guquan zhongchou rongzi guanli banfa (shixing)'" (On the General Solicitation Rule in Private Equity Crowdfunding-Also on the Measures of Private Equity Crowdfunding [Draft]), *Faxuejia* (The Jurist), No. 5 (2015), pp. 95–104.

59 Wu Chaopeng, Wu Shinong, Cheng Jingya, and Wang Lu, "Fengxian touzi dui shangshi gongsi tourongzi xingwei yingxiang de shizheng yanjiu" (The Role of Venture

Capital in the Investment and Financing Behavior of Listed Companies: Evidence from China), *Jingji yanjiu* (Economic Research Journal), No. 1 (2012), pp. 105–119; Gou Yannan and Dong Jing, "Fengxian touzi jinru shiji dui qiye jishu chuangxin de yingxiang yanjiu" (The Relationship between Timing of Venture Capital Investment and the Technological Innovation of Firms), *Zhongguo ruan kexue* (China Soft Science), No. 3 (2013), pp. 132–140; Wu Cuifeng, Wu Shinong, and Liu Wei, "Fengxian touzi jieru chuangye qiye pianhao jiqi fangshi yanjiu-Jiyu zhongguo chuangyeban shangshi gongsi de jingyan shuju" (A Study on the Investment Preference and Pattern of Venture Capital: Evidence from Chinese Listed Companies on the GEM), *Nankai guanli pinglun* (Nankai Business Review), No. 5 (2014), pp. 151–160.

60 Shen Wei, "Face Off: Is China a Preferred Regime for International Private Equity Investments? Decoding a 'China Myth' from the Chinese Company Law Perspective," *Connecticut Journal of International Law,* Vol. 26, No. 1 (2010), pp. 89–160.

61 Tao Liang, "The Enforceability of Anti-dilution Provisions in Private Placement Transactions in China," *Tsinghua China Law Review,* Vol. 6, No. 1 (2013), pp. 46–63.

62 Shen Wei, "Uncertainties in Implementing a Multiple-Class Share Structure under the PRC Corporate Law and Possible Mitigation Strategies," *Company Lawyer,* Vol. 31, No. 9 (2010), pp. 280–290.

63 Shen Wei, "China's Dilemma: How Can a Weak Company Law Regime Support a Strong Market for International Private Equity Investments?-A Real 'Piggybacking' Case," *Business Law International,* Vol. 11, No. 3 (2010), pp. 195–224.

64 William T. Allen and Han Shen, "Assessing China's Top-Down Securities Markets," in *Capitalizing China,* edited by Joseph Fan and Randall Morck (Chicago: University of Chicago Press, 2011), p. 150.

65 Lu Li, "Zizhi ruhe xingcheng-Dui zhengquan jiaoyisuo falii diwei de lishi bijiao" (How to Form Self-Governance: A Historical Comparison Concerning the Legal Status of Security Exchange in the PRC), *Xiandai faxue* (Modern Law Science), No. 4 (2004), pp. 130–131; Feng Guo and Tian Chunlei, "Linyuanxianyu moruo tuierjiewang—Guanyu woguo zhengquan jiaoyisuo zuzhi xingshi gaige de yidian fansi" (Better to Go Back and Make a Net Than Long for the Fish by Merely Staring into the Water—Rethinking the Reform of Organization Form of China's Stock Exchange), *Faxue pinglun* (Law Review), No. 5 (2009), p. 28.

66 Allen and Shen, "Assessing China's Top-Down Securities Markets."

67 Tang Yingmao, "Siren qiye weihe qu haiwai shangshi-Zhongguo falü dui hongchou moshi haiwai shangshi de jianguan" (Why Private Enterprises Choose Overseas IPOs-China's Legal Supervision on the Red Chip Mode of Overseas IPOs), Zhengfa luntan (Tribune of Political Science and Law), No. 4 (2010), pp. 144–146.

68 Chen Su, "Shangfa jizhi zhong zhengfu yu shichang de gongneng dingwei" (The Government and Market's Functional Orientation in Commercial Law Mechanisms), *Zhongguo faxue* (China Legal Science), No. 5 (2014), pp. 44–46; Zhang Shouwen, "Zhengfu yu shichang guanxi de falii tiaozheng" (Legal Regulation on the Relationship between Government and Market), *Zhongguo faxue* (China Legal Science), No. 4 (2015), p. 66.

69 He Donghang and Kong Fanbin, "Gonggong zhengce zhixing de zhongguo jingyan" (China's Experience in Public Policy Implementation), *Zhongguo shehui kexue* (Social Sciences in China), No. 5 (2011), pp. 72–74.

70 Nicholas Howson, "Enforcement without Foundation? Insider Trading and China's Administrative Law Crisis," *American Journal of Comparative Law,* Vol. 48, No. 4 (2012), pp. 955–1002.

71 Tang Xin, "Siren susong yu zhengquan zhifa" (Private Action and Securities Law Enforcement), *Qinghua faxue* (Tsinghua Law Review), No. 3 (2007), pp. 106–109; Guo Li, "Zhengquan qizha falil zeren de bianjie xinjin meiguo zuigao fayuan xujia chenshu panli yanjiu" (The Boundary of Legal Liability for Securities Fraud-Study

on Recent Cases of False Statement from the United States Supreme Court), *Zhongwai faxue* (Peking University Law Journal), No. 4 (2010), pp. 632–633; Wu Guangming, "Zhengquan tuanti susong wenhua zhi tantao-Meiguo yu woguo taiwan diqu bijiaofa jiaodu zhi guancha" (Study on the Culture of Securities Group Action-Observation on the Comparative Law View between the United States and Taiwan Region of China), *Jiao da faxue* (SJTU Law Review), No. 3 (2014), pp. 120–121.

72 Hui Huang, "Private Enforcement of Securities Law in China: A Ten-Year Retrospective and Empirical Assessment," *American Journal of Comparative Law,* Vol. 42, No. 3 (2013), pp. 757–798.

73 Luo Peixin, "Legal Construction for the Harmonious Ecological Environment of China's Securities Market-From the Perspective of Philosophy," *Chinese Legal Science,* Vol. 4 (2005), p. 97; Wu Yue and Ma Hongyu, "Zhengjianhui yu zhengquan jiaoyisuo jianguanquan peizhi shizheng fenxi" (An Empirical Analysis of Supervision Power Allocation between the Securities Supervision Committee and Stock Exchanges), *Shehui kexue* (Journal of Social Sciences), No. 4 (2008), pp. 98–99.

74 Benjamin L. Liebman and Curtis J. Milhaupt, "Reputational Sanctions in China's Securities Market," *Columbia Law Review,* Vol. 108 (2008), pp. 929–983.

75 Peng Bing, "Zhengquan jiaoyisuo jianguan gongneng yanjiu-Cong qiye zuzhi de shijiao" (Study on the Regulatory Function of the Securities Exchange-From the Perspective of Enterprise Organization), *Zhongguo faxue* (Chinese Legal Science), No. 1 (2005) l, p. 84; Miao Yinzhi, "Lun zhengquan jiaoyisuo jingzheng yu jianguan de guanxi jiqi dingwei" (Securities Regulation Exchange: Regulation from the Perspective of Competition), *Shidai faxue* (Present Day Law Science), No. 6 (2008), pp. 71–77.

76 Nicholas C. Howson and Vikramaditya S. Khanna, "Reverse Cross-Listings—The Coming Race to List in Emerging Markets and the Enhanced Understanding of Classical Bonding," *Cornell International Law Journal,* Vol. 47, No. 3 (2015), pp. 607–629.

77 Kong Ningning and Yan Xi, "Jiaocha shangshi yu gongsi chengzhang-Laizi zhongguo A+H gu de jingyan zhengju" (Cross-Listing and Firm Growth-Evidence from China's 'A+H' Shares), *Jinrong yanjiu* (Journal of Financial Research), No. 7 (2009), p. 143; Liu Xiaoyuan and Jin Yuanyuan, "Kuajing shuangchong shangshi gongsi zhili yingxiang yanjiu pingshu" (A Review on the Effects of Cross Listing on Corporate Governance), *Shoudu jingmao daxue xuebao* (Journal of the Capital University of Economics and Business), No. 3 (2011), pp. 106–108.

78 Qin Jiaqi, He Qing, and Li e'juan, "Kuajing shuangchong shangshi yu gongsi touzi xiaolv fenxi" (Analysis on Cross-Border Dual Listing and Investment Efficiency of Companies), *Zhengquan shichang daobao* (Securities Market Herald), No. 10 (2009), pp. 59–60; Jiang Huining, "Kuaguo zhengquan rongzi falii jianguan mubiao de heli xuanze" (Reasonable Choice for Legal Regulatory Targets of Transnational Securities Financing), *Faxue* (Law Science), No. 2 (2013), p. 89.

79 Wang Yaxing, Ye Ling, and Yang Li, "Jiaochashangshi, xinxi huanjing yu jingji xiaoguo-Laizi A+H gu shichang de jingyan shuju" (Cross-Listing, Information Environment and Economic Consequence-Evidence from the Market of A Shares and H Shares), *Zhengquan shichang daobao* (Securities Market Herald), No. 12 (2012), p. 73.

80 Howson and Khanna, "Reverse Cross-Listings."

81 John C. Coffee, Jr., "The Future as History: The Prospects for Global Convergence in Corporate Governance and Its Implications," *Northwestern University Law Review,* Vol. 93 (1999), p. 674.

82 Howson and Khanna, "Reverse Cross-Listings."

83 Ibid.

84 Yue Caishen and Wang Ju, "Jianguan lilun de fazhan yu zhengquan jianguan zhidu wanshan de lujing xuanze" (Development of Supervision Theories and Approaches to Improvement of Securities Supervision), *Xiandai faxue* (Modern Law Science), No. 2 (2006), p. 120.

85 Allen and Shen, "Assessing China's Top-Down Securities Markets"; Yang Dian, "Gongsi zhili yu qiye jixiao-Jiyu zhongguo jingyan de shehuixue fenxi" (Corporate Governance and Firm Performance: A Sociological Analysis Based on the Chinese Experience), *Zhongguo shehui kexue* (Social Sciences in China), No. 1 (2013), p. 92.

86 Deng Feng, "Zhongguofa shang dongshihui de juese, zhineng ji sixiang yuanyuan: Shizhengfa de kaocha" (Sources of the Role, Function and Philosophy of the Board of Directors in Chinese Law: An Empirical Study), *Zhongguo faxue* (China Legal Science), No. 3 (2013), p. 108.

87 Geng Lihang, "Lun woguo gudong paisheng susong de chengben chengdan he sifa xuke" (On the Burden and Cost of Our Country's Shareholder Derivative Suit), *Falü kexue* (Science of Law), No. 1 (2013), pp. 170–182.

88 Liu Guiqing, "Gudong dui dongshi zhi zhijie susong-Dui xin gongsifa di 153 tiao fali jichu de fansi yu chonggou" (Direct Action Conducted by Shareholders to Directors-Rethinking and Reconstruction on the Jurisprudential Basis of the New Company Law Article 15), *Faxue pinglun* (Law Review), No. 3 (2006), pp. 70–74; Zhang Guoping and Wang Yaping, "Lun woguo gudong zhijie susong guize de buzu yu wanshan" (Study on the Faults and Improvements of the Direct Suit Rule in the PRC), *Zhengzhi yu falü* (Political Science and Law), No. 9 (2012), pp. 90–97.

89 Ma Xinyan, "Neimu jiaoyi chengfaxing peichang zhidu de goujian" (Construction of a System of Punitive Damages for Insider Trading), *Faxue yanjiu* (Chinese Journal of Law), No. 6 (2011), pp. 112–125; Liu Xianquan, "Lun neimu jiaoyi fanzui zuixin sifa jieshi ji falii shiyong" (On the Latest Judicial Interpretation and Judicial Application of the Crime of Insider Trading), *Faxuejia* (The Jurist), No. 5 (2012), pp. 39–51; Zeng Yang, "Zhengquan neimu jiaoyi zhuti shibie de lilun jichu jiqi luoji zhankai" (The Theoretical Basis and Logical Expansion of the Scope of Securities Insider Trading), *Zhongguo faxue* (China Legal Science), No. 2 (2014), pp. 158–182.

90 Nicholas C. Howson, "Punishing Possession—China's All Embracing Insider Trading Enforcement Regime," in *Research Handbook on Insider Trading,* edited by Stephen Bainbridge (Northampton, MA: Edward Elgar, 2013), p. 330.

91 Chen Jie and Zeng Yang, "Dui '8·16' guangda shijian neimu jiaoyi dingxing zhi zhiyi" (Question on the Determination of the Nature of Insider Trading in the '8.16' Guangda Incident), *Faxue pinglun* (Law Review), No. 1 (2014), p. 191.

92 Zuo Chuanwei, "Woguo gongsi jian xianghu chigu de falii guizhi" (Legal Regulation on Cross-Shareholdings among Companies in China), *Fashang yanjiu* (Studies in Law and Business), No. 4 (2011), p. 86.

93 Li Huai, Wang Dong, and Lv Yanfang, "Woguo chanye zhenghe qushi, jili jiqi jixiao fenxi-Jiyu 2003–2008 nian shangshi qiye binggou anli de weiguan shijiao" (Analysis on Tendency, Mechanism and Performance of China's Industrial Integration-Based on the Cases of Listed Companies in Mergers and Acquisitions from 2003 to 2008), *Hongguan jingji yanjiu* (Macroeconomics), No. 10 (2011), p. 30.

94 Lin Zhang, "The Political Rise of Hostile Takeovers in China: Efficiency, Politics and Law," *China: An International Journal,* Vol. 12, No. 3 (2014), pp. 136–154.

95 Hua Cai, "Bonding, Law Enforcement and Corporate Governance in China," *Stanford Journal of Law, Business & Finance,* Vol. 13, No. 1 (2007), pp. 82–120.

96 Although private enforcement is generally more cost-effective, its exact cost is difficult to ascertain and the approach is susceptible to criticism that it externalizes the cost of instigation and enforcement, thereby limiting the recourse of poorer investors.

97 Zhang Mubin, "Woguo shangshi gongsi kongzhiquan shichang zhili xiaoli yanjiu-Jiyu guquan jizhongdu de guding xiaoying mianban fenxi" (Study on the Effectiveness of China's Listed Corporation's Control Rights on Market Governance-Based on Panel Analysis on the Fixed Effect of the Equity Concentration Ratio), *Nanjing shehui kexue* (Social Sciences in Nanjing), No. 11 (2007), p. 35.

98 Wang Dan, "Paisheng susong zijin jili wenti yanjiu" (An Analysis of Establishing an Adequate Funding Incentive for Shareholder Derivative Litigation), *Bijiaofa yanjiu* (Journal of Comparative Law), No. 5 (2015), p. 165.

99 Chen Qunfeng, "Dui woguo gudong paisheng susong de fansi-Baochi jili yu zhiyue jizhi de pingheng" (Reflection on Shareholder Derivative Suits in Our Country: Maintaining Balance between the Incentive and Restraint Mechanisms), *Hebei faxue* (Hebei Law Science), No. 11 (2013), p. 66.

100 Liu Xiaoyuan and Jiatao, "Woguo jituanxing qiye xindai fengxian fenxi ji fangfan duke" (Analysis of Group Enterprise Credit Risk in China and the Preventative Countermeasures), *Zhongyang caijing daxue xuebao* (Journal of the Central University of Finance & Economics), No. 1 (2008), p. 38.

101 Han Wenxiu, "Guoji jinrong weiji xia de zhongguo jingji fazhan qianjing" (China's Economic Development Prospects under the Background of the International Financial Crisis), *Jingjixue dongtai* (Review of Economic Research), No. 6 (2009), pp. 20–24.

102 Wang Yuanlong and Wenbin, "Jiaru WTO hou guoduqi: Zhongguo yinhangye de yingdui" (The Post-Accession Era after China's Entry into the WTO), *Guoji jinrong yanjiu* (Studies of International Finance), No. 5 (2005), p. 7.

103 Wu Yanbing, "Guoyou qiye shuangchong xiaolv sunshi yanjiu" (The Dual Efficiency Losses in Chinese State-Owned Enterprises), *Jingji yanjiu* (Economic Research Journal), No. 3 (2012), p. 26.

104 Gu Gonggen, "Lun guozi guoqi shenhua gaige de zhengce mubiao yu fazhi zouxiang" (On the Policy Goal and Tendency of Rule of Law), *Zhengzhi yu falu* (Political Science and Law), No. 11 (2014), pp. 80–87.

105 Li-Wen Lin and Curtis J. Milhaupt, "We Are the (National) Champions: Understanding the Mechanisms of State Capitalism in China," *Stanford Law Review,* Vol. 65 (2013), pp. 698–759.

106 Lin Shangli, "Jieji, suoyouzhi yu zhengdang: Guoyou qiye dangjian de zhengzhixue fenxi" (Class, System of Ownership and Political Parties: A Political Analysis of the Party Building in State-Owned Enterprise), *Tianjin shehui kexue* (Tianjin Social Sciences), No. 1 (2010), 55–57.

107 Xie Shengfeng, "Gonggong touzi fubai: Jingji xiaoying, zhidu tanyuan yu zhili" (Corruption in Public Investment, Economic Effect, Origin and Governance), *Guojia xingzheng xueyuan xuebao* (Journal of China National School of Administration), No. 1 (2006), pp. 28–31; Fan Ziying, "Zhuanyi zhifu, jichu sheshi touzi yu fubai" (Fiscal Transfer, Infrastructure Investment and Corruption), *Jingji shehui tizhi bijiao* (Comparative Economic & Social Systems), No. 2 (2013), pp. 179–192.

108 Zhou Xuan, "Heishi shijian de fansi yu zhongguo zhuquan caifu jijin yunying celue de jianyi" (Rethinking the Blackstone Incident and Advice on Operation Strategies of Chinese Sovereign Wealth Funds), *Jingji tizhi gaige* (Reform ofEconomic System), No. 3 (2010), pp. 123–127.

109 Shen Wei, "FG Hemisphere Associates v. Democratic Republic of the Congo (2011) 14 H.K.C.F.A.R. 395," Vol. 108, No. 3 (2014), *American Journal of International Law,* pp. 776–782.

110 Jean-Marc F. Blanchard, "The China Investment Corporation: Power, Wealth or Something Else?," *China: An International Journal,* Vol. 12, No. 3 (2014), pp. 155–175.

111 Zhang Ming, "Zhuquan caifu jijin yu zhongtou gongsi" (The Sovereign Wealth Fund and CIC), *Jingji shehui tizhi bijiao* (Comparative Economic & Social Systems), No. 2

(2008), pp. 93–100; Guo Li, "Zhongtou: Zhuquan caifu jijin de konggu gongsi lujing" (CIC: The Holding Company Path for Sovereign Wealth Funds), *Zhongwai faxue* (Peking University Law Journal), No. 4 (2009), pp. 533–534; Zhang Ming, "Quanqiu jinrong weiji beijing xia zhongguo zhuquan caifu jijin touzi xingwei de zhuanbian" (Change of Investment Behavior of Chinese Sovereign Wealth Funds under the Background of Financial Crisis), *Guoji jingji pinglun* (International Economic Review), No. 5 (2010), pp. 99–109.

112 Li Guo, "Demystifying the Chinese Sovereign Wealth Fund amidst U.S. Financial Regulation," *Tsinghua China Law Review,* Vol. 2, No. 2 (2010), pp. 353–379.

113 Gu Xiaomin and Zhu Junyong, "Woguo jinrong jituan de fazhan xian-zhuang he jianguan duice" (The Development Status and Regulatory Countermeasures of China's Financial Group), *Shanghai jinrong* (Shanghai Finance), No. 3 (2005), pp. 33–34; Yao Dequan and Wang Shuai, "Zhongguo chanyexing jinrong konggu jituan fazhan moshi yanjiu" (The Development Model of Industrial Financial Holding Companies in China), *Caijing lilun yu shijian* (The Theory and Practice of Finance and Economics), No. 168 (2010), pp. 2–7.

114 Li Guo, "Financial Conglomerates in China: Legality, Model and Concerns," *Peking University Journal of Legal Studies,* Vol. 1 (2008), pp. 255–273.

115 Wang Guanjie, "Zhongguo guoyou qiye de zhengzhi gongneng: wenti, tiaozhan yu yingdui" (The Political Function of Chinese State-Owned Enterprises: Problems, Challenges and Countermeasures), *Jingji yanjiu cankao* (Review of Economic Research), No. 63 (2012), pp. 37–38.

116 Wu Fan and Lu Yangchun, "Woguo guoyou qiye gongsi zhili cunzai de zhuyao wenti yu duice" (Main Problems Existing in Governance of Our Country's State-Owned Enterprises and Their Countermeasures), *Jingji tizhi gaige* (Reform of Economic System), No. 5 (2010), p. 69.

117 Zhaofeng Wang, "Corporate Governance under State Control: The Chinese Experience," *Theoretical Inquiries in Law,* Vol. 13, No. 2 (2012), pp. 487–502.

118 Cai Xinlei, "Woguo duli dongshi zhidu de shijian yu fansi" (The Practice and Rethinking of the Independent Director System in China), *Xibei daxue xuebao* (Journal of Northwest University [Philosophy and Social Sciences Edition]), No. 2 (2010), p. 40.

119 Liu Cheng, Yang Jidong, and Zhou Sijie, "Shehui guanxi, duli dongshi renming yu dongshihui dulixing" (Social Relations, the Appointment of Independent Directors and Independence of Boards of Directors), *Shijie jingji* (Journal of World Economy), No. 12 (2012), p. 99.

120 Chien-Chung Lin, "The Chinese Independent Director Mechanism under Changing Macro Political-Economic Settings: A Review of Its First Decade and Two Possible Models for the Future," *American University Business Law Review,* Vol. 1, No. 2 (2011–2012), pp. 263–336.

3

DO ALL ROADS LEAD TO CHINA?

Chinese Commercial Law Scholarship in the Past Decade (Part 2)

Wei Shen and Casey G. Watters

Source: China Review, 16, 3, 2016, pp. 213–237.

Abstract

China's recent development of a modern legal system coupled with unparalleled economic growth have drawn substantial attention from commercial law scholars. This review summarizes Chinese- and English-language commercial law academic literature from the past decade contributed by both Chinese and non-Chinese scholars while discussing their differences. China's use of vague laws that rely upon implementation rules resulted in a substantial proportion of articles focusing on policy discussions and comparison to foreign approaches. Subsequently, a common theme in both Chinese and English literature was transplantation of foreign law. Chinese scholars often took a nationalistic approach, primarily assessing laws on their impact on China, whereas non-Chinese scholars advocated the adoption of foreign laws or legal structures to create clear standards and provide certainty for investors, which in turn is believed to facilitate continued growth of the Chinese economy. The literature is grouped into subject categories, allowing for discussion of important works and representative articles from leaders in their respective fields.

4. Private land use in commercial law

This first step in the analysis is to ask why private ownership matters. The proffered answer is essentially an economic model under which private property will presumably be used for economic benefit, while public land will be controlled by disinterested bureaucrats. Here, disinterest assumes a lack of corruption on the part of officials. Property ownership is a complex area of law encompassing a wide range of issues and types of property.[1] While some argue that China falls short of protecting property rights, Donald Clarke claims that private ownership has been virtually restored to China's ownership structure.[2] Of primary concern in recent years have been land use rights – an area where legal theory and application diverge greatly in China.[3]

In a country transitioning from a planned economy to a highly regulated market economy, the implications of private equity ownership are an important tangential issue when examining property law. Even in the absence of a planned economy, the market dependence on state-owned enterprises (SOEs) allows the state significant control over the market and places pressure on regulators to protect the interests of such enterprises. However, one recent article argues that ownership interest does not paint an accurate picture of the government's power to control enterprises and Chinese government has more control over private enterprise and less over SOEs than commonly assumed.[4] The political logic of corporate governance in the context of state capitalism is a dynamic legitimacy management scheme,[5] which explains and justifies a dominant political control over SOEs.

In reality, the boundary between privately held businesses and SOEs is not always clear in China with mixed ownership common.[6] However, even when ownership is entirely separate, the majority shareholders of privately held corporations in China also tend to have close government relationships that likely result in the same benefits SOEs are believed to receive by virtue of their state status.[7] In essence, the state's control over enterprises, both private and state owned, is through regulatory control – essentially capture.[8] As discussed above, the government retains a near monopoly on banking, and access to financing is one of the ways the government is able to maintain control over private enterprises. This dynamic makes it difficult to ascertain when companies should be treated as private, state owned, or, in some cases, state actors. This confusion, compounded by multiple statutory provisions and treatise, "has thorny implications for many U.S. and multilateral economic regulatory regimes, which pivot on 'state' versus 'private' ownership of enterprise."[9]

Similar to the misconception regarding government control of SOEs and private enterprise is the role of land ownership in China. While the state, by virtue of the people, officially owns all land and permits usage under something likened to a leasehold estate, in reality property rights substantially similar to a fee simple estate have been attained.[10] Tenure insecurity is a primary concern of landowners and academics,[11] and therefore a primary argument for developing an official system of land ownership. The decision to allow renewal of the "leasehold" period with compensation effectively recognized real estate property rights without undermining the Chinese system. Ownership by the state flows from the revolution and holds an important symbolic place in the Chinese legal system.[12] In the same way the party and government exist in a mutually beneficial symbiotic relationship, providing virtually unhindered land use rights while officially maintaining state ownership, which demonstrates the role of government while allowing sufficient economic freedom to foster investment and continued development.

5. International trade law and the WTO

To someone with a basic familiarity with China and Chinese commercial law, it may appear strange at first glance that a review of commercial law literature lacks a section dedicated to foreign investment but addresses the WTO and trade agreements. From the perspective on investors, Chinese foreign investment law and the Procedures for Administration of Foreign Investment in Commercial Sectors are of substantial importance and the WTO and other treaties, requiring state action to implement provisions to bring grievances, seem almost inapplicable to real-world business decisions. However, in academia the two are interconnected as China's entrance into the WTO was part of a larger strategy of economic reform and subsequent treaties, including bilateral investment treaties, to further liberalize the Chinese economy.[13] "China's commitments have had a large impact on its domestic legal system even without being directly enforceable. . . . China's commitments have in a sense constitutionalized the current policy of economic reform and made reversal of this course not only difficult domestically but also a violation of China's international law obligations."[14]

Entrance into the WTO required China to assent to multiple reforms including allowing foreign companies entrance to previously protected industries and reducing protection of domestic markets and other barriers to trade.[15] Articles focusing on trade agreements fit into several categories. The first category is articles discussing the necessary reforms and their impacts.[16] Articles of this category may focus on the impact on China and the rule of law, economic reforms, the impact of agreements on everyday people, or how the business landscape has changed and will change for foreign investors. The second category of articles is discussions of grievances filed by or against China in the WTO.[17] The details and angles of such articles vary greatly and are often largely political but with great legal and economic significance.

The Trans-Pacific Partnership (TPP) has spurred substantial debate and a number of publications focusing on Sino-U.S. relations and the geopolitical ramifications of such an agreement.[18] The legal analysis, at least with respect to commercial law, lags behind for two reasons. First, parties to the negotiation have not reached specific terms, and without detailed terms it is difficult to make a comprehensive legal analysis or argument. Speculation adds little to legal academic discourse, especially seeing as once a decision is made a predictive article is rendered obsolete. The second reason is that many Western journals, in particular U.S. law journals, take a couple years between submission and final publication. This means speculative articles may be preempted by treaty or other decisions, and because the TPP is a recent proposal, articles may not have reached publication.

6. International investment law, BITs, FTAs, and the TPP

China's bilateral investment treaty (BIT) program is a fascinating field with the substance, rationale, and implications of China's BITs a key focus of research for both Chinese and foreign scholars. A major feature of modern bilateral investment treaties is to allow investors to access international tribunals such as ICSID for the resolution of disputes between the investor and the host state.[19] Recent research scrutinizes key aspects of the investor-state arbitration clauses in Chinese BITs from BIT jurisprudential and practical perspectives and shows that, compared to older-Chinese BITs, China is becoming increasingly liberal in allowing investors to resort to international arbitration for domestic disputes. This liberalization, in turn, promotes unity in BIT activities in the region.[20]

In stark contrast to the explosion of bilateral investment treaties, the development of multilateral agreements in the field of international investment protection has been slow and had a less significant impact on trade.[21] In the Asian region, the most recent multilateral achievements are the investment treaty signed by ASEAN and China in 2009 and a trilateral investment agreement signed by China, Japan, and South Korea in 2011. Scholars have scrutinized major substantive standards such as national treatment,[22] most-favored-nation treatment,[23] fair and equitable treatment,[24] full protection and security,[25] expropriation,[26] and capital transfer[27] by reference to Chinese investment treaty jurisprudence. A thorough comparative review indicates that, regardless of its economic and political significance, China's multilateral investment treaties represent an increasingly liberal stance both ASEAN and China have recently taken in offering substantive protection standards to foreign investors, which will facilitate investment, improve transparency of investment rules and regulations, strengthen cooperation in investment, and ultimately liberalize the investment regime in the ASEAN-China region.[28] Over the past decade, China has increased its speed of liberalization with respect to BIT law and practice with Chinese and foreign scholars offering insights into the procedural and substantive standards of Chinese BITs. In this vein, scholars have attempted to group and divide the approximately 129 Chinese BITS into several generations.[29]

There has been a well-known "China disequilibrium" in the universe of investment treaty arbitration. On the one hand, the People's Republic of China has already concluded 129 BITs, which ranks second only to Germany (136).[30] In addition, China has been actively negotiating and concluding free trade agreements (FTAs) with various developing and developed countries, and these FTAs often include a chapter providing for investment protections. On the other hand, although the number of BIT cases has exploded globally in the 21st century,[31] and China is an active player in negotiation and conclusion of BITs, China is comparatively absent from BIT arbitration activities.[32] Both China's involvement in the BIT arbitration cases and the utility of Chinese BITs are indeed extremely limited. Thus far, there has been only one arbitration case brought by a foreign investor against China under any Chinese BIT.

Two reasons have been offered for this "China disequilibrium." First, BITs entered into prior to 1998 lack an effective dispute resolution provision for foreign investors, and thus the investor-state arbitration clauses *de facto* blocked international arbitration for potential disputes between foreign investors and China.[33] The second argument is that the Chinese law and legal system provide sufficiently high standards to protect foreign investors, thereby alleviating the need for investors to turn to international arbitration under BITs.[34] The validity of this hypothesis is questionable due to both foreign parties' reliance on arbitration as means to avoid litigation in Chinese courts over contract disputes and recent commercial disputes between China and other nations. These include tension between China and the

United States regarding Google's operations in China,[35] as well as between Australia and China concerning Rio Tinto's four employees arrested on charges of taking bribes and stealing commercial secrets.[36]

The first Chinese BIT dispute to be arbitrated, *Tza Yap Shum* v. *Republic of Peru*, was decided in 2009,[37] and slightly rebalanced the "China disequilibrium." In addition, the case offered a full menu of resources, an award on the jurisdiction, an award on merits, and an award on annulment, for understanding how a large number of Chinese BITs are interpreted and applied by tribunals in practice.[38] The practical value of these awards is not only to enrich Chinese BIT jurisprudence but also to show how Chinese BITs can be more effectively utilized by the foreign investment community. Therefore, the case has drawn substantial attention from the investment arbitration circle. Both Chinese and foreign academics have offered in-depth analyses of the technical and jurisprudential sides of these awards. Such research has enriched Chinese BIT jurisprudence.[39]

Chinese scholars' writings have appeared China-centric, which is in line with research in other fields, especially in the field of public international law. For instance, an emphasis has been placed on China's stance in international law and policy as well as its role in international relations as a rising great power.[40] A global perspective may also justify China's international engagement, which constitutes a sensible part of the Kantian project: building international institutions and strengthening commercial interdependence.[41] Against this backdrop, Chinas BIT law and practice have a hybrid feature: they are used not only to attract foreign inbound investment but also to protect Chinese outbound investment.[42] Under the growing pressure of the TPP negotiation, China's BITs and FTAs are used to counter the TPP's potential impact on squeezing China out of the global trade and investment rule-making process. China's strategy in negotiating and signing FTAs has been described as multilateralism and regionalism, which have significant implications for China and the rest of the world.[43] By doing so, China has joined the mainstream of globalization.[44] This multilateral strategy is evidenced by China's attempt to be a member, rather than a bystander, of the Energy Charter Treaty.[45]

There is also a domestic dimension to China's BIT law and practice. China's greater willingness to recognize and accept a higher level of substantive standards in protecting foreign investors also matches China's domestic efforts to improve its rule of law and legal system. Locally, China recently amended its constitution, granting individuals the right to own property, and enacted a property rights law to solidify interests in land.[46] It also tried to improve the land taking regime and administrative litigation regime.[47] These domestic law reforms allow China to make more liberal promises at the international stage while negotiating BITs and FTAs. One obvious example is China's acceptance of creeping or indirect expropriation as well as a Hull formula type of compensation clause in its new-generation BITs and FTAs.[48] This new liberalism reflected in its BIT/FTA law and practice is in line with China's tendency of leaning toward a rule-based property rights protection regime,[49] with more broadly shared norms.[50]

A close correlation between China's domestic reform and international engagement is clearly indicated in China's establishment of a free trade zone in Shanghai and three additional zones thereafter. One key reform implemented in the Shanghai free trade zone is to reform China's current foreign investment approval regime and apply the negative list approach toward the foreign investment projects.[51] The negative list of non-conforming measures, together with pre-establishment national treatment and transparency requirements, has become one of the key hurdles in China's ongoing negotiation of its BIT with the United States.[52] Part of the plan to have these free trade zones in China is to make use of them as a testing ground upgrading China's foreign investment governance regime and its rights protection standards.[53] The overall strategy is also clear: China wants to be not only a stakeholder by piggybacking on the current international trade and investment system to benefit its growing economy but also a shareholder by leading the rule-making process to sustain its growing role in the international economic governance system.[54] The most effective way to counter U.S. efforts to exclude China from the TPP negotiation is therefore to upgrade its own foreign investment law regime and multilateralize its investment treaty regime.[55]

The FTA network, as observed, is built up and attached to the importance of boosting the development of its services industry and services trade. China's services FTAs are modeled on GATS while going beyond GATS commitments to sectoral coverage.[56] Yet, this does not seem enough to liberalize trade services. The reason for this slow progress is the existing regulatory constraints in services areas. In order to further liberate the services trade, China needs to couple the negotiation of services provisions with its regulatory reform in services areas.[57] This again confirms a close connection between China's international engagement and domestic reform.

7. Enforceability of commercial agreements and arbitration

Another area unique to the international discourse of Chinese commercial law is the focus on enforceability of agreements, including arbitral awards,[58] and the role of Chinese courts in adjudicating commercial disputes.[59] The latter includes an abundance of literature suggesting judicial reform through the adoption of foreign judicial standards, or, alternatively, utilizing international commercial arbitration via the New York Convention to circumvent the discretion of Chinese judicial bodies. In most jurisdictions, the enforcement and procedural mechanisms are dealt with separately. However, the nature of the Chinese legal system makes treatment of international commercial dealings a vital concern to any deal because, both in academic literature and practice, the substantive and procedural intertwine themselves inseparably, requiring an examination of both in any comprehensive review of Chinese commercial law. The enforceability of commercial agreements in China, as with the literature on the topic, can be broken down into three areas: choice of law, enforcement through a trial, and arbitration.

a. Choice of law

Choice of law issues are of particular concern to foreign scholars and parties because the question of applicable law arises in contracts between Chinese and foreign entities. If the laws of each jurisdiction would provide alternate outcomes, the issue of applicable law would necessarily be litigated upon breach of the contract if the parties did not incorporate a choice of law clause in the contract. Chinese scholars are less inclined to focus on the subject because courts will naturally apply Chinese law and to elect foreign law to govern the contract there must be a foreign party or substantial foreign element to the transaction.[60] While choice of law is an essential element in cross-border contractual relationships, it is rarely the main topic of an article. Instead, it usually appears as part of a discussion on arbitration. There has been a fresh focus on conflicts of law after the promulgation of the Law on the Application of Law for Foreign-Related Civil Legal Relationships of the PRC, the first ever legislation in the history of China to deal systemically with conflicts of laws. Specific provisions and the impacts on foreign countries have been the focus of research with a study confirming that modern conflicts of laws doctrines have been embraced in the conflicts of laws code.[61] Ultimately, how these modern doctrines are interpreted and applied depends on Chinese courts.

b. Trials and judicial enforcement

Determining whether the court will enforce an agreement is essential to commercial law and the ability of parties to contract. Several issues arise in this regard including courts refusing to hear cases, corruption, susceptibility to pressure from the public or government, and whether court judgments will be enforced.[62] Contrary to the commonly held view in the West that the Chinese government is disconnected from the citizenry, research shows the Chinese courts are highly susceptible to public opinion: "[P]rotesting, petitioning, or simply threatening to do either is a successful means for litigants to pressure courts to rule in their favor or to alter decided cases. The ability of individuals to influence court decisions through petitioning is linked to other better-known problems in the Chinese legal system. Courts' sensitivity to the threat of unrest reflects the facts that party officials continue to interfere in court decisions and that individual judges and court leaders are dependent on party officials for their positions."[63]

The ability of external parties to influence court decisions introduces an element of unpredictability into Chinese litigation.[64] There are countless academic articles discussing the role of Chinese courts, but few offer substantial new arguments because little information is available and the Chinese government treats information regarding the courts as sensitive.[65] However, this is changing as demonstrated by some recent empirical research, which attempted to overhaul conventional views on Chinese courts and commercial litigation. Based on intensive interviews and in-depth investigations in the Pearl River Delta, local courts in this region were said to be effective and efficient in enforcing commercial judgments. The empirical findings that the enforcement process is relatively efficient, the problem of local protectionism is not serious, the enforcement outcomes are reasonable, and the plaintiffs' view on courts is positive changed the long-standing assumption that Chinese courts were far less than efficient and effective.[66] The fact that limited data are available and this research challenges conventional academic and business wisdom regarding the ability of Chinese courts to address commercial disputes signal the need for additional independent research to corroborate the results. Nonetheless, these findings not only fill the gap in existing literature but also affirm the correlation between the functioning of the judicial system and economic development.[67] Meanwhile, as far as pure domestic disputes are concerned, the stronger parties are more likely to win cases by a large margin and institutional litigants fare better than individual litigants.[68] The institutional fact that the organizational and social status of government-related parties has a greater impact on the outcome of the cases itself triggers a more dynamic interpretation to the roots of the law and the nature of the courts in China.

With the unpredictability of Chinese courts and the fact that Chinese courts rarely enforce foreign judgments, and are particularly resistant to U.S. judgments,[69] parties to contracts that may require enforcement in China are increasingly turning to arbitration. To address this problem, judicial cooperation must be improved in enforcement of judgments. Mutual recognition and enforcement of judgments can be established through the abandonment of the reciprocity requirement, an approach that would provide a foundation for Chinese and U.S. courts to move forward.[70] The other approach providing for recognition is presumed reciprocity. Reciprocity can be reasonably seen as established if one country's judgments may be recognized and enforced according to the statutory law or the case law of the other country. In the end, the United States and China need to negotiate and work out a bilateral legal instrument to delineate the scope of mutual enforcement. Currently, the case study on *Sanlian* v. *Robinson* (Sanlian), the first Chinese judgment recognized and enforced by U.S. courts, though a breakthrough between the two countries, showed a high cost involved in such mutual recognition and enforcement cases and the necessity of a bilateral treaty for the purpose of enhancing transnational justice in a cross-border context.[71] A survey of Chinese law pertaining to the key issues by the Hague Choice of Court Convention demonstrates the comparability of the two, which naturally supports China's ratification of the Hague Choice of Court Convention with the aim of promoting order and predictability for foreign investors in China.[72]

Domestically, some Western scholars have rightly observed "a turn against law" in China where leaders de-emphasize the role of formal law in favor of reviving court mediation practices.[73] While this observation is correct, the underlying political logic behind such a turn against law movement is incomplete. Social stability concerns may play a role in the deviation from the rule of law course,[74] through improving access to courts by improving the efficiency and efficacy of court adjudication. For instance, the amended Civil Procedure Law mandates the use of mediation in litigation with the goal of decreasing appeals and increasing litigants' faith in the courts.[75] This changing face of Chinese courts deserves an insightful investigation with solid evidence, and should not be misinterpreted through random comparison. Rather, it should be interpreted in a dynamic mediation-adjudication framework. The incorporation of mediation into the formal trial process creates a series of internal contradictions due to an obvious mismatch between a flexible and non-legalistic mediation and the rigid format of formal litigation.[76]

c. *Arbitration of commercial disputes in China*

In many respects, enforceability of international commercial arbitration is straightforward through application of the New York convention. However, to operate in China a business must establish a Chinese business entity, which will be treated as a Chinese legal person. As a result, domestic arbitration has become a center of academic attention.[77] Under Chinese law, ad hoc arbitration is unenforceable and for an arbitration clause to be valid it must specify a legal arbitration commission. Of particular importance is the recent division of the China International Economic and Trade Arbitration Commission (CIETAC), whereby CIETAC in Beijing claims that CIETAC Shanghai and Shenzhen are subcommittees but the regional commissions severed their ties and no longer answer to CIETAC in Beijing.[78] Arbitral awards rendered by the Shanghai and Shenzhen CIETACs are being enforced by Chinese courts, but the organizations previously received their status as commissions legally authorized to conduct arbitration through CIETAC in Beijing and, therefore, an argument can be made as to whether awards issued by the now independent commissions are legally enforceable.

The issue of enforceability extends to arbitration agreements because if a party listed CIETAC Shanghai or Shenzhen as the place of arbitration then CIETAC will argue that by disassociating with CIETAC the "branches" became ineligible to hear the cases. While this issue has spurred academic debate, by continuing with the arbitration parties will have waived their right to object to enforceability in court, and local courts, answering to the local government, are unlikely to rule in favor of a party claiming the local arbitration commission lacks legal authority.

In addition to traditional arbitration, some investment treaties provide dispute resolution mechanisms. BITs "are designed to protect foreign investors against expropriation and regulatory uncertainty."[79] Increasingly, BITs allow parties to bring actions against a sovereign through a form of international arbitration.[80] Without such treaties, investors would risk expropriation of their assets when making an investment in the target country – making BITs an important area of commercial law connected to arbitration that receives substantial academic attention.

With the exception of arbitration, a common theme among academic literature is the argument that China should adopt laws similar to those in the United States or other Western countries.[81] Arguments are common for the separation of powers,[82] ending currency controls,[83] and relaxing limitations on foreign investment in the banking sector.[84] In addition, scholars might call for establishing a system of land ownership similar to the British fee simple to facilitate investment and development. However, China has a unique system with a legal tradition that developed reflecting its government and culture. As China continues to develop and reform its legal system, the rule of law will become increasingly important. Nevertheless, the academic literature should focus on how proposed reforms will impact China and not on seeking to duplicate a Western legal regime.

8. Conclusion

The preceding overview of recent Chinese commercial law scholarship illustrates a variety of approaches utilized by Chinese and non-Chinese scholars, who, in addition to holding unique perspectives based on nationality, represent a range of economic, political, and jurisprudential philosophies. Across the ideological spectrum, transplantation of foreign law remains a common solution to perceived gaps in the Chinese legal regime as it lags behind economic development and the accompanying changes to industry and society. This section summarizes the academic literature through two distinctive sets of often contradictory views: insider versus outsider and empirical research versus case or comparative study. It then concludes with final thoughts on the picture academics paint of the future of Chinese commercial law development.

a. Insider versus outsider

While Chinese and Western scholars share many similarities in their arguments and approaches to articles, the varying experience of both groups nonetheless color the academic discourse. In this regard, Western scholars differ from Chinese in their willingness to criticize the Chinese legal regime while utilizing their legal rules and standards as benchmarks to measure China's legal system. The interconnectedness of the law and wide discretion afforded by law to Chinese officials bring a range of seemingly disconnected issues under the prevue of commercial law, allowing for the flexible adoption of foreign legal standards by academics. The Chinese adoption of Western law regarding independent directors is illustrative of this point. Whereas domestic scholars, recognizing current problems with the system, are more likely to praise the adoption of independent director standards as a step toward greater minority shareholder protection and better corporate governance, foreign scholars are quick to dismiss the reform as ineffective by comparing it to the standards of minority shareholder protection in the West. Often in the commercial context, legal standards and business practice must align to provide parties the highest degree of legal protection – a process that takes time in countries like China that are still establishing their legal regime. In this light, under theorization of independent directors was quoted as the key reason for the existence of inconsistent rules.[85] This explanation over simplifies the problems inherent in transplanting foreign law, as a concentrated shareholding structure of listed companies is likely to lead to regulatory failure as the independent directors appointed by the majority shareholders do not possess independence and are heavily influenced by the majority shareholders.

This comparative methodology is also used by Chinese scholars to justify legal transplant of other corporate governance instruments such as shareholder activism. The widespread adoption of shareholder proposal rules in other jurisdictions is used as justification for adopting similar rules in China. While borrowing from the legal experience and jurisprudence of other jurisdictions can be beneficial, direct reliance upon other countries' reception of a particular corporate governance tool to justify legal reform is overly simplistic and will often fall short of the desired results without first adapting the system to China's unique domestic conditions.

Urban land reform is the other area where a comparison can be easily made. Unlike in China's Western counterparts, urban land use rights are not equal to title or ownership. In other words, the land use rights, the dominant form of land tenure, are less than full fee simple ownership. Using the full fee simple ownership as a benchmark, an immediate conclusion is that re-privatization is a necessary step for continued economic reform because such an incomplete ownership system must be improved before incomplete property rights drag on economic development.[86] In practice, the legal protection afforded property "owners" in China far exceeds the theoretical underpinnings of the state as the sole owner of real property. While room for limited reform exists, the land being owned by the people with the government acting as steward and the legitimacy of the one-party state are ideologically intertwined. In this context, re-privatization offers limited immediate economic value when weighed against its political costs and societal stability. While re-privatization may be a direction, it will not result in any constructive paradigm without political and ideological reform. As with land reform, Chinese and non-Chinese scholars hold opposing views on a variety of legal reforms in the sense that non-Chinese are more insistent on Western-style legal reform while Chinese scholars may be more tolerant of informal arrangements. These ideological differences illuminate a stark distinction between a Western-centric and a China-centric viewpoint, or between legalism and pluralism, when it comes to the same legal issue within a changing context.

b. Empirical study versus case study or comparative study

The conventional methodologies in studying Chinese law are comparative study and case study. Comparatists tend to bemoan their chosen field due to the scarcity of decent comparative legal scholarship and the lack if a theoretical foundation for the study of comparative law. As illustrated in this article, a more sanguine, yet critical, view of commercial law in China can be produced. Sanguine, since a sympathetic reading of contemporary comparative scholarship on China demonstrates that there is more than enough such scholarship to generate a lively debate on commercial law works within a comparative framework. Critical, since the existing literature can be improved to have a form of paradigmatic discourse. More recently, empirical study has been deployed to investigate the real effect of transplanted doctrines and rules.[87] The empirical methodology has been employed to investigate China's cases adjudicated under the statutory veil-piercing regime and has affirmed the uncertainty and complexity of the adjudication of veil-piercing cases.[88] Empirical work also demonstrates the limits to which the transplanted bankruptcy law norms such as company reorganization procedures and insolvency administrators will be effective and the complexity of the financial distress problems that remain to be resolved in the Chinese context.[89]

Based on such empirical research, more reflective suggestions can be made to clarify and improve legislation and court adjudication.[90] However, limited public information including published cases, lack of judicial reasoning in cases, and government control of available information hinder empirical research and cause many, especially foreign, scholars to question conclusions derived from empirical research. In addition, empirical research relies upon "inside" information through access to the judiciary or government officials. Scholars wishing to maintain the privileged status of such inside connections may be reluctant to publish negative information, which could in turn harm their career or that of their information source. Also, over-emphasis on positive empirical findings will strengthen scholars' relationships with their government counterparts and subsequently benefit the scholars' careers through a continuing stream of information. This reliance in part explains why empirical research often provides a comparatively positive picture of the Chinese legal environment than other methodologies. Nonetheless, empirical research remains limited and is necessary to fill a gap in Chinese legal scholarship and challenge theoretical models as they develop out of the comparative discourse. In addition to the need for personal government contacts and the reluctance of foreign scholars to trust the finding of empirical research, another possible explanation for the scarcity of empirical studies is that comparative study enables comparative scholars to rest comfortably in the warm confines of their own scholarship without being challenged by questions regarding their methodological stances and research bias.

Case study is a conventional approach taken by Western scholars. For example, the role of courts in adjudicating commercial or corporate disputes has been investigated through a review of more than 1,000 disputes reported between 1992 and 2008 along with interviews with sitting judges and relevant officials. Such a case study, as reasonably anticipated, has shown Chinese courts' increasingly technical competence together with their inconsistent institutional autonomy.[91] This conclusion is in line with the old saying that well illustrates the Chinese context: one step forward and two steps backward. The problematic side of this case study approaches its finding of a natural dimension any person may reasonably expect to see. In other words, the case study is not to discover but confirm a possible rule of law paradox. As such, case studies fall on the opposite side of the research spectrum from empirical research, offering limited additional substance to the academic discourse. The reliance on this method by Western scholars may stem from the value case studies provide practitioners in a common law context and Western scholars' familiarity with the method.

c. *The future of Chinese commercial law discourse*

It appears that the contemporary academic literature on Chinese commercial law contains a wide array of arguments. The mainstream thinking is that a gap needs to be filled with an emphasis on legislative developments, an area relevant to all aspects of Chinese commercial law.[92] The contract-out approach to transnational transactions embraced by practitioners and subsequently the focus of substantial commercial law scholarship does not suggest a lack of domestic law – a misconception easily construed by foreign scholars' omission of research regarding purely domestic commercial law. A piggybacking strategy may rationalize the overutilization of foreign law, and to some extent its use as benchmarks in Chinese transactions, and advocate a contract-out approach. As Chinese courts become increasingly sophisticated and China continues to adopt more comprehensive regulatory regimes, the motivation to piggyback will reduce and scholarship should increasingly focus on domestic law. The existing body of comparative research should facilitate the development of a theoretical context for continued discourse allowing continued comparative discourse with deeper analysis than the mere advocating for transplantation of foreign legal systems without adapting them to the Chinese environment.

Although all roads may lead to Rome, it does not seem to be the case for China. While the scholarship on Chinese commercial law itself is rich and has a wide coverage, the purposes, objectives, methodologies, logic, and ideologies can vary. Fortunately, one point of consensus seems to be reached by all scholars, that is, commercial law that should be used is an amalgam of public and private rule making, and is of critical importance not only to investment and economic activities but also to reshaping a top-down society.

Notes

* The authors thank the two reviewers for their constructive comments on previous drafts of this article and acknowledge Yu Tao's research assistance in completing citations of Chinese-sourced materials.

1 Chen Pu, "Zuowei suoyouquan yundong xingshi de xintuo – Yige jiejue xintuo caichan suoyouquan guishu wenti de lilun changshi" (Trust Acting as a Form of Transferring Property Ownership – Theoretically Trying to Solve the Problem of Trust Property Ownership Attribution), *Hebei faxue* (Hebei Law Science), No. 12 (2010), pp. 86–93; Feng Yujun, "Zhongguo zongjiao caichan de fanwei he guishu wenti yanjiu" (Study on the Problem of Scope Regarding Ownership of Religious Property in China), *Zhongguo faxue* (China Legal Science), No. 6 (2012), pp. 87–98; Sun Xianzhong, "Zailun woguo wuquanfa zhong de yiti chengren pingdeng baohu yuanze" (On the "Common Acceptance and Equal Protection" Principle in Our Country's Property Law), *Fashang yanjiu* (Studies in Law and Business), No. 2 (2014), pp. 67–72.

2 Donald Clarke, "China's Stealth Urban Land Revolution," *American Journal of Comparative Law*, Vol. 62, No. 2 (2014), pp. 323–366.

3 Zhang Qianfan, "Chengshi tudi 'guojia suoyou' de kunhuo yu xiaojie" (Confusion and Digestion of "State-Owned" Urban Land), *Zhongguo faxue* (China Legal Science), No. 3 (2012), pp. 178–190; Zhan Zhongle, "Woguo tudi shiyongquan shouhui leixinghua yanjiu" (Typology Study on Taking Back the Land Use Right in China), *Zhongguo faxue* (China Legal Science), No. 2 (2012), pp. 98–107; Zhang Shanbin, "Jiti tudi shiyongquan liuzhuan de zhangai paichu yu zhidu wanshan" (Typology Study on Removing Obstacles and Improving the Land Use Rights Transferring System), *Faxue pinglun* (Law Review), No. 2 (2014), pp. 90–97.

4 Curtis J. Milhaupt and Wentong Zheng, "Beyond Ownership: State Capitalism and the Chinese Firm," *Georgetown Law Journal*, Vol. 103 (2015), pp. 665–722.

5 Jiangyu Wang, "The Political Logic of Corporate Governance in China's State-Owned Enterprises," *Cornell International Law Journal*, Vol. 47, No. 3 (2014), pp. 631–669.

6 Jing Leng, *Corporate Governance and Financial Reform in China's Transition Economy* (Hong Kong: Hong Kong University Press, 2009).

7 Dong Ming, "Zhuanxingqi zhongguo de zhengzhi jingjixue yu minying qiye zhengzhi xingwei" ("Plutonomy" and Political Behavior of Private Enterprises during the Transition Period of China), *Xuexi yu tansuo* (Study & Exploration), Vol. 2 (2012), pp. 54–58.

8 Milhaupt and Zheng, "Beyond Ownership."

9 Ibid.

10 Clarke, "China's Stealth Urban Land Revolution," p. 323.

11 Peter Ho, "The 'Credibility Thesis' and Its Application to Property Rights: Secure Land Tenure, Conflict and Social Welfare in China," *Land Use Policy*, Vol. 40 (September 2014), pp. 13–27.

12 Cui Shuanlin, "Guojia suoyouquan xingzhi wenti yanjiu – Zhendui guoyou ziben de fenxi" (Study on the Essence of State-Ownership Based on the Management of State-Owned Capital), *Hebei faxue* (Hebei Law Science), No. 9 (2008), p. 44.

13 Li Yumei and Zhang Qi, "Zhongguo qianshu shuangbian touzi xieding de yinzi xiaoying – Jiyu 1994–2013 nian mianban shuju de shizheng fenxi" (The Effects of Bilateral Investment Agreements on Attracting FDI Inflow to China), *Yatai jingji* (Asia-Pacific Economic Review), Vol. 4 (2015), pp. 132–137.

14 Donald C. Clarke, "The Chinese Legal System since 1995: Steady Developments, Striking Continuities," *China Quarterly*, Vol. 191 (2007), p. 565.

15 Tom Tong, "Chinese Retail and Wholesale Markets Open Slowly to Foreign Investors," *International Trade Law Journal*, WTR Currents, Vol. 14 (2005), pp. 43–44.

16 Julia Ya Qin, "The Impact of WTO Accession on China's Legal System: Trade, Investment and Beyond" (Wayne State University Law School Research Paper No. 07–15, 2007), http://ssrn.com/abstract=985321.

17 Wu Xiaohui, "Lun WTO maoyi zhengduan anjian zhong zhongguo de 'chaochanggui yiwu'" (On the "Unconventional Obligations" of China in WTO Trade Dispute Cases), *Fazhi yanjiu* (Research on the Rule of Law), No. 12 (2011), pp. 30–36.

18 Inkyo Cheong, "Negotiations for the Trans-Pacific Partnership Agreement: Evaluation and Implications for East Asian Regionalism" (ADBI Working Paper No. 428, 2013), http://papers.ssrn.com/sol3/papers.cfm?abstract id=2292899; Peter A. Petri and Michael G. Plummer, "The Trans-Pacific Partnership and Asia-Pacific Integration: Policy Implications," (Peterson Institute for International Economics Policy Brief, 2012), http://ssrn.com/ abstract=2108399.

19 Yang Caixia and Qin Quan, "Guoji touzi zhengduan jiejue zhong de wumoqi zhongcai chutan" (Preliminary Research on Arbitration without Privity in International Investment Dispute Resolution), *Bijiaofa yanjiu* (Journal of Comparative Law), No. 3 (2011), p. 108.

20 Shen Wei, "Is This a Great Leap Forward? – A Comparative Review of the Investor-State Arbitration Clause in the ASEAN-China Investment Treaty: From BIT Jurisprudential and Practical Perspectives," *Journal of International Arbitration*, Vol. 27, No. 4 (2010), pp. 379–419.

21 Li Yumei and Sang Baichuan, "Guoji touzi guize bijiao, qushi yu zhongguo duice" (A Comparison of International Investment Rules: Trends and Chinese Countermeasures), *Jingji shehui tizhi bijiao* (Comparative Economic & Social Systems), No. 1 (2014), pp. 179–181.

22 Zhu Wenlong, "Woguo zai guoji touzi xieding zhong dui guomin daiyu de xuanze" (China's Choice of National Treatment in International Investment Agreements), *Hebei faxue* (Hebei Law Science), No. 3 (2014), pp. 179–187.

23 Shen Wei, "Lun zhongguo shuangbian touzi xieding zhong xianzhixing touzi zhengduan jiejue tiaokuan de jieshi he shiyong" (Interpretation and Application of Dispute Resolution Provisions Restricting Investment in Chinese Bilateral Investment Treaties), *Zhongwai faxue* (Peking University Law Journal), No. 5 (2012), p. 1060.

24 Han Ying, "Guoji touzi xieding zhong 'gongping yu gongzheng daiyu'zhi qushi – ICSID zuixin zhongcai anli pingxi" (Trends of "Just and Fair Treatment" in International Investment Agreements: Analysis of the Latest Cases of the ICSID), *Shehui kexuejia* (Social Scientist), No. 9 (2010), p. 72.

25 Shen Wei, "Zhongguo touzi xieyi shiti baohu biaozhun de ziyouhua he duobianhua yanjin" (Liberal and Multilateral Movement of Substantive Protection Standards in Chinese Investment Treaties), *Faxue yanjiu* (Chinese Journal of Law), No. 4 (2015), pp. 195–197.

26 Wang Xiaolin, "Guoji touzi jianjie zhengshou de zhongguo guanqie" (China's Concern over the Issue of Indirect Expropriation against International Investment), *Beifang faxue* (Northern Legal Science), No. 2 (2015), 84–92.

27 Zhang Lei, "Lun zhongmei shuangbian touzi xieding taben guanyu waihui zhuanyi tiaokuan de fenqi" (The Differences in the Model Bilateral Investment Treaties of China and the United States on the Foreign Currency Transference Clause), *Shanghai jinrong* (Shanghai Finance), No. 10 (2013), pp. 93–94.

28 Shen Wei, "Leaning Towards a More Liberal Stance? – An Evaluation of Substantive Protection Provisions under the New ASEAN-China Investment Agreement in Light of Chinese BIT Jurisprudence," *Arbitration International* Vol. 26, No. 4 (2010), pp. 549–595.

29 Stephan W. Schill, "Tearing Down the Great Wall – The New Generation Investment Treaties of the People's Republic of China," *Cardozo Journal of International and Comparative Law*, Vol. 15, No. 1 (2007), pp. 73–118.

30 UNCTAD, Recent Developments in International Investment Agreement, IIA Monitor No. 3 (UNCTAD/WEB/ITE/IIA/2007/6, 2007), www.unctadxi.org/templates/DocSearch_779.aspx.

31 Susan D. Franck, "The Legitimacy Crisis in Investment Arbitration: Privatizing Public International Law through Inconsistent Decisions," *Fordham Law Review*, Vol. 73 (2005), p. 1521.

32 Qi Tong, "Lun 'zhongguo haiwai touzizhe dui guoji touzi zhongcai jizhi de liyong" (Chinese Overseas Investors' Utilization of International Investment Arbitration Mechanisms), *Dongfang faxue* (Oriental Law), No. 3 (2014), p. 93.

33 See, e.g., Schill, "Tearing Down the Great Wall"; Kathryn Sanger, "Basic Principles of Investment Treaties," in *Investor-State Arbitration – Lessons for Asia*, edited by Michael Moser (Huntington, NY: Juris, 2008), p. 22.

34 See, e.g., Yuqing Zhang, "The Case of China," in Moser, *Investor-State Arbitration*, p. 159.

35 "Google v China," *Financial Times*, 23 March 2010, p. 14 (remarking on Google's closure of Google.cn and debate on internet freedom with China); Kathrin Hille et al. "China Gets Tough on Google," *Financial Times*, 24 March 2010, p. 1 (reporting Google's decision to end compliance with local censors and move search engines to Hong Kong).

36 Patti Waldmeir and Peter Smith, "Rio Tinto's Top Iron Ore Salesman in China Admits Bribe Allegations," *Financial Times*, 24 March 2010, p. 1 (arguing that Rio's practice in China was in line with industry practices but one of the biggest problems for foreigners operating in China is vague and ill-forced law); William MacNamara and Patti Waldmeir, "Rio Seeks to Rebuild Relations with Beijing," *Financial Times,* 23 March 2010, p. 17 (alleging that the "arrests were payback for Rio's touch stance in negotiation of iron ore sales with the Chinese steel industry").

37 *Tza Yap Shum* v. *Republic of Peru,* ICSID Case No. ARB/07/6, Decision on Jurisdiction and Competence of 19 June 2009. Note, however, the decision was not made public until August 2009, even though the decision was rendered on 19 June 2009. References made herein are based on the English translation of the decision, available at www.htttp://ita.law.uvic.ca.

38 Huang Yueming, "ICSID zhongcaiting kuoda guanxiaquan de tujing jiqi yingdui – Cong 'xieyeshen' an qieru" (The ICSID Tribunal's Paths to Expanding Its Jurisdiction and Corresponding Countermeasures – Cut in through the "Xie Yeshen Case"), *Huadong zhengfa daxue xuebao* (Journal of the East China University of Political Science and Law), No. 5 (2013), pp. 64–75.

39 An Chen, "Should the Four Great Safeguards in China-Foreign BITs Be Hastily Dismantled? – Comments on Provisions concerning Dispute Settlement in Model U.S. and Canadian BITs," *Journal of World Investment & Trade*, Vol. 7, No. 6 (2006), pp. 899–993; An Chen, "Distinguishing Two Types of Countries and Properly Granting Differential Reciprocity Treatment – Re-comments on the Four Safeguards in China-Foreign BITs Not to Be Hastily and Completely Dismantled," *Journal of World Investment & Trade*, Vol. 8, No. 6 (2007), pp. 771–778; Shen Wei, "Conceptuality or Textuality? Understanding the Notion of Expropriation in the Context of Tza Yap Shum v. The Republic of Peru," *Journal of East Asia and International Law* Vol. 7, No. 2 (2014), pp. 379–407; Shen Wei, "The Good, the Bad or the Ugly? – A Critique of the Decision on Jurisdiction and Competence in Tza Yap Shum v. The Republic of Peru," *Chinese Journal of International Law* Vol. 9, No. 1 (2011), pp. 55–95.

40 Congyan Cai, "New Great Powers and International Law in the 21st Century," *European Journal of International Law*, Vol. 24, No. 3 (2013), pp. 755–795.

41 Manik V. Suri, "Conceptualizing China within the Kantian Peace," *Harvard International Law Journal* Vol. 54, No. 1 (2013), pp. 219–258.

42 Lu Jinyong and Li Xiu'e, "Zhongguo shuangbian ji quyu touzi zhidu anpai: Tedian, zuoyong ji jianyi" (China's Bilateral and Regional Institutional Arrangements on Investment: Characteristics, Effects and Suggestions), *Yataijingji* (Asia-pacific Economic Review), No. 1 (2013), pp. 99–104.

43 Jun Zhao and Timothy Webster, "Taking Stock, China's First Decade of Free Trade," *University of Pennsylvania Journal of International Law*, Vol. 33, No. 1 (2011), p. 116.

44 Guiguo Wang, "China's FTAs: Legal Characteristics and Implications," *American Journal of International Law* Vol. 105, No. 3 (2011), pp. 493–516.

45 Sheng Zhang, "The Energy Charter Treaty and China: Member or Bystander?" *Journal of World Investment and Trade*, Vol. 13 (2012), pp. 597–617.

46 Michael T. Stanczyk, "Enter the Dragon's Lair: The New Socialism and Private Property Ownership in the People's Republic of China," *St. Johns Journal of Legal Commentary*, Vol. 22, No. 3 (2008).

47 Shen Wei, "Expropriation in Transition: Evolving Chinese Investment Treaty Practices in Local and Global Contexts," *Leiden Journal of International Law*, Vol. 28, No. 3 (2015), pp. 579–604.

48 Ibid.

49 Ibid.

50 Wang, "China's FTAs."

51 Shen Wei and Matthias Vanhullebucsh, "Where Is the Alchemy? The Experiment of the Shanghai Free Trade Zone in Freeing the Foreign Investment *Regime in China,"* European Business Organization Law Review, *Vol. 16, No.* 2 (2015), pp. 321–352.

52 Jie Huang, "Challenges and Solutions for the China-US BIT Negotiations: Insights from the Recent Development of FTZs in China," *Journal of International Economic Law*, Vol. 18, No. 2 (2015), pp. 1–33.

53 Gong Baihua, "Guojihua he fazhihua shiye xia de shanghai zimaoqu ying- shang huanjing jianshe" (The Origins of the Business Environment of the Shanghai FTPZ from the Perspective of Internationalization and Legalization), *Xueshu yuekan* (Academic Monthly), No. 1 (2014), pp. 39–40.

54 Zhang Lin, "Guoji jingmao xinguize: Zhongguo zimaoqu de shijian yu tansuo" (New Rules on International Economy and Trade: Practice and Exploration of the Chinese Free Zone), *Shijie jingji yu zhengzhi luntan* (Forum of World Economics & Politics), No. 5 (2015), pp. 155–156.

55 Congyan Cai, "Trans-Pacific Partnership and the Multilateralization of International Investment Law," *Journal of East Asia and International Law*, Vol. 6, No. 2 (2013), pp. 385–413; Rafael Leal-Areas, "China's Attitude to Multilateralism in International Economic Law and Governance: Challenges for the World Trade System," *Journal of World Investment & Trade*, Vol. 11, No. 2 (2012), pp. 259–273. There is a separate school arguing that China's deep engagement in the international investment rule making is a mitigating strategy to lower the potential risks for its outbound investment. Matthew T. Simpson, "Mitigating Volatility: Protecting Chinese Investment in Post-Conflict Regions," *Journal of World Investment & Trade*, Vol. 9, No. 2 (2008), pp. 317–332.

56 Li Mosi, "Quyu fuwu maoyi ziyouhua de xin quxiang – Jiyu GATS HE NAFTA leixing xieding de bijiao" (New Trends in Regional Liberalization of Trade in Services: Based on a Comparison of GATS-Type and NAFTA-Type Agreements), *Shanghai duiwai jingmao daxue xuebao* (Journal of Shanghai University of International Business and Economics), No. 3 (2015), pp. 5–16.

57 Jingxia Shi, "Services Liberalization in China's Free Trade Agreements," *China Legal Science*, Vol. 1, No. 4 (2013), pp. 96–117.

58 Xiao Fang, "Guoji touzi zhongcai caijue zai zhongguo de chengren yu zhixing" (Recognition and Enforcement of International Investment Arbitration Awards in China), *Faxuejia* (Jurist), Vol. 6 (2011), pp. 94–107.

59 Wu Dechang, "Guowai fayuan shiyong 'guoji shangshi hetong tongze' de sifa shijian yu fail tanxi" (An Analysis of Foreign Courts' Juridical Practice in the Application of "Principles of International Commercial Contracts" and Jurisprudence), Jiangxi shehui kexue (Jiangxi Social Sciences), No. 6 (2010), pp. 164–169.

60 Mo Zhang, "Choice of Law in Contracts: A Chinese Approach," *Northwestern Journal of International Law & Business*, Vol. 26 (2006), pp. 297–298; Mo Zhang, "Codified Choice of Law in China: Rules, Processes and Theoretic Underpinnings," *North Carolina Journal of International Law & Commercial Regulation*, Vol. 37, No. 1 (2011), p. 85 (providing a good overview of the history of Choice of Law in China beginning with the Tang dynasty); *Zhonghua Renmin Gongheguo Shewai Minshi Guanxi Falu Shiyong Fa* (Law of the People's Republic of China on the Laws Applicable to Foreign-Related Civil Relations) (promulgated by the Standing Comm. Nat'l People's Cong., 28 October 2010, effective 1 April 2011).

61 Guangjian Tu, "China's New Conflicts Code: General Issues and Selected Topics," *American Journal of Comparative Law*, Vol. 28, No. 2 (2011), pp. 562–590.

62 A successful plaintiff in a China court must still rely upon the government to collect the rendered judgment.

63 Benjamin L. Liebman, "A Populist Threat to China's Courts?," in *Chinese Justice: Civil Dispute Resolution in Contemporary China*, edited by Margaret Y. K. Woo and Mary E. Gallagher (Cambridge: Cambridge University Press, 2011), p. 269.

64 Zhang Hongtao, "Zhongguo fayuan yali zhi xiaojie – Yizhong falv zuzhixue jiedu" (How to Dispel the Stress of China's Courts: An Interpretation from Legal Histology), *Faxuejia* (Jurist), No. 1 (2014), p. 34.
65 Donald C. Clarke, *"Emprical Research into the Chinese Judicial System"*, available at file:///C:/Users/yutao/Downloads/SSRN-id412660.pdf, at 1–33 (last visited on 26 August 2016).
66 Xin He, "Enforcing Commercial Judgments in the Pearl River Delta of China," *American Journal of Comparative Law*, Vol. 39, No. 2 (2009), pp. 419–456.
67 Ma Mingzhi, "Falv zhidu dui jingji fazhan de zuoyong jiqi zai woguo de shixian lujing" (Role of the Legal System on the Economic Development and Its Realization Path in China), *Hebei faxue* (Hebei Law Science), No. 12 (2013), pp. 161–167.
68 Xin He and Yang Su, "Do the 'Haves' Come Out Ahead in Shanghai Courts?," *Journal of Empirical Legal Studies*, Vol. 10, No. 1 (2012), pp. 120–145.
69 Donald C. Clarke, "The Enforcement of United States Court Judgments in China: A Research Note" (Legal Studies Research Paper No. 236, 2004).
70 Xie Xinsheng, "Tiaoyue yu huhui queshi shi zhongguo panjue de yuwai zhixing – Yi meiguo fayuan zhixing zhongguo minshangshi panjue diyi'an wei shijiao" (Extraterritorial Enforcement of Chinese Courts' Judgments without Treaties or Reciprocal Provision: From the Perspective of the First Chinese Civil and Commercial Cases Enforced by a U.S. Court), *Huanqiu falvpinglun* (Global Law Review), No. 4 (2010), pp. 152–160.
71 Qisheng He, "The Recognition and Enforcement of Foreign Judgments between the United States and China: A Study of *Sanlian v. Robinson*," *Tsinghua China Law Review*, Vol. 6, No. 1 (2013), pp. 24–44.
72 Guangjian Tu, "The Hague Choice of Court Convention – A Chinese Perspective," *American Journal of Comparative Law*, Vol. 55, No. 2 (2007), pp. 347–365.
73 Zhang Bo, "Lun tiaojie yu fazhi de paichi yu jianrong" (Discussion on the Exclusion and Compatibility of Mediation and Rules of Law), *Faxue* (Law Science), No. 12 (2012), pp. 55–61.
74 Carl Minzner, "China's Turn Against Law," *American Journal of Comparative Law*, Vol. 50, No. 4 (2011), pp. 935–984.
75 Feng Yuqing and Cao Qing, "Popularised Judiciary in Rural China: Paternalistic Approaches and Enchanted Legal Consciousness," *Hong Kong Law Journal* Vol. 44, No. 2 (2014), pp. 651–676.
76 Xin He and Kwai Hang Ng, "Internal Contradictions of Judicial Mediation in China," *Law & Social Inquiry*, Vol. 39, No. 2 (2014), pp. 285–312; Pan Jianfeng, "Lun minshi sifa yu tiaojie guanxi de dingwei" (Discussion on the Relationship between Civil Adjudication and Mediation), *Zhongwai faxue* (Peking University Law Journal), No. 1 (2013), pp. 185–196; Li Hao, "Tiaojie gui tiaojie, shenpan gui shenpan: minshi shenpan zhong de tiao shen fenli" (Mediation and Trial Are Separate: The Separation of Mediation and Trial in Civil Judgments), *Zhongguo faxue* (China Legal Science), No. 3 (2013), pp. 5–18.
77 William Leung, "Enforcement of Arbitral Award Made by China's Newly Proclaimed Foreign-Related Arbitration Commissions – A Tale of Two Cities," *Dispute Resolution International* Vol. 7, No. 1 (May 2013), pp. 41–53. For more on CIETAC, see Tom Christopher Prostler, "The Rise of an Arbitration Giant: An Overview of the Development of the Chinese Law on Arbitration and the CIETAC Rules," *Vindobona Journal* Vol. 15 (2011), p. 217.
78 China International Economic and Trade Arbitration Commission, "Zhongguo guoji jingji maoyi zhongcai weiyuanhui guanyu Zhongguo guoji jingji maoyi zhongcai weiyuanhui shanghai fenhui, Zhongguo guoji jingji maoyi zhongcai weiyuanhui huanan fenhui youguan shiyi de gonggao" (Notice on Relevant Issues of CIETA Shanghai Branch and CIETA South China Branch Issued by CIETA), *Zhongguo lvshi* (Chinese Lawyer), No. 2 (2013), pp. 2–3.

79 See, e.g., Tom Ginsburg, "International Substitutes for Domestic Institutions: Bilateral Investment Treaties and Governance," *International Review of Law and Economics,* Vol. 25, Issue 1 (2005), pp. 107–121.

80 Ibid.

81 Gao Hongjun, "Meiguofa quanqiuhua: Dianxing lizheng yu fail fansi" (Globalization of U.S. Law: Typical Cases and Reflection), *Zhongguo faxue* (China Legal Science), No. 1 (2011), pp. 6–24.

82 Chen Weidong, "Sifa jiguan yifa duli xingshi zhiquan yanjiu" (Research on the Independent Exercise of Authority by Judicial Organs in Accordance with the Law), *Zhongguo faxue* (China Legal Science), No. 2 (2014), pp. 20–49.

83 Zhang Bin, "Renminbi huilv gaige: Zhezhong de fang'an" (Reform on the Renminbi Exchange Rate: A Proposal for Compromise), *Guoji jingji pinglun* (International Economic Review), No. 1 (2010), pp. 65–85.

84 Liu Jiasong, "Waizi cangu yinhangye yu jinrong anquan de xinxing shichang guojia bijiao yanjiu" (Comparative Study on Foreign Capital's Participation in Banking and Financial Security in Emerging Market Economies), *Hongguan jingji yanjiu* (Macroeconomics), No. 9 (2013), p. 39.

85 Donald C. Clarke, "Three Concepts of the Independent Director," *Delaware Journal of Corporate Law*, Vol. 32 (2007), pp. 73–111.

86 Clarke, "China's Stealth Urban Land Revolution."

87 Cheng Jinhua, "Sibei lilv guize de sifa shijian yu chonggou: Liyong shizheng yanjiu jiejue guifan wenti de xueshu changshi" (Juridical Practice and Reconstruction of the Rule of Four-time Rate: An Academic Attempt to Resolve Normative Problems by Empirical Research), *Zhongwai faxue* (Peking University Law Journal), No. 3 (2015), pp. 684–716.

88 Hui Huang, "Piercing the Corporate Veil in China: What Is It Now and Where Is It Heading," *American Journal of Comparative Law*, No. 3 (2012), pp. 743–774; Huang Hui, "Zhongguo gongsifa renge fouren zhidu shizheng yanjiu" (An Empirical Study on Disregarding the Corporate Personality System in Chinese Corporate Law), *Faxue yanjiu* (Chinese Journal of Law), No. 1 (2012), pp. 3–16.

89 Roman Tomasic and Zinian Zhang, "From Global Convergence in China's Enterprise Bankruptcy Law 2006 to Divergent Implementation: Corporate Reorganisation in China," *Journal of Corporate Law Studies*, Vol. 12, No. 2 (2012), pp. 295–332.

90 Cheng Jinhua, "Zhongguo gongsi shangshi de dili yu zhili – Dui zhengquan shichang xingzheng zhili de zaichanshi" (Geography and Governance of Chinese Company Listing: A Reinterpretation of Administrative Governance on Security Markets), *Zhengquan fayuan* (Securities Law Review), No. 3 (2010), pp. 54–85.

91 Nicholas Howson, "Corporate Law in the Shanghai People's Courts, 1992–2008: Judicial Autonomy in a Contemporary Authoritarian State," *East Asia Law Review*, Vol. 5 (2012), pp. 303–442.

92 Lutz-Christian Wolff, "China's Private International Investment Law: One-Way Street into PRC Law?," *American Journal of Comparative Law*, Vol. 36, No. 3 (2008), pp. 1039–1074.

4

A DYNAMIC CHINA MODEL

The Co-Evolution of Economics and Politics in China

Ling Chen and Barry Naughton

Source: Journal of Contemporary China, 2017, 26, 103, pp. 18–34.

Abstract

China's economic success derives from the co-evolution of the political and economic systems. There is no single 'China model'. Rather, three successive generations of China model can be identified, corresponding to 'growth equilibria' that emerged when policy responded effectively to specific economic challenges. The structure of interaction between economic and political is determined by the basic governance strategy of the Chinese Communist Party.

Introduction

If a 'China model' exists, it will be found in the economic sphere. Advocacy of a China model almost always relies on an appeal to China's remarkable economic growth. Yet attempts to base a China model on the economy quickly collide with the fact that the most distinctive feature of China's political economy is the presence of a strong, intrusive government and the dominance of the political. This article presents a dynamic and evolutionary version of a China political economy model. The key feature is the sustained interplay between political and economic (sub-) systems. The two sub-systems have co-evolved, constantly interacting so that each shapes and is shaped by the other. This dynamic evolutionary process has led not to a single 'China model', but rather to three successive but quite different generations of 'China model' between the 1980s and today.

The governance strategy of the Chinese Communist Party (CCP) and the Chinese government provides the framework within which the model is developed. That is, economic and political systems co-evolve, but within the boundaries established by the Party itself. In order to maintain the continuity of CCP authority, the leaders of the government and Party seek legitimacy through performance and inclusiveness. These objectives lead them to initiate successive waves of liberalizing economic reform, followed by adaptation in the political system. In order to understand these dynamic features more fully, a simplified model is presented in which changes run back and forth between political and economic sub-systems. This simplified dynamic is traced through three successive equilibria, evolutionary stages that define generations of the China model.

The next section discusses the existing China model literature, identifying shortcomings and introducing some basic concepts. The structure and dynamics of the model are described in the third section, and the three following sections narrate the Chinese experience since 1978 as a story of the dynamic creation of three generations of China model. The final section discusses some issues that arise and their implications. A final section summarizes and shows how the model contributes to understanding the current situation in China and the future.

An unresolved issue in the 'China model' literature

The China model literature developed in order to explain the systemic elements behind China's high speed economic development. There are many different versions of the 'China model', but they all contain some common features. most authors take the 'China model' to include three things: (1) a strong and decisive government which is capable of steering the economy through aggressive investment and macroeconomic policy, and which may include a large state sector; (2) a system of personnel management that effectively incentivizes lower level officials and promotes higher quality officials; and (3) a rational and pragmatic ruling party, that frequently adopts an experimental, adaptive and incremental approach to reform.[1] Most authors take for granted the fact that China is a market economy, or at least moving in that direction. The strong state and relatively rational ruling party are universal characteristics of China models, although different authors assess the positives and negatives attached to these features in different ways.[2]

At the center, then, of virtually all versions of a 'China model' is the interrelationship of a strong government and a market economy. However, almost nothing in this literature analyzes the economic motives and objectives of the government or CCP, or the way in which these objectives might change with changing economic conditions. This omission is particularly striking in the polemic advocacy literature on the 'China model' which repeatedly celebrates China's strong government, while simply taking it for granted that the government's goals will be economic growth and the emergence of a strong China. The objectives and actions of the CCP, the Chinese government and Chinese society are merged into a single undifferentiated and unexamined entity.[3] The resulting attempt to distill a unique idealized essence of the Chinese experience without analyzing the key components or dynamics will never yield useful conclusions. Instead, a useful discussion of the 'China model' ought to apply a generalizable logic based on key actors and structured dynamics. This can illuminate the Chinese experience and isolate features that might be applicable outside China.[4] In this article, such a logic provides the basis for an evolutionary account of the system of relations between government and the economy in China.

A starting point for analyzing government – economy relations in China can be found in the crucial distinction developed by North and Weingast in their classic analysis of the emergence of constitutional government in England in 1688.

North and Weingast point out that a ruler can establish credibility in one of two ways: either through a pattern of 'responsible behavior' or by choosing to be 'constrained to obey a set of rules that do not permit leeway'.[5] Pessimistic about the feasibility of the first choice, North and Weingast argue that the English sovereign accepted the constraints of constitutional rule in order to achieve the benefit of credibility. By contrast, the CCP has taken the alternate approach: it has committed itself to 'responsible behavior', and consistently declined to be constrained by 'rules that do not permit leeway'. The lack of constraints gives the CCP and the government the ability to act powerfully and decisively.

It is this fundamental choice by the ruling party that really sets China apart: 'China model' proponents are implicitly arguing that the CCP made the right choice to decline the constraints of constitutional rule, because this enhanced the CCP's capacity for decisive action and sharpened the CCP's focus on responsible behavior. Since 1978, the regime's own definition of responsible behavior has included two main components: performance – especially economic performance – and inclusiveness. It is already widely accepted that the Communist Party committed itself to growing the economy and providing benefits to almost the entire population in order to achieve 'performance legitimacy'.[6] Indeed, this view has become a kind of folk wisdom, sometimes described as an implicit bargain between the CCP and the Chinese population, in which economic well-being is traded for political acquiescence. However, the implications of the ruling CCP's choice for 'responsible behavior' are rarely analyzed further. In this article, the government and CCP commitment to 'responsible behavior' is presented as the central element of CCP governance strategy, because it is the means through which the CCP aims to sustain its political authority through establishing credibility and legitimacy. The co-evolution of economic and political mechanisms in China unfolds in the wake of the CCP's choice to establish its legitimacy by making a sustained commitment to good performance and inclusive governance.

Theoretical framework: co-evolution

To build and sustain legitimacy, the CCP commits itself to 'responsible behavior' in the terms of North and Weingast, consistently pursuing two interrelated objectives: performance and inclusiveness.[7] The pursuit of each of these objectives generates new social demands, which impose costs on the CCP and require it to provide additional services and governance goods. The CCP's objectives are never perfectly aligned with social demands, and so the CCP response includes elements of adaptation, compromise and pressure, as it searches for a low cost outcome. This process can be seen with each of the twin objectives of the CCP's legitimation strategy.

Performance and credible rules

'Performance' is whatever delivers economic growth. Economic growth is a crucial part of the Party's legitimacy, and the pursuit of it repeatedly leads the Party to economic reform. However, because the Party's commitment is to performance rather than liberalization *per se*, other less market-friendly policies are also adopted. The Party's commitment to marketization is generally instrumental, and subordinate to the growth objective.

Once the marketization process is begun, it unleashes a set of demands from newly empowered economic actors. Specifically, it creates a demand for 'credible rules' within the economic system. Dispersed market actors can constitute a common market only if they are subject to the same rules of conduct. As a result, rules that facilitate the basic system of market exchange have gradually been set up, with the active engagement of the CCP. These rules are embedded in the market economy, and create an ongoing demand that government maintain and uphold the rules, and develop new rules to cover new situations.

Inclusiveness and contestation

Inclusiveness is the second pillar of the CCP's claim to legitimacy. The meaning of inclusiveness can be sharpened by the distinction introduced by Robert Dahl almost 50 years ago between competition and participation. Democracy is characterized by different degrees of competition – or contestation – and participation – or inclusiveness; different realizations of these features lead to different types of regime.[8] The Party asserts that its responsibility and fundamental nature is to represent the national interest of China, including the interests of all major social groups. When a new social group emerges, the Party begins a political process to incorporate that group into its governance structure. 'Inclusiveness' means that the Party has an obligation to listen to and respond to the interests of new social groups, and also that it seeks to ensure that no social group can have an independent power base to challenge the regime from the 'outside'. The CCP implicitly acknowledges the low level of contestation in the Chinese system, but argues that legitimacy is ensured by a high degree of inclusiveness. Advocates of the 'China model' agree, and tout 'consensus' as a major advantage of the system.

The political system seeks ways to incorporate new interest groups into a system of consultation, while the interest groups themselves look for ways to influence policy. Market competition raises efficiency, but it also leads to competition among interest groups, competition for policy preferences and competition over rule-setting. Interest groups accept policy consultation in which they have a 'voice', but they seek a system in which their voice has greater weight, which often leads them to prefer a system with greater contestation.

Tension and equilibrium

Each of the two basic pillars of the regime legitimation strategy thus elicits a demand that is in tension with the regime's fundamental strategic choice. The drive for economic performance creates a demand for credible rules. The drive for inclusiveness creates a demand for contestation over policy and fair competition in the marketplace. The CCP accedes to these demands to a certain extent,

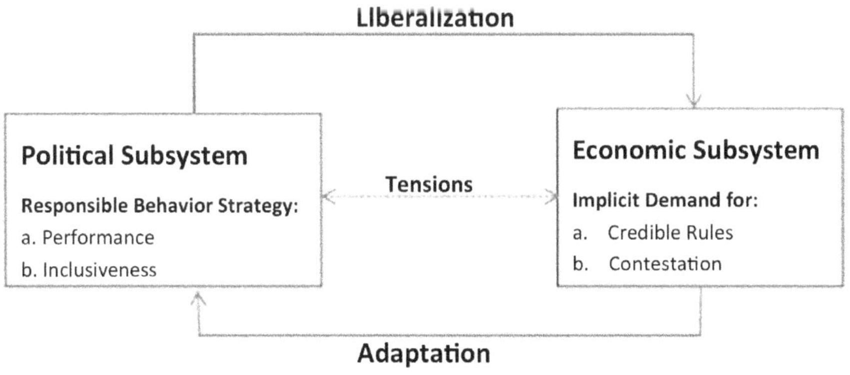

Figure 4.1 Dynamics of evolution

but seeks to limit their applicability. The Party concedes the need for rules and competition in the economic arena, and also seeks to rationalize and improve the performance of the government bureaucracy. As a result, the system has generally moved in the direction of clearer rules and fair contestation.

However, there is an insurmountable boundary that limits the spread of rules and contestation. The CCP insists on maintaining its own discretionary power and resists any externally imposed rules or contestation. Indeed, the purpose of the commitment to responsible behavior is precisely to fend off the constraints of constitutional order, or 'rules that do not permit leeway', in North and Weingast's words. Thus, while performance and inclusiveness are the two basic premises of the CCP's governance model, credible rules and contestation are two basic demands that arise within the economic system. Therefore, the political sub-system and the economic sub-system consistently produce conflict and tension, which drives system development. The basic dynamics of the model are shown schematically in Figure 4.1.

Over time, the balance among the different elements changes continuously. Consistent with the 'China model', the strong and decisive government responds in adaptive and incremental fashion to the challenges of the day, but those challenges can be quite different during different periods. The interactions among economic and political systems can be analyzed in terms of five basic movements or stages.

A. *Initiation: crisis and challenge*

The history of the People's Republic has been marked by repeated systematic crises, and the underlying logic of these crises is consistent. The political system prevented the free play of market forces: as a result, policy-makers lacked the information needed to steer the economy responsibly. Individuals faced incentives incompatible with sustained economic growth. The absence of appropriate information and incentives has repeatedly led to the accumulation of risk at the system level, and eventually to crisis.

B. Policy movement to economic liberalization

The Party initiates liberalization selectively in order to deal with crisis. In Chinese experience, liberalization has repeatedly led to quick and vigorous economic response. Market development reveals critical information to policy-makers about where the growth potential is in the economy, and policy-makers have learned to carry out 'experiments' to facilitate this process. The development of the economy creates new levels of complexity, and also new demands for further liberalization. New market actors develop a voice and a concept of their own interests. The vigorous economic response threatens to create a positive feedback loop, in which liberalization increases impetus for future liberalization. This creates a new source of tension in the system.

C. Movement from economics to politics: government adaptation

Economic change, even as it is successful, challenges the Party's existing stance and requires actions to revitalize the twin bases of legitimacy, performance and inclusiveness. First, leaders move to increase the capability and effectiveness of government in order to support economic performance. New institutions are devised as economic progress puts pressure on governmental authorities to raise their game. This interaction, to be sure, is part of the general development process in many countries, but China does it in a distinctive fashion. China's experimental and adaptive processes work well at this phase. Second, leaders adopt measures to re-establish and increase inclusiveness. Liberalization creates new interest groups and types of organization. This makes the Party's existing mechanisms of inclusion obsolete, and the Party looks for new ways to incorporate these groups into its interest aggregation system. They do so by creating new sets of governance structures and new policy processes, including those discussed by deLisle and Yang in this issue. New interests are accorded legitimacy and expert opinion is given special attention, while the Party moves to co-opt newly emerging groups into the hierarchical political system.

D. Emergence of new equilibrium

As a result of liberalization and adaptation, both the economic and political systems reach a more sophisticated level, and a new equilibrium emerges between them. The development of the economy and the complex of policies associated with 'political upgrading' creates a new generation of 'China model'. The compatibility of institutions triggers a new surge of economic growth and leads to quick efficiency gains. The system moves out of crisis and gains renewed vitality. Efficiency gains are distributed as rents and channeled into new investment, including physical and human capital investments and investments in the system itself.[9] A new 'growth equilibrium' develops.

E. Tensions and 'substitution strategy'

Despite rapid growth and increased wealth, the tension between the economic and political systems has not disappeared and may actually increase. Two types of pressure threaten to disrupt the new equilibrium. On the one hand, with economic growth the sophistication and complexity of the economy increases, putting new demands on the political system. With growth, the complexity of interest groups and the need for information both increase. On the other hand, actions taken within the political system can undermine economic gains. In the face of inevitable economic shocks, the government often adopts 'substitution strategies', which we define as occurring whenever the government uses administrative or political measures to replace market-based policy instruments in the face of potential crisis or market failure. Given that 'responsible behavior' is defined by the outcomes of economic growth and inclusiveness, the leadership is not fully committed to liberalization as the means to this end. When economic prosperity or social stability is threatened, the Party responds with the most immediate tools at its disposal, and so is continuously tempted to substitute administrative intervention for market outcomes. Macroeconomic challenges are met with aggressive government intervention. This may cause an erosion of market forces and a re-assertion of administrative powers, which cultivates a new type of crisis and initiates a new cycle of dynamics.

In related fashion, the incorporation of interest groups into the Party's governance structure becomes more selective and subtly restricts information by reducing the salience of dissenting and minority views. After welcoming emerging market groups under the Party's umbrella, the Party ends up rewarding selected interest groups for their participation in the system. Insider voices may come to dominate the policy conversation, and selected insiders are insured against some of the risks of market competition. Individual risks are converted into systemic risk.[10] Rapid economic growth also serves to disrupt existing arrangements. In other words, the equilibrium begins to decay. Equilibrium is temporary and policy-makers face new challenges and, possibly, a new phase of crisis.

There is no single 'China model' but rather successive generations of equilibrium among economic and political forces. The interaction produces three distinct generations of China model since 1978. Rather than being a static achievement of the Chinese political system, the China model is shown to be a provisional outcome of a set of dynamically interacting and co-evolving sub-systems. The logic of this dynamic interaction and co-evolution, in turn, is transformed into specific institutional outcomes through the consistent and distinctive governance strategy of the Communist Party which is designed to maintain its ruling status.

The first generation of the China model

A. Crisis and the beginning of reform in 1978–1979

By the end of the Cultural Revolution, China was in a serious economic crisis, and the Party was faced with a catastrophic loss of legitimacy. The December

1978 declaration of the Third Plenum of the 11th Party Congress was notably short of specifics, declaring only that 'socialist modernization' would heretofore be the Party's 'overall mission'. It gave no hint of the economic reforms to follow because, in fact, those reforms remained to be discovered by the process of liberalization and opening itself.

B. Liberalization

The economic reforms that followed the policy turn of 1978–1979 have been well-documented and analyzed.[11] Text Box 2.1 lists a few of the most important, proceeding from the bottom up.

Text Box 2.1 Main liberalization measures in 1978–1985

1. **Farmers** were given decision-making autonomy, better prices, and, ultimately, control of their land through the contract responsibility system.
2. **Rural townships and villages** were allowed to set up non-agricultural enterprises in almost any sector, and this right was gradually extended to **private businesses**.
3. **State-owned enterprises** were given more autonomy, including the right to retain funds and spend them on investment or worker welfare.
4. **Dual-track pricing** was introduced. Since the plan was fixed in size, allowing enterprises (including state enterprise) to buy and sell on the market allowed the economy to gradually 'grow out of the plan'.
5. **Special Economic Zones** were created where foreign investment was welcomed and new trade rules were piloted.

During this period, the experimental and adaptive approach to reform – sometimes known as 'crossing the river by groping for stepping stones' – became well established. For the first time, a potential 'China model', a distinctive approach to economic reform and transformation, was discernible. Reforms were primarily bottom-up, involving millions of dispersed actors and with extremely limited knowledge, an environment especially suited to the experimental approach. These reform policies quickly unleashed potential and created an explosion of economic growth. Since entry of new producers was the main form in which commercial and industrial reforms occurred, millions of new market actors, overwhelmingly small-scale and low-tech, were created virtually overnight. The economic policy worked well, and quickly achieved results that solidified and built support for the reform process.

C. Political adaptation

Political adaptation to these momentous economic changes began immediately. At the 1978 Third Plenum, the Party gave a new definition of responsible behavior, and committed to it. By taking ownership of the objective of modernization, the Party put itself symbolically at the head of China's modernization drive. This meant that all of the Party's formidable resources of persuasion, reward and intimidation could now be legitimately deployed in the service of economic development. The Plenum re-positioned the Party as the driver of the development process, and thereby established 're-purposing' as a repeatedly employed instrument of China's reform process. Basic principles of cadre management were introduced that included retirement (except for the top leaders) and increased training and education. Other crucial features of political adaptation are listed in Text Box 2.2, proceeding from the top down.

Text Box 2.2 Main provisions of political adaptation, 1979–1989

1. **'Socialist modernization'** adopted as CCP goal. Clear communication that economic development was top priority, while Deng's 'four Cardinal Principles' set limits to liberalization.
2. **Political reform** based on separation of government and Party (first floated in 1980, partially implemented in 1987–1988).
3. **Norms of retirement** and **educational credentials**. Cadres needed to be 'young, educated, professional and revolutionary'.
4. **'Target responsibility system'** brought strong incentives into the hierarchy, with steep reward functions. Local governments forced to become entrepreneurial.
5. **'Factory manager responsibility system'** gave authority to SOE managers.
6. **Village representative assemblies** created.

Crucially, the incentives of grassroots cadres were adapted to make them compatible with the burgeoning market economy. Incentives for rural governments had been transformed organically as township and village officials became deeply invested in building local township and village enterprises (TVEs). In the mid-1980s, similar incentives were incorporated into the formal governance system through explicit evaluation criteria for most government and party officials. Target responsibility systems established success indicators for bureaucrats at all levels, gave them explicit weight in an evaluation function, and linked monetary rewards to that evaluation.[12] Moreover, promotion was significantly influenced by good performance on indicators such as fiscal revenue and GDP growth specified in target responsibility systems.[13] Although the importance of these success indicators in the Chinese system is universally recognized, it needs to be stressed how unusual it is for such high-powered incentives to be introduced into government bureaucracies. Normally, when publicly accountable officials have to trade off multiple objectives, high-powered incentives are avoided, because incentivizing one or two targets draws effort away from other objectives.[14] Such an incentive system only made sense because of the overwhelming priority given to economic development by the CCP leaders.

The Chinese political system became much more inclusive as class struggle was abandoned along with the Cultural Revolution. Many suppressed social groups were brought back into normal society, including the intellectuals, scientists, technicians and specialized bureaucrats; individual businesses and entrepreneurs; and households with overseas family connections, all of whom had been attacked during the Cultural Revolution. In 1977–1978, Deng Xiaoping revived the policy meeting system that had been halted during the Cultural Revolution and brought the democratic Parties back into the political arena. In the free-wheeling environment of the 1980s, consultation was mainly ad hoc, but certainly increased. Village representative assemblies were set up and spread.

D. A new equilibrium: late 1980s 'China model 1.0'

In a short time, a new political economic system came into existence, which we label 'China model 1.0'. This system was not very institutionalized, but it was highly flexible and marked by substantial consistency of institutions and incentives. The rules for larger, state-owned firms had changed enough (through the 'dual track' system) that all firms could do business with each other, contributing to the emergence of a national market system. Ownership forms co-existed, with entry driving the *de facto* privatization of the most competitive sectors. Growth accelerated, especially after 1983, driven from the bottom up by the entry of millions of small-scale actors. Shortages of basic consumer goods, pervasive in the 1970s, were eliminated by the mid-1980s. Yasheng Huang has called this a golden age of grassroots entrepreneurial activity and bottom-up growth.[15]

The institutional framework of China model 1.0 has been well described in the literature. Localities began to see themselves as being in competition with other areas for economic development, in a system classified as 'fiscal federalism' or labeled 'decentralized authoritarianism'.[16] These descriptions located the essence of the early system in some combination of top-down control, local autonomy and inter-jurisdictional competition. Modern national institutions – financial, fiscal, legal, property rights – were almost completely absent. Nevertheless, reforms created a relatively consistent set of institutional arrangements that provided new incentives for economic growth and encouraged the movement away from the traditional command economy. Enough authority was decentralized to local governments that they had incentives to invest and to create innovative institutions. Better incentives and human capital began to generate growth, a bigger surplus and more wealth. This gave the system greater resources to resolve problems and in turn gave birth to more diversified demand for property rights, more effective and accountable government, and for the broader set of institutions required for a market economy.

E. Tensions, substitution strategy, and renewed crisis

The positive economic conditions and fragile young equilibrium was over-turned in the turmoil of 1989. Leadership consensus shattered spectacularly as top leaders split over how to handle economic disruption and social demands for change. The most dynamic reformers were purged from the leadership, and the post-1989 leadership announced their intention to bring back planning, terminate dual-track markets for producer goods, implement price controls, and direct scarce energy and material resources to state firms. This was the most extreme of all possible 'substitution strategies': the political leadership literally intended to substitute a revived planning system for the market economy that had begun to develop. But while the top leadership abandoned China model 1.0 after 1989, there was actually no going back. The robust set of complementary institutions established in the 1980s certainly did not disappear, and in fact displayed consistent vitality well into the 1990s. Though reforms were halted from 1989 to 1991, the basic resilience of the system created in the 1980s quickly became obvious as the economy bounced back from the 1989–90 recession. The inflation that planners were worried about was gone within a year; and TVEs re-emerged as the most dynamic sector despite temporary central government discrimination against them. Local governments quickly resumed their role as growth promoters. The system proved robust and the economy sprang back to life quickly after Deng's 1992 Southern Tour.

The second generation China model

A. The crisis

The conservative post-1989 leadership was unable to undermine China model 1.0, but a deeper looming crisis compelled a response in the 1990s. This was a crisis of state capacity that resulted from the lack of a national fiscal and financial superstructure. From the very beginning of reform, the processes of de-centralization and de-monopolization had been eroding the resources and revenues available to the government, especially the central government. This steady decline in fiscal revenues reached a point of crisis as revenues fell below 13% of GDP in 1993. The leadership was finally galvanized to action after 1993, launching a series of fundamental reforms. The fundamental cause of this crisis was the fact that the grassroots economy had outgrown the fiscal and financial institutions that had once been adequate in China's smaller and less competitive economy, and until that time nothing had been put in to replace them.

B. Liberalization

A new wave of liberalization began after the declaration that China was a 'socialist market economy' in October 1992. What followed was an astonishing period of radical and comprehensive institutional reforms, especially those concentrated between 1993 and 1999. Liberalization gave not just TVEs, but also foreign-invested and private firms new spaces in which to operate and compete under reasonably fair conditions. Most impressively, the institutional development necessitated by the preceding fiscal crisis was used to provide a 'level playing field' to these different types of ownership. Wu Jinglian sees this as the beginning of the comprehensive reform that created the basis for China's market economy.[17] Not surprisingly, the overall policy package was quite different from that in the first period. Reforms were designed in a top-down manner. There actually was a 'reform blueprint', outlined in the declaration of the 1993 Third Plenum, which was largely implemented. Moreover, reform was on balance recentralizing, as it restored resource flows to the central government. Since these policies have been covered in the literature, we simply summarize a few main points in the following Text Box 2.3.

Text Box 2.3 Main provisions of economic reform, 1993–1999

1. **Fiscal system** restructured in 1994–1995, with new tax system and a generally recentralizing division of revenues between center and locality.
2. **Local governments** were given broader economic management authority, eventually including land and commercial development.
3. **Commercial banks** separated from a newly empowered **central bank**.
4. **New foreign trade** system with current account convertibility adopted.
5. **State enterprises** given new corporate code (1995); major down-sizing of state sector (1998–2000). Loss-making firms allowed to go bankrupt.
6. **Individual mobility** is permitted and rural-to-urban migration on a mass scale begins.

Again, the economic response was rapid. By the turn of the century, central government resources had clearly recovered and were now consistent with more moderate government goals. The crisis of state capacity was resolved. Entrance into the World Trade Organization (WTO) in 2001 locked in the main institutional changes. The restructuring and listing of state-owned commercial banks that culminated in 2004–2006 marked the last high point of this reform era. The package of reforms created a sufficiently rule-based economy that individuals had a degree of predictability and incentives to work within the system: economic growth accelerated again after 2002.

Along with rapid growth came a further expansion in the number of economic actors. Firms of all ownership types proliferated as the state sector shrank. In the city, housing reform made most residents into property owners. As the flow of farmers leaving the countryside gradually became a flood, all social arrangements had to be reconstructed. The traditional dualistic society, enforced by the *hukou* system, was completely inadequate. The advent of the Internet meant a revolution in people's access to information. These enormous changes created an across-the-board demand for a new set of social institutions that could respond to an unprecedented volume and diversity of social demands.

C. Political adaptation

Just as the economic reform program of the 1990s involved much more institutional design and implementation than had been evident before, so the political adaptations of the CCP represented a much more systematic effort to reconstruct China's political institutions. Some of the most important adaptive provisions are shown in Text Box 2.4.

Text Box 2.4 Main provisions of political adaptation, 1992–2010

1. China was declared a 'socialist market economy' (in 1992) and the **CCP was formally 're-purposed'** as a 'governing Party' (in 2004).
2. **Civil Service System** was formally introduced in 1993, introducing professional standards, job classification, ranks and incentive pay.
3. Broad program of **cadre reform** created formal **age limits, term limits and job credentialing.**
4. Functions of **government radically re-oriented** as industrial ministries were abolished (1998) and new social service functions significantly expanded (post-2005).
5. New systems of **industrial and technology policy** introduced to steer market economy.

Just as had been the case in 1978, a clear re-statement of purpose by the CCP initiated this period. By adopting the 'Socialist market economy', the Party clearly demonstrated that its definition of responsible behavior henceforth fully incorporated a market economy. The restructuring of the cadre system – which began with the introduction of a government civil service in 1993 – culminated at the September 2004 issuance of the 'decision on enhancing the Party's governing Capacity', which laid out a systematic vision for the entire bureaucracy, under the guise of improving the Party's management of cadres. Shambaugh has called this 'probably the most important party meeting and document to be published since the critical Third plenum in 1978'.[18] Critically, the 'decision' was accompanied by a set of documents formalizing a comprehensive set of procedures for Party and government management. Most important among these procedures were the regular turnover rules that created rational and reasonably predictable career paths. A combination of age limits and term limits was put in place that guaranteed a predictable set of career trajectories in which expectations were clearly formed and actually realized. Credible turnover at the top is the keystone of the arch, creating stable expectations about promotion and career paths.[19] Credentials (especially educational credentials) and evaluation procedures were required for promotion. The result was a high-powered, incentive-compatible system that led to the accumulation of skills within the system (Text Box 2.4, Item 3).

The overall structure of the government was overhauled in a series of changes beginning in 1998. The industrial ministries were abolished and the planning agencies severely downgraded. Beginning in 2004, the concept of a 'service-oriented government' was endorsed.[20] Government outlays for education, medical insurance and pensions increased steadily, and a crisis management system was introduced at every government level and department after the SARS crisis in 2003. At the top of the government apparatus, Wen Jiabao presided over important changes in the policy formulation process that opened up the policy process to systematic expert input, bringing in scientists, economists and academics of many disciplines into the policy process.[21] Wen Jiabao was particularly adept at structuring and shaping the policy consultation process.

The second strand of political adaptation was the CCP's drive to re-establish inclusiveness as a pillar of its legitimacy. The doctrine of the 'Three Represents' was elaborated by Jiang Zemin in a 1 July 2001 speech commemorating the 80th anniversary of the CCP. According to this doctrine, the Party should represent the advanced productive forces, advanced modern culture and the interests of the vast majority of the people. The Three Represents finally abandoned the obsolete class-based identification of the Party, and replaced it with a formula that was at once inclusive and elitist. Hu Jintao after 2003 introduced 'Scientific Developmentalism' and the 'harmonious society', designed to bring the interests of previously neglected groups into the scope of decision-making. As policy stressed inclusiveness, institutional innovations were taken to incorporate more social groups into the Party's consultation (and control) system. Labor unions have traditionally been weak in China. Now, the government gave the official Unions higher status and defined a set of worker rights in the 2008 Labor Law. At the same time, workers' grievances were taken out of the courts and placed in a custom-built arbitration process, with representatives from the union, employer and local government labor bureaus.[22]

D. A new equilibrium, 1998–2012: the 'China model 2.0'

The most immediate difference between 'China model 2.0' and its predecessor is that 'China 2.0' (for short) is founded on a set of institutional arrangements that were much more robust, more comprehensive and that had been intentionally designed. 'China 1.0' had been founded on a modest set of *ad hoc* arrangements between central and local governments, combined with bottom-up market liberalization. China 1.0 had been fully successful only at the grassroots levels. China 2.0 was based on a far more sustainable set of power arrangements; a much more complete set of institutional arrangements; and a set of human skills that were increasingly adequate and in command of the information resources they needed to make decisions. A complete set of rules governing the careers of Party and government bureaucrats was put in place; and a full panoply of institutions governing the government and economy created. In short, the system became far more institutionalized.

On the economic side, financial institutions were largely borrowed from developed countries, but adapted to Chinese conditions. In the state-run industrial economy, a new ownership agency, the State Asset Supervision and Administration Commission (SASAC), was set up in 2003 and instituted a system of managerial evaluation and appointment procedures that borrowed from Western practice but was integrated into the Party's personnel management system.[23] On the political side, the institutional innovations were thoroughly distinct. These combined an authoritarian power structure with high-powered incentives and a comprehensive set of regulations governing evaluations and career paths. This is certainly an unusual and distinctive combination.

Even though many of the policies that created China 2.0 were centralizing, entrepreneurial local governments continued to play a critical role in the system. The focus shifted from rural to urban governments: to compensate them for the loss of budgetary revenues (to the center), local officials were given much greater latitude in managing their local economy.[24] Local governments could no longer simply harvest revenues from their public enterprises (many of which had gone bankrupt), but they could devise creative strategies for restructuring them, unlocking the value of the land they sat on. Local governments had always had implicit control over urban land, and after about 2000 began to leverage land as a critical asset. Local officials became deal-makers and played a much broader developmental role, and the role of urbanization in the development process accelerated.

As a result of these changes, China 2.0 was dramatically scalable. The model was adequate to incorporate the gigantic central government state-owned enterprises (SOEs) that are among the largest corporations in the world. The institutions are sufficient to govern macroeconomic relationships in the second largest economy in the world. This dramatically bigger system was also able to incorporate diverse social groups in a way that was inconceivable in the 1980s: spending for universities and science and technology increased, while intellectuals were given a voice in policy deliberations; workers had a portfolio of explicit rights and approved channels to defend those rights; private business people made their accommodations with the system and devoted their efforts to earning profit and expanding their business.

There was a fundamental complementarity among the different elements of this new system. This is most easily seen from the perspective of a local government official who now faced clearly defined and fully aligned incentives. He was rewarded for investing and promoting economic growth according to clear articulated indicators; he faced stable expectations of promotion if he succeeded; and he generally had access to the resources needed to achieve these goals. In the wake of the consolidation of China 2.0, China's economic growth accelerated. Budgetary revenues recovered, and the central government's position was stabilized. From 2003 through 2008, China's GDP growth surged above 10% for six successive years – from a moderately high base – fundamentally transforming China's economy and position in the world.

E. Tensions and substitution strategies

With the consolidation of China 2.0 in the mid-2000s, the impetus for further economic reform declined dramatically. After the completion of bank restructuring in 2006, Wen Jiabao presided over no major market-oriented reforms. Instead, to achieve key objectives or deal with external shocks, Wen Jiabao adopted 'substitution strategies'. For example, to achieve the objective of technological upgrading, the government under Wen Jiabao began to re-create sectoral technology and industrial policies, which proliferated after 2005 to total more than 50 by 2010. These led to a significant increase in government intervention in industrial product markets. Even more important was the government's response to the global financial Crisis (GFC) in 2008. China's stimulus program was not merely massive, RmB4 trillion in fiscal expansion plus RmB9 trillion in credit expansion; in addition, it was delivered directly to local leaders through the Party/government hierarchy, with banks firmly instructed to accommodate the massive increase in investment projects.[25] This crucial characteristic meant the stimulus increased the politicization of investment allocation and substantially 'softened' the budget constraints faced by local government officials. Once launched, these funds proved impossible to cut off, and credit expansion remained high for the next five years. The stimulus program was an effective policy when precisely what was needed was to counter-act market forces and stop the GFC from spilling over into China. However, in a context where market-oriented reforms had stalled out, and with 'substitution strategies' eroding the power of market forces, the dynamism of China 2.0 was potentially compromised. Questions began to be raised about the adaptability and dynamism of the China 2.0 set-up.

The third generation: A 'Xi Jinping model'?

A. The crisis

When Xi Jinping came to power in 2012, the potential for crisis once again threatened the China model. In the first place, changes in exogenous conditions demanded new responses. With the end of the 'miracle growth' phase, the potential growth rate has dropped dramatically from over 10% to an unknown figure somewhere between 5% and 8%, largely due to a dramatic decline in labor force growth. The response to these rapidly changing conditions has become more difficult because of the substitution strategies followed by the political leadership. The rapid increase in debt caused by China's stimulus response to the GFC proved impossible to limit. Much of the debt was acquired by local governments, with uncertain ability to repay. Even more worrisome, with softer budget constraints, debt spread through multiple channels ('shadow banking') to local government funding vehicles and private and public corporations. The potential for a debt crisis grew significantly.

Substitution strategies were of limited effectiveness in responding to these external changes. Rapid credit growth was used to prevent the inevitable slowing of the economy, piling up risks for the future. It is widely agreed that in response to the slow-down, the economy should shift toward services and 'innovation-led' growth, but the industrial and technology policies developed by Wen Jiabao did little to reveal what those sectors actually were, despite the expenditure of hundreds of billions of yuan. In fact, even beyond these specific problems, worry seemed to grow about the ability of the system to adapt in fundamental ways. Perhaps due to the influence of interest groups and corruption, the system seemed to have developed a much higher degree of inertia, which seemed to policy-makers to threaten their ability to resolve accumulated issues or respond to the largest exogenous change in economic conditions since 1978.

B. Liberalization

The Xi Jinping administration laid out an ambitious program of economic reform and liberalization in November 2013 (Text Box 2.5). Implementation of this program has been extremely uneven, and the actual program is still in its infancy.

Text Box 2.5 Liberalization measures proposed in 2013–2015

1. **Market Administration:** abolition of many administrative approval requirements, experimentation with 'negative lists', permitting any economic activity not explicitly limited.
2. **Financial reform**: liberalization of interest rates, lowering entry barriers to financial firms, expansion of capital market, and opening of the capital account.
3. **State Enterprises:** change the model of SOE management to one of 'managing capital' combined with 'mixed ownership'.
4. **Fiscal reform:** restructure local government debt; create new tax revenue sources; drastically reduce local government dependence on real estate.
5. **Internationalization:** domestic firms encouraged to invest abroad; increased use of RMB outside China.

However, the program, if implemented, would redraw the boundaries between government and market, and provide substantially greater scope for the operation of market forces, particularly through the financial system. The slogan 'give the market the determining role in resource allocation' is a reasonably good description of the objective of this bundle of policies. The proposed reforms are undoubtedly significant; however, as of mid-2016 they had been only partially and unevenly implemented.

C. Political adaptation

Major political adaptations have occurred since the beginning of the Xi Jinping administration, beginning with subtle and not-so-subtle shifts in the definition of responsible behavior and inclusiveness. Most clearly, the objective of economic growth no longer has absolute priority in the definition of responsible behavior. More non-economic considerations shape and constrain policy-making than in the past, including rooting out corruption, improving environmental conditions and ensuring a higher degree of ideological conformity, along with the constant of ensuring social stability. Text Box 2.6 summarizes the important initiatives launched under Xi.

Text Box 2.6 Political adaptation during 2013–2015

1. **'China Dream.'** Demotion of economic growth from its previous position as dominant objective; incorporation of nationalist and ideological objectives, as well as environmental considerations.
2. **Anti-corruption campaign.** Expansion of authority of Central discipline Inspection Commission.
3. **Party leadership**. Expansion of Party policy-making leadership small groups; more direct participation and oversight by the Party in policy and strategic decision-making.
4. **Leadership evaluation** emphasized in cadre promotion decisions.
5. **Ideological controls** tightened.

The most obvious political change in China in the past three years has been the prominence of anti-corruption efforts. The authority and organization of the Central Disciplinary Inspection Commission (CDIC) been substantially enhanced. Central Discipline Inspection Teams – essentially mobile audit teams that squat in a locality or enterprise and search for corruption or other malfeasance – have been dispatched to every province and most large central SOEs. It is not simply that many high-profile corruption cases have been reported, but rather that new institutions have become important and the balance of power among existing institutions has shifted.

The CCP drive for inclusiveness has also been re-defined and raised to a new level under Xi Jinping. Xi's 'China dream' seeks to merge the aspirations of individual Chinese into the realization of a historical revitalization of the Chinese nation. Xi's 'four Comprehensives' wrap the regime's policy priorities in a single all-encompassing package: Build a moderately Prosperous Country; Deepen Reform; Rule the Country by Law; and Strictly Govern the Party. The 'four Comprehensives' subtly display the fact that economic growth no longer has absolute priority, and also combine inclusiveness with stronger top-down leadership. At the same time, the drive for inclusiveness has acquired a harder edge, with stricter ideological controls, closer monitoring of non-governmental organizations and targeting of regime critics, as described by Yang and deLisle in this issue. Redefinition is an important part of governmental adaptation in China.

D. A new equilibrium? The 'China model 3.0'

The 'China model 3.0' is just emerging, and neither the economic liberalization policies nor the government adaptations have been fully fleshed out, much less realized in practice. It is far too early to pass judgment on this China model 3.0, but it is possible to pose some preliminary questions. First, is this in fact a new equilibrium? It is certainly new. The Xi administration is different enough from the previous regime that it represents a clear break with the previous equilibrium. In important respects, 3.0 policies seem to emerge specifically out of the perceived problems of 2.0, and are designed to break down the systemic inertia deemed to characterize 2.0. Most of the important initiatives of 3.0 are top-down, and seem to be designed to give top policy-makers the maximum possible freedom of action. In that sense, 3.0 Shows the Xi administration strongly re-affirming the basic CCP strategic choice for 'responsible behavior' and against any external constraints. Yet they also break with the institutional arrangements of 2.0 which accorded substantial latitude to local governments and social organizations; and depart from Party norms that emphasized predictable (and limited) career paths.

Is China 3.0 an equilibrium? Here we must be more cautious. In the first place, the economic liberalization measures have been only partially and slowly implemented since they were unveiled in the fall of 2013. Those measures have the potential to unlock a new phase of productivity growth, but they have to be effectively implemented for that to happen. At the same time, it is unclear whether or not the political adaptations are consistent with the liberalization measures. Certainly, an effective anti-corruption program and market liberalization are complementary, each increasing the effectiveness of the other. By drawing clear lines between government and the market, and reducing government discretionary authority, 3.0 seeks to control the scope for rent-seeking behavior by administrators, leaving more space for markets. Moreover, the concentration of authority could potentially be used to push through difficult reforms over the opposition of entrenched interest groups. The potential for complementarity is present. However, we will not be able to observe these benefits until an effective liberalization program is actually pushed through. In the meantime, the re-definition of responsible behavior and inclusiveness creates uncertainty among new market actors. For the economy to reap efficiency gains, market actors must be convinced that they will have access to new opportunities. There is potential for China 3.0 to become a new equilibrium, but it is still several steps away from that now. The shift away from purely economic definitions of performance could be either complementary to market reforms or a source of heightened conflict with the aspirations of market actors.

A further unresolved question is the extent to which incentives are aligned in any emergent China model 3.0. This is best seen by focusing on the role of local governments, which face many kinds of overlapping uncertainty. The objectives that they should strive to achieve have changed and become more diverse, and the principles upon which promotion will be judged are currently unclear. They face risk from the anti-corruption campaign, and from the ways in which the rules of doing business are changing. At the same time, the traditional resources that local government officials could call on to get things done are in question. In particular, land revenues have declined and their future is uncertain. New policies have undermined the position of local governments as local business conglomerates by reducing local government regulatory powers, restricting their financial flexibility, and reducing access to land revenues that had been the basis of much local wealth. Tax reforms will change their resource base in ways that are hard to predict. In sharp contrast to China 2.0, local officials in China 3.0 face uncertainty and conflicting objectives. By extension, this means that the traditional system of high-powered incentives ('target responsibility systems') have lost their usefulness, since these work poorly when managers are being called on to balance numerous competing objectives. Yet this has been one of the fundamental pillars of the Chinese growth model for the past 30 years.

So far, the China model 3.0 is still far from maturity, and also far from displaying the same kind of coherence as China 2.0. Steps can still be taken to improve that coherence. Complementary institutions with respect to taxation, regulation and regulatory institutions have yet to make an appearance, but could make a large difference. Financial reforms and opening could also have a positive effect. Whether these complementary institutions develop will determine whether new efficiency gains can be generated; then and only then would a new sustainable growth equilibrium come into existence.

Conclusion

This simplified account of China's evolution since 1978 has demonstrated the inter-dependence between economic and political developments. While the economic system has generally evolved toward greater marketization, and the political system towards greater rationality, neither of these developments was linear, nor can either be understood in isolation. Each process is embedded in the other, and the coherence of the process, when it is visible, is visible only when the interdependent parts are considered together. Moreover, such coherence can only be realistically understood by separately and explicitly analyzing the CCP as the crucial actor, whose 'moves' shape the responses of all the other actors. It is the CCP's strategy to maintain legitimacy that gives coherent shape both to the political response to economic developments and to the policies that shape economic growth.

As is true of other China models, the validity of the arguments made here ultimately depends on an appeal to China's remarkable economic growth. However, in this model, sustained economic growth in China is the result of particular periods of policy-making breakthrough that overcame growth limitations and created growth equilibria that lasted for a decade or more. The pursuit of responsible behavior by the CCP has indeed led to a high performing economy, but only because of those extraordinary periods in which dedicated reform leaders pushed through difficult economic changes. When that occurred, complementary political adaptations also took place. However, at other times, the same underlying political calculus has led leaders to delay reforms and follow substitution strategies, and the long-term performance of the economy has suffered.

This analysis identifies three generations of the 'China model'. Each of these represents a potential equilibrium, but not a permanent state of affairs. They are equilibria because they align incentives and reveal crucial information about the economy's potential at that stage of development. Existing institutions have been adapted and re-purposed to bring some coherence to the overall institutional framework. This has produced efficiency gains that are available to reward participants for their continued adherence to the norms and requirements of that framework. It gives the CCP and government resources to re-invest in the creation of complementary institutions and human capital. The result is a degree of social stability and a phase of sustained fast economic development.

However, these equilibria are not eternal. The long-term tension persists between the principles guiding the political system (performance and inclusiveness), and the credible rules and fair contestation demanded by economic actors. In this sense, the institutionalization observed, especially in China 2.0, is of a very particular type: the CCP and government invest in more effective organizations and procedures as instruments for achieving responsible behavior. These institutions do not, however, constrain policy-makers in the same way as institutions would that had grown as part of a broader commitment by the sovereign to a constitutional order. The institutions can always be changed, even a strikingly complex and interrelated set of institutions such as those created in the China model 2.0.

The model does not produce any straightforward predictions about China's future. Positive outcomes are entirely possible, since the economy still displays remarkable resilience and dynamism, but only so long as the political system is able to adapt and upgrade its capacity. At the same time, there is no assurance that an efficiency-enhancing equilibrium will be reached. Policy-makers face internal and external pressures that may alter the definition of 'responsible behavior'. As growth inevitably slows, old ways of steering the economy no longer work very well, and the demand for independent regulatory institutions is increasing. New sources of growth are required, and this means that new markets are opening up in multiple areas. Meanwhile, a clear line separating government and market has already been announced as part of the (aspirational) economic agenda. With China's growth, economic policymakers have to face global capital markets, and be actively embedded into the global governance system, neither of which was particularly important in the two previous generations. Without doubt, the need to supply responsible behavior and include global partners in networks of cooperation will cause unprecedented systemic tensions. The shape of the China model 3.0 is not yet fixed, and there may be alternative paths to a productivity-enhancing growth equilibrium. New economic challenges will require further changes in the model; but new economic capabilities mean the potential for efficiency gains is high, if policy-makers can forge a new period of institutional adaptation.

Acknowledgement

Ling Chen acknowledges support from the National Natural Science foundation of China (NSFC).

Disclosure statement

No potential conflict of interest was reported by the authors.

Notes

1 For example, Daniel Bell, characterizes his 'China model' as 'democracy at the bottom, experimentation in the middle, and meritocracy at the top'. Daniel Bell, *The China Model: Political Meritocracy and the Limits of Democracy* (Princeton, NJ: Princeton University press, 2015), p. 180.

2 The China model literature is vast. Examples of polemically 'pro-China model' authors include Bell, *The China Model*; Wei Pan, 当代中华体制：中国模式的经济、政治、社会解析 [*The Contemporary Chinese System: The Economic, Political and Social Analysis of the China Model*] (Hong Kong: Joint publishing, 2010); and Weiwei Zhang, *The China Wave: Rise of a Civilizational State* (Hackensack, NJ: World Century, 2012). Balanced analytical descriptions include Suisheng Zhao, 'The China model: can it replace the Western model of modernization?', *Journal of Contemporary China* 19(65), (2010), pp. 419–436, and Yongnian Zheng, 中国模式：经验与挑战 [*The China Model: Experience and Challenge*] (Beijing: CITIC Press, revised edition, 2015); Minglu Chen and David S. G. Goodman, 'The China model: one country, six authors', *Journal of Contemporary China* 21(73), (2012), pp. 169–185, provide an overview.

3 The 'civilizational state' described by Weiwei Zhang, *The China Wave*, is an extreme example of this tendency. Zhang brings history and culture into the mix, and explicitly celebrates a uniquely Chinese ability to merge all interests into a single collectivity.

4 The 'China model' occupies a very different space in the intellectual landscape *outside* China than it does *inside* China, but the relationship between government and the economy is still at the core. Outside China, the 'China model' is usually counterposed

to a 'Washington consensus' model of market fundamentalism (leading to the irresistible but misleading term 'Beijing consensus'). In this sense, the 'China model' is used to legitimize both stronger roles for an interventionist state and incremental models of policy reform. See Barry Naughton, 'China's distinctive system: can it be a model for others?', *Journal of Contemporary China* 19(65), (2010), pp. 437–460.

5 Douglas North and Barry Weingast, 'Constitutions and commitment: the evolution of institutions governing public choice in seventeenth-century England', *The Journal of Economic History* XLIX(4), (1989), p. 804.

6 For example, see Yuchao Zhu, '"Performance legitimacy" and China's political adaptation strategy', *Journal of Chinese Political Science* 16(2), (2011), pp. 123–140.

7 This statement requires an important caveat. The Party itself claims that its legitimacy arises from its historic role in making the revolution in China, and not from performance or responsible behavior. This is explicitly stated in the preamble to the Chinese Constitution, which justifies the supremacy of the Party in the political system. The strategy of performance and inclusiveness is imputed to the CCP, not declared or acknowledged by the Party.

8 Robert Dahl, *Polyarchy: Participation and Opposition* (New Haven, CT: Yale University Press, 1971). See also Michael Coppedge, Angel Alvarez and Claudia Maldonado, 'Two persistent dimensions of democracy: contestation and inclusiveness', *The Journal of Politics* 70(3), (2008), pp. 632–647.

9 For a theory of economic interaction in which successful cooperation leads to new rents and investment, see Masahiko Aoki, *Toward a Comparative Institutional Analysis* (Cambridge, MA: MIT Press, 2001).

10 This is consistent with Mancur Olson's general theory of interest group entrenchment, but has special Chinese characteristics because of the CCP's resistance to externally imposed constraints. Mancur Olson, *The Rise and Decline of Nations: Economic Growth, Stagflation, and Social Rigidities* (New Haven, CT: Yale University Press, 1984).

11 For additional detail on this and the next period, see Barry Naughton, *The Chinese Economy: Transitions and Growth* (Cambridge, MA: MIT press, 2007), pp. 85–111.

12 Susan H. Whiting, *Power and Wealth in Rural China: The Political Economy of Institutional Change* (New York: Cambridge University Press, 2001); Hon S. Chan and Jie Gao, 'Performance measurement in Chinese local governments' [with translated documents], *Chinese Law and Government* 41(2–3), (2008), pp. 4–111.

13 An extensive literature was initiated by Hongbin Li and Li-An Zhou, 'Political turnover and economic performance: the incentive role of personnel control in China', *Journal of Public Economics* 89(8–9), (2005), pp. 1743–1762.

14 Daron Acemoglu, Michael Kremer and Atif Mian, 'Incentives in markets, firms and governments', *Journal of Law, Economics and Organizations* 24(2), (2008), pp. 273–306; Barry Naughton, 'Market economy, hierarchy and single party rule', in Janos Kornai and Yingyi Qian, eds, *Market and Socialism Reconsidered (with Particular Reference to China and Vietnam)* (London: Macmillan, for the international economic association, 2008), pp. 135–161.

15 Yasheng Huang, *Capitalism with Chinese Characteristics: Entrepreneurship and the State* (Cambridge: Cambridge University Press, 2008).

16 For 'fiscal federalism', see Gabriele Montinola, Yingyi Qian and Barry Weingast, 'Federalism, Chinese style: the political basis for economic success in China', *World Politics* 48(1), (1995), pp. 50–81; for 'decentralized authoritarianism', see Chenggang Xu, 'The fundamental institutions of China's reforms and development', *Journal of Economic Literature* 49(4), (2011), pp. 1076–1151.

17 Jinglian Wu, *Understanding and Interpreting Chinese Economic Reform* (Singapore: Gale Asia Cengage learning, 2015); see also Naughton, *The Chinese Economy*, pp. 100–107.

18 David Shambaugh, *China's Communist Party: Atrophy and Adaptation* (Washington, DC: Woodrow Wilson Center, 2008), p. 124.
19 Pierre Landry, *Decentralized Authoritarianism in China: The Communist Party's Control of Local Elites in the Post-Mao Era* (New York: Cambridge University Press, 2008); Barry Naughton, 'Inside and outside: the modernized hierarchy that runs China', *Journal of Comparative Economics* 44(2), (2016), pp. 404–415.
20 Lan Xue and Kaibin Zhong, 'Domestic reform and global integration: public administration reform in China over the last 30 years', *International Review of Administrative Sciences* 78(2), (2012), pp. 284–304.
21 Ling Chen, 'Bureaucratic system and negotiation network: a theoretical framework for China's industrial policy', *OECD Reviews of Innovation Policy: China* (Paris: OECD, 2008), pp. 595–612; Ling Chen, 制度，精英与共识：寻求中国政策过程的解释框架 [*System, Elites and Consensus: In Search of a New Explanatory Framework for China's Policy Process*] (Beijing: Tsinghua University Press, 2011); Shaoguang Wang and Peng Fan, 中国试共识性决策：开门与漠河 [*The Chinese Model of Consensus Decision-Making: A Case Study of Healthcare Reform*] (Beijing: Renmin University Press, 2013).
22 Christina Chen, *The Politics of Labor Protection in Authoritarian Systems: Evidence from Labor Law and Enforcement in Post-Reform China*, unpublished Ph.D. dissertation, University of California, San Diego, 2011.
23 Naughton, 'China's distinctive system'.
24 Fubing Su and Ran Tao, 'The China model withering? Institutional roots of China's local developmentalism', *Urban Studies*, published online before print, (7 July 2015), DOL: 10.1177/0042098015593461; Christopher McNally, 'Strange bedfellows: Communist party institutions in the corporate governance of Chinese state holding corporations', *Business and Politics* 4(1), (2002), pp. 91–115.
25 Barry Naughton, 'Understanding the Chinese stimulus package', *China Leadership Monitor* 28, (2009), available at: www.hoover.org/publications/clm/issues (accessed 12 April 2016).

5

CHINA INCORPORATED

The First Corporation Law of the People's Republic of China

Robert C. Art and Minkang Gu

Source: Yale Journal of International Law, 20, 2, 1995, pp. 273–308.

Effective since 1994, the first national corporation law of the People's Republic of China ("PRC" or "China")[1] pursues a distinctive mission: to meld the organizational structure of Western capitalist business into a political and economic regime that maintains socialist principles and goals. The Eighth National People's Congress adopted the Corporation Law ("Law") in 1993, plainly modeling it on American and other Western corporation codes. The Law, however, should not be expected to produce business entities comparable to American corporations in the near future.

The Corporation Law represents a key element in the program of economic reform that China began in 1978.[2] Through this program, the Chinese government aims to standardize and modernize enterprise organization and practice.[3] The Corporation Law of 1993 thus supersedes provisional corporate regulations of the central government and two municipalities.[4] It also constitutes one part of a general process of "legalization," the replacement of the traditional emphasis on policy and propriety[5] with codified law and legal institutions.[6]

The primary purposes of the law are (1) to restructure the organization and management of state-owned enterprises; (2) to address serious, chronic, and seemingly intractable problems of inefficiency; (3) to promote competition and productivity; and (4) to remove the state from detailed management of business operations. This reform, however, should not be confused with privatization; the state will maintain ultimate control and majority ownership of the largest enterprises pursuant to a policy we term "corporatization."

A secondary function of the Corporation Law is to countenance, and even to promote, the development of small private enterprises. The Law envisions the private sector not as a substitute for state industry but rather as a necessary supplement that will be particularly useful in ameliorating current problems of unemployment and inefficiency in the national economy.

Like much of the recent legislation,[7] the Corporation Law uses forms and conventions drawn from American and other Western law and represents an important step toward international business practices. For example, the Law provides for stock with par value and dividends; shareholders with limited liability, preemptive rights, and the power to elect directors; and directors with fiduciary duties and the power to appoint officers.

Differences from Western models bracket this general similarity at both the broad level, in ideology and overall objective, and the technical level, in details and specific rules. The melding of Western forms with the goal of promoting a "socialist market economy"[8] has produced a Corporation Law with distinctly Chinese characteristics.

Most fundamentally, the Corporation Law focuses on state-owned enterprise rather than on entrepreneurial, capitalist business. Western corporate principles are blended with traditional concepts in Chinese law such as the "legal representative," an individual who has the authority to bind a legal entity and who is personally liable for misconduct. Other distinctive elements of the Corporation Law include an extraordinarily extensive grant of power to shareholders and provision for a "board of supervisors" to oversee the board of directors.[9] In addition, workers play a role in determining corporate policy, and the rules governing profit allocation incorporate workers' welfare. Finally, the Law relies primarily on administrative sanctions rather than on derivative actions to deter and punish misconduct by managers.

After briefly reviewing the historical and economic context in which the Law arises, this Article will analyze the ideological and policy underpinnings of the Corporation Law. Its core purpose was to remove government from routine, close business management without abandoning the central socialist precept that the people own the primary means of production. The Article then examines the specific provisions adopted to pursue these goals, including the rules of corporate organization and governance, liability, and stock and dividends.

The Conclusion reflects on the importance of the Corporation Law as a milestone in the development of Chinese ideology and policy. The Law establishes an organizational blueprint that offers great promise for solving China's chronic economic problems and, ultimately, for fully privatizing business. Success, however, will depend on the government's resolve to enact reforms well beyond corporate law. Unless the government accepts the full rigor of the market system by withdrawing state subsidies and permitting uneconomic state enterprises to fail, the result will be a mere facade of a modernized economy. In that event, the Corporation Law is likely to join a long succession of unsuccessful past efforts to reform Chinese state enterprise.

I. Economic and historical context of the current reforms

Contemporary corporate legislation in China must be understood as the outgrowth of earlier twentieth century attempts to reform the nation's economic policy. Such attempts have been aimed, in successive and distinct stages, at two issues – how to reform and reorganize state-owned enterprise for greater efficiency and productivity, and what place, if any, private business should occupy in China's overall economy.

A. Persistent problems in managing state-owned enterprise

Since the country was established, the dominant feature of economic organization in the People's Republic has been enterprise owned by the state as the representative of "the whole people." State-owned enterprises are the principal producers of energy, transportation, telecommunications, raw and semi-finished materials, and industrial and technical equipment.[10] In 1993, the state sector employed nearly 110 million workers, vastly more than collectives and private sector businesses combined (though vastly fewer than the agricultural sector).[11]

State-owned enterprises, which constitute only 19 percent of total enterprises, are also the main source of national revenue. The 71,600 state-owned industrial enterprises in China produced 53% of the country's total industrial output in 1993. State-owned enterprises also provided over 67% of state revenues and financed state policies to benefit enterprises operated by collectives as well as by private, foreign, and other business owners.[12]

Despite its dominance in China's economy, the state-run system has suffered chronically from losses, inefficiency, and insufficient productivity. Chinese government statistics show that approximately one third of state-owned enterprises are losing money, largely because of poor management.[13] Many state enterprises are billions of dollars in debt.[14] Some, although faced with insufficient demand, rely on loans from state banks to maintain production and merely stockpile their products.[15] A substantial portion of workers officially employed by state enterprises are in fact *xia gang*, or "off-post" – a euphemism for workers who are employed on paper but are not expected to report for work and thus are paid only a fraction of their previous income.[16] Subsidies to keep those enterprises in operation lay a heavy burden on the government, a burden the current reforms are intended to relieve.[17]

Three problems underlie the condition of state-owned enterprises: lack of autonomy (the inability of an individual enterprise to manage its own production and make other key decisions), lack of initiative, and lack of adequate incentives for efficiency and productivity. Traditionally, state ownership of the means of production meant that factory managers were responsible to the relevant ministry's bureaucracy.[18] Furthermore, China rejected two practices that amount to fundamental tenets of Western capitalist systems: paying higher wages for more or better work and discharging workers for unsatisfactory performance.[19]

China adopted central planning to avoid the perceived defect of "blind competition" in a free market economy. Chinese Marxist theoreticians understood Adam Smith's theory of the "invisible hand," wherein individual firms, each oriented toward its own benefit, unintentionally maximized aggregate efficiency and productivity. They nonetheless deemed the byproduct of that process – periodic economic crisis, including depressions and high unemployment – to be unacceptable. Organizing enterprises to work cooperatively within an overall plan seemed more productive but in practice stripped each enterprise of the freedom and incentive to manage its operations efficiently.

In addition, the government's use of state enterprises for both production and delivery of welfare services constitutes a further structural impediment.[20] Chinese enterprises routinely provide their workers with housing, medical care, pensions, and a host of other social services and benefits as part of the "iron rice bowl" of lifetime employment and social benefits.[21] The work-unit system performs these welfare services that Western countries deliver not through business organizations but through government agencies.[22] Thus, for China's state-owned enterprises, profitability is neither the central goal nor a likely outcome.

To reform the system, the Chinese government has tried a succession of approaches with little success. For instance, in 1961, the government designated state industrial enterprises "companies," but these operations remained essentially administrative units of the government.[23] The government next experimented with economic organizations called "trusts" that integrated manufacturing and distribution functions in the industrial and communication sectors.[24] In 1985 and 1986, State Council regulations authorized "economic unions" with a similar purpose.[25]

Concurrently with these later reforms, the government worked towards a new company law, drafting seven versions over a ten-year period.[26] A significant ideological development occurred during the drafting process at the Plenary Session of the Communist Party Central Committee in 1984. As part of a call for comprehensive economic reform, including greater autonomy for enterprises, the central committee indicated that ownership and management of state-owned enterprises "may be appropriately separated."[27]

The People's Congress codified this ideological shift in 1988 when it enacted the Law on Industrial Enterprises Owned by the Whole People.[28] The law assigned responsibility for management to enterprise managers but preserved the roles of the Communist Party and of government agencies in controlling business operations.[29] Enterprise managers received "operating rights" designed to permit greater autonomy in the use of state-owned assets, but these rights were vague and poorly designed.[30] That same year, the government adopted the "responsibility contract system," in which state enterprises and their supervising governmental agencies agreed on the means of management and distribution of profits. Because the government retained the authority to appoint managers, specify profits, and dictate the terms of the agreement, however, this reform effected little improvement[31]

The reforms of this progression shared a common failure to provide meaningful enterprise autonomy or incentives for enterprise efficiency.[32] As a result, none succeeded in adequately improving productivity or profitability.

In the mid- to late 1980s, Chinese economists began developing new theories on stock companies.[33] Building on a reference by Karl Marx, scholars explored the stock company as a possible form of capital ownership by the organized working people. They argued that the corporate form and advanced business management skills developed in capitalist countries could benefit a socialist system as well.[34]

This approach was analogous to China's decision to abandon its commitment to "austere self-reliance" and to encourage the importation of foreign technology.[35] That policy reversal claimed to "make foreign things serve China and achieve greater, faster, better, and more economical results in building socialism."[36] In the same vein, the government opened the path to reform by recasting Western corporate law not as wedded to laissez-faire capitalism, but rather as a foreign construction readily adaptable to serving China in accordance with socialist principles.

Finally, on December 29, 1993, the Fifth Session of the Standing Committee of the Eighth National People's Congress adopted the first Corporation Law for China. This legislation is expected to play a major role in the standardization of business organizational structure and business practice for large sectors of the socialist market economy. It is also seen as an important first step in China's development of a modem enterprise system.[37] Under the new law, the corporation will become the most important form of Chinese enterprise organization.[38]

B. The role of private business in the overall economy

National policy and attitudes regarding privately owned enterprise have fluctuated dramatically during the history of the People's Republic. After 1949, all pre-revolutionary laws, including a company law, were initially abolished.[39] Nonetheless, more than 10,000 private companies continued to exist, and securities exchanges operated in Tianjin and Beijing until around 1952.[40] Provisional Regulations issued in 1950 and 1951 recognized several business forms, some of which offered limited liability to investors.[41]

The 1954 constitution, however, announced a policy "to use, restrict and transform" capitalist business, and to "gradually replace capitalist ownership with ownership by the whole people."[42] By 1956, China had transformed virtually all private businesses into joint state-private enterprises, thereby eliminating the last vestiges of capitalism.[43] Some individual firms were restored between 1957 and 1965, only to be later ruthlessly suppressed during the Cultural Revolution as the "tails of capitalism."[44] The 1975 Constitution recognized socialist ownership only[45]

In 1978, Communist Party policy shifted from strict adherence to socialist state ownership to modernization and economic reform. New policies permitted small-scale individual and household businesses with limited authority to hire outside workers. Later policies imposed even fewer restrictions on private businesses.[46] The 1982 Constitution and 1986 General Principles of Civil Law further encouraged the growth of the private economy by allowing businesses to hire larger numbers of employees.[47] Moreover, an amendment of the constitution in 1988 expressly authorized the development of a private economy.[48]

Such efforts to stimulate private industry have been quite successful. In 1993, private enterprise employed approximately 15 million workers. Although this number comprises only a fraction of those employed in the state sector, it is growing far more rapidly.[49] Five years earlier, only 3.7 million people had worked in private enterprises.[50]

Stock exchanges opened in Shanghai in 1990 and in Shenzhen in 1991.[51] In 1992, Deng Xiaoping endorsed the operation of such capitalist instruments as securities and stock markets to operate within the socialist system.[52]

This expansion of private enterprise has not been without difficulties. Notably, in 1989, the government, motivated in part by concern over "bourgeois liberalism," pursued many private businesses for tax evasion and other offenses. That campaign, however, appears to have run its course.[53]

II. Motivation and ideological issues

The Corporation Law is designed both to restructure state enterprises on international capitalist models and to legitimate a much smaller private sector. The Chinese government's pursuit of these goals entails major ideological adjustments. At one time, the Chinese government prohibited even discussion about establishing corporations or private ownership of stock because it deemed such concepts inconsistent with, or even heretical to, China's political and economic system.[54] The Law now endorses notions previously anathema to Chinese domestic law, such as profits[55] and dividends, that once meant income derived from exploiting the working class.[56]

A. Reforming state enterprises: corporatization, not privatization

In most countries, a policy of privatization shifts control over industries and production from the state sector to private hands. The state relinquishes ownership by sale of entire enterprises to investors, typically in the form of shares. In the short term, the government enjoys the liquidity of the cash received; in the long term, it reaps the advantage of greater efficiency and improved management that results when industry is freed from close governmental control and subjected to the rigors of the market.[57]

This form of privatization is neither a motivation for, nor consistent with, the intent of recent reforms in China. The Corporation Law repeatedly reaffirms China's commitment to socialism. Indeed, the Law's very first pronouncement is the purpose of "maintaining the social economic order and promoting the development of a socialist market economy."[58]

China's program is not privatization of the sort experienced by the nations of formerly communist Eastern Europe.[59] A better description of it is "corporatization," a more limited reform. Corporatization entails restructuring state enterprises, adopting the corporate form, and instituting stock ownership and trading without necessarily relinquishing the state's controlling interest in the means of production.[60]

A critical feature of corporatization is the Chinese government's retention of majority ownership in state enterprises that it has converted to the corporate form.[61] By retaining this stake, the government preserves the Marxist-Leninist principle of ownership of the means of production by the people, as represented by the state.[62] Sale of minority interests in these corporations' stock allows the government to draw private capital into state enterprises without ceding ultimate control.[63]

This policy of corporatization supports several goals of the Chinese government. First, it channels the massive private savings of Chinese citizens into productive ventures.[64] Second, it may diminish the potential threat that private financial resources pose for the government.[65] Third, and of central importance, it will improve management of state enterprises, which suffer from chronic low productivity, inefficiency, and poor management. In sum, then, the state will continue to regulate the economy, but as a sovereign implementing policies of general application rather than as an owner micro-managing individual enterprises.[66] Even with this new orientation, however, political pressures will prod the government to intervene in some specific decisions, such as wage levels.[67]

One tactic the Chinese government is using to fulfill these goals is the assignment of state-owned shares to local state property administration departments.[68] Formerly, state shares were assigned to the enterprise's president who had no direct stake in the state property. As a result, these representatives for the state's shares often failed to ensure that the state received the proper bonus shares and dividends, thereby causing a drain on state assets.[69]

Under a 1994 pilot program, the State Economic and Trade Commission announced that government departments will launch wholly state-owned investment or holding companies to separate ownership of state enterprises from management more clearly.[70] A few of these holding companies have already been organized in areas at the forefront of enterprise reform, such as Shenzhen, Shanghai, and Beijing.[71] The assignment prevents the government from nominating a state enterprise's senior staff. Instead, the holding company's directors, themselves selected in accordance with the Corporation Law, choose the general managers.[72]

Ceding increased autonomy to enterprises does not, by itself, ensure either accountability or efficiency. Indeed, the decentralization and deregulation in recent years have sometimes resulted in managerial abuses. Without the discipline of the stock exchanges and the oversight of government officials, some managers have treated state assets like their own private property. Some, for instance, have purchased expensive foreign automobiles and other luxuries nominally for the enterprise.[73] In the words of one local government official, "[m]any state factories have become an empire, with the general manager as the emperor who is accountable to nobody."[74] These enterprises have nevertheless continued to rely on the government for subsidies and loans and for protection against business failure. Many enterprises not only pay little or no taxes, but in fact drain government finances.[75]

Supporters of the new law hope that the participation of private shareholders in selecting directors and managers will increase managerial accountability and improve economic performance. Permitting employees to own stock may also increase their performance incentives at the shop floor level.[76]

The full potential of corporatization, however, will be realized only if the government permits market forces to operate with their full rigor and accepts certain attendant painful consequences like unemployment and dislocation. Subsidies must be removed and economically unviable state enterprises must be permitted to fail. Until that happens, managers and corporations will lack the incentives to improve efficiency and productivity as the reforms envision.

The government recognizes in the abstract that some state enterprises will not be able to compete on the free market and will be forced into bankruptcy.[77] To date, however, examples of such bankruptcies are few, and the process of bankruptcy is deemed experimental.'[78] A principal reason bankruptcy remains rare is the absence of a state-operated unemployment compensation or other social insurance system to ameliorate the effects of bankruptcy on workers.[79] Moreover, permitting enterprises to default on loans from state banks – which have often granted funds to enterprises to keep them in operation even when their production was not needed – would inflict huge losses on those state banks.[80] Until inefficient state enterprises are in fact subjected to bankruptcies and similar painful adjustments, the practical effect of the new Corporation Law will thus remain questionable.

B. Private enterprise as a supplement to state industry

Another key aspect of the Corporation Law is that it offers small, private business ventures greater opportunity for expansion. Authorizing private enterprise presents greater difficulties to a socialist state than modifying the organizational form of state enterprises because private business potentially conflicts with socialist ideology. During the 1980s, the Chinese state resolved this conflict by distinguishing between "individual" enterprises (*geti jingji*) and "private" enterprises (*siying jingji*). Individual firms were based essentially on a person's own labor although they might employ a few workers without changing their nature. In contrast, private firms relied on hired labor and hence raised serious issues of worker exploitation.[81] Regulations used eight employees as the demarcation between the two categories, based on a number derived ultimately from Marx's analysis in *Capital*.[82]

Theoreticians could reconcile individual firms with socialist ideology fairly readily. Although the state sector must remain the leading economic force, other forms could provide a "valuable adjunct" by contributing to society's wealth.[83] Individual firms hired workers who would otherwise be unemployed and used only small amounts of capital. These firms thus dovetailed with socialism in that they did not exploit workers, served socialist goals, and merely supplemented the dominant state economy.[84]

Private firms, on the other hand, presented greater ideological challenges because they employ large numbers of workers and large amounts of property. Firms of this type are, in some cases, operated by entrepreneurs who appear to be capitalists – not engaging in labor, yet becoming rich.

The ideological difficulty was finally resolved at the Communist Party's National Congress in 1987. Zhao Ziyang, then the General Secretary, advanced the theory that China was in the "primary stage of socialism," which began in the 1950s and was expected to last one hundred years thereafter. In this stage, the main goal is to develop production to meet the material needs of the people. Public ownership must predominate, but a private sector may contribute production and employment that the state cannot currently provide.[85] The 1988 Constitution adopted this pragmatic view and thereby legitimized profit-seeking private enterprise.[86]

Today, large numbers of small businesses operate throughout China's economy. Traders run shops on small lanes and busy streets. Self-employed merchants sell goods from stalls in specialized markets, from rented counters in state-owned department stores, and at market fairs.[87] These businesses account for a substantial share of commerce in which larger and state-owned enterprise are not engaged. For example, many small businesses in Beijing transfer goods from Fujian and Guangdong to the north or from rural areas to the city by purchasing wholesale and distributing within local communities.[88] In previous decades, the government would have classified many of these activities as "speculation" or "profiteering" and would have subjected them to criminal prosecution.[89]

In another ground-breaking move, the Chinese government has encouraged individuals and private firms to buy small state-owned enterprises and become full owners.[90] The enterprises placed for sale are ones that the government deems itself unable to manage successfully. They fall mainly into three categories: (1) enterprises that are insolvent or near bankruptcy; (2) businesses that are suffering from losses or earning minimal profits over an extended term; or (3) those selected for sale "to perfect the structure of industry." Such sales relieve the government of the burden of maintaining unsuccessful enterprises and provide an opportunity to revive them through private ownership.[91]

Though significant, this program of selling selected small state-owned enterprises must be kept in perspective. It does not evince a current policy or goal to privatize the bulk of the Chinese economy. Instead, it reflects an intention to permit the co-existence of private ownership as a supplement to state ownership, which will continue to play the leading role in the Chinese economy.

The development of private enterprise is proceeding at an impressive rate, albeit from a minute base. According to a 1994 Chinese government report, private firms in China numbered 328,000, had registered capital of more than 100 billion yuan ($11.8 billion), and employed slightly over five million people.[92] Those figures reflect substantial percentage increases over the figures from previous years[93] but must be evaluated in light of the sheer enormity of the country. China has a gross domestic product exceeding 3.1 trillion yuan and a population exceeding 1.1

billion.[94] Clearly, private business currently plays a minor, supplementary role in an economy overwhelmingly based on state-owned enterprise.

III. The privilege and forms of incorporation

The new Corporation Law establishes the basic organizational structure for Chinese enterprises, both in the dominant state sector and in the supplementary private sector. Although some provisions specifically aim toward converting state-owned enterprises into the corporate form, most of the Law applies equally well to state and private enterprises.

Three features of the statute merit special consideration. One major prerequisite under the new legislation is the registration of a corporation, which permits the state to maintain control over the privilege of incorporation. A key structural element distinguishes between two corporate forms: the Limited Liability Company (primarily for closely held enterprises) and the Joint Stock Company (primarily for publicly traded corporations). Finally, the principle of a "legal representative," carried over from prior civil law, adds another distinctively Chinese characteristic to the Law.

A. Incorporation by approval, not by right

The law tightly regulates incorporation, maintaining state control over this form and its attendant privilege of limited liability. Government departments wielding authority granted by the State Council or the provinces[95] must approve the establishment of a company, and may do so only after the enterprise meets certain conditions.[96] Each company must apply for registration and obtain a "certificate of operation."[97] The scope of a corporation's permissible operations is limited to those specified in the registration unless the government department approves an amendment to the registration.[98] Public stock offerings require State Council permission[99] and are subject to detailed rules.[100]

The processes of incorporation, operation, and capitalization of a business are thus plainly matters of governmental control and permission, not of right. The Law condones and even endorses private business activity but handles it warily nevertheless. The operative attitude appears to be that corporations are a necessary evil to be closely regulated rather than an economic engine to be encouraged and released.[101]

The current Chinese approach is comparable to the "special" incorporation processes followed in England and the United States until the early 1800s. At that time, each instance of incorporation required special legislation. Current American policy, in contrast, grants corporate status to any enterprise fulfilling nominal filing requirements.[102]

Chinese legislators consciously considered whether to require prior approval to incorporate, and deemed such approval necessary. They concluded that this prior screening would ensure the healthy development of corporations and would "protect against corporations being established wantonly."[103] In addition, registration protects the public fisc because the enterprise must arrange to pay taxes on business income[104] and obtain all licenses necessary to conduct its particular line of business before being incorporated.

Most importantly, the prior registration requirement is designed to minimize fraud and abuses. In particular, registration may forestall the organization of "briefcase" companies – private corporations that have no greater substance than the contents of a briefcase and that enter into business deals and then disappear after receiving the first payments. Registration is also intended to prevent foreigners from persuading Chinese investors to contribute equipment and other resources to enterprises in which foreigners contribute only a small down payment and empty promises to contribute more later. The funds that these fly-by-night operators appear to have may be borrowed or subsequently diverted to other purposes. Similarly, promoters may promise to contribute capital in stages: a portion at the outset and the rest in the future. The future amounts may never materialize, or if they do, they may be the original contributions that the promoter has surreptitiously withdrawn. Creditors then suffer the consequences when the company cannot pay its obligations.[105]

In a mature private economy, experienced businesses and individuals contemplating substantial transactions are accustomed to protecting themselves. They investigate the credit and reputation of the other party and often demand collateral, letters of credit, or other forms of protection. The principle of *caveat emptor* is familiar. Parties are suitably cautious.

China presents different circumstances. The vast majority of enterprises in China continue to be government-owned, accustomed to dealing only with other government-owned entities. These enterprises are oriented toward meeting production goals and administrative requirements, not generating profit Sharp or dishonest entrepreneurs may easily mislead or cheat them. Registration serves to deter or minimize such abuse by assuring, for example, that a corporation meets minimum capitalization requirements.

Despite the burden of registration prior to incorporation, the Corporation Law relaxes regulation to some extent. Establishment of a new enterprise previously required approval to engage in the intended activity from the administrative agency in charge of the particular industry. The administrative agencies followed rigid, highly centralized planning processes. A new enterprise could seek registration as a legal entity only after receiving this preliminary approval. The new legislation, consistent with the policy to establish a socialist market economy, removes this first prerequisite in almost all cases.[106]

B. Two forms of corporation: the limited liability company and the joint stock company

The Act provides for two forms of corporations which correspond roughly to the British distinction between the Limited Company (or Ltd.) and the Public Limited Company (p.l.c.), or the American distinction between the closely held (or close) corporation and the larger (including the listed) corporation.[107] The Chinese terms are *You Xian Ze Ren Gong Si* or Limited Liability Company ("LLC"),[108] and *Gu Feng You Xian Gong Si* or Joint Stock Company.[109] Provisions outside the Corporation Law authorize other business forms with unlimited liability.[110]

Enterprises formed by foreign investors almost always take the corporate form and are regulated by any of three other laws: the Law on Joint Ventures Using Chinese and Foreign Investment, the Law on Wholly Foreign-Owned Enterprises, or the Law on Chinese-Foreign Contractual Joint Ventures.[111] These acts basically parallel the Corporation Law with regard to such matters as establishing and managing the company, but differ in some special provisions. For example, foreign-owned corporations must assign either the position of chairman or vice-chairman of the board of directors to a Chinese citizen, with the other to be held by a foreign investor. Different time restrictions also apply to investments.[112] Because of these differences, the Corporation Law provides that "this law shall apply also to a limited liability company owned by a foreign businessman, but if this company is regulated by other laws concerning joint venture, contractual joint ventures, or wholly foreign-owned enterprise, the other laws shall be applied."[113]

The Limited Liability Company form is generally for smaller corporations, defined in terms of the number of investors and amount of registered capital. Yet, a state institute or department that wishes to corporatize one of its enterprises without relinquishing any ownership or control also may adopt the LLC form.

In most cases, a Chinese LLC must have between two and fifty shareholders[114] and a minimum registered capital ranging from 100,000 to 500,000 yuan, depending on the type of business (unless other regulations set a higher minimum).[115] In addition, it may not publicly offer its stock.[116]

A Joint Stock Company typically is larger than an LLC. It may have any number of shareholders but must have registered capital of at least ten million yuan.[117] A Joint Stock Company may distribute stock via either the "promoter method" or the "share float method."[118] In the first option, the promoters purchase all the shares by subscription; in the second, the company offers shares to the public, but the promoters must still purchase thirty-five percent of the stock.[119] Under either method, promoters must retain their stock for three years.[120] The requirement that they buy and retain stock seeks to inhibit, or at least to delay, promoters' selling highly risky securities to public investors while avoiding any personal assumption of risk.[121] By design, promoters generally are subjected to substantial personal risk during the corporation's start-up phase.[122]

Both vehicles are available to convert state enterprises to the corporate form. When the sole investor in an LLC is from a state investment company or department, the LLC is termed a "wholly state-owned company"[123] and is relieved of certain organizational requirements normally applied to LLCs. For example, the institute or department may dispense with shareholder meetings, directly appoint and change directors, hire and dismiss managers, and make key decisions concerning merger, division, dissolution, and issuance of securities.[124] Thus, a wholly state-owned LLC is essentially an administrative unit of a government agency, clothed in a corporate form.

A state-owned enterprise that converts into a Joint Stock Company need not meet the usual requirement of five promoters. Nevertheless, it still must use the share float method.[125] The promoter in this instance would be the pre-existing state enterprise, contributing the enterprise's assets rather than cash. In this case the stock offering requirement serves to draw additional capital into the enterprise from the private sector.

C. Liability for corporate obligations: shareholders and "legal representatives"

One particularly important element of the 1993 Corporation Law is its adoption of the principle of limited liability for shareholders – a concept fundamental to Western corporate law, but relatively new to China. The Corporation Law does not adopt limited liability wholesale, however. Instead, the law provides for the distinctively Chinese concept of a human "legal representative" who is subject to sanction for improper corporate activities.

The idea that those operating a business should be entitled to enjoy the profits if it succeeds, but be insulated from liability for losses if it fails, is neither intuitively appealing nor obvious. The concept inevitably denies recovery not only to contract claimants, but also to personal injury tort victims when the corporation is bankrupt Western capitalist countries decided long ago that the benefits to society of encouraging commerce in this manner outweighed the detriment to such claimants. Only the long history of that policy decision in capitalist countries makes the principle appear basic or commonplace. In China, which lacks a comparable history of orientation toward private enterprise, acceptance of the limited liability principle could not be assumed. Earlier versions of company regulations provided for limited liability in only some forms of company organization.[126]

It is therefore significant that the Corporation Law adopted principles of liability for corporate obligations parallel to Western – in particular American – practice in key respects. For instance, the Corporation Law adopts the familiar principle that a corporation is a "legal person," an entity that enjoys civil rights and owes civil responsibilities to the full extent of its assets.[127] In addition, the law explicitly protects shareholders from liability beyond their capital contributions,[128] and does not mention "piercing the corporate veil" or any other limitation on shareholder immunity.[129]

Nevertheless, the Corporation Law integrates the distinctively Chinese concept of the *fading daibiaoren*, or "legal representative," as an encroachment on limited liability. A legal representative is the natural person authorized to act on behalf of and to bind the company[130] in a manner similar to the "agent" in American corporate law. The Chinese legal representative, however, serves an expanded role bearing greater risks than an agent under American law. The legal representative of a corporation is the chairman of the board of directors or president,[131] or, in a small LLC that chooses not to have a board, the executive director.[132] He or she must perform such functions as applying for a certificate for a branch company.[133]

Most importantly, the Civil Code subjects a legal representative to sanctions for the legal person's misconduct.[134] For example, the legal representative is personally at risk if the corporation engages in business beyond its authorized scope, conceals facts from registration and tax authorities, or hides property to evade repayment of debts.[135] While the legal representative is not personally liable for corporate debts, the extent of responsibility is nevertheless serious. He or she may be fined or subjected to administrative sanctions, including warnings, reprimands, probation, and dismissal from office,[136] with attendant loss of prestige, status, and face. Moreover, if the offense constitutes a crime, the legal representative may be prosecuted.

IV. Internal governance

The Corporation Law details permissible forms of internal corporate organization and governance. Distinctive features include a supervisory committee to oversee the board of directors, extensive shareholder authority in major managerial decisions, and specific references to the rights of workers.

A. Board of directors and supervisory committee

Every corporation must have a board of directors,[137] generally elected by the shareholders for terms of up to three years.[138] A small LLC may have a single executive director instead,[139] but an LLC that is formed by more than two state-owned entities must have a board that includes representatives democratically elected by the workers.[140]

The board selects managers and makes other key business decisions.[141] The Communist Party Committee no longer dominates the management decisions of the factory directors.[142] The board's procedures and powers are largely analogous to those in American corporate practice, with a few minor variations.[143]

One of the more distinctive variations from the American law is the supervisory committee, a concept adopted from German law.[144] Supervisory committees are optional for LLCs and Joint Stock Companies. If a company opts to have one, the supervisory committee must be comprised of at least three individuals, each with a term of three years.[145] Some members are elected by shareholders, others by workers, in a ratio specified by company regulations.[146] Directors, managers, and personnel in charge of financial affairs may not serve concurrently as supervisors.[147]

The supervisory committee oversees the board of directors and assures that it pursues the policies fixed by the shareholders. Its members attend meetings of the board of directors in a non-voting capacity and inspect the company's financial affairs.[148] The Corporation Law imposes upon supervisors the responsibility "to prevent the board of directors and company managers from violating laws, regulations, and the company's by-laws," and "to force the directors to correct their mistakes if their actions have harmed the interests of the company."[149]

Both directors and supervisors owe fiduciary duties to the corporation and are subject to liabilities for breach. The statute specifies that they must obey administrative rules and company regulations and that they are responsible for damages if a breach harms the corporation.[150] Directors and supervisors must fulfill their duties "sincerely and diligently,"[151] a prescription that corresponds to American law's duties of loyalty, good faith, and care.

B. Shareholders' rights and powers

Shareholders have extensive powers in Chinese corporate law. The Law provides that the "shareholders' meeting is the most powerful authority."[152] The shareholder holding the most equity calls and presides over the first shareholders' meeting.[153] Thereafter, in addition to mandatory annual meetings,[154] shareholders, directors, or supervisors may call special meetings.[155] At this meeting, shareholders elect and dismiss directors and members of the supervisory committee, set their salaries, and consider their reports.[156] Shareholders have the right to inspect financial records, to decide on issuance of additional shares, and to vote on such fundamental changes as mergers, dissolution, and liquidation.[157] Shareholders may vote by proxy.[158]

These rights resemble those of shareholders under American law,[159] but the Chinese statute adds others. Unlike their American counterparts, shareholders of Chinese corporations "decid[e] the policy of management and the plan of investment of the company," approve the budget, and vote on the issuance of bonds.[160] Perhaps most notably, the shareholders "consider[] and approv[e] the plan of distribution of profits and recovery for losses"[161] and decide whether to issue dividends.[162] American corporate law, in contrast, places those decisions exclusively within the scope of the directors' authority.[163]

Shareholders also have the right to sue for an injunction and damages if a decision of the board "violates laws and administrative rules, and invades the legal interests of the shareholders."[164] The statute does not specify whether a shareholder's action is direct (asserting the shareholder's own rights) or derivative (asserting rights on behalf of the corporate entity), or even whether that distinction is recognized.[165] Apparently a shareholder may bring such suits directly. The statute does not provide expressly for derivative actions, wherein a shareholder asserts rights on behalf of the corporate entity.

The extraordinary power accorded to shareholders is consistent with the Corporation Law's overall approach to managing state-owned enterprises. The government, which will be a huge shareholder in corporatized companies, did not intend to relinquish ownership or ultimate control over China's productive enterprises. Rather, it sought to remove itself from the micro-management of enterprise decisions. By assigning management authority to the board of directors, while retaining majority stock ownership and a strong role for shareholders, the government can maintain the level of control that it chooses.

C. Workers' role in corporate governance

The right of workers to participate in corporate decision-making is codified in the Corporation Law. Those rights do not include voting and, at least by the Law's express terms, appear far more limited than the rights provided for under earlier legislation. Previous law, for example, accorded workers the rights to remove the director of an enterprise, subject to government approval, and to decide matters directly affecting the workers.[166]

Under the Corporation Law, a company must "hear the opinions" of workers and their union before making a decision affecting their vital interests.[167] Vital interests include salary, welfare, work safety, labor insurance, important decisions over production and operation, and significant rules and systems.[168] Workers or their union representatives may attend directors' meetings.[169] They do not, however, have veto power or even the right to vote at these meetings.[170]

The Corporation Law confers additional powers on workers in certain situations. For instance, corporations formed by more than two state-owned enterprises or state-owned investing bodies must include democratically elected representatives of the workers on the board of directors. The statute is silent, however, as to the number or percentage of worker directors.[171]

Similarly, if a corporation has an optional supervisory board, then at least one of the members must be a democratically elected workers' representative. The statute provides that worker representatives must be in "the proper ratio," but it leaves the definition of that critical term to the corporation's regulations.[172]

The aggregate of explicit powers accorded to workers by these various provisions is not extensive. Workers in Chinese corporations appear to have less power than their peers in Germany, for example, which has statutorily mandated nearly equal representation of workers and shareholders on the board of supervisors.[173]

Nevertheless, in practice, Chinese workers may well wield great influence because of the extensive power of the Communist Party. An official commentary on the reforms stated that, within enterprises, "the Party organization will continue to play its role as the political nucleus, and workers and staff will participate in democratic management"[174] If they follow past practice in selecting their leaders, workers will probably elect Party members to be their representatives on the board of directors or the supervisors' committee. Because the "leading role" of the Party is enshrined in the Constitution and pervades the economy, the presence of Party members on these governing boards will result in substantial influence, particularly in corporations where the state maintains majority ownership. This Party influence does not depend on Party members' having extensive formal voting powers on the boards of directors.[175]

D. Safeguards against malfeasance

The Corporation Law specifies in detail the penalties for violating its various rules, duties, and requirements. Enforcement of these specific provisions is based on administrative and criminal processes rather than on derivative civil liability actions brought by shareholders. The Law does not even mention derivative actions, and such actions, if allowed, would in all likelihood be unsuccessful. Under current conditions, few if any Chinese corporate officers or directors would be financially able to pay a substantial civil judgment for breach of a fiduciary duty and thus could provide little relief to aggrieved shareholders suing derivatively.

The enforcement scheme of the Law relies on progressive discipline. As a first step, those who make false reports or statements relating to such matters as registration capital and accounting shall be, in the statute's terms, "ordered to correct their mistakes."[176] When the offense involves cheating creditors, investors, or society, fines are imposed.[177] The Law defines the range of fines by amount (typically between 10,000 and 100,000 yuan)[178] or percentage (such as between 1% and 5% of illegally raised capital,[179] or between 5% and 10% of illegally withdrawn subscription amounts).[180]

Directors, supervisors, and managers are subject to "administrative sanctions," which pose a serious threat to the individual's position and career. Other laws lend meaning to this term, specifying as included in "administrative sanctions" such penalties as probation, demerits, demotion, and dismissal.[181] In addition, any improper gains, i.e., those derived from accepting bribes, appropriating corporate capital or lending it to others,[182] or operating a business in competition with the corporation,[183] are subject to forfeiture.

Criminal liability potentially attaches to all violations of the Corporation Law.[184] The punishment for white-collar crimes can be severe, including the death penalty.[185] For example, a corporate president convicted of embezzlement, bribery, and selling bonds through a pyramid scheme was executed in 1994.[186]

Short of these extreme sanctions, the Law imposes procedures and requirements in an effort to minimize the opportunities for abuse. Such safeguards are deemed necessary to prevent fraud and misappropriation in the creation and operation of corporations. The danger of such abuses is apparent, particularly because potential investors are not yet sophisticated and because control by private parties of the state's property invites misappropriation.

To safeguard against these abuses, the Law precludes individuals from holding office as a director or manager if they have committed any crime involving corruption, embezzlement, or offenses against the social economic order, or if they have held office in a company whose operating license was revoked for illegal acts.[187] State officials are also disqualified,[188] presumably to reduce the risk of improper influence. Corruption of government officials, in forms including insider trading of securities,[189] has been a serious problem.[190]

Besides requiring corporate officers to have clean records and imposing general principles of fiduciary duty, the statute specifically prohibits misappropriation of company funds, deposit of company funds in personal bank accounts, and use of company assets as surety for a director's personal debts.[191] Directors may not conduct business with the company except as provided in the bylaws or in resolutions promulgated by the shareholders.[192]

V. Stocks and dividends

Issuance of corporate securities has significance beyond the fortunes of particular corporations and their investors; it represents allocation of a portion of society's capital or investment resources to particular enterprises. Securities sales also present the danger of fraud against investors and, particularly when control of state enterprises shifts to private owners, against the corporation. Accordingly, the Corporation Law provides for close regulation of the issuance of equity and debt securities. By imposing a unique system for controlling the distribution of profits and dividends, other provisions of the Law represent a transitional stage between the traditional social-service role of state enterprises and the profit-driven model of corporations.[192]

A. Characteristics of stock

Issuance of shares must conform to the "open, fair and impartial principles; shares of the same class must have equal rights and profits for each share."[193] The reference to "class" indicates that corporations may divide their stock into common, preferred, and other classes.

Curiously, the Corporation Law is entirely silent on one of the most distinctive features of Chinese corporate stock: classes defined not by the characteristics of the shares, but rather by the status and nationality of the shareholders. "Class A" stock is available for purchase by Chinese citizens only, "Class B" is for foreigners, and "Class H" stock has been used for transactions on the Hong Kong stock exchange.[194] The prevalence of B and H shares is a useful indicia of China's openness to foreign investment. At the end of 1992, the Shanghai and Shenzhen stock exchanges listed the stock of seventy companies, including eighteen issues of B shares.[195] In addition, nine state enterprises were selected for listing in Hong Kong.[196]

The statute, unfortunately, does not indicate how the holders of A, B, H, and other stock classes may exercise their rights. In particular, it makes no mention of whether they vote in common with all other shareholders or whether they vote by class, in which case the vote of each class would be necessary to approve a resolution. Class voting can be vital, particularly for foreigners holding "B" shares, because a corporation might adopt a rule of equal application on its face that is actually far more onerous to some. For example, a rule requiring transfers of shares to be made by registration in person at corporate headquarters would affect foreigners far more than Chinese shareholders. Without voting rights as a class, B shareholders would have no effective remedies.[197]

Shares may, but need not be, in the form of a paper certificate.[198] Thus, Chinese corporations may follow current American trends toward "book entry" or uncertificated stock transactions.[199] In some cases, stock certificates may be preferable, for they provide tangible, verifiable evidence of ownership that may be useful to counteract fraud.

Corporations may issue shares in registered or bearer form.[200] Shares sold to promoters or government departments[201] must be registered, making their identities and holdings known to the corporation.[202] The general public may purchase bearer shares, for which corporations do not maintain records of ownership. The statute does not provide a mechanism for identifying the owner of bearer shares for voting or disbursing dividends. Presumably, the owners will have to present their certificates to the corporation.[203]

Existing shareholders have priority in contributing to an LLC's newly added capital.[204] This right appears comparable to the Western concept of preemptive rights, which allows shareholders to purchase new stock in proportion to their previous percentage ownership so they can maintain their percentage of ownership and control. The Chinese statute, however, merely mentions a "priority" without providing details. The Law does not specify the quantify or percentage of stock that a shareholder may purchase, the price or procedures, the remedy for violations of the priority right, or whether the right applies when the company sells stock for property or services.

Shareholders of an LLC may transfer their stock subject to restrictions that balance the rights of the selling shareholder and of the remaining shareholders. The seller must obtain permission from a majority of the other shareholders. If the shareholders approve the sale, they have the first chance to purchase the stock. If they disapprove the sale, the shareholders who voted against the sale must purchase the stock.[205] Hence, this mechanism assures the selling shareholder the right to dispose of the stock and guarantees the remaining shareholders control over the purchaser's identity.

A corporation may not repurchase its stock unless the corporation amends its registration to reduce its capital.[206] The effect of this restriction is to prevent a corporation from buying its stock at depressed prices and selling it later at higher prices. The provision is an example of strict governmental control over the allocation of capital, at the expense of enterprise flexibility.

B. Going public and issuing bonds

A "public company" is a Joint Stock Company that has issued stock to the public with permission from the State Council.[207] Such companies must have at least fifty million yuan in capital and at least one thousand shareholders. Furthermore, public shareholders, i.e., government entities, must hold at least twenty-five percent of the stock.[208] The state also requires public companies to disclose and periodically publish records of their financial affairs and operations.[209]

To issue stock or to maintain a listing on a stock exchange, a Joint Stock Company must have existed and earned profits for the past three years.[210] The profit requirement protects investors against buying shares of failing companies. That protection, however, has a troubling consequence. Companies in difficult financial circumstances are deprived of capital even when additional investment would facilitate a recovery. Excluding those companies from the capital markets at the moment of their greatest need may doom them and exacerbate the losses to creditors, employees, and shareholders.

Wholly state-owned LLCs and Joint Stock Companies may also raise capital by issuing bonds. Privately held LLCs may not.[211] Like stock, bonds may take either registered or bearer form.[212] The statute also allows public companies to issue convertible bonds – bonds that the holder may convert into stock at will.[213] Like stock, bonds may be traded on exchanges.[214]

A host of restrictions apply to bond issuance. These restrictions assist in combatting fraud, which has already appeared in the bond market,[215] and secure the government's control over the use of investment capital. Any bond issue must conform to the state's industrial policy[216] and receive the State Council's approval.[217] Further standards ensure that only large and profitable companies may issue bonds. Each company must already have minimum capitalization and must not issue bonds in excess of forty percent of net capital.[218] In addition, the issuer's profits over the last three years must cover interest payments, and the proceeds of the issuance cannot be used to make up losses.[219] Failure to make payments on previous bonds or default on other debt disqualifies a company from issuing bonds.[220] Although these provisions tend to protect new investors, they also deprive struggling companies of the ability to borrow money possibly essential to their survival and growth.

C. Consideration for shares

The financial provisions of the Law apply the concept of par, or face value, for stock. Although American corporate law is abandoning the concept of par,[221] it may serve a useful purpose in China, at least temporarily, as the country grows more experienced with the corporate form.

Chinese corporations may not issue stock for less than par value.[222] This provision assures that all investors pay the same amount per share and hence effects an element of equity. A simple and age-old device called "low par" can readily and routinely defeat this approach,[223] but the Law precludes use of "low par" unless a government agency permits it in a particular case.[224]

Other problems concerning the amount of consideration for stock arise from the use of tangible and intangible property. Directors may assign an excessively high value to certain property received in exchange for stock. This dilutes the value of other public investors' shares, which they purchased at full value. Because foreigners often have the assets that Chinese companies need, they are particularly well placed to take advantage of a corporation by demanding excessively high valuations for property contributed in exchange for stock.[225]

Conversely, the state worries that the value assigned to its contribution will be too low and will unfairly transfer some of the nation's wealth to a private or foreign entity.[226] Private entities, and even local governments, have reaped windfalls as state-owned assets are sold.[227]

The United States and China have chosen contrasting solutions to this problem. In the United States, a corporation's board of directors assigns values to assets, subject to judicial review only in the case of fraud. China has opted for greater regulation. Companies may issue shares for noncash consideration, including goods, industrial rights, unpatented technologies, and land use rights, but they must appraise all such consideration in accordance with laws and regulations.[228] Pursuant to these regulations, a specialized government office performs the appraisal, not the board of directors.[229] Moreover, the statute caps a corporation's swaps for industrial property rights or technology at only twenty percent of its stock.[230]

D. Dividends and allocation of profits

The Chinese statute imposes detailed restrictions and requirements on balance sheets for shareholder equity accounts. The statute models some of these procedures on rules traditionally followed in American corporation laws. While the American rules have been largely abandoned as outmoded and ineffective, they are still familiar to American corporations and attorneys. Other restrictions reflect the unique accommodations necessary to adapt a capitalist organizational form to a socialist goal and the historical role of Chinese enterprises as vessels for delivering social services to workers.

When a corporation sells stock, the statute labels aggregate par value "registered capital." If the stock sells for more than par value, the excess value is placed in an account called a "capital accumulation fund."[231] Traditional American corporation acts used the same procedures, though with different terminology ("stated capital" rather than registered capital, and "capital surplus" rather than capital accumulation fund).

The Corporation Law provides that revenues from stock transactions and business operations be accounted for separately. Although traditional American statutes also use a separate account for business revenues, labeled earned surplus by the statutes and retained earnings by accountants, the similarity ends there. The Chinese statute controls the allocation of the corporation's profits and protects specified interests of corporate constituencies other than shareholders.

The "statutory collective accumulation fund" is the ongoing balance of a portion of the company's profits, minus all of its losses, dividends, and other transfers. The account starts at zero when the company is first organized. When the company suffers a business loss, as calculated on its Income Statement (also known as Profit and Loss Statement), the amount will be subtracted from the statutory collective accumulation fund. The number this calculation produces may be negative. As long as that account remains negative, all future profits must be allocated exclusively to the account.[232]

When the corporation earns profits (and the statutory collective accumulation fund is positive), then the statute mandates certain allocations. The corporation must dedicate ten percent of its profits to the statutory collective accumulation fund[233] as a reserve for possible future losses and for reinvestment in the business.[234] The corporation cannot use this fund to justify dividends to shareholders.[235] The corporation must also allocate five to ten percent of profits to a "statutory public welfare fund"[236] to provide for the collective welfare of workers.[237] Interestingly, the allocation requirement does not apply if the statutory collective accumulation fund has reached fifty percent or more of registered capital.[238] Thus, a corporation that has been successful enough to accumulate profits equal to half of the original investment is freed from the obligation to set aside a fund for its workers' benefit because it is considered sufficiently reliable to provide for them adequately.

After the mandatory allocations, a corporation has discretion in distributing its profits. It may allocate profits to a "discretionary collective accumulation fund" – essentially retaining the profits in the business. Alternately, it may distribute the amount as dividends to shareholders. Overall the Corporation Law is less restrictive in this area than previous law because it does not impose ceilings on the rate of return from stocks and bonds.[239]

This regulation of profit allocation is but a pale reflection of the traditional role Chinese enterprises played in providing lifetime employment, housing, medical care, retirement, and other social services to its workers. Requirements for "welfare funds" and regulation of the use of "accumulation funds" appear oriented toward maintaining, in some measure, the traditional social functions and responsibilities of enterprises for their workers.

The profit allocation requirements are not onerous, but to date there is no evidence that the state is substituting those requirements for the more encompassing, traditional obligation of state enterprises to provide social services to their work units. If Chinese corporations are to develop into independent, profit-maximizing economic entities on the international model, they must be relieved of their social welfare burdens. Organizing social services through enterprises worked only because extensive state subsidies kept each enterprise operating. The government must construct a new network of social welfare agencies to fill the gap[240] – a mammoth task far beyond the scope of the Corporation Law.

VI. Conclusion: Chinese characteristics of the 1993 law

Though the PRC's Corporation Law of 1993 closely follows Anglo-American and Western patterns, it aims for different goals and will produce different results. Most fundamentally, China's Corporation Law is not primarily oriented to entrepreneurial, capitalist business in the Western sense. Instead, it is designed to restructure state-owned enterprise, which can be expected to remain the dominant feature of the Chinese economy for the foreseeable future. While the state intends to step out of direct management, it maintains ultimate control through majority stock ownership. The Law addresses private business only as a subsidiary goal. It governs, facilitates, and legitimizes private business merely as a supplement to the state economy.

The provisions for internal corporate governance include a number of distinctively Chinese characteristics. For example, the statutes call for a "legal representative," an individual capable of binding the corporation who is personally liable for misconduct. Other examples include the option to have a supervisory committee to oversee the board of directors and the specification of a role for workers in determining corporate policy. Further, the Corporation Law defines the powers of shareholders broadly so the government may exercise its ultimate powers over enterprises through stock ownership. Protections for workers and investors are built into the law. For instance, administrative sanctions for managers' breaches of duty substitute for the derivative actions used in corporate law outside China. Moreover, profit allocation is regulated in a unique fashion, reflecting the historical role of work units as providers of social services to workers.

Despite its promise for stimulating investment and improving enterprise management, China's social, economic, and political environment inherently limit the statute's potential effect. Courts may not effectively and accurately enforce rights and standards established by statute.[241] The effect of national legislation in various regions is not uniform. The Communist Party's continued role within state-owned corporations may also inhibit or retard change. The Corporation Law may in the end merely mimic the jargon it borrows from the West without providing the full legal and social infrastructure necessary to make it meaningful and reliable.[242]

Current reforms represent corporatization, not privatization. Still, corporatization is a major step toward achieving international standards of business organization and motivation. Moreover, once state enterprises are converted into a corporate form with private ownership and transferability of shares, it will be logical and relatively easy for them to sell additional shares to the private sector.

Overall, China's new Corporation Law is an important reform from both pragmatic and ideological perspectives. In the small private sector, the new law is likely to be highly useful. In the far larger state sector, which now and in the near future will dominate China's non-agricultural economy, the effect is less clear. Repackaging state enterprises in the garb of Western capitalism will have merely cosmetic consequences if the underlying incentives remain unchanged. Success of the central goal of promoting efficiency and productivity depends on resolve and policies beyond the Corporation Law. The state must relieve state enterprises of their social-service functions and must resist pressures to intervene in, manage, and subsidize inefficient enterprises. Corporations unable to compete must be permitted to fail. Without such resolve and discipline, the Corporation Law may be doomed to the fate of a series of previous failed efforts to reform inefficient state enterprises.

Notes

1 Zhonghua Renmin Gongheguo Gongsifa [The Corporation Law of the People's Republic of China] (enacted Dec. 29, 1993). A published translation may be found in 2 China L. For. Bus.: Bus. Reg. (CCH Int'l) ¶ 13–518 (July 4, 1994). This Article relies on a translation that Minkang Gu prepared prior to the CCH publication (hereinafter cited as Corporation Law). All subsequent citations to the Corporation Law refer to Gu's translation.

2 In December 1978, the Chinese Communist Party Central Committee announced that its primary emphasis would shift from class struggle to economic development. *See*

Zhongguo Gongchandang Di-shiyijie Zhongyang Weiyuanhui Di San Ci Quanti Huiyi Gongbao [Communique of the Third Plenum of the 11th Central Committee of the Communist Party of China], adopted Dec. 22, 1978, *cited in* Donald C. Clarke, *What's Law Got to Do With It? Legal Institutions and Economic Reform in China,* 10 UCLA PAC. BASIN LJ. 1, 4 n.5 (1991).

3 Wu Naitao, *Guarantee for Modern Enterprise System,* BEIJING REV., Apr. 4–10, 1994, at 14.

4 The forerunner of the Corporation Law on the national level was the *Opinion on Standards for Companies Limited by Shares,* 3 China L. Foreign Bus.: Bus. Reg. (CCH Austl.) ¶ 13–570 (1993), issued in May 1992 by the State Commission for Restructuring the Economic System. This opinion assumed the legal effect of a ministry-level regulation on May 15, 1993. On the local level, the Shenzhen and Shanghai municipal governments issued separate guidelines. Provisional Regulation of Shanghai Municipality Concerning Joint Stock Limited Companies (promulgated May 18, 1992), *translated in* BAKER & MCKENZIE, SELECTED COMPANY REGULATIONS OF THE PEOPLE'S REPUBLIC OF CHINA 1 (1992); Provisional Regulations of Shenzhen Municipality Concerning Joint Stock Limited Companies (promulgated Mar. 17, 1992), *translated in id.* at 26.

The best sources in English on Chinese corporation law prior to the 1993 legislation are Matthew D, Bersani, *Privatization and the Creation of Stock Companies in China,* 1993 COLUM. BUS. L. REV. 301,308 (summarizing state of company law in China prior to 1993 enactment of current Corporation Law); Alison W. Conner, *To Get Rich is Precarious: Regulation of Private Enterprise in the People's Republic of China,* 5 J. CHINESE L. 1,18–31 (1991) (emphasizing limitations on number of shareholders and stock issuance); and Henry R. Zheng, *Business Organization and Securities Law of the People's Republic of China,* 43 BUS. LAW. 551, 608-J5 (1988) (noting that 1988 law did not provide mechanism for shareholder participation in management).

5 The Confucian concept of "li," or standards of social conduct, was traditionally considered far superior to narrow legalistic rules, known as "fa." Codified law was seen as unnecessary and abhorrent. Since 1979, however, this view has bowed to the demands of foreign investors, and modifications of traditional ideology and a "frenzy of codification" have resulted. Barbara Campbell Potter, *China's Equity Joint Venture Law: A Standing Invitation to the West for Foreign Investment?,* 14 U. PA. J. INT'L BUS. L. 1,4–6 (1993).

6 Twenty laws were promulgated in 1993, and many of them went into effect in 1994. These include the Corporation Law, the Law on Combatting Unfair Competition, the Law on Protecting the Rights and Interests of Consumers, and the Teachers' Law. Reports indicate that the National People's Congress is currently intensively drafting or deliberating on 152 laws, including 54 concerning economic legislation. Geng Yuxin, *Reform Advance Relies on Legislation – Coverage of the NPC and CPPCC Sessions,* BEIJING REV., Mar. 14–20, 1994, at 4 [hereinafter Geng Yuxin, *Reform Advance*]. Gaps in the statutory framework are readily apparent. For example, despite the pervasiveness of embezzlement, corruption, bribery, and other misconduct, China lacks laws to combat or deter these abuses. Huang Wei, *Call to Promote Socialist Culture and Ethics,* BEIJING REV., Apr. 25-May 1, 1994, at 9, 13.

7 A *Beijing Review* article ascribes the rapid progress in legislation in 1993 and 1994 to "the steadfast all-out efforts of the NPC and its Standing Committee," and to "the bold use and absorption of foreign legislative achievements and the introduction of international practices," particularly in areas important to a market economy. Geng Yuxin, *Reform Advance, supra* note 6, at 4. In reference to securities laws specifically, the government stated its intention to "absorb foreign countries' experience while taking into account China's situation." *China's Stock Markets to be More Active,* Xinhua General News Service, Nov. 22, 1992, *available in* LEXIS, Nexis Library, XINHUA

File, Andrew Xuefeng Qian, *Riding Two Horses: Corporatizing Enterprises and the Emerging Securities Regulatory Regime in China,* 12 UCLA PAC. BASIN L.J. 62, 63 n.5 (1993).

8 Article 1 of the Corporation Law announces its purpose, "to promote the development of a socialist market economy." Similarly, Chapter 2, Section 3, which covers wholly state-owned corporations, reflects the spirit of the Chinese Constitution: "The basis of the socialist economic system of the People's Republic of China is socialist public ownership of the means of production, namely, ownership by the whole people and collective ownership by the working people." XIANFA [Constitution] art. 6 (P.R.C.).

9 The use of a board of supervisors appears to derive from the German corporation code. For a description of supervisory boards in Germany and Europe, see Klaus J. Hopt, *Labor Representation on Corporate Boards: Impacts and Problems for Corporate Governance and Economic Integration in Europe,* 14 INT'L REV. L. & ECON. 203 (1994). *See also West European Managers Lose Footing: Ways of Running Firms Set to Change Amid Challenges,* WALL ST. J., Aug. 29, 1994, at A6 (reporting on debates about whether German and French corporations should abandon supervisory board system and move toward American model).

10 Geng Yuxin, *Reform of State Enterprises to Enter New Stage*, BEIJING REV., NOV. 21–27, 1994, at 4 [hereinafter Geng Yuxin, *Reform of State Enterprises*].

11 Chinese employment figures for 1993 outlined the following division of labor: 440 million rural workers, 108.7 million employed in the state sector, 35.5 million in collectives, and 14.9 million in the private sector. Joseph Kahn & Craig Smith, *Unemployment Boosts Tensions in China,* WALL ST. J., Feb. 6, 1995, at A8 (citing statistics from Morgan Guaranty Trust Co., Economic Research).

12 Geng Yuxin, *Reform of State Enterprises, supra* note 10, at 4; Li Tieying, *15 Years of Reform for State-Owned Enterprises,* BEIJING REV., Jan. 9–15, 1995, at 15, 17 (written by state councillor and minister of State Commission for Restructuring Economy); Wu Naitao, *'95 Goals for Reform of State-Owned Enterprises*, BEIJING REV., Jan. 9–15, 1995, at 7.

13 Jiang Yaping, *Five Years of China's Bankrupts Law: Problems and Prospects,* BEIJING REV., Feb. 7–20,1994, at 21. Money-losing enterprises typically resist declaring bankruptcy because the attitudes toward bankruptcy are so negative and because the workers would lose their jobs with little prospect of finding new ones in a competitive market *Id.*

14 Wallace W. Wang, *Reforming State Enterprises in China: The Case for Redefining Enterprise Operating Rights,* 6 J. CHINESE L. 89, 92 n.7 (1992) (citing article from Agence France Presse).

15 *Shenzhen Gives Firms Freedom*, CHINA DAILY, Feb. 6, 1995, at 4.

16 Governmental reluctance to admit true levels of unemployment masks the reality that as many as 20 million urban workers and 5 million government employees may be effectively unemployed. Kahn & Smith, *supra* note II, at A8.

17 Wang, *supra* note 14, at 131.

18 *Id.* at 101.

19 *See, e.g.,* Potter, *supra* note 5, at 30–31, (noting, for instance, that management of foreign joint ventures could not hire and fire according to worker's performance except in Special Economic Zones).

20 Wang, *supra* note 14, at 92–93.

21 State enterprises' services to employees encompass housing, medical care, public security, local police stations, nurseries, schools, savings banks, and tax offices. Geng Yuxin, *Reform of State Enterprises, supra* note 10, at 4. The state, through work units, also provides extensive benefits to seventy percent of China's 147 million nonfarm workers. These benefits include housing, medical care, schools, and entertainment, such as the free use of skating rinks and amusement parks. Jesse Wong, *In China, the*

Welfare State Hangs On, Burdening Already-Stressed Companies, WALL ST. J., Aug. 23, 1994, at A9.

22 Wang, *supra* note 14, at 93, 131; Geng Yuxin, *Reform of State Enterprises, supra* note 10, at 4; Wu, *supra* note 12, at 7.

23 JIANG PING, GONGSIFA JIAOCHEN [A COURSE IN COMPANY LAW] 18–19 (1992).

24 The Chinese government established two kinds of trusts: the national unified trust (such as the Automobile Industrial Company) and the local trust (such as the Yangzhi River Shipping Company). The term "trust" denotes something similar to the form of business structure that American "antitrust" laws target, but without the negative connotations. *Id.* at 19.

25 *See, e.g.,* Guowuyuan Guanyu Jinyibu Qinli he Zhengdun Gongsi de Tongzhi [The Information Regarding Furtherance of Selection and Consolidation of Companies] (Aug, 20, 1985); Gongsi Dengji Guanli Zanxing Guiding [The Interim Provisions Regarding Registration and Management of Companies] (Aug. 25, 1985) (promulgated by Chinese Administrative Bureau for Industry and Commerce); Gongshang Qiye Mingcheng Dengji Guanli Zanxing Guiding [The Interim Provisions Regarding Registration and Management of the Name of Commercial Business and Industrial Enterprises] (June 15,1985) (promulgated by Chinese Administrative Bureau for Industry and Commerce). Particularly important was Guowuyuan Guanyu Jinyibu Tuidong Hengxiang Jingji Lianhe Ruogan Wenti de Guiding [The Provision Concerning Several Issues about Further Promoting Horizontal Economic Unions], issued on Mar. 23,1986 by the State Council, which authorized economic unions within a field of production, between production and scientific research, between production and distribution of commodities, within a field of distribution, between military industry and civil industry, etc. The State Council passed the Interim Regulations Concerning Promoting Economic Unions in 1986 and proposed to organize various forms of "economic union." The Council intended to consolidate particular industries from the manufacturing stage through the product distribution stages into a single entity. Economic unions would be formed voluntarily, not by administrative order. The form would not be restricted to certain occupations, districts, or types of property; economic unions could be group enterprises, enterprise blocs, integrated complexes, etc. Either existing enterprises or new investment initiatives could create new economic unions. *Id.*

26 *Zhongguo "Gongsifa" Jijiang Shishi [The Chinese "Corporate Law" Will Be Put Into Effect],* ASIA TODAY, July 14–20, 1994, at 7 [hereinafter *Corporate Law Will Be Put Into Effect*].

27 Decision of Chinese Communist Party Central Committee on Reform of the Economic Structure, (adopted Oct. 20, 1984), *cited in* Zheng, *supra* note 4, at 604 n.38S.

28 Law of the People's Republic of China on Industrial Enterprises Owned by the Whole People (adopted April 13, 1988), *available in* LEXIS, Intlaw Library, CMnalaw File.

29 Wang, *supra* note 14, at 98–99. Communist Party representatives within each enterprise remained responsible for promoting Party principles, and government agencies continued to enforce extensive rules. Directors wielded some discretionary power, subject to approval by a workers representative assembly and various government departments.

30 "Operating rights" seemed to provide the rights to possess, use, and dispose of state-owned property. Significant regulatory restrictions circumscribed each of these rights, however. The rights also could not be asserted against the state. Thus, for example, the state could reassign operating rights to particular property to a different enterprise without incurring liability and could regulate the use of the property. Moreover, operating rights did not include the right to benefit from the rights of possession, use, and disposition. *Id.* at 102–12. Overall, the statute provided enterprise managers little opportunity for independent decision making and did not improve efficiency. *Id.* at 98–100.

31 *Id.* at 119. A more positive interpretation of the course of reform from 1978 to the current Corporation Law comes from the Minister of the State Commission for Restructuring the Economy. *See* Li Tieying, *supra* note 12, at 15.
32 Wang, *supra* note 14, at 118–19.
33 Zheng, *supra* note 4, at 604 (citing four articles published in 1986 from Chinese publications).
34 *Wang,* supra *note 14, at 119–21; Zheng,* supra *note 4, at 604–05* (citing Tong Dalin, *Gufenhua Shi Shehut Zhuyi Qixe De Yige Xinjidian* [*Stock Company Being a New Starting Point of Socialist Enterprises*, J PEOPLE'S DAILY, Aug. 8, 1986, at 2).
35 Jennifer A. Meyer, *Let the Buyer Beware: Economic Modernization, Insurance Reform, and Consumer Protection in China*, 62 Fordham L. REV. 2125, 2129 (1994); Xang Bin Xue & George D. Wilson, *Capital and Technology: China Rejoins the Modern Business World – An Analysis of China's Equity Joint Ventures Law,* 25 U.S.F. L. *REV.* 511, 514 (1991).
36 Meyer, supra note 35, at 2131–32 (quoting ROBERT KLEINBERO, CHINA'S OPENING TO THE OUTSIDE WORLD: THE EXPERIMENT WITH FOREIGN CAPITALISM 24 (1990) (advocating application of Western principles of insurance law to China)).
37 Wu, *supra* note 3, at 14.
38 *Corporate Law Will Be Put Into Effect, supra* note 26, at 7.
39 Westem-style companies operated in China well before 1949. After the Opium War of 1840 until the 1920s, foreign companies and some Chinese companies issued shares that were traded on exchanges in Beijing and Shanghai. In 1929, the Kuomintang government promulgated a company law (modified in 1946 and still applied in Taiwan). During the 1930s and 1940s, under the Japanese occupation and the Nationalist government, Shanghai continued to house securities trading. PING, *supra* note 23, at 18.
40 Qian, *supra* note 7, at 64–65 (citing ZHONGGUO ZHENGQUAN SHOUCE [CHINA SECURMES HANDBOOK] 513–16, 527–29 (Liu Hongru ed., 1992)). The PRC's provisional constitution, the Common Program, provided that the government would "encourage the active operation of all private economic enterprises beneficial to the national welfare and the people's livelihood." Zhongguo Renmin Zhengzhl Xieshang Huiyi Gongtong Gangling [Common Program of the Chinese People's Political Consultative Conference] art. 31 (adopted Sept. 29,1949), *cited in* Conner, *supra* note 4, at 3 n.6.
41 The 1951 rules provided for five business forms: a limited liability company, an unlimited liability company, a company established by both a limited and an unlimited liability company, a company with limited liability and ownership by shares, and a company established by both unlimited and limited liability shareholders. The regulations were Siying Qiye Zanxing Tiaoli [The Provisional Regulation on Private Enterprises] (promulgated Dec. 30, 1950) and Siying Qiye Zhanxing Tiaoli Shixing Banfa [The Implementing Measures for the Provisional Regulations on Private Enterprises] (promulgated Mar. 3,1953), *cited in* Conner, *supra* note 4, at 4 n.9.
42 Conner, *supra* note 4, at 4 (citing ZHONGHUA RENMIN Gongheguo XIANFA (adopted Sept 20, 1954) [Constitution] art. 10 (P.R.C.)).
43 *Id.*
44 *Id.* at 5.
45 ZHONGHUA RENMIN GONGHEGUO XIANFA [Constitution] (adopted Jan. 17, 1975) (P.R.C.), *reprimed in* 1 XIANFA ZILIAO XUANBIAN [COLLECTION OF CONSTITUTIONAL LAW MATERIALS] 293 (1980) *and cited in* Conner, *supra* note 4, at 5 n.20.
46 In December of 1978, the Third Plenum of the Eleventh Central Committee of the Communist Party paved the way for new small businesses. These entities could not hire workers at first, but later regulations allowed two "assistants" and five "apprentices." Conner, *supra* note 4, at 5–6.

47 ZHONGHUA RENMIN GONGHEGUO XIANFA [Constitution] (adopted 1982) (P.R.C.); Zhonghua Renmin Gongheguo Minfa Tongze [General Principles of the Civil Law of the P.R.C.] (adopted Apr. 12, 1986), *cited in* Conner, *supra* note 4, at 6.

48 Article 11 of the 1982 Constitution, as amended in 1988, provides as follows: The state permits the private sector of the economy to exist and develop within the limits prescribed by law. The private sector of the economy is a complement to the socialist public economy. The state protects the lawful rights and interests of the private sector of the economy, and exercises guidance, supervision and control over the private sector of the economy. Amendment to the Constitution of the People's Republic of China (Adopted at the First Session of the Seventh National People's Congress on April 12, 1988 and promulgated for implementation by Proclamation No. 8 of the National People's Congress on April 12, 1988).

49 Kahn & Smith, *supra* note 11, at A10. The state sector employs 108.7 million people, and the rural sector employs 440 million. Private sector employment grew by thirty percent during these five years while state and collective employment stagnated. *Id.* (based on statistics from Morgan Guaranty Trust Co. Economic Research).

50 Conner, *supra* note 4, at 6–8.

51 Qian, *supra* note 7, at 66; *see also* Zheng, *supra* note 4, at 607.

52 In 1992, in southern China, Deng Xiaoping stated:

> Are securities and stock markets good or bad? Is there any danger in adopting such things? Do they exist exclusively in capitalism? Can they also be adopted in a socialist system? People are allowed to consider such matters further, but resolute action must be taken to experiment with such things.

Qian, *supra* note 7, at 84 n.88 (citing Deng Xiaoping's Tour Gives Rise to Stock Heat, 2 *Shenzhou Xueren* [*China's Scholars Abroad*] (1993), at 23); *see also* Bersani, *supra* note 4, at 301.

53 Conner, *supra* note 4, at 33–42. General Secretary Jiang Zemin accused private entrepreneurs of profiteering, tax evasion, and exploitation. Party pronouncements emphasized the need for better supervision of private businesses, though continuing to characterize them as a helpful and necessary supplement to the socialist economy. Tax enforcement increased as well. Policies had moderated by 1991. *Id.*

54 Qian, *supra* note 7.

55 Potter, *supra* note 5, at 14 (noting that terms such as "profits" in 1979 Joint Venture law lacked meaning in socialist legal system and made statute too vague to provide certainty to foreign investors).

56 Zheng, *supra* note 4, at 604 n.387 (citing 2 XU DIXIN, DICTIONARY OF POLITICAL ECONOMICS 40 (1980)).

57 These motivations are clearly present, for example, in the former Soviet Union and Eastern European countries. *See, e.g.*, Andrei A. Baev, *Civil Law and the Transformation of State Property in Post-Socialist Economies: Alternatives to Privatization,* 12 UCLA PAC. BASIN LJ. 131, 145, 150–51 (1993); David Gordon, *Privatization in Eastern Europe: The Polish Experience,* 25 L. & POL'Y INT'L BUS. 517 (1994); William C. Philbrick, *The Paving of Wall Street in Eastern Europe: Establishing the Legal Infrastructure for Stock Markets in the Formerly Centrally Planned Economies,* 25 L. & POL'Y INT'L BUS. 565, 577 (1994).

58 Corporation Law, art. 1.

59 Gordon and Philbrick analyze the Eastern European experience. Gordon, *supra* note 57, at 523; Philbrick, *supra* note 57, at 577. Baev focuses on the Russian experience. Baev, *supra* note 57, at 145.

60 *See, e.g.*, Qian, *supra* note 7, at 91–92.

61 Bersani, *supra* note 4, at 303. The government has retained 51%–80% of the enterprises listed on stock exchanges. Ren Kan, *The State of the States's Shares,* BUS. WKLY., CHINA DAILY, May 3, 1993, at 3, *cited in* Bersani, *supra* note 4, at 306 n.9.

According to another commentator, "Safeguards in the securities laws will guarantee the state's controlling ownership and interest in shareholding enterprises." Qian, *supra* note 7, at 63. As early as 1986, Chinese scholars developing the ideological foundation for integrating the corporate form into a socialist system addressed the concern of dilution of public ownership. They stressed that the state would remain the majority shareholder in most instances. Zheng, *supra* note 4, at 605 (citing Tong Dalin, *Gufenhua Shi Shehui Ztuiyi Qixe De Yige Xinjiduan* [*Stock Company Being a New Starting Point of Socialist Enterprises*], PEOPLE'S DAILY, *Aug. 8, 1986, at* 2).

62 As stated in Article 6 of China's 1982 Constitution, "The basis of the socialist economic system of the People's Republic of China is socialist public ownership of the means of production, namely, ownership by the whole people and collective ownership by the working people." XIANFA [Constitution], translation *available in* LEXIS, Intlaw Library, Chinalaw File. Indeed, ownership of the means of production may be seen as a primary justification for the existence of the state. Privatization would therefore undercut the ideological basis of the government Bersani, *supra* note 4, at 305; Gordon, *supra* note 57, at 519. Bersani cites a constitutional amendment, approved by the National People's Congress on March 29, 1993, changing the designation of state enterprises from "state-run" to "state-owned," XIANFA [Constitution] *amended by* art. VII, and a statement by Premier Li Peng of the government's determination to create independent management for public enterprises. Bersani, *supra* note 4, at 304.

63 Bersani, *supra* note 4, at 303; *see also* Dai Yannian, *Spotlight on China's Modern Enterprise System,* 37 BEIJING REV., Feb. 28-Mar. 6,1994, at 4 (explaining that state will continue to own dominant portion of society's total assets, but that corporations will manage them, together with other assets, in improved manner with clearly defined property rights). This new variation has been called "Market Leninism." *See, e.g.,* Nicholas Kristof, *China Sees "Market-Leninism" as Way to Future,* N.Y. TIMES, Sept. 6, 1993, at Al, A5 [hereinafter, Kristof, *Way to Future].* Some Chinese intellectuals are concerned that China may develop in the direction of fascism, with state-controlled corporations competing under market conditions but in an authoritarian political system. *Id.* (referring to "some young Chinese intellectuals"). Chairman Mao warned of this risk in 1963: "We are afraid that we will stop being a revolutionary country and will become a revisionist one. When that happens in a socialist country, it becomes worse than a capitalist country. A Communist Party can turn into a fascist party." *Id.* at A5. Others think that free markets will lead China to a more open political system. *See, e.g.,* Marcus W. Brauchli, *Chaotic Change: Beijing's Grip Weakens as Free Enterprise Turns into Free-for-All,* WALL ST. J., Aug. 26, 1993, at Al. Concern that economic reforms might create a new bourgeoisie, threatening socialism, was one factor behind a campaign against private business in 1989, which appears to have run its course. Conner, *supra* note 4, at 33–42.

64 Bersani, *supra* note 4, at 304. In 1992, PRC citizens held U.S. $310 billion in private savings, in comparison to only $240 billion in assets held by the state. *Id.* at 304 n.4 (citing E. ECON. REV., April 1, 1993, at 83). A 1993 report noted that savings deposits of urban and rural residents increased 27.9 percent over the 1992 figures and that "energetic efforts to absorb savings deposits" were a priority of government financial policy. *Statistical Communique of the State Statistical Bureau of the People's Republic of China on the 1993 National Economic and Social Development (February 28,1994),* BEIJING REV., Mar. 14–20, 1994, at 24 [hereinafter *Statistical Communique].*

65 Bersani, *supra* note 4, at 304; *see also* Kristof, *Way to Future, supra* note 63, at 5.

66 Clarke, *supra* note 2, at 15–16 (analyzing roles of law and direct state management in Chinese policy); Dai, *supra* note 63, at 4 (reforms are "designed to separate government administration from enterprise management, gaining expanded decision-making power and altering management methods"). A clear and comprehensive statement of the government's rationale for the Corporation Law and allied reforms is in Wu, *supra* note 12, at 7.

67 In 1993, in response to public indignation, the government issued specific directives on wage increases that seemed to contradict its previous promise to limit itself to macro-economic policies. Brauchli, *supra* note 63, at Al.

68 Liu Weiling, *State Acts to Protect Its Shares*, CHINA DAILY SUPPLEMENT: BUS. WKLY., March 28, 1994, at 3.

69 Under the new policy, the representative of state shares will be the local state property administration department, an institution that is responsible to the state and therefore more likely to demand better treatment for the state shares. *Id.*

70 *State Enterprises Face Further Reforms,* BEIJING REV., Oct. 17–23,1994, at 5 [hereinafter *Further Reforms*].

71 *Shenzhen Gives Firms,* CHINA DAILY, *supra* note 15, at 4.

72 *Further Reforms, supra* note 70, at 5. Electing directors under the Corporation Law, of course, does not preclude the government from determining who is on the board when the government is the majority shareholder.

73 Julia Leung and Craig S. Smith, *Some Chinese Factory Bosses Live It Up: Economic Transition Gives Managers Wide Autonomy,* WALL ST. J., Mar. 15, 1994, at A21. Among the examples cited was a fleet of six Mercedeses, including a convertible, owned by Guangdong Kelon Electrical Holding Co., a refrigerator manufacturer in Shunde, China.

74 *Id.* (quoting Liu Shiyi, vice mayor of Shunde, China). He added, "They hardly pay taxes. Instead, they squander the money on fancy office buildings and fast cars, and we have no way of restraining their lavish spending." Some managers even pass on managerial control to their sons or other relatives. *Id.*

75 *Id.* One example is Shougang Corporation, a Beijing-based steelmaker that purchased an iron mine in 1992, paying more than double the amount offered by the next highest bidder. Unlike other steelmakers, the company is not accountable to the Ministry of Metallurgical Industry. Instead, it reports directly to the State Council. Even though its managers are free to run the company as they see fit, they can still count on government help such as an emergency loan from the People's Bank of China.

76 Bersani, *supra* note 4, at 305.

77 Geng Yuxin, *Reform of State Enterprises*, *supra* note 10, at 5.

78 Current policy calls for "experimental trials with enterprise bankruptcy." At the time this Article went to press, the State Council was expected to promulgate a Circular on Issues Concerning the Trial Practice of the Bankruptcy of State-Owned Enterprises in Selected Cities. Wu, *supra* note 12, at 12.

79 *Id.* Government sensitivity to the issue is reflected in the delicate terminology and the corrective measures it uses. Whereas Western capitalists might simply fire excess employees, the Chinese discuss "Appropriately rearranging redundant employees" and "encouraging redundant employees to seek new jobs." *Id.*

80 *Shenzhen Gives Firms Freedom, supra* note 15, at 4. This article described 1995 as China's "year of enterprise reform" and Shenzhen as a pioneering city in the effort However, state enterprises in Shenzhen, operating before reforms without regard to profitability, had taken out heavy bank loans to maintain production even when their products were being stockpiled. Though current policy permits poorly managed enterprises to go bankrupt, the resulting losses to banks hinder implementation of the policy. *Id.*

81 Conner, *supra* note 4, at 9–10.

82 *Id.* at 10 (citing regulations governing "individual" firms and writings of several Chinese writers).

83 Conner, *supra* note 4, at 12 (citing, *inter alia,* Zhonggong Zhongyang Guanyu Jingji Tizhi Gaige de Jeuding [Decision of the Chinese Communist Central Committee on the Reform of the Economic Structure] (adopted Oct 20, 1984)).

84 *Id. at 13* (Citing *S.* HU ET AL,, MINFA TONGZE JIANGHUA [LECTURES ON THE GENERAL PRINCIPLES OF CIVIL LAW] *193 (1986); R.* TONG ET AL., MINFA YUANLI [PRINCIPLES

OF CIVIL LAW] *180–81 (2d ed. 1985);* L. WANG ET AL., *2* MINFA XINLUN [NEW DISCUSSIONS ON CIVIL LAW] *177–78 (1988).*

85 Conner, *supra* note 4, at 14–15 (citing, *inter alia,* General Secretary Zhao Ziyang, Yanzhe You Zhongguo Tese de Shehuizhuyi Daolu Qianjin [Advance Along the Road of Socialism with Chinese Characteristics], Address Before the Communist Party's Thirteenth National Congress (Oct, 25, 1987), *translated in* BEIJING REV., Nov. 9–15, 1987, at 23).

86 ZHONGUA RENMIN GONGHEGUO XIANFA [Constitution] (P.R.C.), art. 11 (amended Apr. 12, 1988), provided: "The state permits the private economy to exist and develop within the limits prescribed by law. The private economy is a supplement to the socialist public ownership economy. The state protects the lawful rights and interests of the private economy and exercises guidance, supervision and control over it" Amendment to the Constitution of the People's Republic of China, Proclamation No. 8, April 12, 1988 by the First Session of the Seventh National People's Congress.

87 *See generally* Shi Xianmin, *The Classification of Privately-Owned Small Businesses in Beijing,* 15 SOC. SCI. IN CHINA 95 (1994). The article identifies five categories of private small business *(getihu)* and describes each one's management patterns, interests and external relationships, sense of affiliation, lifestyle, and value orientation.

88 *Id.* at 100.

89 Zhonghua Renmin Gongheguo Xingfa, art. 118 [Criminal Law of the People's Republic of China] (adopted July 1,1979, effective January 1,1980) (translation *available in* LEXIS, Intlaw Library, Chinalaw File). Article 118 provides:"Whoever makes a regular business of smuggling or illicit speculation, smuggles or speculates in huge amounts or is the ringleader of a group that smuggles or engages in illicit speculation shall be sentenced to fixed-term imprisonment of not less than three years and not more than ten years, and may concurrently be sentenced to confiscation of property."

90 Guanyu Chushou Guoyou Xiaoxing Qiye Chanquan de Zanxing Banfa [The Interim Measures Concerning Sale of Title of Wholly State-owned Small-size Enterprises] (issued February 19,1989). These measures, issued by the Committee of System Reformation, The Ministry of Finance and the Administrative Bureau of State-owned Property, provide that "The buyer can be wholly state-owned enterprises, or collectively-owned enterprises, or 'Joint Ventures, Wholly Foreign-owned Enterprises and Chinese-Foreign Contractual Joint Ventures,' or private enterprises, or partnerships and individuals." Corporation Law, art. 6 "After sale, the buyer shall apply for a change in the certification from the Administrative Department for Industry and Commerce. The nature of the ownership of the enterprises shall follow the nature of ownership of buyer. The enterprise shall be managed based on the newly defined nature of ownership." *Id.* art. 18.

91 Corporation Law, art. 4.

92 These statistics were released by the Chinese State Administration for Industry and Commerce. *Private Ventures,* CHINA DAILY, Sept 27, 1994, at 2.

93 In 1993, private firms numbered 238,000 (70 percent more than in 1992), had registered capital of 68 billion yuan (twice as much as the figure for 1992), and employed 3.72 million people (60 percent more than the prior year). *Private Firms Burst into Boom,* BEIJING REV., Mar. 14–20, 1994, at 5.

94 *Statistical Communique, supra* note 64, at 26. Specifically, GDP was 3138 billion yuan, up 13.4% over 1992, *id.* at 19, and the population was 1.185 billion, up 13 million over 1992, *id.* at 26.

95 Corporation Law, art. 77.

96 The prerequisites for establishing a corporation are set out in Articles 19 (for LLCs) and 73 (for Joint Stock Companies). Administrative regulations provide more details. A corporation must: 1) have its own name, organizational structure, and articles of association; 2) have a fixed place of business and the necessary facilities; 3) have

funds and personnel of an amount and number which conform with State regulations and which are in proportion with the scale of its production and services; 4) have the ability to bear civil liability independently; and 5) have a scope of business that conforms with the provisions of State laws, statutory regulations, and policies. Administrative Regulations of the People's Republic of China Governing the Registration of Legal Corporations, art. 7, promulgated June 3, 1988 by the State Council. The Administrative Regulations of the People's Republic of China Concerning the Registration of Corporations (promulgated July 1, 1994 by the State Council) also state detailed items of registration concerning the establishment of a corporation.

97 Corporation Law, arts. 94–95.

98 *Id.* art. 11. Companies might circumvent this regulation of operations by investing in another company. The statute limits that possibility by prohibiting any company from investing more than fifty percent of its assets in another company. *Id.* Art. 12.

99 *Id.* arts. 84–85.

100 *Id.* Art. 86–91.

101 One commentator expressed these reservations in relation to China's joint venture law as applied to foreigners. Potter, *supra* note 5, at 34.

102 In the early years of the United States, and in England during that period, corporate status and limited liability were regarded as extraordinary privileges, or "concessions" of governmental power. The sovereign (the Crown, Congress, or state legislature) granted corporate charters only in specific instances, and only for companies with an evident connection to public welfare, such as railroads, banks, and traders with foreign lands. NORMAN LATTIN, THE LAW OF CORPORATIONS § 54, at 174–75 (2d ed. 1971). Corporate powers and purposes were defined narrowly, which generated litigation over "ultra vires" actions – conduct by a corporation outside the lines of business permitted to it Subsequently, Jacksonian populists viewed the requirement of special legislation for each grant of corporate status as unfairly benefitting the rich and powerful. The solution was "general incorporation" legislation, under which corporate status became inexpensive and freely available to anyone fulfilling fairly minimal filing requirements. *Id.* at 181. In the United States, general incorporation acts appeared first in New York in 1811 and became standard between 1875 and 1925. *Id.* at 175–76. These modem statutes authorize corporations to engage in "any lawful purpose" – which means virtually any conduct permitted to a natural person. *Id.* at 177.

103 Quanguo Renda Falu Weiyuanhui Guanyu "Zhonghua Renmin Gongheguo Gongsifa (Chaoan)" Shenyijieguo de Baogao [The Law Committee of the National People's Congress, Report Concerning the Examination of Chinese Corporation Law (draft)] (Dec. 17, 1993).

104 Business income taxes are new to China, and the system of assessment and collection remains uncertain. In the case of Sino-foreign mining joint ventures, for example, a government official said that the 33% profit tax and 17% value-added tax applicable to other businesses would apply. However, those ventures would also be subject to a "resources-compensation tax" at a rate that has not yet been decided. Julia Leung, *As China Opens Up Mining, Foreigners are Confused about Ownership, Taxes,* WALL ST. J., Mar. 21, 1994, at A7.

105 *The Chinese "Corporate Law" Will Be Put into Effect, supra* note 26, at 7. For a discussion of abuses of the company form prior to the new Corporation Law, see Zheng, *supra* note 4, at 580.

106 The Corporation Law preserves the possibility of requiring approval, if laws and regulations outside the Corporate Law so provide. Corporation Law, art. 8. This provision could apply, for example, to aircraft production. The provision follows the pattern of prior Chinese regulation of companies, which prohibited private enterprises from engaging in military or financial industries or dealing in cultural objects, antiques, jewelry, stamps, firearms, ammunition, cars, and explosives. Conner, *supra* note 4, at

24. Some literature uses the term "socialist market economic macro-control system" to describe the policy of regulating only at the macroeconomic level, not at the level of the individual enterprise. *See, e.g.*, Geng Yuxin, *Greeting the Year for Enterprise Reform*, BEIJING REV., Jan. 2–8, 1995, at 4.

107 *See* HARRY G. HENN & JOHN R. ALEXANDER, LAWS OF CORPORATIONS § 259, at 704 (3d student ed. 1983). Separate statutory treatment for small corporations, typically defined by the number of shareholders, is common in the United States and Europe. *Id.* § 259; Colin McFadyean, *The American Close Corporation and its British Equivalent*, 14 BUS. LAW 215 (1958); ROBERT B. THOMPSON & FAYE L. KATT, O'NEAL'S CLOSE CORPORATIONS: LAW AND PRACTICE § 1.13, 1.18 (3d ed. 1994).

108 Literally, *You Xian* Ze *Ren Gong Si* translates as "limited liability company." Liability is limited to the shareholders' equity. The term *gongsi*, meaning company or corporation, has been used to refer to a level of administrative authority over government-owned enterprises, but can also apply to private enterprises.

The Chinese term, "Limited Liability Company," must be distinguished from the same term as it is used in American legislation. Many American states have authorized a new form of business organization, which they label a "limited liability company," in order to permit businesses to qualify for some tax benefits that partnerships typically receive while retaining the corporation's protection of investors. An American LLC, unlike a Chinese LLC, is not considered incorporated and enjoys extensive discretion to establish its own internal governance structure.

109 Literally, *Gu Feng You Xian Gong Si* translates as "shareholding limited company." An alternative is "company limited by shares," which is used in the translation published by CCH International. *See supra* note 1. That alternative is an accurate translation of the Chinese, but seems confusing in English. How do shares limit a company? What the term denotes is that the company is characterized by share ownership and provides limited liability to shareholders. Because all corporations provide limited liability, this Article uses the phrase "Joint Stock Company" as the most descriptive translation.

110 Some experts suggested that the Law should have also included the unlimited liability company and the joint company, i.e.; a company formed by shareholders, some of whom are protected by limited liability, along with others subject to unlimited liability. *See* Quanguo Renda Falu Weiyuanhui Guanyu "Zhonghua Renmin Gongheguo Gongsifa (Chaoan)" Shenyijieguo de Baogao [Law Committee of National People's Congress, Report Concerning Examination of Chinese Company Law (draft)] (Dec. 17,1993). THE COMPANY LAW of the PEOPLE'S REPUBLIC OF CHINA 59 (1993). The final version omitted these other forms of economic organization.

Enterprises with unlimited liability can be treated as partnerships, which the Civil Law of China regulates. *See* CHINESE CIV. P. LAW, art. 52, which provides that a jointly operated business established by different enterprises or units can be subject to unlimited responsibility based on the requirements of relevant laws or their contract

111 Translations available in LEXIS, Intlaw Library, Chinalaw File, Numbers 41, 345,463.

112 Quanguo Renda, *supra* note 110, at 60.

113 *Id.* at 60

114 Corporation Law, art. 20.

115 Scientific, technological, consulting, and service companies need capitalization at the low end of the range; commercial retail companies lie in the middle; and production, management, and wholesale companies need the most capitalization. *Id.* art. 23. One-hundred thousand to five-hundred thousand yuan is equivalent to approximately U.S. $12,500 to $62,500.

116 *Id.* art. 99 (permitting an LLC to publicly float stock only after receiving approval to convert into joint stock company).

117 *Id.* arts. 73, 78. Ten million yuan equals approximately U.S. $1.25 million.

118 *Id.* art. 74.

119 *Id.* arts. 74, 83.

120 *Id.* art. 147.

121 In American securities law, a similar restriction on resales assures that insiders bear the economic risk of their investment for at least two years. *See* 17 C.F.R. §§ 230.502(d), 230.144(d).

122 Promoters not only must complete the formal requirements of organizing the corporate entity, but must also assume multiple responsibilities. If the company cannot be established, the promoters are jointly liable for all expenses incurred in the attempt and must repay any amounts received for subscriptions with interest If the "promoters' negligence" during establishment injures the company, the promoters must pay compensation. Corporation Law, art. 97.

123 *Id.* art. 64.

124 *Id.* arts. 65–69.

125 *Id.* art 75.

126 The 1951 regulation, for example, provided for some companies with limited liability, others with unlimited liability, and others with a combination of the two. *See supra* note 41.

127 Corporation Law, arts. 3,4. For a description of the "legal person" concept in the Chinese Civil Code, see Zheng, *supra* note 4, at 553–57.

128 Article 3 provides that shareholders in an LLC assume liability limited to "the amount of capital that they invested," and that shareholders in a Joint Stock Company "assume . . . liability equal to the amount of shares purchased." The difference in phrasing might suggest that capital can be contributed to an LLC in a form other than share purchases, but the Law does not reflect that concept elsewhere.

129 Under American law, courts in exceptional cases disregard the corporate entity to impose personal liability on shareholders for debts incurred by the enterprise. This practice, called "piercing the corporate veil," stems entirely from common-law equitable principles, not express statutory authority. The cases typically involve fraud, disregard of corporate formalities, and grossly inadequate capitalization. Tort claimants are more likely to succeed than contractual claimants, because contractual claimants chose to deal with the corporation; tort victims often do not. The defendants most likely to suffer liability are active shareholders who personally caused the corporation to engage in improper conduct rather than passive investors with no participation in corporate affairs beyond their shareholding. *See, e.g.*, ROBERT C. CLARK, CORPORATE LAW §2.4 (1986); ALFRED F. CONARD, CORPORATIONS IN PERSPECTIVE §§ 270–77 (1976); HARRY G. HENN & JOHN R. ALEXANDER, Laws of Corporations § 146 (1983).

130 The "legal representative" concept has a long history in Chinese law. For the current general statement of the rule, see The General Principles of Civil Law of the People's Republic of China, art. 43, Apr. 12, 1986, *available in* LEXIS, China law library. File No. 346 [here in after Civil Law].

131 Corporation Law, arts. 45 (applicable to most LLC's), 68 (applicable to LLC's wholly owned by the state), 113 (applicable to joint stock companies).

132 *Id.* art. 51.

133 *Id.* art. 96.

134 *Id.* art. 49.

135 *Id.*

136 *Id.* (stating that legal representative is subject to administrative sanctions). The term "administrative sanctions" is defined in, for example, Zhonghua Renmin Gongheguo Xingzheng Jiancha Tiaoli (The Provisions of Administrative Supervision of PRC), passed on November 23,1990 by the State Council and issued on December 9,1990 by the 69th decree of the State Council of PRC. Sanctions include warning, minor and severe reprimands, probation, demotion, dismissal, and discharge.

137 An LLC may have between three and thirteen directors, *id.* art. 45, and a Joint Stock Company may have between five and nineteen, *id.* art. 112.
138 *Id.* art. 115.
139 *Id.* art. 51. An executive director may serve concurrently as manager of the LLC.
140 *Id.* art. 45.
141 *Id.* art. 46 (listing powers of directors).
142 The government urged transition from the system of overall responsibility by the factory director, under the leadership of the CPC Party Committee, to exercising a system of overall responsibility by the factory director alone. *See* Zhonggong Zhongyang, Guowuyan Guanyu Renzheng Guanche Zhixing Quanmin Suoyuzhi Gongyeqiye Sange Tiaoli de Buchong Tongzi [The Central Committee of the Chinese Communist Party and the State Council, Additional Information of Conscientiously Carrying Out Three Provisions Regarding Wholly State-owned Industrial Enterprise] (Nov. 11, 1986). This system changed the CPC from the primary organization in an enterprise to an active supporter of the factory director. *See* Zhongguo Gongchandang Quanmin Suoyuzhi Gongyeqiye Jicengzuzhi Gongzuo Tiaoli [The Working Provisions For CPC Primary Organization In the Wholly State-owned Industrial Enterprise] (issued on September 15, 1986 by the Central Committee of CPC and the State Council).
143 For example, the Corporation Law specifies the number of directors, limits terms to three years, and allows directors not attending a meeting to vote by proxy. Corporation Law, arts. 112, 115, 118. In comparison, American corporation laws typically set no standards on the number of directors, limit terms to one year in most cases, and do not allow directors to vote by proxy. Revised Model Bus. Corp. Act. §§ 8.03 (one or more directors), 8.05 (one year term unless terms are staggered over either two or three years), 8.20 (directors may participate without being present in person if communications allow all to hear each other, but proxies are not sanctioned) (1991).
144 The German concept of supervisory councils, with labor representation, has been used in newly adopted corporation acts in Eastern Europe. Gordon, *supra* note 57, at 546–48. For a description of the German model, see Gregory *J.* Thwaite & Jurgen Pesch, *A Guide for the Perplexed: Some Aspects of German Merger and Acquisition Law Explained for Foreign Counsel,* 20 INT'L BUS. LAW. 566,571 (1992); Hopt, *supra* note 9, at 203.
145 The provisions for LLCs are substantially identical to provisions for Companies Limited by Shares. Compare Corporation Law, arts. 52 and 53 with Corporation Law, arts. 124 and 125.
146 Corporation Law, arts. 52 (for LLCs), 124 (for Joint Stock Companies).
147 *Id.*
148 *Id.* arts. 54 (for LLCs), 126 (for Joint Stock Companies).
149 *Id.* art. 54.
150 *Id.* arts. 63, 128.
151 *Id.* art. 128.
152 *Id.* arts. 37 (for LLCs), 102 (for Joint Stock Companies).
153 *Id.* art. 42.
154 *Id.* art. 104.
155 In LLCs, interim meetings may be called by more than one quarter of the shareholders, one third of directors, or one third of the supervisors. *Id.* art. 43. In Joint Stock Companies, interim meetings must be called if requested by a ten percent shareholder, the directors, or the supervisors (with no percentage vote specified). Meetings must be called if the number of directors falls below the statutory requirements or if losses reach one third of paid-up capital. *Id.* art. 104.
156 *Id.* art. 38 (for LLCs), 103 (for Joint Stock Companies).
157 *Id.* A two-thirds majority can approve fundamental changes. *Id.* art. 39.
158 *Id.* art. 108 (describing Joint Stock Companies).

159 *See, e.g.*, Revised Model Bus. Corp. Act §§ 7.01 (annual meeting), 7.02 (special meeting), 7.21 (voting entitlement of shares), 7.28 (voting for directors), 8.08 (removal of directors by shareholders), 8.11 (compensation of directors), 10.03 (amendment by Board of Directors and Shareholders), 11.03 (action on plan), 14.02 (dissolution by Board of Directors and Shareholders), 16.02 (inspection of records by Shareholders) (1994). American law has no counterpart to the Chinese Supervisory Committee.

160 Corporation Law, art. 38.

161 *Id*, (for LLCs).

162 *Id.* art. 103(7) (for Joint Stock Companies).

163 *See, e.g.*, Revised Model Bus. Corp. Act § 8.01(b) (1994), stating the general rule: "All corporate powers shall be exercised by or under the authority of, and the business and affairs of the corporation managed under the direction of, its board of directors. . . ." More specific powers of directors are provided in, e.g, the Revised Model Bus. Corp. Act §§ 6.21 (issuance of shares), 6.40 (distributions to shareholders) (1994).

164 *Id.* art. 111 (describing Joint Stock Companies).

165 For summaries of the concepts and procedures of shareholder direct and derivative actions in American corporate law, see ROBERT C. CLARK, CORPORATE LAW §§ 15.1–15.9 (1986); NORMAN D. LATTIN, *The* LAW OF CORPORATIONS *§§ 102–116 (1971).*

166 The Law of the People's Republic of China on Industrial Enterprises Owned by the Whole People, adopted by the People's Congress in 1988, provided for a Workers' Representative Assembly. Through the assembly, workers could not only advise management but "elect and remove the enterprise director subject to government approval . . . and decide on plans regarding workers." Wang, *supra* note 14, at 99.

167 Corporation Law, art. 55.

168 *Id.* arts. 55, 56.

169 *Id.* art. 55.

170 *Id.*

171 *Id.* art. 45.

172 *Id.* art. 124.

173 Hopt, *supra* note 9, at 204 (citing German statutes).

174 Dai, *supra* note 63, at 5. This *Beijing Review* editorial on the current economic reforms described the new approach to enterprise organization, but emphasized that public ownership would remain dominant in the economy. *Id.* An analysis of the 1988 Law of the People's Republic of China on Industrial Enterprises Owned by the Whole People noted that although the Workers' Representative Assemblies created by that law seem to assure that workers have representation in management, realistically they "sometimes provide[] a channel for Party officials to wield power." Wang, *supra* note 14, at 99.

175 The widespread concern that the death of Deng Xiaoping may fundamentally alter the course of reforms and government policy, even though Deng has relinquished all his offices, suggests that real power in China does not always require formal trappings.

176 Corporation Law, arts. 206, 209, 211.

177 *See, e.g., id.* arts. 206–12.

178 Fines between 10,000 and 100,000 yuan may be imposed for submitting false documents relating to registration, *id.* art. 206, keeping a false set of accounting records, *id.* art. 211, and providing false reports of financial affairs, *id.* art. 212.

179 *Id.* art. 210.

180 *Id.* art. 209.

181 For a definition of "administrative sanctions" see *supra* note 136.

182 Corporation Law, art. 214.

183 *Id.* art. 215.

184 At least 15 separate articles state that in addition to the other more specific sanctions, criminal liability (which is not defined in the Corporation Law) applies "in accordance with the law." *Id.* arts. 206–14, 217–24.

185 Robert Steiner, *Big Chinese Bank, Citing Fraud, Won't Honor Letter of Credit*, ASIAN WALL ST. J., June 23, 1993, at 3. For instance, the Xinhua News Agency reported that the president of a Chinese company who embezzled about $375,000 was executed in April 1994; that a vice-minister was sentenced to 20 years in prison in the same case; and that a company president was executed for embezzlement and bribery totaling $373,500. *Chinese Executive Convicted of Embezzlement Executed*, OREGONIAN, Apr. 12, 1994, at A4.

186 Shen Taifu, former president of the Beijing Changcheng [Great Wall] Machinery and Electronics Group, was convicted of embezzling two million yuan and taking a ten percent patent commission on all company transactions. He also devised a national pyramid scheme, selling bonds by promising interest rates of 43% and defrauding approximately 100,000 investors of more than one billion yuan. Finally, he paid bribes for favors. Shen was executed, and all of his personal property was confiscated. His wife, Sun Jihong, a vice president of the company, was convicted of converting one million yuan of company money, sentenced to fifteen years in jail, and deprived of political rights for three years. Jiang Jiang, *Finally, Alarm Bells Sound,* BEIJING REV., May 2–8, 1994, at 13.

187 Corporation Law, art. 57.

188 *Id.* art. 58.

189 Investors in A-share stock markets, which are open only to Chinese citizens, frequently complain of rampant insider trading by government officials and private citizens such as business leaders and stockbrokers who have undisclosed information about regulatory policies and corporate developments. One brokerage firm has been found guilty of trading on advance knowledge of a corporate takeover, forced to disgorge its profits, fined, and shut down for two months. Joseph Kahn, *China Fines Broker in First Crackdown on Insider Trading,* WALL ST. J., Feb. 7, 1994, at All. In 1993, the Communist Party's top disciplinary committee formally banned party officials from playing the stock market. Brauchli, *supra* note 63, at Al.

190 President Jiang Zemin has warned that corruption has grown so common that it threatens to ruin the Communist Party. Party and army officials have stolen billions of yuan, engaged in massive smuggling and other rackets, and sought bribes and payoffs. *Way to Future, supra* note 63, at 5.

191 Corporation Law, art. 60.

192 *Id.* art. 61.

193 *Id.* art. 130 (specifying further that all shares issued at same time shall have equal conditions of issue and price, and that any unit or individual buying shares shall pay equal value). *But see id.* art. 135 (reserving power in State Council to "regulate other shares not provided for by this Act," which might be interpreted to permit preferred or other classes of stock, in addition to common shares).

194 Authorities have considered relaxing the ban on foreigners holding A shares but have not yet done so. Joseph Kahn, *Rescue Plan Spurs Jump in China's Stock Markets,* WALL ST. J., Aug. 2,1994, at Cl.

195 Qian, *supra* note 7, at 67.

196 *Id.*

197 A commentator offered this example in his discussion of the provisional corporate law regulations that the Corporation Law superseded. Bersani, *supra* note 4, at 322. The point is equally valid under the 1993 legislation.

198 Corporation Law, arts. 129 (requiring share certificates), 132 (specifying contents of certificate).

199 *See, e.g.,* Alexandria Peers, *"Paperless" Wall Street is Due Next June,* WALL ST. J., June 7, 1994, at Cl (describing federal deadline to eliminate stock certificates, unless investors pay extra for them as part of program to expedite settlement and delivery of stock after trades on exchange).

200 Corporation Law, art. 134. These types are also called "name" and "non-name," respectively.
201 *Id.* art. 133.
202 Article 134 provides for a shareholders' list of name shares.
203 The provision most relevant to these procedures specifies that, when a company has bearer shares, the company must announce the issues to be discussed at a meeting 40 days prior to thc mceting, and the holders of these shares must hold their stock 5 days prior to the meeting. Corporation Law, art. 105.
204 *Id.* art. 33.
205 *Id.* art. 35.
206 *Id.* art. 149.
207 *Id.* art. 151.
208 *Id.* art. 152.
209 *Id.* art. 156.
210 *Id.* arts. 152(3) (requirements for applying for listed shares), 157 (suspension of listed shares).
211 *Id.* art. 159.
212 *Id.* art. 168.
213 *Id.* arts. 172, 173 (available only to public companies with State Council approval).
214 *Id.* art. 171.
215 In 1993, for example, the Great Wall Machinery & Electronics Corp. of Beijing sold bonds worth $175 million to more than 200,000 investors through the lure of a promise of annual returns of 24%. The corporation failed shortly thereafter. Brauchli, *supra* note 63, at Al, A5.
216 Corporation Law, art. 161(4).
217 *Id.* art. 164.
218 Joint stock companies must have net capital of 30 million yuan, and LLCs must have net capital of 60 million yuan. *Id.* arts. 161(1), (2).
219 *Id.* arts. 161(3), 161 (final paragraph).
220 *Id.* art. 162.
221 Anglo-American corporation law traditionally recognized par as a way to protect both investors and creditors of a corporation. The modern trend in American law, however, has been to abandon the concept of par, and all of its elaborate restrictions, in recognition of serious conceptual flaws in its structure. For example, the Revised Model Business Corporation Act now being adopted throughout the United States does not assign any legal significance whatsoever to par. *See* Robert C. Art, *Corporate Shares and Distributions in a System Beyond Par: Financial Provisions of Oregon's New Corporation Act, 24* WILLAMETTE L. REV. 203,204 (1988).
222 Corporation Law, art. 131.
223 Stock is called "low par" when par value is lower than the price received. To illustrate, a corporation may set par at one dollar, or even one cent, and then sell the shares to the public at twenty dollars per share, their fair market value. The corporation then sells additional shares of the same class to certain favored insiders at only five dollars per share. Because both sales generate at least par value, the company has fulfilled the statutory requirement and fully circumvented the Law's intent to assure that all shareholders are treated equally.
224 The price received for stock cannot be less than "par value," but can be greater if "permitted by [the] securities management department of the State Council." *Id.*
225 The Chinese are sensitive to the perception that foreigners seek to exploit China – a perception with justification in history. Consequently, the joint venture law permits only those ventures that employ advanced technology, modem scientific management methods, innovation, and/or training. Potter, *supra* note 5, at 16. The belief that China should not be a dumping ground for obsolete or unwanted products and equipment

from technologically advanced countries seems also to contribute to the Corporation Law's requirements for appraisal by government offices.

226 In Eastern Europe, for example, privatization of state enterprises often resulted in the enrichment of managers and the *nomenklatura.* Because of the lack of supervision and control, the *nomenklatura* arranged transfers of state assets to companies owned by themselves or friends. Gordon, *supra* note 57, at 523. Abuses experienced include insider dealing and gross undervaluation of assets. Philbrick, *supra* note 57, at 580.

227 *China Limits Sale of Assets Held by State Companies,* WALL ST. *J.* May 17, 1994, at A15. Wen Hui Bao, a government-run newspaper in Shanghai, reported that local government agencies and companies often sell assets or equity formally controlled by Beijing, using the proceeds for their own benefit The central government estimates an annual loss of $3.4 billion due to undervaluation of its contributions to joint ventures with foreign firms.

228 Corporation Law, arts. 26 (applicable to all shareholders), 80 (applicable specifically to promoters). A further provision, *id.,* art. 81, adds that when a state-owned enterprise converts to corporate form, the assets it contributes must be fairly evaluated.

229 *Id.* art. 26.

230 *Id.* art. 80.

231 *Id.* art. 178.

232 *Id.* art. 177.

233 *Id.*

234 *Id.* art. 179.

235 *Id.* (omitting dividends from permitted uses of fund).

236 *Id.* art. 177.

237 *Id.* art. 180.

238 *Id.* art. 177.

239 Zheng, *supra* note 4, at 610–11.

240 Some propose a national pension fund to protect the workers. Presently, work units fund their pensions (sometimes at one hundred percent of pre-retirement pay) out of current operating funds. The work unit and individuals have not funded future pension costs. Jesse Wong, *In China, The Welfare State Hangs On, Burdening Already-Stressed Companies,* WALL ST, J., Aug. 23, 1994, at A10. Chinese officials recognize that reform of state enterprises requires the creation of new structures for social security, pensions, and unemployment insurance. *Further Reforms, supra* note 70, at 5–6; Wu Naitao, *'95 Goals for Reform of State-Owned Enterprises,* BEIJING REV., Jan. 9–15, 1995, at 7, 14.

241 According to one commentator, multiple institutional features limit the ability of China's courts to enforce legal standards. These problems include poorly indexed laws and regulations, inadequate legal training of judges, vulnerability of judges to corruption and outside pressures, and obstacles in the enforcement of judgments. In addition, judges' decisions can be overridden by superiors who do not always follow legal standards. Clarke, *supra* note 2, at 57–71.

242 *See, e.g.,* Potter, *supra* note 5, at 35 (expressing similar reservations regarding China's laws and rales affecting foreign joint ventures).

6

INTRODUCTION TO THE NEW COMPANY LAW OF THE PEOPLE'S REPUBLIC OF CHINA

Steven M. Dickinson

Source: Pacific Rim Law & Policy Journal 16, 1, 2007, pp. 1–11.

Abstract

This article briefly analyzes the new Company Law and its effects on doing business in China. After a brief history of the previous version of the law, this article examines the many changes to management and articles of association, capital requirements, limited liability companies, access to corporate information, piercing the corporate veil, third party loans, and legal remedies for improper actions. It goes on to look at the impact on the structure of foreign investments and discusses the likely effects of the new law in actual practice.

I. Introduction

On October 27, 2005, the People's Republic of China adopted a new Company Law. This law became effective on January 1, 2006.[1] The New Company Law replaces the Old Company Law, which had been adopted in 1993.[2] The New Company Law is a complete revision of the old law. Almost nothing of the old law survived the revision. Drafters estimate approximately ninety percent of the provisions of the new law are unique.

The New Company Law governs two types of corporations: limited liability companies *(youxian gongsi)* and joint stock companies. The changes to limited liability companies are especially important to foreign investors in China because the statutes governing foreign direct investment in China require foreign investors to operate through a Chinese limited liability company.[3] For existing foreign invested limited liability companies, the rules on operation of such companies have substantially changed. Potential new investors must realize the old rules no longer apply and consider the new regime. Because foreign investors are currently prohibited from investing directly in China through joint stock companies, the discussion below will be limited to the New Company Law's changes regarding limited liability companies.

II. Important changes introduced by the New Company Law

A. Management and articles of association

Under the Old Company Law, the articles of association for a limited liability corporation was not a living document. Article 22 of the Old Company Law provided a list of items to be included in the articles. As a matter of practice, companies were required to include those provisions and no others. As a result, articles of association were virtually the same for every company regardless of its size or nature. There was no freedom to revise or adapt the articles to meet the specific needs of a particular company. Under the Old Company Law, the roles of shareholders, directors, and officers were taken as mandatory provisions to be followed by all companies. As a result, the articles of association became little more than a "fill in the blanks" form document adopted by every company without regard to the actual management needs of that company.

The New Company Law abandons the rigidity of the old law and encourages shareholders of limited liability companies to take a flexible approach to company management. The articles of association now are intended to be adaptable to meet the specific needs of each company. The New Company Law provides for management of the company by the shareholders, directors, officers and supervisors and provides default provisions concerning the duties and scope of authority for each.[4] However, with respect to many important provisions related to management of the company, the New Company Law specifically provides that the shareholders are free in the articles of association to adopt specific provisions to meet the needs of the company.[5] There are virtually no provisions related to management that cannot be altered or expanded in a manner determined by the shareholders in the articles of association.

The New Company Law also encourages shareholders to include provisions in the articles of association related to the financial management of the company. For example, the Old Company Law required profits earned by the company to be distributed among shareholders strictly in accordance with the shareholders' ownership interest in the company.[6] Under the New Company Law, shareholders are entitled in the articles of association to provide for distribution of profits in any manner agreed to by the shareholders, even if that distribution differs from the ownership percentage of the respective shareholders.[7] This provides significant flexibility in financing of limited liability companies that was entirely absent under the Old Company Law.

Under the former company law system, officers and directors often used their companies to secure financing of other businesses with which the officers and directors were involved. To restrict such behavior, the New Company Law provides that the shareholders may impose limitations on the authority of the directors and senior management. If officers or directors exceed the authority given them, their actions are void and the shareholders may file suit to compel compliance and for damages.[8]

B. Reduced and simplified minimum capital requirements

Chinese company law emphasizes registered capital requirements as a means to protect creditors. Since credit reporting is still primitive in China, the New Company Law emphasizes registered capital reporting and full capitalization of all new companies.[9] It simplifies and significantly reduces minimum capital requirements in an effort to make the corporate form available to more individual investors and to more investors from China's less developed regions. The Old Company Law imposed minimum capital requirements of 500,000 RMB for manufacturing and wholesale trade businesses, 300,000 RMB for sales businesses and 100,000 RMB for service businesses.[10] Though these limits did not significantly restrict state owned enterprises or individual investors in China's wealthier coastal regions, they imposed significant barriers for individual investors and for businesses in the less developed regions.

The New Company Law eliminates both the high minimum registered capital requirement and the system of capitalization based on the type of business. Under the new system, the minimum capital requirement for limited liability companies with two or more shareholders is reduced to 30,000 RMB.[11] For single shareholder limited liability companies, the minimum capital requirement is set at 100,000 RMB.[12] The minimum capital requirement is the same for all types of business activities. The intent of this change is to channel as much economic activity as possible into companies formed and registered under the New Company Law. The hope is that the protection of limited liability will encourage economic activity, particularly in currently underdeveloped regions of China.

C. Single shareholder limited liability companies

The New Company Law now allows natural persons or legal persons to form single shareholder limited liability companies.[13] Under the Old Company Law, a limited liability company was required to have two or more shareholders.[14] In contrast, the new statute provides for a simplified management structure appropriate to single shareholder entities. However, in order to prevent abuse of the corporate structure in single shareholder companies, the New Company Law provides for a number of restrictions:

- the registered capital requirement is increased to 100,000 RMB,[15]
- the entire registered capital amount must be paid in a single installment,[16]
- a single investor may form only one single shareholder company,[17] and
- if the shareholder fails to maintain adequate distance between the finances of the company and the shareholder's personal finances, the shareholder will lose the protection of limited liability and will have joint financial liability for company debts.[18]

These single shareholder provisions illustrate the manner in which the New Company Law attempts to balance the benefits of limited liability status to potential investors while still providing protection to creditors.

D. Public and shareholder access to company information

The Old Company Law was silent regarding public access to information about companies, and in practice, access was extremely limited. Without the assistance of an attorney or other legal professional, it was generally not possible to access a company's basic registration information.

The New Company Law takes an entirely different and much more public approach. The New Company Law provides that the public has the right to access basic company registration information and further provides that the registration authority must provide consulting assistance in accessing that information.[19] The public will now have access to the following information on limited liability companies:

- name
- registered address
- legal representative
- registered capital
- business classification
- scope of business
- termination date
- identity of shareholders[20]

Under the Chinese system, all of this information is considered essential for creditor protection. The New Company Law takes the reasonable position that creditor protection requires this basic information to be freely available to the public. Since the identity of shareholders is freely available, it is now impossible to use a Chinese limited liability company to conceal the identity of the true party in interest.

The New Company law also significantly expands shareholder access to company information. Under the former system, shareholders had no practical way to obtain information about company operations. This allowed the directors and officers to operate the company for their own benefit and without any effective supervision by the shareholders. Under the new law, the company must maintain the following basic records and make those records available to the shareholder at the shareholder's request:

- articles of association[21]
- minutes of meetings of the board of directors
- minutes of meetings of the board of supervisors
- tax returns and financial reports[22]

The statute also provides for shareholder access to the company's full financial records. In this case, though, the company has the right to deny access if it believes such access will damage it.[23] This could occur, for example, where a shareholder is also a competitor of the company. If the company willfully withholds information from the shareholder, the shareholder may file suit to force the company to release information.

E. Abuse of shareholder rights and piercing the corporate veil

The New Company Law introduces the new concept of the abuse of shareholder rights.[24] This concept is intended to protect both the company and third party creditors. The new law provides that shareholders must exercise their rights in accordance with the law, the regulations, and the company articles of association. The shareholder must not abuse the independent legal person status of the company or his own limited liability rights in a manner that harms the interests of the company or its other shareholders or creditors.

Where such abuse damages the company or other shareholders, the offending shareholder is liable for such loss. Where such abuse is used by the shareholder to escape liability for his own debts in a manner that seriously damages the interests of a creditor of the company, the shareholder is jointly liable for such debts. A similar provision is contained in the single shareholder company section. It provides that the shareholder of a single shareholder company who cannot prove that the finances of the company are independent of his or her own finances will have joint liability for the debts of the company.[25] This "piercing the corporate veil" concept is entirely new to China and though it may be useful to prevent obvious abuses, it could also be used to undermine the concept of limitation of liability, which is the foundation of the corporation law concept.

F. Limitations on third party loans and guarantees

Unrestricted debt guarantees to unrelated companies were a major problem under the former company law system. Large companies that appear to be financially solvent are often actually insolvent because they used their profits to acquire unrelated companies or to guarantee the debts of companies related only through the private financial interests of directors, officers, or controlling shareholders. To the detriment of legitimate creditors, the extent of such loans, guarantees, and other security arrangements are oftentimes not exposed until bankruptcy or insolvency proceedings are commenced.

Articles 15 and 16 of the New Company Law seek to remedy this. Article 15 permits a company to invest in another company, but prohibits it from doing so in a manner such that it becomes jointly liable for the debts of the other company. Article 16 provides additional rules concerning the providing of investment or debt guarantees to third party companies:

- the investment or guarantee must be approved by either the board of directors or by the shareholders, as provided in the articles of association,
- where the articles of association limit the amount of investment or guarantee, such limit may not be exceeded, and
- the shareholders must approve a guarantee provided to a shareholder or to the person actually controlling the company. In such cases, the benefiting shareholder may not participate in the decision and approval must be by a majority of the remaining shareholders.[26]

Under this approach, the senior management of the company and individual directors have no authority to make investments or to provide guarantees. This is a significant departure from former practice. This is also an example of the new approach to the articles of association, where shareholders are encouraged to limit potential abuses by specifically limiting the authority of directors and officers.

G. Legal remedies for improper acts of directors and senior management

As noted above, a major problem affecting companies in China has been that individual directors and senior management operate the company to benefit themselves while disregarding shareholders' interests. The New Company Law seeks to address this matter directly. First, Article 149 expressly prohibits directors and senior management from engaging in the following acts:

> "(1) Misappropriating company funds; (2) Depositing company funds into an individual account; (3) Loaning company funds or providing a company guaranty without shareholder approval; (4) Signing a contract or trading with another company in violation of the articles of association, unless the shareholders expressly consent; (5) Without shareholder consent, seeking business opportunities for oneself or for any other person by taking advantage of one's authority, or operating for oneself or for any other person any business similar to that of the company for which one works, without shareholder consent; (6) Taking commissions on a company transaction; (7) Disclosing company secrets without permission; (8) Other acts inconsistent with the obligation of fidelity to the company."[27]

This detailed list of prohibitions is a good summary of the kinds of problems that occurred under the old system.

The Old Company Law did not provide any clear method for shareholders to protect their rights when directors and managers behaved improperly. It was silent on the power of the shareholders to take action in the court system if such activities occurred. As a result, some courts refused to hear shareholder complaints on the ground that the Old Company Law did not authorize them to interfere in a company's internal affairs.

The New Company Law provides a clear set of procedures for shareholder action and specific authority to appeal to the courts to resolve such matters. Article 152 provides that when a director or senior manager violates the provisions of Article 149, noted above, the shareholder(s) holding one percent or more of the total shares of the company may require the company to file suit in the people's court. If the company refuses to file suit, the shareholder may file suit on behalf of the company. In addition, if the interests of the shareholders are directly affected, then the shareholders may file suit on their own behalf. Article 153 further provides that if any director or senior manager damages a shareholder's interest by violating any law, administrative regulation, or the company's articles of association, the affected shareholders may file suit for compensation.

Under the New Company Law, the court system is intended to be the final authority for protection of shareholder rights and for ensuring that companies comply both with government regulations and with the provisions of their articles of association. These provisions in the New Company Law further underline the importance of the articles of association in governing the company and in protecting shareholder rights.

III. The New Company Law's impact on foreign investors

Direct foreign investment in China may be carried out in three forms: a wholly foreign owned entity,[28] an equity joint venture,[29] or a contractual joint venture.[30] These forms of foreign invested enterprise are organized in China as limited liability companies. The statutes and associated regulations provide for specific and unique provisions concerning each of these three forms of foreign investment in China. Where the unique provisions do not apply, the provisions of the New Company Law will control.[31] The foreign invested enterprise statutes and regulations are concerned with approvals and investment percentages, but not with day to day management issues. Accordingly, the fundamental changes introduced by the New Company Law will significantly impact both existing and future foreign invested enterprises in China.

The three foreign invested enterprises laws provide for special treatment of investors in a limited liability company based on the status of the investor. In this case, the status is foreign nationality. Similar status-based distinctions formerly existed for domestic enterprises. For example, wholly state owned enterprises and town and village enterprises were governed by their own unique statutes and regulations. A primary goal of the New Company Law is to eliminate such status-based distinctions for domestic enterprises. As a result, all Chinese companies are in principle formed under the provisions of the Company Law, regardless of the status of the investor.

This change in principle is not the case for foreign investment, primarily because China still provides significant tax benefits and other incentives to foreign invested enterprises. It is essential to be able to characterize a limited liability company as a foreign invested enterprise to maintain these special benefits.

For example, an extremely favorable tax regime provides foreign invested companies with benefits not available to domestic enterprises.[32] This foreign invested enterprises tax regime provides for numerous tax reductions, including the following:

- a reduced fifteen percent tax rate instead of the normal thirty-three percent rate
- exemption from all income tax for certain periods
- rebates of taxes paid upon reinvestment of profits
- exemption from import duty on imports of equipment[33]

In addition, local authorities are authorized to provide additional tax and related incentives to foreign invested enterprises.

This special regime for foreign investors has survived adoption of the New Company Law. These tax and related benefits give foreign invested enterprises a significant business advantage over purely domestic Chinese competitors in the Chinese market, which makes investment in China more attractive for foreign investors.

IV. Conclusion

The New Company Law intends to make a revolutionary change in the practice of formation and management of corporations in China. However, a mere change in the law is not sufficient to bring about such change. The change will come only if the principles and procedures embodied in the new law are actually adopted and used by entrepreneurs, attorneys and the courts. There is much that suggests that the process of change will be slow and difficult.

Some elements of the New Company Law will have an immediate impact. These are elements that can be applied automatically by local government officials and that do not require the participation of legal professionals or the courts. There are three such provisions that should have such immediate impact: the reduction in the amount of registered capital,[34] the provision allowing single shareholder limited liability companies,[35] and the provisions that allow for a simplified management structure for limited liability companies with a limited number of shareholders.[36]

It is realistic to presume that these provisions will be implemented within the existing Chinese system. Each of these provisions can be implemented without the commitment of resources and in a way that is entirely automatic. For the reduction in registered capital and single shareholder companies, this is obvious. The changes are uniform and are applicable throughout the system without the need for local officials to make discretionary evaluations. Management structure is similar. Local authorities can devise a check box form that allows the party forming the company to choose one of two options: either a full board or a single director. Once the choice is made, the local authorities can then proceed in a rigid and formalized manner that does not require discretion or judgment.

The other, more dramatic changes introduced by the New Company Law will encounter implementation problems. As with most Chinese laws, the New Company Law was drafted by a group of sophisticated legal professionals at the top levels of government but with little input from the public or lower levels of the bureaucratic structure.[37] These changes require demand from the public, legal professionals for implementation, government officials for registration, and a court system for enforcement. Given the weak judiciary system and a bureaucracy unaccustomed to handling complex corporate law questions, the New Company Law likely will have little impact on closely held limited liability companies in China. Absent public or institutional demand for such sweeping legislation, the only way the legislation may have any impact is through a combination of massive, government-imposed education and vigorous government enforcement. Since neither of these may happen in China, the New Company law likely will fail to have the significant impact the drafters hoped for.

Notes

1 Company Law of the People's Republic of China (promulgated by the Standing Comm. Nat'l People's Cong, Oct. 27, 2005, effective Jan. 1, 2006) LAWINFOCHINA (last visited Nov. 5, 2006) (P.R.C.) [hereinafter New Company Law],

2 Company Law of the People's Republic of China (promulgated by the Standing Comm. Nat'l People's Cong., Dec, 29, 1993, amended Dec. 25, 1999 and August 28, 2004), *translated at* www.lawinfochina.com/dispecontent.asp?db=l&id=3656 (last visited Nov. 5, 2006) (P.R.C.) [hereinafter Old Company Law],

3 See the discussion on foreign invested companies, *infra* Section III.

4 *See* New Company Law art. 37–57 (giving the provisions for management of limited liability companies).

5 *See, e.g., id.* art. 42–47, 49–51, 54, 56.

6 Old Company Law art. 33.

7 New Company Law art. 35.

8 *See id.* art. 38,46, 50.

9 See generally *id.* art. 26–32.

10 Old Company Law art. 23.

11 New Company Law art. 26.

12 *Id.* art. 59.

13 *Id.* art. 58–64.

14 Old Company Law art. *20.*

15 New Company Law art. 59.

16 *Id.*

17 *Id.*

18 *Id.* art. 64,

19 *Id.* art. 6, 7.

20 *Id.* art. 7, 25.

21 *Id.* art. 23(3).

22 *Id.* art. 165, 166.

23 *Id.* art. 34, para. 2.

24 *Id.* art. 20.

25 *Id.* art. 64.

26 *Id.* art. 16.

27 *Id.* art. 149.

28 *See generally* Law of the People's Republic of China on Enterprises Operated Exclusively with Foreign Capital (promulgated by the Standing Comm. Nat'l People's Cong., Apr. 12, 1986, effective Oct. 31, 2000) LAWINFOCHINA (last visited Nov. 7, 2006) (P.R.C.).

29 *See generally* Law of the People's Republic of China on Chinese-Foreign Equity Joint Ventures (promulgated by the Nat'l People's Cong., Mar. 15, 2001, effective Mar, 15, 2001) LAWINFOCHINA (last visited Nov. 7, 2006) (P.R.C.).

30 *See generally* Law of the People's Republic of China on Chinese-Foreign Contractual Joint Ventures (promulgated by the Nat'l People's Cong., Oct. 31, 2000, amended Oct. 31, 2000) LAWINFOCHINA (last visited Nov. 7, 2006) (P.R.C.).

31 New Company Law art. 218.

32 *See generally* Income Tax Law of the People's Republic of China for Enterprises With Foreign Investment and Foreign Enterprises (promulgated by the Nat'l People's Cong., Apr. 9, 1991, effective July 1, 1991) LAW INFO CHINA (last visited Nov. 7, 2006) (P.R.C.).

33 *Id.* art. 7, 8, 10.
34 New Company Law, art. 26, 59.
35 *Id.* art. 58–64.
36 *Id.* art. 61, 62.
37 The transparency of the legislative process in China has been studied and criticized by many legal scholars. For a brief treatment of this issue and the Chinese law-making system generally, *see generally*, Congressional-Executive Commission on China, *Legislative Transparency of China's NPC*, www.cecc.gov/pages/virtualAcad/gov/legistransp.php.

7

CHINA'S FINANCIAL SYSTEM AND THE LAW*

Franklin Allen and Jun "QJ" Qian

Source: Cornell International Law Journal, 47, 3, 2014, pp. 499–553.

Law plays a different role in China's financial system than in most developed economies. China's financial system is dominated by a large banking sector. The role of the stock market in allocating resources in the economy has been limited and ineffective. The most successful part of the financial system, in terms of supporting the growth of the overall economy, is a shadow banking sector that consists of alternative financing channels, governance mechanisms, and institutions. These by and large do not rely on the law but on other enforcement mechanisms. The co-existence of this sector with banks and markets can continue to support the growth of the Hybrid Sector (non-state, non-listed firms).

Introduction

In most financial systems, the law plays a crucial role. Finance is a process by which lenders provide money to borrowers now in exchange for payments in the future. The law usually provides a way of making such promises credible. Allen, Qian and Qian (AQQ) point out that China operates differently.[1] During the last thirty-five years or so, China has been one of the most successful economies in terms of growth.[2] In 2014, the IMF predicts that it will overtake the U.S. and become the largest economy in the world in terms of Purchasing Power Parity.[3] China has achieved this despite formal financial institutions, poorly functioning markets, and an ineffective legal system underpinning their operation.

In this paper, we provide a comprehensive review of China's financial system and the legal system associated with it.[4] Almost every functioning financial system includes financial markets and intermediaries (e.g. a banking sector), but how these two standard financial sectors contribute to the entire financial system and economy differs significantly across different countries.[5] In this regard, we discuss what has worked and what has not within the two sectors in China and consider the effects of further development on the entire economy. We also examine a shadow financial sector, which operates outside the markets and banking sectors and consists of alternative financing channels, governance mechanisms, and institutions.

We draw three main conclusions about China's financial system and its future development. First, China's financial system has been dominated by a large banking system. This is clear when China's banking system and financial markets is compared with those of both developed and emerging countries.[6] Even with the entrance and growth of many domestic and foreign banks and financial institutions in recent years, China's banking system is still mainly controlled by the four largest state-owned banks.[7] All of these "Big Four" banks have become publicly listed and traded companies in recent years; the government is the largest shareholder and retains control of these institutions.[8] This ownership structure has served these banks well by avoiding the problems encountered by the major financial institutions in developed countries that were at the center of the 2007–2009 global financial crisis.[9] Continuous improvement of the banking system, including further development of financial institutions outside the Big Four banks and extension of more credit to productive firms and projects, can help stabilize China's financial system in the short run and can be especially timely given the uncertainties in the Chinese and global economies.[10]

Our second conclusion concerns China's financial markets. Two domestic stock exchanges, the Shanghai Stock Exchange (SHSE) and Shenzhen Stock Exchange (SZSE) were established in 1990.[11] The scale and importance of the stock exchanges are insignificant compared to the banking sectors; the stock exchanges have not been effective in allocating resources in the economy, because these stock exchanges remain speculative and driven by insider trading.[12] In recent years, the stock market has witnessed significant development.[13] As such, financial markets are likely to play an increasingly significant role in the economy.[14] We discuss several issues and potential problems related to increasing the size and scope and improving the efficiency of the stock and other financial markets.

Third, we find that the most successful part of the financial system, in terms of supporting the economy's overall growth, is neither the banking sector nor the financial markets. Rather it is a sector of alternative financing channels, such as informal financial intermediaries; internal financing and trade credits; and coalitions among firms, investors, and local governments.[15] This alternative system is often referred to as the shadow banking system.[16] Many of these financing channels do not rely on the law for enforcement but depend on other enforcement mechanisms, such as competition in product and input markets, as well as trust, reputation, and relationships.[17] This alternative financial sector, together with the banking system and the financial markets, has supported the growth of a "Hybrid Sector" with various types of ownership structures.[18] Our definition of the Hybrid Sector includes all non-state, non-listed firms, including privately or individually owned firms, and firms that are partially owned by *local* governments (e.g. Township Village Enterprises or TVEs).[19] The growth of the Hybrid Sector has been much higher than that of the State Sector (state-owned enterprises or SOEs, and all firms where the central government has ultimate control) and the Listed Sector (publicly listed and traded firms, with most of them having been converted from the State Sector).[20] The Hybrid Sector contributes to most of China's economic growth, and it employs the majority of the labor force.[21] The co-existence of the alternative financial sector with banks and markets can continue to fuel the growth of the Hybrid Sector.[22]

This paper draws heavily on our previous work including "Law, Finance, and Economic Growth in China" by Franklin Allen, Jun Qian & Meijun Qian (AQQ (2005)), "China's Financial System: Past, Present, and Future," a chapter in China's Great Economic Transformation, also by Franklin Allen, Jun Qian, and Meijun Qian (AQQ (2008)); and "China's Financial System: Opportunities and Challenges," a chapter in Capitalizing China by Franklin Allen, Jun Qian, Chenying Zhang & Mengxin Zhao (AQZZ (2013)). The remaining sections are organized as follows. In Section I, we briefly review the history of China's financial system, present aggregate evidence on China's financial system, and compare China's financial system to those of developed and other developing countries. In Section II, we examine China's banking system and how it has changed over time. In Section III, we briefly examine the growth and irregularities of financial markets, including the stock market, and listed firms. We also consider the effects of several initiatives to develop new markets and further develop existing markets, as well as changes in corporate governance among listed firms. In Section IV, we examine the shadow financial sector, including alternative financial channels and governance mechanisms. Motivated by the success of this financial sector and firms in the Hybrid Sector, we also compare the advantages and disadvantages of using the law as the basis of finance and commerce. When converting RMB into US dollar, we use the exchange rate of US$1 = RMB 8.28 *(yuan)* for transactions and events occurring before 2005, and we use the spot rate at the end of each year for activities that occur during and after 2005.

I. Overview of China's financial system

A. A brief review of the history of China's financial system

China's financial system was well developed before 1949.[23] One key finding in reviewing the history of this period, including the rise of Shanghai as one of the financial centers of Asia during the first half of the 20th Century, is that the development of China's commerce and financial system as a whole was largely *outside* of the formal legal system.[24] For example, despite the introduction of Western-style courts in Shanghai and other major coastal cities in the early 1900s, most business-related disputes were resolved through mechanisms outside of the courts, including guilds (merchant coalitions), families and local notables.[25] In Section IV.C below, we argue that modern equivalents of these non-legal dispute-resolution and corporate governance mechanisms are behind the success of Hybrid Sector firms in the same areas in the 1980s and 1990s. These alternative mechanisms may be more responsive in adapting to changes in a fast-growing economy like China than the law and legal institutions.

After the founding of the People's Republic of China in 1949, all of the pre-1949 capitalist companies and institutions were nationalized by 1950.[26] Between 1950 and 1978, China's financial system consisted of a single bank – the People's Bank of China (PBOC). This bank was owned and controlled by the central government under the Ministry of Finance. It served as both the central bank and a commercial bank, controlling about 93% of the total financial assets of the country and handling almost all financial transactions.[27] Functioning primarily to finance the physical production plans, the PBOC used both a "cash-plan" and a "credit-plan" to control the cash flows in consumer markets and transfer flows between branches.[28]

The first main structural change began in 1978 and ended in 1984.[29] By the end of 1979, the PBOC dissociated itself from the Ministry and became a separate entity, while three state-owned banks took over some of its commercial banking businesses. The Bank of China[30] (BOC) was given the mandate to specialize in transactions related to foreign trade and investment; the People's Construction Bank of China (PCBC), created in 1954, was set up to handle transactions related to fixed investment, especially in manufacturing; and the Agriculture Bank of China (ABC) was created in 1979 to manage all banking business in rural areas. The PBOC itself was formally established as China's central bank.[31] Finally, the fourth state-owned commercial bank, the Industrial and Commercial Bank of China (ICBC) was formed in 1984, and took over the rest of the commercial transactions of the PBOC.[32]

For most of the 1980s, the development of China's financial system can be characterized by the fast growth of financial intermediaries outside of the "Big Four" banks.[33] Regional banks (partially owned by local governments) were formed in the Special Economic Zones in the coastal areas; in rural areas, a network of Rural Credit Cooperatives (RCCs), which are similar to credit unions in the United States, was set up under the supervision of the ABC; and Urban Credit Cooperatives (UCCs), counterparts of the RCCs in the urban areas, were also founded.[34] Non-bank financial intermediaries, such as the Trust and Investment Corporations (TICs), which operated in selected banking and non-banking services with restrictions on both deposits and loans, emerged and proliferated in this period.[35]

The most significant event for China's financial system in the 1990s was the inception and growth of China's stock market.[36] Two domestic stock exchanges (SHSE and SZSE) were established in 1990 and grew quickly, with respect to the total market capitalization and trading volume, during most of the 1990s and in recent years.[37] The real estate market paralleled the stock market, growing from nonexistent in the early 1990s to being a significant market in recent years. Both the stock and real estate markets have experienced major corrections during the past decade, and are characterized by high volatilities and speculative short-term behaviors by many investors.[38]

These patterns are due, in part, to the fact that the development of a supportive legal framework and institutions has been lagging behind that of the markets.[39] For example, China's first bankruptcy law governing SOEs was passed in 1986 on a trial basis, but the formal Company Law did not become effective until the end of 1999.[40] This version of the Company Law governs all corporations with limited liability, publicly listed and traded companies, and branches or divisions of foreign companies, as well as the organization structure, securities issuance and trading, accounting, bankruptcy, and mergers and acquisitions of those companies.[41] China enacted a new bankruptcy law in August 27, 2006, that became effective June 1, 2007.[42] We provide a brief analysis of the status and problems of the stock market and real estate market in Section V below.

Following the Asian Financial Crisis in 1997, financial sector reform focused on state-owned banks, especially the problem of NPLs.[43] We will further discuss this issue in Section II. China's entry into the WTO in December 2001 marked the beginning of a new era, as we continue to observe increasing competition from foreign financial institutions and more frequent and larger-scale capital flows.[44]

A developed financial system is characterized by, among other factors, the substantial role played by institutional investors.[45] In China, institutional investors began to emerge in the late 1990s: the first closed-ended fund, from which investors cannot withdraw capital after initial investment, was set up in 1997, and the first open-ended fund, from which investors can freely withdraw capital (subject to share redemption restrictions), was established in 2001.[46] By November 2013, there were 89 fund companies.[47] The total net assets value (NAV) increased from RMB 11 billion (or US $1.3 billion) in 1998 to RMB 2.58 trillion or $322 billion in May 2008, which was still small compared to the assets within the banking sector.[48] In 2003, a few Qualified Foreign Institutional Investors (QFII) entered China's asset management industry, where they have been operating through forming joint ventures with Chinese companies.[49] In 2011, China approved the RMB Qualified Foreign Institutional Investors (RQFII), which allows QFII to invest in Chinese stock and bond markets within a predetermined limit.[50] On the other hand, China allowed Qualified Domestic Institutional Investors (QDII) to invest in overseas markets beginning in July 2006.[51]

At the national level, the China Investment Corporation (CIC) was established in September 2007 with the intent of utilizing the accumulated foreign reserves for the benefit of the state, and part of the foreign reserves were placed under management at the establishment.[52] CIC makes occasional announcements about its investments, but the overall transparency of its investment strategy is low.[53] Since inception, CIC has made some aggressive investment decisions, including the well-publicized $3 billion (pre-IPO) investment in private equity group Blackstone, and the $5 billion investment in Morgan Stanley (this took the form of mandatory convertible bonds that can be converted into almost 10% of the firm's equity).[54]

Endowed with limited capital and given the problems with the administration of the pension system, pension funds have not played a significant role in the stock or

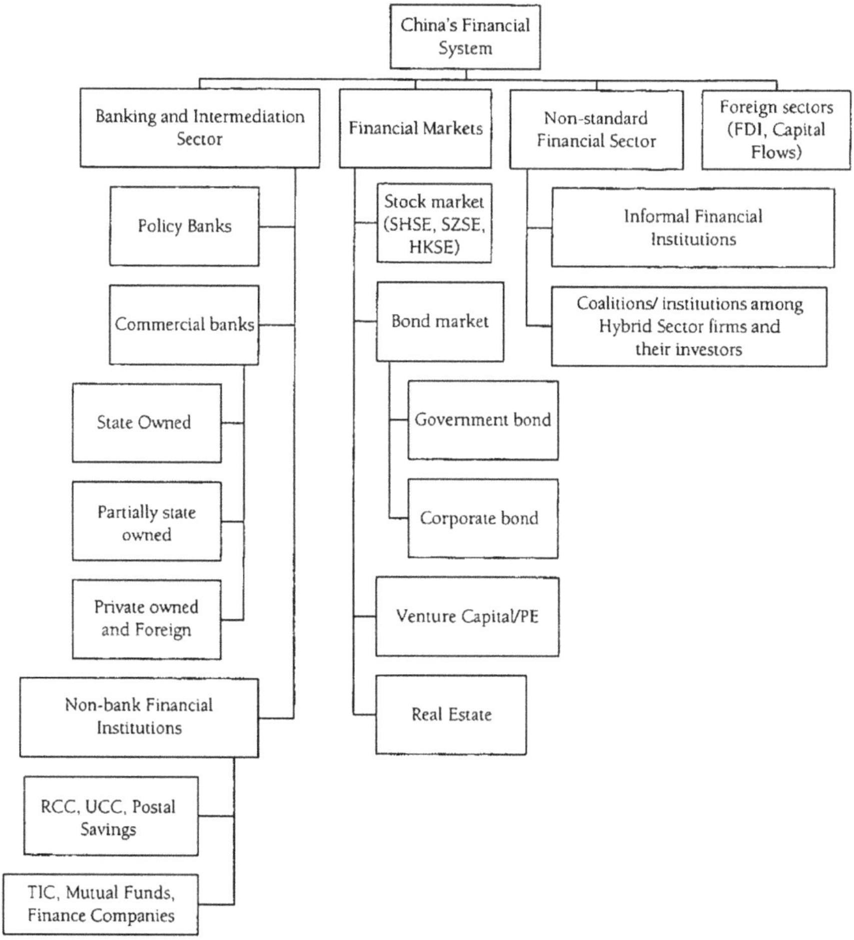

Figure 7.1 Overview of China's Financial System

bond markets.[55] With a fast aging population and the growth of household disposable incomes, further development of a multipillar pension system that includes individual accounts with employees' self-contributed and tax exempt funds that can be directly invested in the financial markets can lead to the development of both the financial system and the fiscal system, as well as the development of social stability.[56]

Figure 7.1 depicts the current structure of the entire financial system. In what follows, we will describe and examine each of the major sectors of the financial system. In addition to the standard sectors of banking and intermediation, and financial markets, we will document the importance of the shadow financial sector.[57]

B. Size and efficiency of the financial system: banks, markets, and alternative finance

In Table 7.1, we compare China's financial system to those of other major emerging economies, with measures for the size and efficiency of banks and markets taken from Levine (2002), Demirgüc-Kunt and Levine, and data from the World Bank's Global Financial Development Database (GFDD). We present average figures from 2001–2011 for each country as well as the average of all the other emerging economies (excluding China). We first compare the size of a country's banks and equity markets relative to that country's gross domestic product (GDP). In terms of total market capitalization, China's stock market, at 63% of its GDP over the period 2001–2011, is slightly larger than the 57% of GDP average of the other major emerging economies.[58] "Value traded" is perhaps a better measure of the actual size of the market than "market capitalization," because the latter includes non-tradable shares or tradable shares that are rarely traded.[59] However, the majority of the bank credit goes to state-owned firms in China and only a small fraction goes to firms in the Hybrid Sector (more evidence of this is given below).[60] In addition, NPLs account for a larger percentage of all the loans in China at 11% than the average percentage in other emerging economies at 8%, indicating that China's banking sector still has room to improve its efficiency.[61]

The next two columns of Table 7.1 (Structure Indices) compare the relative importance of financial markets versus banks, with a lower score indicating that banks are more important relative to markets. China's score for "Structure Size" (log of the ratio of Market Capitalization/Total Bank Credit) is negative, suggesting that the size of total market capitalization is actually smaller than that of bank credit, and the score is lower than the average of other emerging economies. Its score for "Structure Activity" (log of the ratio of Total Value Traded/Total Bank Credit) is negative, indicating that the trading volume of markets is still smaller than bank credit, and its Structure Activity is slightly larger than the average of other emerging economies. Taken together, these numbers suggest that the financial systems of most emerging economies, including that of China, remain bank-dominated.[62] In terms of "Structure Efficiency" (log of product (market capitalization/GDP) x (bank NPLs/bank total loans)), which denotes the relative efficiency of markets versus banks, China has a higher score than most other developing countries, suggesting that its banks are relatively less efficient than markets when compared to the efficiency of other countries.[63] "Structure Regulatory" is based on 2005 data and measures the extent to which commercial banks are restricted in participating in activities outside commercial lending. China's score of 16 is higher than most other countries, suggesting that by law commercial banks in China face tight restrictions in operating in other areas.[64]

We also compare the development of the financial system (Financial Development), including both banks and markets (the last three columns of Table 7.1). China's overall financial market size, in terms of both "Finance Activity" (Log of product of (Total Value Traded/GDP) x (Bank credit/GDP)) and "Finance Size"

Table 7.1 Comparing financial systems: Banks and Markets (average 2001–2011)

This table compares financial markets and banking sector of China with those of other large emerging economies. All the measures on the size and efficiency of banks and markets are based on Levine (2002) and Demirgüç-Kunt and Levine (2001), and data is from the World Bank's Global Financial Development Database (GFDD) which was published in April 2013. We present the 2001–2011 average figures for all countries (except for "Structure Regulatory," which are based on 2005 figures). Average of other emerging economies are (simple) averages across other emerging economies *excluding* China.

Measures	*Size of Banks and Markets*				*Structure Indices: Markets vs. banks**				*Financial Development*** (banking and market sectors)*		
	Bank credit/ GDP	*NPL/ Total Loans*	*Value traded /GDP*	*Market cap. /GDP*	*Structure Activity*	*Structure Size*	*Structure Efficiency*	*Structure Regulatory*	*Finance Activity*	*Finance Size*	*Finance Efficiency*
China	1.11	0.11	0.82	0.63	−0.13	−0.24	−1.17	16	−0.04	−0.15	0.88
Argentina	0.13	0.07	0.03	0.36	−0.68	0.44	−1.59	7	−2.44	−1.33	−0.42
Brazil	0.36	0.04	0.25	0.51	−0.16	0.16	−1.72	10	−1.06	−0.74	0.82
Egypt	0.45	0.18	0.20	0.50	−0.36	0.05	−1.04	13	−1.06	−0.65	0.03
India	0.38	0.05	0.60	0.62	0.20	0.21	−1.48	10	−0.65	−0.63	1.05
Indonesia	0.22	0.09	0.13	0.28	−0.22	0.11	−1.61	–	−1.54	−1.21	0.18
Malaysia	1.08	0.09	0.40	1.31	−0.43	0.09	−0.93	10	−0.36	0.15	0.65
Mexico	0.16	0.03	0.07	0.27	−0.33	0.24	−2.13	12	−1.95	−1.37	0.43
Pakistan	0.24	0.14	0.50	0.23	0.32	−0.02	−1.51	10	−0.93	−1.27	0.56
Peru	0.21	0.06	0.03	0.44	−0.86	0.33	−1.59	8	−2.24	−1.05	−0.31
Philippines	0.28	0.10	0.08	0.47	−0.51	0.23	−1.32	7	−1.63	−0.89	−0.08
Russian	0.28	0.05	0.31	0.54	0.05	0.28	−1.56	–	−1.06	−0.82	0.79
S. Africa	0.69	0.03	0.92	2.03	0.12	0.47	−1.19	8	−0.20	0.15	1.46
Sri Lanka	0.28	–	0.03	0.18	−0.95	−0.18	–	7	−2.07	−1.30	–

(*Continued*)

Table 7.1 (Continued)

Measures	*Size of Banks and Markets*				*Structure Indices: Markets vs. banks**				*Financial Development** (banking and market sectors)*		
	Bank credit/ GDP	*NPL/ Total Loans*	*Value traded /GDP*	*Market cap. /GDP*	*Structure Activity*	*Structure Size*	*Structure Efficiency*	*Structure Regulatory*	*Finance Activity*	*Finance Size*	*Finance Efficiency*
Thailand	0.96	0.09	0.49	0.59	−0.29	−0.21	−1.28	9	−0.33	−0.24	0.75
Turkey	0.24	0.08	0.39	0.26	0.20	0.04	−1.68	12	−1.03	−1.19	0.69
Ave. for Ems	0.40	0.08	0.29	0.57	−0.26	0.15	−1.47	9.46	−1.23	−0.83	0.47

Table 7.1 Notes: *: Structure indices measure whether a country's financial system is market- or bank-dominated; the higher the measure, the more the system is dominated by markets. Specifically, "structure activity" is equal to log (value traded/bank credit) and measures size of bank credit relative to trading volume of markets; "structure size" is equal to log (market cap/bank credit) and measures the size of markets relative to banks; "structure efficiency" is equal to log[(market cap ratio/GDP)×(bank NPLs/bank total loans)] and measures the relative efficiency of markets vs. banks; finally, "structure regulatory" is the sum of the four categories in regulatory restriction, or the degree to which commercial banks are allowed to engage in security, firm operation, insurance, and real estate: 1-unrestricted; 2-permit to conduct through subsidiary; 3-full range not permitted in subsidiaries; and 4-strictly prohibited.

**: Financial development variables measure the entire financial system (banking and market sectors combined), and the higher the measure, the larger or more efficient the financial system is. Specifically, "finance activity" is equal to log (total value traded ratio×private credit ratio), "finance size" is equal to log (market cap ratio×bank private credit ratio), and "finance efficiency" is equal to log (total value traded ratio/bank NPL ratio).

(Log of product of (Market capitalization/GDP) x (Bank credit/GDP)), is larger than the average market size of other emerging countries.[65] For "Finance Efficiency" (Log of (Total Value Traded/GDP)/Bank NPLs Ratio), China's measure is also higher than the average measure of other emerging countries.[66] Based on the evidence from the past decade, we can conclude that China's banks and markets, or at least the formal sectors of the financial system, are, relative to the size of China's economy, as large as or larger than those of other major emerging economies.[67] However, the banking sector does not lend much to the Hybrid Sector, which, as we will see in Section IV, is the dynamic part of the economy.

Related to the size of banks and markets is the question: where do most firms get their capital and funds? As shown in AQQ (2005) and AQQ (2008), the four most important financing sources for all firms in China, in terms of firms' *fixed asset investments*, are domestic bank loans, firms' self-fundraising, the state budget, and FDI, with self-fundraising and bank loans carrying most of the weight. Self-fundraising, falling into the category of alternative finance (non-bank, non-market finance), includes proceeds from capital raised from *local* governments (beyond the state budget), communities, and other investors; internal financing channels such as retained earnings; and all other funds raised domestically by the firms. It is important to point out that equity and bond issuance, which are included in self-fundraising (but fall into the category of formal external finance), apply only to the Listed Sector, and account for a small fraction of this category.[68]

While the Listed Sector has been growing rapidly, SOEs are on a downward trend, as privatization of these firms is still in progress.[69] Around 30% of the funding for publicly traded companies comes from bank loans, and this ratio has been very stable.[70] Around 45% of the Listed Sector's total funding comes from self-fundraising, including internal financing and proceeds from equity and bond issuance.[71] Moreover, equity and bond sales, which rely on the use of external markets, only constitute a small fraction of total funds raised in comparison to internal financing and other forms of fundraising.[72] Combined with the fact that self-fundraising is also the most important source of financing for the State Sector-around 45% to 65% of total funding – we can conclude that alternative channels of financing are important even for the State and Listed Sectors.[73]

Not surprisingly, self-fundraising plays an even more important role for firms in the Hybrid Sector, accounting for close to 60% of total funds raised, while individually owned companies – a subset of the Hybrid Sector – rely on self-fundraising for 90% of total financing.[74] Self-fundraising includes all forms of internal finance, capital raised from family and friends of the founders and managers, and funds raised in the form of private equity and loans.[75] Since firms in this sector operate in an environment with legal and financial mechanisms and regulations that are likely poorer than those available for firms in the State and Listed Sectors, financing sources here may work differently from how they work in the State and Listed Sectors, and may also work differently from self-fundraising conducted in developed countries.[76]

II. The banking and intermediation sector

In this section, we examine the status of China's banking and intermediation sector. After reviewing aggregate evidence on bank deposits and loans, we review evidence on the growth of non-state banks and financial intermediaries.

A. Aggregate evidence on bank deposits and loans

As in other Asian countries, China's household savings rates have been high throughout the reform era.[77] Given the growth of the economy, the sharp increase in personal income, and limited investment opportunities, it is not surprising that total bank deposits from individuals have been growing quickly since the mid-1980s.[78] From Figure 7.2-A, residents in metropolitan areas contribute the most to total deposits beginning in the late 1980s, while deposits from enterprises (including firms from all three sectors) provide the second largest source. The role of deposits

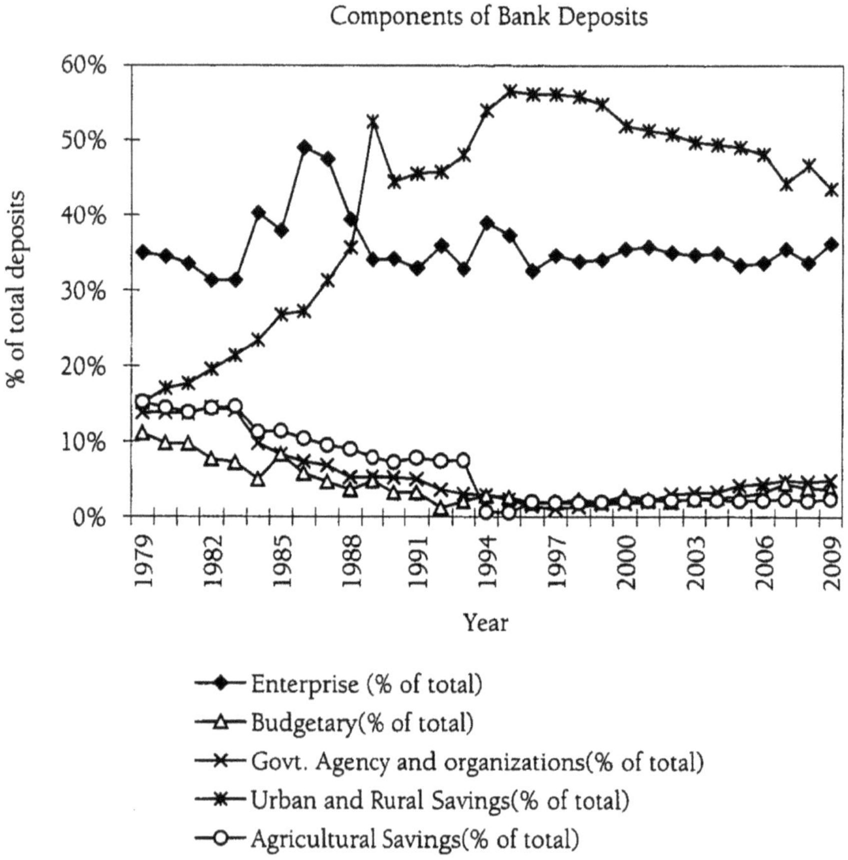

Figure 7.2-A Sources for Bank Deposits in China

from government agencies and organizations (including non-profit and for-profit organizations, not shown in the figure) has steadily decreased over time.[79]

Table 7.2-A compares total savings and bank deposits in China, Japan, South Korea, and India, during the period of 1997–2012. In terms of the ratio of Time and Savings Deposits/GDP, China maintains the highest or second highest level (an average of over 90% in recent years), while Japan leads the group in terms of total amount. Looking at the breakdown of bank deposits, interest-bearing "savings deposits" are by far the most important form of deposits in China, providing a good source for bank loans and other forms of investment. Figure 7.2-B compares total (non-state) bank credit (over GDP) extended to Hybrid Sector firms in China and privately owned firms (including those publicly listed and traded) in Taiwan and South Korea. For South Korea, we also plot the bank credit ratios during its high economic growth period of the 1970s and 1980s (each year appearing on the horizontal axis indicates the time period for China, while a particular year *minus* 20 indicates the time period for South Korea). We can see that the scale and growth of China's 'hybrid' bank credit during 1991–2009 are far below those of the private bank credit of Taiwan and South Korea in the same period, but are similar to those of South Korea twenty years ago.

Table 7.2-B breaks down China's bank loans by maturities, loan purposes, and borrower types during the period of 1994–2012.[80] While there has been a shift from short-term to long-term loans (first two columns), the majority of loans goes to SOEs in manufacturing industries (Industrial Loans and Commercial

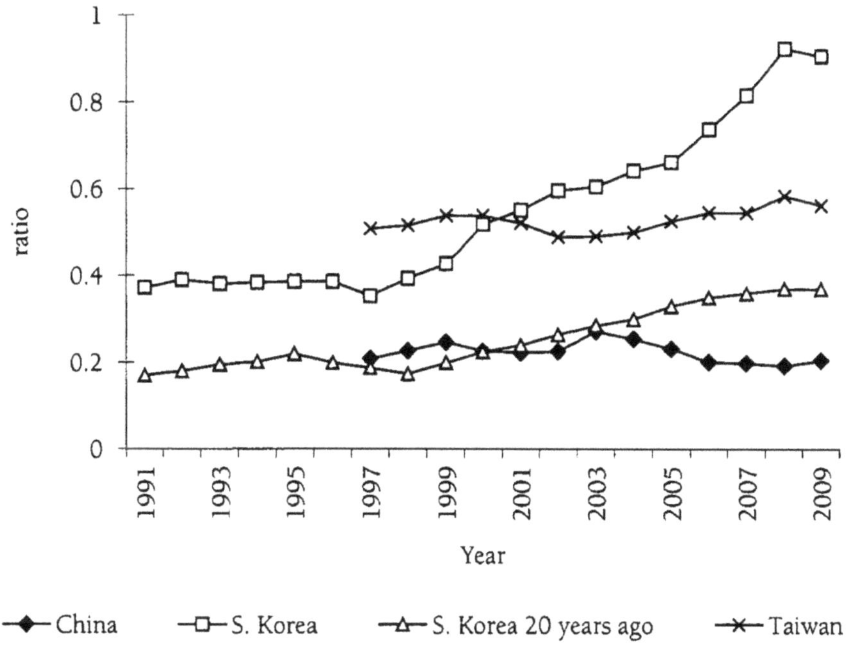

Figure 7.2-B Comparing Total Bank Credit extended to private/hybrid sectors

Table 7.2-A Comparisons of Total Savings and Deposits (in US$ billions)

	1998	*1999*	*2000*	*2001*	*2002*	*2003*	*2004*	*2005*	*2006*	*2007*	*2008*	*2009*	*2010*	*2011*	*2012*
China															
Demand deposits[“]	320	391	465	533	647	777	899	1030	1265	1671	1931	2683	3337	3778	4038
Savings deposits[6]	606	674	722	820	961	1143	1445	1748	2069	2363	3187	3811	4556	5575	6540
Time deposits[0]	100	114	136	171	199	253	307	410	676	878	1205	1661	2153	2633	3115
Time & Savings Dep/GDP	68%	73%	72%	75%	80%	85%	91%	95%	101%	92%	100%	114%	111%	110%	117%
Japan															
Demand deposits[“]	1793	2259	2073	1838	2567	3523	3795	3541	3523	3683	4560	–	–	–	–
Time, savings & foreign currency deposits	7921	8997	8059	5351	5383	5416	5448	4642	4536	4778	6160	–	–	–	–
Time & Savings Dep/GDP	181%	185%	184%	142%	131%	118%	114%	109%	106%	106%	110%	–	–	–	–
South Korea															
Demand deposits[”]	18	22	23	27	36	38	46	54	67	66	50	63	68	71	80
Time, savings & foreign currency deposits	185	251	289	315	383	410	467	485	546	543	471	574	681	731	825
Time & Savings Dep/GDP	46%	54%	61%	64%	63%	64%	58%	57%	56%	52%	58%	63%	66%	68%	69%
India															
Demand deposits[“]	24	28	31	32	35	44	60	71	89	114	96	119	145	122	118
Time, savings & foreign currency deposits	140	161	175	198	235	277	333	368	460	647	653	800	983	987	1079
Time & Savings Dep/GDP	34%	36%	39%	42%	45%	45%	45%	45%	47%	51%	56%	58%	57%	59%	59%

Source: IMF and CEIC database

Notes: “: Demand deposits, balance of the accounts can be withdrawn on demand of customers (e.g., check-writing); [b]: Savings deposits, interest-bearing accounts that can be withdraw but cannot be used as Money (e.g., no checking writing); [c]: Time deposits, savings accounts or CD with a fixed term.

Table 7.2-B Breakdown of Bank Loans (end-of-year figures in RMB billions)

Year	*Total Loans*	*Short-term Loans*	*Industrial Loans*	*Commercial Loans*	*Infrastructure Construction Loans*	*Agricultural Loans*	*Loans to TVEs*	*Privately Owned Firms*	*Joint Ventures & Cooperative Firms*
1994	3,997.60	2,694.87	994.83	1,050.98	61.72	114.39	200.24	15.59	79.23
1995	5,054.41	3,337.20	1,177.47	1,283.71	79.93	154.48	251.49	19.62	99.91
1996	6,115.66	4,021.00	1,421.33	1,533.26	97.38	191.91	282.19	27.98	134.63
1997	7,491.41	5,541.83	1,652.66	1,835.66	159.11	331.46	503.58	38.67	189.10
1998	8,652.41	6,061.32	1,782.15	1,975.24	162.87	444.42	558.00	47.16	248.75
1999	9,373.43	6,388.76	1,794.89	1,989.09	147.69	479.24	616.13	57.91	298.58
2000	9,937.11	6,574.81	1,701.93	1,786.85	161.71	488.90	606.08	65.46	304.98
2001	11,231.47	6,732.72	1,863.67	1,856.34	209.96	571.15	641.30	91.80	326.35
2002	13,129.39	7,424.79	2,019.05	1,797.31	274.80	688.46	681.23	105.88	269.74
2003	15,899.62	8,366.12	2,275.60	1,799.44	300.21	841.14	766.16	146.16	256.94
2004	17,819.78	8,684.06	2,389.66	1,707.41	278.01	984.31	806.92	208.16	219.84
2005	19,469.04	8,744.92	2,251.67	1,644.76	298.37	1,152.99	790.18	218.08	197.53
2006	22,534.72	9,853.44	2,865.4	1,667.15	361.26	1,320.82	622.20	266.76	183.27
2007	26,169.09	11,447.79	3,362.33	1,783.33	374.19	1,542.93	711.26	350.77	206.91
2008	30,339.46	12,518.17	3,614.29	1,773.22	368.46	1,762.88	745.4	422.38	227.08
2009	39,968.48	14,661.13	3,876.92	1,948.33	364.68	2,162.25	902.9	712.10	218.03
2010	47,919.56	16,623.34	–	–	–	–	–	–	–
2011	54,794.67	20,313.26	–	–	–	–	–	–	–
2012	62,990.96	24,827.28	–	–	–	–	–	–	–

Source: Statistical Yearbooks of China, CEIC database (1985–2012)

Loans).[81] Most of the "Infrastructure/Construction Loans" (a small component of total loans) fund government sponsored projects, while the size of "Agricultural Loans" is much smaller.[82] More importantly, the size of loans made to TVEs, privately- and collectively-owned firms, and joint ventures (last three columns), all of which belong to the Hybrid Sector, is also much smaller.[83]

B. Growth of non-state financial intermediaries

The development of both non-state banks and other (state and non-state) financial institutions will allow China to have a stable and functioning banking system in the future.[84] In addition to boosting the overall efficiency of the banking system, these financial institutions provide funding to support the growth of the Hybrid Sector.[85]

Recent development of shadow banking

Due to the strong demand of capital by the real economy, shadow banking – which includes trust loans, entrusted loans, loans by small-scale lending companies, corporate bonds, and informal finances, etc. – has been growing rapidly since 2009.[86] We will leave the development of corporate bonds for Part IV and informal financing for Part V. In this part we will elaborate on trends of trust loans, entrusted loans and loans by small-scale lending companies. The growth of banks' wealth management products also reflects the development of the shadow banking system.[87] However, here we do not include wealth management products into shadow banking as this would involve double counting.

Due to the limited loan quota of the banking system and the strong demand of capital by the real economy, financing through shadow banking has been growing rapidly since 2009.[88] First, we examine the entrusted loans, trust loans and corporate bonds, all of which are included in the total social financing. The term Total Social Financing (TSF), first introduced by the governor of the PBOC, Xiaolian Hu, in her speech on December 24, 2010, is a liquidity measure which covers loans in local currency, loans in foreign currency, entrusted loans, trusted loans, bank acceptance bills, net corporate bond financing, and non-financial enterprise equity financing.[89] The PBOC elaborated on the statistics' details and the meanings of this term in *China's Monetary Policy Report Quarter Four of 2010* in January 2011,[90] and it started to publish monthly data for this indicator. Since then, this indicator has been seen as one of the most important monetary indicators in China, because traditional monetary indicators such as M2 fail to take all of the social financing sources into account.[91] Table 7.3-A describes the breakdown of China's total social financing from 2002 to 2012. During that period, trust loans, entrusted loans, and net corporate bond financing ranked in the top three sources for social financing in terms of average annual growth, with the rate of 58.0%, 53.7%, and 51.0%, respectively.[92] The average annual growth rate of total social financing from 2002 to 2012 is 22.9%, much higher than the growth rate of M2 (18.3%) and that of the outstanding bank loans (17.0%) within the same period, indicating that the other sources of financing have been growing dramatically in the recent years.[93] By 2012, loans in both local and foreign currency accounted for 57.9% of total social financing.[94] Entrusted loans, trust loans, and net corporate bond financing accounted for only 8.1%, 8.1% and 14.3%, respectively, but are on an upward trend.[95] Besides these three sources, loans by small-scale companies also have been growing rapidly since 2010.[96] By September 2013, the amount of outstanding loans by small-scale lending companies was RMB 753.5 billion.[97] The total number of small-scale lending companies grew from about 2,500 in December 2010 to 7,398 in September 2013.[98]

The high growth of credit through shadow banking is driven by the following factors. First, the bank loan quota is still restricted by the regulatory requirements.[99] Thus, the funding demand is much higher than the supply of bank loans.[100] In this situation, shadow banking has been growing rapidly to meet the demand of funds by the real economy.[101] Second, due to the restrictions on real estate loans, the funding demand in real estate and for local government financing platforms cannot be satisfied.[102] In this case, those real estate enterprises can only get funds through trust loans or other sources.[103] Third, the growth rate of bank deposits was much lower than that of bank loans for a long period starting from 1979, except the years of 1984 to 1986, 1988, and 1997.[104] Since 2009, the opposite situation has started to take place.[105] This is partly due to the restricted deposit interest rate and the relatively higher required return of financial assets by Chinese households, and also partly due to the drop of trade surplus and capital inflows after 2009.[106] In order to meet the requirement of the ratio of loan to deposit (LTD) set by the CBRC, banks have to raise funds by issuing wealth management products.[107]

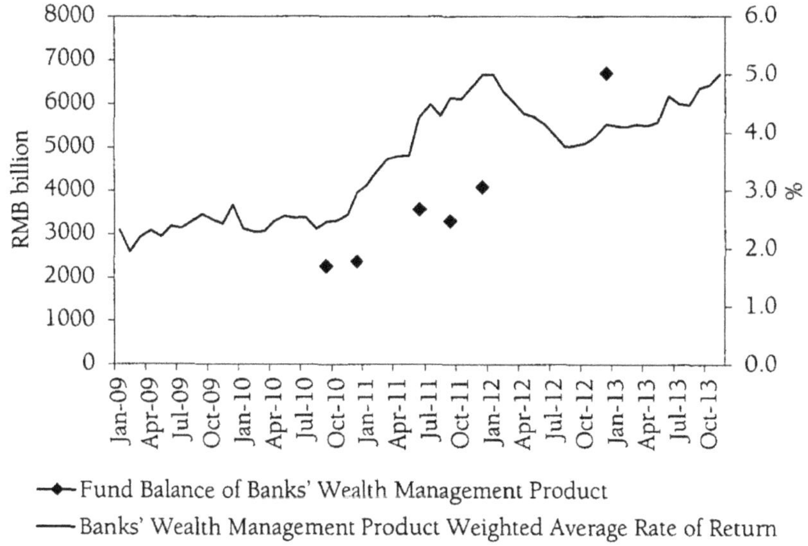

Figure 7.2-C Recent Growth of Banks' Wealth Management Products (2009–2013)

Table 7.3-A Breakdown of Total Social Financing in China (RMB billion)

Year	*Total amount of Social Financing*	*Loan in Local Currency*	*Loan in Foreign Currency*	*Entrusted Loan*	*Trust Loan*	*Bank Acceptance Bill*	*Net Corporate Bond Financing*	*Non-financial Enterprise Equity Financing*
2002	2,011.2	1,847.5	73.1	17.5		(69.5)	36.7	62.8
2003	3,411.3	2,765.2	228.5	60.1		201.1	49.9	55.9
2004	2,862.9	2,267.3	138.1	311.8		(29.0)	46.7	67.3
2005	3,000.8	2,354.4	141.5	196.1		2.4	201.0	33.9
2006	4,269.6	3,152.3	145.9	269.5	82.5	150.0	231.0	153.6
2007	5,966.3	3,632.3	386.4	337.1	170.2	670.1	228.4	433.3
2008	6,980.2	4,904.1	194.7	426.2	314.4	106.4	552.3	332.4
2009	13,910.0	9,594.2	926.5	678.0	436.4	460.6	1,236.7	335.0
2010	14,019.0	7,945.1	485.5	874.8	386.5	2,334.6	1,106.3	578.6
2011	12,829.0	7,471.5	571.2	1,296.2	203.4	1,027.1	1,365.8	437.7
2012	15,763.0	8,203.8	916.3	1,283.8	1,284.5	1,049.9	2,255.1	250.8

Source: Aggregate Statistics from the People's Bank of China (China's Central Bank) and CEIC, 2002–2012.

Table 7.3 B State-owned and Private Banks in China (RMB billion)

Types of Banks	*Total Assets*	*Total Deposits*	*Outstanding Loans*	*Profit*[1]	*NPL rate (%)*
2012					
Big Five Banks	60,040.0	–	–	754.6	1.0
Other Commercial Banks	35,874.0		–		–
1) Joint Equity	23,527.0		–	136.8	0.7
2) City Commercial Banks	12,347.0	–	–	252.6	0.8
Foreign Banks	2380.4	1307.2	–	16.34	0.5
Urban Credit Cooperatives	–	3.3(-Sep.)	–	–	–
Rural Credit Cooperatives	7,953.5	5,974.0	–	65.4	–
2011					
Big Five Banks	53,634.0			664.7	1.1
Other Commercial Banks	28,363.5	–	–	–	–
1) Joint Equity	18,379.0	–	–	200.5	0.6
2) City Commercial Banks	9,984.5	–	–	108.1	0.8
Foreign Banks	2153.5	1220.2	934.63	16.7	0.4
Urban Credit Cooperatives	3.0	5.5	3.46	0.02	–
Rural Credit Cooperatives	7,204.7	5,570.3	3955.12	53.1	–
2010					
Big Five Banks	46,894.0	–	–	515.1	1.3
Other Commercial Banks	22,756.6	–	–	–	–
1) Joint Equity	14,904.0		–	135.8	0.7
2) City Commercial Banks	7,852.6	–	–	77.0	0.9
Foreign Banks	1742.3	967.7	818.54	11.9	0.5
Urban Credit Cooperatives	2.2	9.7	6.78	0.01	–
Rural Credit Cooperatives	6,391.1	5,050.0	3601.63	23.3	–
2009					
Big Five Banks	40,089.0	29,506.5	20,151.7	400.1	1.8
Other Commercial Banks	17,465.0	15,041.5	9,606.6	–	–
1) Joint Equity	11,785.0	10,548.7	6,707.4	92.5	1.0
2) City Commercial Banks	5,680.0	4,492.8	2,899.2	49.7	1.3
Foreign Banks	1,349.2	668.8	727.1	6.5	0.9
Urban Credit Cooperatives	27.2	39.5	–	0.2	–
Rural Credit Cooperatives	5,492.5	4,742.1	5,421.3	22.8	–
2008					
Big Five Banks	31,836.0	23,696.1	15,029.3	354.2	2.8
Other Commercial Banks	12,941.2	11,072.2	7,162.4	–	
1) Joint Equity	8,809.2	7,801.8	5,054.5	84.1	1.5
2) City Commercial Banks	4,132.0	3,270.4	2,107.9	40.8	2.3
Foreign Banks	1,344.8	533.5	762.1	11.9	0.8

(*Continued*)

Table 7.3-B (Continued)

Types of Banks	*Total Assets*	*Total Deposits*	*Outstanding Loans*	*Profit*[1]	*NPL rate (%)*
Urban Credit Cooperatives	80.4	76.2	–	0.62	–
Rural Credit Cooperatives	5,211.3	4,173.6	3,753.2	21.9	
2007					
Big Five Banks	28,007.0	20,067.7	13,850.9	246.6	8.05
Other Commercial Banks	10,589.9	9,023.3	5,684.4	–	–
1) Joint Equity	7,249.4	6,432.0	4,001.9	56.4	2.15
2) City Commercial Banks	3,340.5	2,591.4	1,682.6	24.8	3.04
Foreign Banks	1,252.5	390.0	700.0	6.1	0.46
Urban Credit Cooperatives	131.2	134.1	84.7	0.77	–
Rural Credit Cooperatives	4,343.4	3,534.9	3,256.1	19.3	–
2006					
Big Five Banks	24,236	18,285.1	11,426.2	197.5	9.22
Other Commercial Banks	8,038.4	7512.8	5526.6	–	–
1) Joint Equity	5,444.6	5,396.5	4,156.9	43.4	2.81
2) City Commercial Banks	2,593.8	2,116.2	1,369.7	18.1	4.78
Foreign Banks	927.9	244.0	485.9	5.8	0.78
Urban Credit Cooperatives	183.1	157.9	100.7	1.0	–
Rural Credit Cooperatives	3,450.3	3,040.2	2,747.6	18.6	–
2005					
Big Five Banks[2]	21,005.0	16,283.8	10,224.0	156.1	10.49
Other Commercial Banks	6,502.2	6,261.1	4,576.6	–	–
1) Joint Equity	4,465.5	4,570.0	3,487.7	28.9	4.22
2) City Commercial Banks	2,036.7	16,91.2	1,088.9	12.1	7.73
Foreign Banks	715.5	179.3	363.8	3.7	1.05
Urban Credit Cooperatives	203.3	181.3	113.1	0.9	–
Rural Credit Cooperatives	3,142.7	2,767.4	2,319.9	12.0	–
2004					
Big Four Banks	16,932.1	14,412.3	10,086.1	45.9	15.57
Other Commercial Banks	4,697.2	4,059.9	2,885.9	50.7	4.93
1) Joint Equity	–	–	–	17.6	5.01
2) City Commercial Banks	1,693.8	1,434.1	904.5	8.5	11.73
Foreign Banks	515.9	126.4	255.8	18.8	1.34
Urban Credit Cooperatives	171.5	154.9	97.9	0.4	–
Rural Credit Cooperatives	3,101.3	2,734.8	1,974.8	9.65	–
2003					
Big Four Banks	16,275.1	13,071.9	9,950.1	196.5	19.74
Other Commercial Banks	3,816.8	3,286.5	2,368.2	–	7.92
1) Joint Equity				14.6	6.5
2) City Commercial Banks	1,465.4	1,174.7	774.4	5.4	14.94

Types of Banks	*Total Assets*	*Total Deposits*	*Outstanding Loans*	*Profit*[1]	*NPL rate (%)*
Foreign Banks	333.1	90.7	147.6	18.1	2.87
Urban Credit Cooperatives	148.7	127.1	85.6	0.01	–
Rural Credit Cooperatives	2,674.6	2,376.5	1,775.9	4.4	–
2002					
Big Four Banks	14,450.0	11,840.0	8,460.0	71.0	26.1
Other Commercial Banks	4,160.0	3,390.0	2,290.0	–	–
1) Joint Equity	2,990.0	–	–	–	9.5
2) City Commercial Banks	1,170.0	–	–	–	17.7
Foreign Banks	324.2	–	154.0	15.2	–
Urban Credit Cooperatives	119.0	101.0	66.4	–	
Rural Credit Cooperatives	–	1,987.0	1,393.0	–	–
2001					
Big Four Banks	13,000.0	10,770.0	7,400.0	23.0	25.37
Other Commercial Banks	3,259.0	2,530.7	1,649.8	12.9	–
1) Joint Equity	2,386.0	1,849.0	1,224.0	10.5	12.94
2) City Commercial Banks	873.0	681.7	425.8	2.4	–
Foreign Banks	373.4	–	153.2	1.7	–
Urban Credit Cooperatives	128.7	107.1	72.5	2.6	–
Rural Credit Cooperatives	–	1,729.8	1,197.0	–	–

Source: Almanac of China's Finance and Banking 2000–2012, CEIC data base, Quarterly Monetary Report of PBOC

Table 7.3-B Notes:

1. It is before tax profit up to 2006, and after tax profit from 2006–2012.
2. Big four (stated owned) banks refer to Bank of China, China Construction Bank, Industrial and Commercial Bank of China, and Agricultural Bank of China. Big five banks are the Big four Banks and the Bank of Communications.

Development of other non-state banks

Table 7.3-B provides a (partial) breakdown of the different types of banks. Although the largest four or five banks (the fifth largest bank is the Bank of Communications, also state-owned) dominate in every aspect of the banking sector during the period of 2001–2012, the role of other banks in the entire banking sector cannot be ignored.[108] Table 7.4-C provides evidence on the growth of non-bank intermediaries. Overall, the growth of these non-bank intermediaries has been impressive since the late 1990s.[109] Among them, "other commercial banks" (many are state-owned), RCCs, and TICs hold the largest amount of assets; the size of foreign banks and mutual funds (not listed in the table) is minuscule, but these are likely to be the focus of development in the near future.[110] In an effort to boost lending to the private sector and improve competition in the banking system, the CBRC granted private capital the same entry standards to the banking industry as other

Table 7.3-C Comparison of Assets Held by China's Non-Bank Intermediaries (RMB billion)

This table compares *total assets* held by banks and non-bank intermediaries during the period 1995–2012.

Year	*State-owned Banks*	*RCCs*	*UCCs*	*Insurance Companies*	*TICs*	*Non-deposit Intermediaries*	*Other Commercial Banks*	*Foreign Banks*
1995	5,373.3	679.10	303.92	–	458.60	48.97	536.91	42.90
1996	6,582.7	870.66	374.78	–	563.70	82.02	769.98	55.30
1997	7,914.4	1,012.20	498.94	–	636.40	100.42	948.61	75.80
1998	8,860.9	1,143.11	560.63	–	802.50	120.97	1,128.18	118.40
1999	9,970.6	1,239.24	630.15	260.4	907.50	137.08	1,376.89	191.40
2000	10,793.7	1,393.06	678.49	337.4	975.90	160.82	1,828.26	379.20
2001	11,188.2	1,610.80	780.02	459.1	1,088.30	223.67	2,255.70	341.80
2002	13,549.6	2,205.21	119.23	649.4	1,544.10	408.10	2,997.72	317.90
2003	16,275.1	2,674.62	148.72	912.3	–	495.58	3,816.80	331.10
2004	16,932.1	3,103.30	171.50	1,185.4	–	–	4,697.20	515.90
2005	21,005.0	3,142.7	203.3	1,529.6	–	–	6,502.2	715.5
2006	24,236.0	3,450.3	183.1	1,973.1	–	–	8,038.4	927.9
2007	28,007.0	4,343.4	131.2	2,900.4	–	–	10,589.9	1,252.5
2008	31,836.0	5,211.3	80.4	3,341.8	–	–	12,941.2	1,344.8
2009	40,089.0	5,492.5	27.2	4,063.5	–	–	17,465.0	1,349.2
2010	46,894.0	6,391.1	2.2	5,048.2	–	–	22,756.6	1,742.3
2011	53,634.0	7,204.7	3	6,013.8	–	–	28,363.5	2,153.5
2012	60,040.0	7,953.5	–	7,354.6	–	–	35,874.0	2,380.4

Source: Aggregate Statistics from the People's Bank of China (China's Central Bank) and CEIC, 2000–2012.

capital in May 2012.[111] The CBRC indicated that private companies may buy into banks through private stock placements, new share subscription, equity transfers, and mergers and acquisitions.[112] Further, private investment is also welcomed in trust, financial leasing, and auto-financing companies.[113] As a development on this front, after the Third Plenum of the 18th CPC Central Committee in November 2013, the government also allowed private investors that meet certain requirements to set up small and medium-sized banks and other financial institutions.[114] Finally, our coverage of non-bank financial institutions excludes various forms of informal financial intermediaries, some of which are deemed illegal but overall provide a considerable amount of financing to firms in the Hybrid Sector.

III. Financial markets

In this section, we examine China's financial markets, including the stock markets, and the recent addition of venture capital and private equity markets as well as asset management industries. We also compare, at the aggregate level, how firms raise funds in China and in other emerging economies through external markets in order to determine if China's experience is unique. We then briefly review publicly traded companies' financing and investment decisions. Finally, we discuss the further development of financial markets as well as corporate governance and the performance of listed firms.

A. Overview of stock markets

After the introduction of China's domestic stock exchanges in 1991, the SHSE and SZSE initially underwent rapid growth.[115] However, in the long run they have not done so well.[116] Figure 7.3 compares the performance of some of the major stock exchanges around the world, as measured by the "buy-and-hold" return in the period January 1992 and December 2013.[117] The figure plots inflation-adjusted real returns. Over this period, the performance of the value-weighted SHSE index (the calculation for the SZSE is similar) is below that of the DAX (Germany), which has the best performance among the group, and that of the S&P 500 (U.S.), FTSE (U.K.), CAC (France), and only slightly better than the Nikkei Index (Japan), the worst among the group. By the end of 2013 it was at about the same level in real terms as at the start of 1992.

As Table 7.4-A indicates, at the end of 2013, the SHSE was ranked the seventh largest market in the world in terms of market capitalization, while the SZSE was ranked the eleventh. The Hong Kong Stock Exchange (HKSE), where selected firms from mainland China have been listed and traded, was ranked the seventh largest in the world. Needless to say, the Chinese financial markets will play an increasingly important role in world financial markets.[118] Also from Table 7.4-A, "turnover velocity" is the annual total turnover for all the listed firms expressed as a percentage of the total market capitalization, and the figures for SZSE and SHSZ are among the highest, suggesting that there is a large amount of speculative

Table 7.4-A A Comparison of the Largest Stock Markets in the World in December 2013

Ranking	*Stock Exchange*	*2013 Dec Market cap US bn*	*2013 Dec share turnover*
1	NYSE Euronext (US)	17,950	70.9%
2	NASDAQ OMX (US)	6,085	144.6%
3	Tokyo SE Group	4,543	129.6%
4	London SE Group	4,428	46.5%
5	NYSE Euronext (Europe)	3,584	355.2%
6	Hong Kong Stock Exchange	3,101	40.9%
7	Shanghai SE	2,497	151.6%
8	TMX Group	2,114	62.6%
9	Deutsche Börse	1,936	67.8%
10	SIX Swiss Exchange	1,541	45.4%
11	Shenzhen SE	1,452	269.3%
12	Australian SE	1,387	57.7%
	China (SHSE, SZSE, HKSE)	7,050	127.14%

Notes: All figures are from www.world-exchanges.org, the web site of the international organization of stock exchanges. Turnover velocity is the total turnover of domestic stocks for the year expressed as a percentage of the total market capitalization.

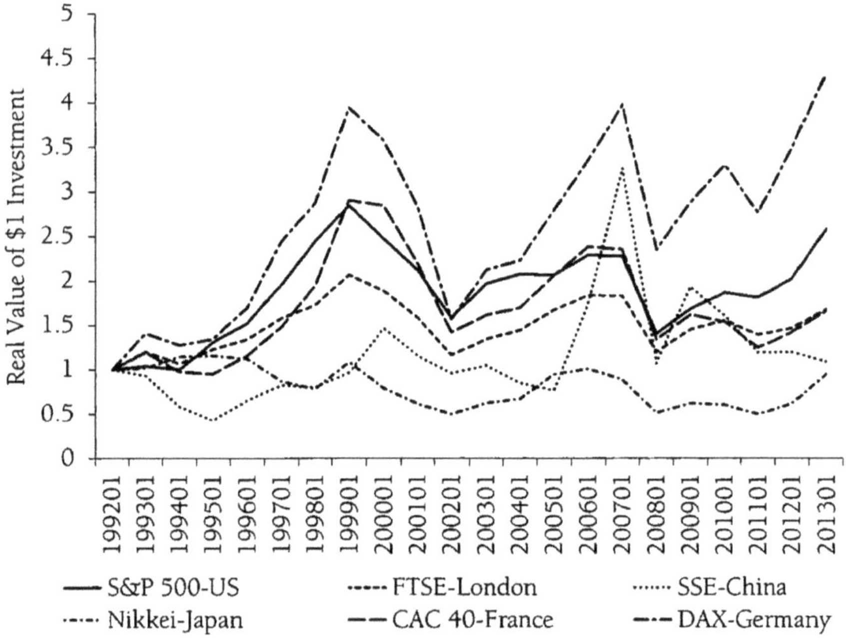

Figure 7.3 A Comparison of Performance of Major Stock Indexes (Buy-and-hold returns of $1 between Jan. 1992 and Dec. 2013)

trading especially among small- and medium-cap stocks in the Chinese markets, as these stocks are more easily manipulated than large cap stocks.[119]

There are two other markets established to complement the two main exchanges.[120] First, a fully electronically-operated market ("*Er Ban Shi Chang*" or "Second-tier Market," similar to the NASDAQ) for Small and Medium Enterprises (SMEs) was opened in June 2004.[121] It was designed to lower the entry barriers for SME firms, especially newly established firms in the high-tech industries.[122] By the end of February 2007, there were 119 firms listed in this market.[123] Second, *San Ban Shi Chang* or "Third-tier Market" was established to deal primarily with de-listing firms and other over-the-counter (OTC) transactions.[124] Since 2001, some publicly listed firms on both SHSE and SZSE that do not meet the listing standards have been delisted and the trading of their shares shifted to this market.[125] In 2006, "New Third-tier Market" (or "Xin San Ban Shi Chang") was established to deal with the equity transactions of non-listed shareholding companies' in a high-tech zone (with the name of "Zhong Guan Cun") in Beijing.[126] The companies on this market can be transferred to the GEM or small and medium-sized plate if approved by the CSRC.[127] On October 23, 2009, China launched a NASDAQ-style Growth Enterprises Market (GEM, or "Chuang Ye Ban") with 28 companies that were mainly from the hi-tech, electronic, and pharmaceutical industries.[128] The main purpose of GEM is to provide financing for small and medium sized private enterprises.[129] The first ten firms seeking to list on the GEM drew a combined RMB 784 billion in subscriptions in September 2009, while the second and third sets had eighteen firms, including Huayi Brothers Media, China's largest privately owned film company.[130] In June and August 2010, the SZSE started to release the index of GEM-ChiNext and ChiNext Composite, respectively.[131] Since 2012, the development of China's stock market has been accelerated.[132] On July 8, 2012, the State Council approved the National Equities Exchange and Quotations to extend the "new third-tier market" to a nation-wide market in Beijing, Tianjin, Shanghai, and Wuhan.[133] On December 14, 2013, the State Council finally decided to enlarge the volume of the new third-tier market, allowing all kinds of small and medium enterprises to do equity transactions on this market.[134] Other recent developments in the stock market include the pilot of preference shares and the possible IPO transformation from an approval-based system to a registration-based system.[135] Preference shares are a mature species in the stock market of developed countries, whereas in China they were just promoted soon after the Third Plenary Session in November 2013.[136] Thus, the pilot program has been seen as a major innovation in China's stock market.[137] First, the pilot helps to accelerate the development of direct financing and to provide investors with more diversified investment channels.[138] Second, it helps commercial banks to innovate capital instruments to meet regulatory capital requirements, as the issue of preference shares is included in Tier-1 capital.[139] The other surprisingly aggressive reform in November 2013 for the stock market was a pledge by the central government to turn the current approval-based system of IPOs into a registration-based one, potentially removing a stumbling block that has distorted supply and demand, and artificially inflated valuations of new stock offerings.[140] The approval-based system has long been criticized as one of the fundamental deficiencies in China's stock market.[141]

Despite rapid recent development in China's stock market, there is evidence that the market is still not efficient because prices and investor behavior are not necessarily driven by the fundamental values of listed firms.[142] For example, Morck et al. find that stock prices are more "synchronous" in the sense that stock prices move up and down together in emerging countries like China than in developed countries.[143] They attribute this phenomenon to poor minority investor protection and the imperfect regulation of markets in emerging countries.[144] In addition, there have been numerous lawsuits alleging insider trading and manipulation.[145] In many cases, unlike well-known companies in developed markets stricken by corporate scandals like Enron, managers and other insiders from Chinese companies did not use any sophisticated accounting and finance maneuvers, even by China's standards, to hide their losses.[146] These cases reveal that the inefficiencies in the Chinese stock markets can be partially attributed to poor and ineffective regulation.[147] We discuss below issues relating to regulation, market efficiency, and the further development of China's financial markets.

B. Overview of bond markets

Table 7.4-B provides information on China's bond markets. The government bond market had an annual growth rate of 22.2% during the period of 1990–2012 in terms of newly issued bonds, while total outstanding bonds reached RMB 7,199.36 billion (or $1137.7 billion) by the end of 2012.[148] The second largest component of the bond market is called "policy financial bonds." These bonds are issued by "policy banks," which operate under the supervision of the Ministry of Finance; the proceeds of bond issuance are invested in government-run projects and industries, such as infrastructure construction (similar to municipal bonds in the United States).[149] Compared to government-issued bonds, the size of the corporate bond market is relatively small. However, it has been growing quickly in recent years.[150] In terms of the amount of outstanding bonds, the size of the corporate bond market was less than one fourth of the size of the government bond market in 2008, and has grown to around 63% by 2012.[151]

The small size of the bond market, especially the corporate bond market, relative to the stock market, is common among Asian countries.[152] AQQ (2008) compares different components (bank loans to the private sectors or the Hybrid Sector of China; stock market capitalization; public/government and private/corporate bond markets) of the financial markets around the world at the end of 2003.[153] Compared to Europe and the U.S., we found that the size of both the government (public) and corporate (private) bond markets is smaller in Asia (Hong Kong, South Korea, Malaysia, Taiwan, Singapore, Indonesia, Philippines, and Thailand), excluding Japan; even in Japan, the size of the corporate bond market is much smaller compared with its government bond market.[154] We also found that the

Table 7.4-B China's Bond Markets: 1990–2012 (Amount in RMB billion)

This table presents the development of China's bond markets. "Policy Financial Bonds" are issued by "policy banks," which belong to the Treasury Department, and the proceeds of bond issuance are invested in government run projects and industries such as infrastructure construction (similar to municipal bonds in the U.S.)

Year	*Treasury Bonds*			*Policy Financial Bonds*			*Corporate Bonds*		
	Amount Issued	*Redemption Amount*	*Balance*	*Amount Issued*	*Amounts Redemption*	*Balance*	*Amounts Issued*	*Amounts Redemption*	*Balance*
1990	19.72	7.62	89.03	6.44	5.01	8.49	12.4	7.73	19.54
1991	28.13	11.16	106.00	6.69	3.37	11.81	24.9	11.43	33.11
1992	46.08	23.81	128.27	5.50	3.00	14.31	68.37	19.28	82.20
1993	38.13	12.33	154.07	0.00	3.43	10.88	23.58	25.55	80.24
1994	113.76	39.19	228.64	0.00	1.35	9.53	16.18	28.20	68.21
1995	151.09	49.70	330.03	–	–	170.85	30.08	33.63	64.66
1996	184.78	78.66	436.14	105.56	25.45	250.96	26.89	31.78	59.77
1997	241.18	126.43	550.89	143.15	31.23	362.88	25.52	21.98	52.10
1998	380.88	206.09	776.57	195.02	32.04	512.11	15.00	10.53	67.69
1999	401.50	123.87	1,054.20	180.09	47.32	644.75	15.82	5.65	77.86
2000	465.70	152.50	1,367.40	164.50	70.92	738.33	8.30	0.00	86.16
2001	488.40	228.60	1,561.80	259.00	143.88	853.45	14.70	0.00	100.86
2002	593.43	226.12	1,933.60	307.50	155.57	1,005.41	32.50	0.00	133.36
2003	628.01	275.58	2,260.36	456.14	250.53	1,165.00	35.80	0.00	169.16
2004	692.39	374.99	2,577.76	414.80	177.87	1,401.93	32.70	0.00	201.86
2005	704.20	404.55	2,877.40	585.17	205.30	1,781.80	204.65	3.70	401.81
2006	888.33	620.86	3144.87	898.00	379.0	2,300.80	393.83	167.24	553.29
2007	2313.91	584.68	4874.10	1109.02	413.36	2992.68	505.85	288.09	768.33
2008	855.82	753.14	4976.78	1082.30	406.38	3668.6	843.54	327.78	1285.06
2009	1792.70	707.15	5795.00	1167.80	374.53	4481.88	1662.90	440.00	2440.59
2010	1977.83	1004.34	6768.49	1319.27	564.84	5236.32	1549.15	509.92	3467.18
2011	1710.01	1095.85	7382.65	1997.27	731.70	6501.88	2354.80	1021.56	4645.68%
2012	1615.42	1798.71	7199.36	2141.50	–	–	3736.55	–	–
Yearly Growth	22.17%	28.19%	22.10%	30.21%	26.79%	37.20%	29.62%	26.18%	29.76%

Source: Aggregate Statistics from the People's Bank of China (China's Central Bank) 2000–2012 and the Statistical Yearbook of China 2000–2012.

size of all four components of China's financial markets are small relative to that of other regions and countries, including bank loans made to the Hybrid Sector (private sector) in China (other countries).[155] Moreover, the most under-developed component of China's financial markets is the corporate bond market (labeled "private" bond market).[156]

C. Evidence on the listed sector

In this section, we briefly examine publicly listed and traded companies in China. It is worthwhile to first clarify that firms from the Hybrid Sector can become listed and publicly traded.[157] AQQ (2005) found that 80% of their sample of more than 1,100 listed firms were converted from former SOEs.[158] In recent years, the government has attempted to change the composition of listed firms by relaxing regulations toward Hybrid Sector firms, including the establishment of the recently opened GEM.[159]

Until the share reform announced in 2005 and implemented in 2006–2007, listed firms in China issued both tradable and non-tradable shares (Table 7.5-A).[160] The non-tradable shares were either held by the government or by other state-owned legal entities (i.e., other listed or nonlisted firms or organizations).[161] Table 7.5-B shows that, in 2009, non-tradable shares constituted around half of all shares (53%, column 2), but fell rapidly from 2010 to 2012.[162] By the end of 2012, the non-tradable shares constituted around 24% of all shares, and the rest majority of tradable shares were Class A shares.[163] Among the tradable shares, Class A and B shares are listed and traded in either the SHSE or SZSE. Originally, Class A shares were issued to and traded by Chinese investors while Class B shares were issued to and traded by foreign investors including those from Taiwan and Hong Kong and QFIIs.[164] While the two share classes issued by the same firm are identical in terms of shareholder rights (e.g. voting and dividend rights), B shares were traded at a significant discount relative to A shares and were traded less frequently than A shares.[165] The "B share discount" has been reduced significantly since the CSRC allowed Chinese citizens to invest and trade B shares with foreign currency accounts in 2001.[166] In addition, Class H shares, issued by companies registered in mainland China and approved by the CSRC to get listed in HK, are traded on the HKSE.[167] Finally, there are N shares and S shares for firms listed in the U.S. and Singapore but operating in China (we omit discussions on these shares since they are not listed on the domestic exchanges).[168] After the share reforms discussed below government shares became G shares and are tradable.

We next describe standard corporate governance mechanisms in the Listed Sector. First, according to the 2005 Company Law, listed firms in China have a two-tier board structure: the Board of Directors (five to nineteen members) and the Board of Supervisors (at least three members), with supervisors ranking above directors.[169] The main duty of the Board of Supervisors is to monitor firms' operations as well as the activities of top managers and directors; the board consists mostly of representatives of shareholders and employees, with the rest of the board

Table 7.5-A Types of Common Stock Issued in China

Tradable?		*Definition*
No (Private block transfer possible)	State-owned shares* (G shares after recent reform and tradable)	Shares that are controlled by the central government during the process when firms are converted into a limited liability corporation but before listing. These shares are either managed and represented by the Bureau of National Assets Management or held by other state-owned companies, both of which also appoint firms' board members. After reforms announced in 2005 and implemented in 2006–7 state shares became G shares and are tradable.
	Entrepreneur's shares	Shares reserved for firms' founders during the same process described above; different from shares that founders can purchase and sell in the markets.
	Foreign owners	Shares owned by foreign industrial investors during the same process.
	Legal entity holders	Shares sold to legal identities (such as other companies, listed or non-listed) during the same process.
	Employee shares	Shares sold to firm's employees during the same process.
Yes (Newly issued shares)	A Shares	Shares issued by Chinese companies that are listed and traded in the Shanghai or Shenzhen Stock Exchange; most of these shares are sold to and held by Chinese (citizen) investors.
	B Shares	Shares issued by Chinese companies that are listed and traded in the Shanghai or Shenzhen Stock Exchange; these shares are sold to and held by foreign investors; starting in 2001 Chinese investors can also trade these shares.
	H Shares	Shares issued by selected Chinese companies listed and traded in the Hong Kong Stock Exchange; these shares can only be traded on the HK Exchange but can be held by anyone.

*: There are sub-categories under this definition

represented by either officials chosen from government branches or executives from the parent companies; directors and top managers of the firms cannot hold positions as supervisors.[170] The company has the discretion to decide the number of representatives of employees on the Board of Supervisors, but representatives of employees must account for at least one third of the board.[171] The Board of

Table 7.5-B Tradable vs. Non-tradable Shares for China's Listed Companies

Year	*Shanghai SE: State/total shares*	*Nontradable/ total shares*	*Tradable/ total shares*	*A/total shares*	*A/Tradable shares**
1992	0.41	0.69	0.31	0.16	0.52
1993	0.49	0.72	0.28	0.16	0.57
1994	0.43	0.67	0.33	0.21	0.64
1995	0.39	0.64	0.36	0.21	0.60
1996	0.35	0.65	0.35	0.22	0.62
1997	0.32	0.65	0.35	0.23	0.66
1998	0.34	0.66	0.34	0.24	0.71
1999	0.43	0.65	0.35	0.26	0.75
2000	0.44	0.64	0.36	0.28	0.80
2001	0.50	0.64	0.36	0.29	0.80
2002	0.52	0.65	0.35	0.26	0.74
2003	0.57	0.64	0.35	0.27	0.76
2004	0.58	0.64	0.36	0.28	0.77
2005	0.57	0.62	0.38	0.30	0.78
2006	0.36	0.65	0.35	0.27	0.81
2007	0.37	0.69	0.31	0.28	0.90
2008	0.47	0.58	0.42	0.37	0.91
2009	0.49	0.53	0.47	0.50	0.98
2010	–	0.32	0.68	0.58	–
2011	–	0.26	0.74	0.61	–
2012	–	0.24	0.76	0.64	–

Source: China Security Regulation Committee Reports (2000–2006), CEIC database and www.csrc.gov.cn

Non-tradable shares include "state-owned" and "shares owned by legal entities"; This column is calculated as "(Non-tradable in Shanghai SE + Non-tradable in Shenzhen SE)/(Market cap in Shanghai SE + Market cap in Shenzhen SE)"

*: tradable shares include A, B, and H shares;

Directors serves similar duties as its counterpart in the U.S., including appointing and firing CEOs.[172] According to the "one-share, one-vote" scheme adopted by firms in the Listed Sector, shareholders including the state and legal person shareholders that typically own the majority of shares appoint the board members.[173] Specifically, the Chairman and one or two Vice Chairmen of the Board are elected by the remaining directors who have the majority of votes; with the approval of the Board, the CEO and other top managers can become members of the Board.[174] The CSRC requires at least one third of the board and a minimum of two people on the Board to be independent.[175]

Since the law does not specify that every member of the Board must be elected by shareholders during general shareholder meetings, in practice some directors are nominated and appointed by the firms' parent companies; the nomination process is usually kept secret, particularly when nominating board members for former SOEs.[176] Since not all members of either board are elected by shareholders, a major problem with the board structure is the appointment of and contracting with the CEOs.[177] Based on firm-level compensation data which has been available since 1998 due to disclosure requirements, Fung et al. (2003) and Kato and Long (2004) concluded that no listed firms grant stock options to CEOs or board members.[178] The situation is somewhat different now.[179] Among overseas listed SOEs, barriers to exercising stock options have been overcome, and some senior executives have been granted stock options and have received substantial rewards; examples include the former chairman of CNOOC Wei Liucheng and Bank of China-Hong Kong former chairman Liu Mingkang *(Caijing* Magazine, 2008). However, the cash-based compensation level for CEOs is still much lower than the compensation level for their counterparts in developed countries, and the consumption of perks, such as company cars, is prevalent.[180]

Second, the existing ownership structure, characterized by the large amount of non-tradable shares including cross-holdings of shares among listed companies and institutions, makes it difficult for value-increasing M&As.[181] In many deals, a Hybrid Sector non-listed firm acquires a listed firm that is converted from an SOE, but the large amount of non-tradable shares held by the state remain intact after the transaction.[182] Such an acquisition can be the means through which low quality, non-listed companies bypass listing standards and access financial markets (e.g., Du et al., 2008).

Third, one factor contributing to the occurrence of corporate scandals is the lack of institutional investors (including non-depository financial intermediaries) as they are a recent addition to the set of financial institutions in China.[183] Professional investors would perhaps not be so easily taken in by simple deceptions.[184] Another factor is that the enforcement of laws is questionable due to the lack of legal professionals and institutions.[185]

Fourth, the government plays the dual roles of regulator and blockholder for many listed firms, including banks and financial services companies.[186] The main role of the CSRC, whose functional counterpart in the U.S. is the SEC, is to monitor and regulate stock exchanges and listed companies.[187] The government exercises its shareholder control rights in listed firms through the Bureau of National Assets Management, which holds large fractions of nontradable shares, or other SOEs (with holdings of non-tradable shares).[188] Moreover, the government's dual roles can lead to conflicting goals, such as maximizing profits as shareholder versus maximizing social welfare as regulator or social planner, in dealing with listed firms, which in turn weaken the effectiveness of both of the government's roles.[189] Based on a sample of 625 firms with 28% of the CEOs being ex- or current government bureaucrats, Fan et al. (2007) find that the three-year post-IPO average stock returns of the sample underperform the market by 20%, and the underperformance of firms with such politically-connected CEOs exceeds those without politically-connected CEOs by almost 30%.[190] Firms with politically-connected CEOs are also more likely to appoint other bureaucrats, and not personnel with relevant professional experience to boards of directors.[191]

D. Private equity/venture capital and the funding of new industries

Allen and Gale (1999, 2000a) have suggested that stock market-based economies, such as the U.K. in the 19th century and the U.S. in the 20th century, have been more successful in developing *new* industries than intermediary-based economies such as Germany and Japan.[192] They argue that markets are better than banks for funding new industries, because evaluation of these industries based on experience is difficult, and there is wide diversity of opinion.[193] Stock market-based economies such as the U.S. and U.K. also tend to have well-developed systems for the acquisition and distribution of information, so the cost of information to investors is low.[194] Markets then work well because investors can gather information at low costs and those that anticipate high profits can provide the finance to the firms operating in the new industries.[195]

A key part of this process is the private equity and venture capital sector.[196] Venture capitalists are able to raise large amounts of funds in the U.S. because of the prospect that successful firms will be able to undertake an IPO.[197] With data from 21 countries, Jeng and Wells (2000) found that venture capital is less important in other countries, and the existence of an active IPO market is the critical determinant of the importance of venture capital in a country.[198] This is consistent with the findings of Black and Gilson (1998); after comparing the U.S. and Germany, Black and Gilson found that the primary reason venture capital is relatively successful in the U.S. is because of the active IPO market.[199]

These facts imply that the development of active venture capital and private equity markets can increase the financing for China's new industries.[200] What is unusual about China is that it currently has the ability to develop both traditional industries, such as manufacturing, and in the near future new, high-tech industries, such as aerospace, computer software, semiconductors, and bio-genetics.[201] China's development is different from the experience of South Korea and Taiwan in the 1970s and that of most other emerging economies in the 1990s, because the latter countries focused on developing manufacturing industries first.[202] In relation to developing traditional industries like Korea and Taiwan in the 1970s, China has already followed suit in first introducing advanced[203] technologies from developed countries and "nationalizing" these technologies within designated companies before moving toward the more advanced technologies.[204] Allen and Gale (1999, 2000a) argue that banks are better than financial markets for funding mature industries because there is wide agreement on how they are best managed, so the delegation of the investment decision to a bank works well.[205] This delegation process, and the economies of scale in information acquisition through delegation, makes bank-based systems more efficient in terms of financing the growth in these industries.[206] Therefore, the banking system can contribute more in supporting the growth and development of these industries than markets.[207]

E. *Asset management industries*

The mutual fund industry in China has gone through three stages of development.[208] The first stage is between 1992, when China's first fund *LiuBo* was established, and 1997, when the first version of the mutual fund regulation was drafted and passed by the CSRC.[209] The *LiuBo* Fund was a closed-end fund with NAV RMB100 million RMB ($12.5 million) and began to trade on the SHSE in 1993.[210] While the industry experienced fast growth in the few years after 1992, lack of regulation and problems associated with fund trading hampered the further development of the industry.[211] The first open-end fund *Hua An Chuangxin* was established in September of 2001, following the announcement of the proposal for open-end fund investment by the CSRC, a milestone for China's mutual fund industry.[212]

Figure 7.4 shows the development of the mutual fund industry in China. The total net assets value increased from RMB 11 billion ($1.3 billion) in 1998 to about RMB 2.80 trillion ($456.6 billion) in the fourth quarter of 2013.[213] In 2001, the NAV of all funds was about 0.8% of GDP and 1.19% of total national savings; these figures rose to 5.39% of GDP and 10.56% of total savings in 2012.[214] The growth of open-end funds contributed to most of the growth in the industry.[215] The most popular investment style is actively managed domestic equity, with only a few index funds and exchange traded funds (ETFs).[216]

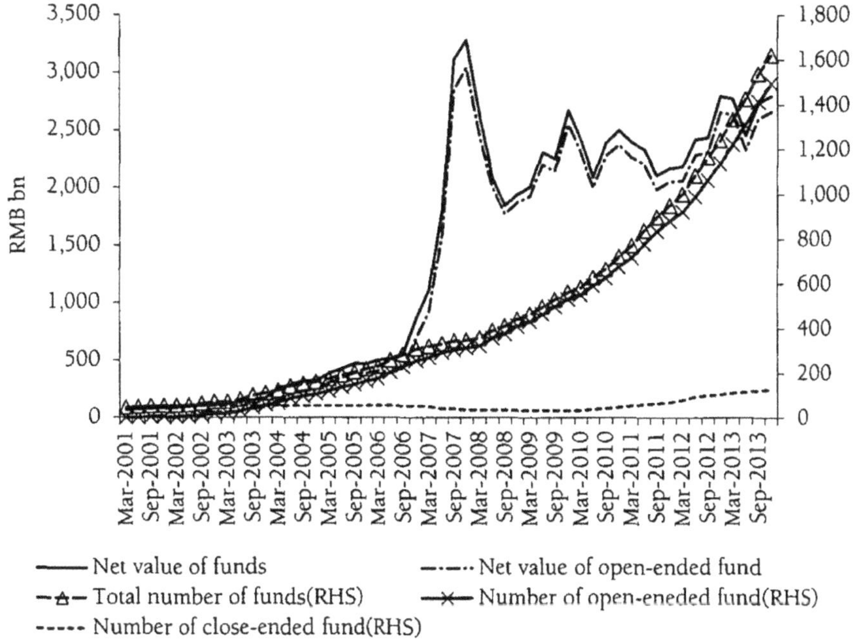

Figure 7.4 Growth in China's Mutual Fund Industry (1998–2013)

Many mutual fund companies are owned by securities and other financial services companies.[217] Like their counterparts in the U.S., management fees are the major source of income for fund companies, accounting for about 80% of total income.[218] Administration fees account for 9% of total income, and the rest of the income comes from investment and other incomes.[219] More than half of the fund managers have a master-level or higher academic degree, and the majority of them are 36 to 45 years old.[220]

The first fund managed by a qualified foreign institutional investor (QFII) was set up in 2002.[221] The State Administration of Foreign Exchange (SAFE) is the government agent that regulates the QFII funds.[222] The QFII Act allows foreign investors to invest in Chinese securities, with the intention of introducing sophisticated foreign investors to the Chinese market and with the hope that their presence would improve market efficiency.[223] In addition, with the exercise of their shareholder rights, the presence of foreign investors can also help improve corporate governance of the Listed Sector.[224] However, the original QFII rules imposed restrictions on foreign investors, such as a capital lock-up period of one to three years limiting capital withdrawal (and leaving China) and other operating restrictions.[225] In August 2006, the CSRC revised QFII rules to promote more participation from foreign investors.[226] Under the new rules, there has been a significant increase in applications from foreign investors for QFII quotas.[227]

Most of the institutions in the first group of QFII applicants were securities companies and investment banks, with other financial services companies such as insurance companies and pension fund companies also on the list.[228] By the end of July 2006, China had approved a total of $7,495 billion foreign investment capital quota from 45 QFIIs, or three quarters of the then ceiling of $10 billion capital inflow through QFIIs.[229] In December 2007, the investment quota tripled, rising from $10 billion to $30 billion.[230] In September 2009, draft rules were issued by SAFE to increase the upward limit of investment for an individual QFII institution to $1 billion from the previous $800 million.[231] As of November 2013, there were a total of 251 approved QFIIs operating in China.[232] With the development of RMB internationalization, RMB Qualified Foreign Institutional Investors (RMBFII) was approved by the State Council in August 2011, allowing foreign institutional investors to invest in domestic securities market within an approved quota.[233] The initial quota was RMB 20 billion ($3.2 billion) in January 2012 and was increased to RMB 144.6 billion ($23.3 billion) in November 2013.[234]

The approval of qualified domestic institutional investors (QDII) to invest in overseas markets came after QFII, in July 2006.[235] The QDII funds invest in stocks, bonds, real estate investment trusts and other mainstream financial products in markets such as New York, London, Tokyo and Hong Kong.[236] Similar to the QFII scheme, it is a transitional arrangement that provides limited opportunities for domestic investors to access foreign markets at a stage in which a country/territory's currency is not freely convertible and capital flows are restricted.[237] As of early 2008, ten fund companies had obtained the approval to launch QDII.[238] The total number of QDII funds reached 75 in July 2009.[239] The performance of the QDII funds has been less than stellar.[240] Going forward, the probable continuing appreciation of the RMB against major international currencies including the dollar is a major concern for QDII investors.[241]

IV. The shadow financial sector and evidence on hybrid sector firms

In this section we study how the shadow financial sector supports firms in the Hybrid Sector to raise funds and to grow from start-ups to successful industry leaders. We also examine the alternative governance mechanisms employed by investors and firms that can substitute for formal corporate governance mechanisms. Due to data limitations, much of this evidence is by necessity in the form of anecdotes or the results of a survey.[242]

We first compare the Hybrid Sector with the State and Listed Sectors to highlight the importance of its status in the entire economy in Section A. Second, we consider survey evidence in Section IV.B. Finally, Section IV.C provides discussions and comparisons of alternative financing channels and governance mechanisms that support the growth of the Hybrid Sector versus formal financing channels (through banks and markets) and governance mechanisms (laws and courts).

A. Comparison of hybrid sector vs. state and listed sectors

Figure 7.5-A compares the level and growth of *industrial output* produced in the State and Listed Sectors combined vs. that of the Hybrid Sector from 1998 to 2012.[243] The output from the Hybrid Sector has been steadily increasing during

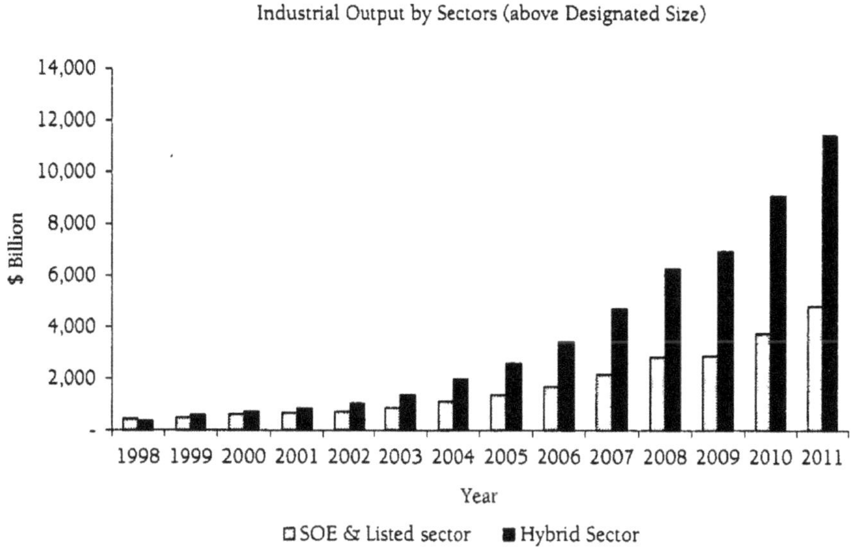

Figure 7.5-A Comparing the Sectors – Industrial Output

this period and exceeded that of the other two sectors in 1998. The total output in 2011 is almost $11,444 billion for the Hybrid Sector, while it is around $4,812 billion in the State and Listed Sectors combined.[244] The Hybrid Sector grew at an annual rate of over 30% between 1998 and 2011, while the State and Listed Sectors combined grew at around 20% during the same period.[245] In addition, the growth rates for investment in fixed assets of these sectors are comparable (*China Statistics Yearbooks*, and AQQ (2005)), which implies that the Hybrid Sector is more productive than the State and Listed Sectors. In fact, with large samples of firms (from sources) with various ownership structures, Liu (2007) and Dollar and Wei (2007) find that the returns to capital figure is much higher in non-state sectors than the State Sector, and that a capital reallocation from state to private sectors will generate more growth in the economy[246] Fan et al. (2006) and Li et al. (2007) find that state-owned firms in China have a much easier access to the debt market and accordingly higher leverage than non-state firms.[247] One reason for the differences is that due to government protection (for economic and social/political reasons) the costs for bankruptcy and financial distress are much lower for state-owned firms.[248] These firms also have easier access to bank loans, especially credit extended by state-owned banks.[249]

All of the above facts make the growth of the Hybrid Sector even more impressive. Not surprisingly, there has been a fundamental change among the State, Listed, and Hybrid Sectors in terms of their contribution to the entire economy. In 1980, the State Sector contributed more than two thirds of China's GDP and (non-agricultural) privately owned firms, a type of Hybrid Sector firm, were negligible contributors; but in 2011, the State Sector only contributed 15% of the GDP (*China Statistical Yearbook*, 1998–2012).[250] The above trend of the Hybrid Sector replacing the State Sector is likely to continue in the near future.[251]

Figure 7.5-B presents the number and growth of non-agricultural employees in the three sectors. The Hybrid Sector is a much more significant source of

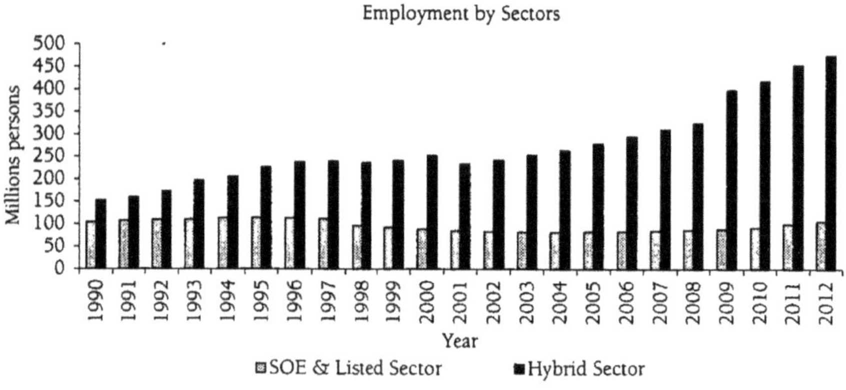

Figure 7.5-B Comparing the Sectors – Employment

employment opportunities than the State and Listed Sectors.[252] Over the period from 1990 to 2012, the Hybrid Sector employed an average of over 73% of all non-agricultural workers; the TVEs (part of the Hybrid Sector) have been the most important employers providing (non-agricultural) jobs for residents in the rural areas, while (non-agricultural) privately-owned firms employ more than 40% of the workforce in the urban areas.[253] Moreover, the number of employees working in the Hybrid Sector has been growing at 5.3% over this period, while the labor force in the State and Listed Sectors has been shrinking.[254] These patterns are particularly relevant for China, given its vast population and potential problem of unemployment.[255]

B. Survey evidence

Much of the information concerning the Hybrid Sector comes from surveys.[256] We focus on evidence in AQQ (2005) and Cull and Xu (2005). The most significant findings of these surveys regarding financing channels are the following. First, during the startup stage, funds from founders' family and friends are an essential source of financing.[257] Banks can also play an important role.[258] Since 2010, peer-to-peer lending, which refers to direct lending through special websites to unrelated individuals without the involvement of any financial institution as an intermediary, has grown rapidly.[259] Second, internal financing, in the form of retained earnings, is also important.[260] During a firm's growth period, financing from private credit agencies (PCAs) and trade credits, rather than banks, are key channels for firms in AQQ's sample.[261] As documented by Tsai (2002) PCAs take on many forms, from shareholding cooperative enterprises run by professional money brokers, lenders, and middlemen, to credit associations operated by a group of entrepreneurs (raising money from group members and from outsiders to fund firms; *zijin huzushe)*, to pawnshops and underground private money houses.[262]

As far as corporate governance is concerned, when asked about what type of losses concern them the most if the firm failed, every firm's founders/executives (100%) included in the AQQ study said reputation loss is a major concern, while only 60% of them said economic losses are of major concern.[263] Competition also appears to be an important factor ensuring firms are well run.[264]

Cull and Xu (2005) find that firms in most regions and cities rely on courts to resolve less than 10% of business-related disputes (the highest percentage is 20%), with a higher reliance on courts in coastal and more developed areas.[265] One reason that firms go to courts to resolve a dispute is because the courts are authoritative; the dispute will be resolved, even though the resolution may not be fair (e.g., Clarke et al. 2008).[266]

C. Discussion on how the shadow financial sector works

In this subsection, we first discuss mechanisms within the shadow financial sector in supporting the growth of the Hybrid Sector. We then compare these alternative institutions that operate outside the legal system with the law and legal institutions that have been widely regarded as the basis for conducting finance and commerce. There are two aspects to alternative financing channels in the Hybrid Sector.[267] The first is the way in which investment is financed.[268] The second is corporate governance.[269] We consider each in turn.

Oncc a firm is established and doing well, internal finance can provide the funds necessary for growth.[270] AQQ (2005) find that about 60% of the funds raised by the Hybrid Sector are generated internally.[271] Of course, internal finance is fine once a firm is established. However, use of this method raises the issue of how firms in the Hybrid Sector acquire their "seed" capital, which may be the most crucial financing during a firm's life cycle.[272] AQQ present evidence on the importance of alternative and informal channels, including funds from family and friends, and loans from private (unofficial) credit agencies (see also Tsai (2002)).[273] There is also evidence that financing through illegal channels, such as smuggling, bribery, insider trading and speculations during early stages of the development of financial markets and real estate market, and other underground or unofficial businesses can also play a critical role in the accumulation of seed capital.[274]

Perhaps the most significant corporate governance mechanism is competition in product and input markets, which has worked well in both developed and developing countries (e.g., McMillan 1995, 1997; Allen and Gale 2000b).[275] What we see from the success of Hybrid Sector firms in WenZhou and other surveyed firms recounted in AQQ suggests that it is only those firms that have the strongest comparative advantage in an industry (of the area) that survived and thrived. A relevant factor for competition in an industry is entry barriers for new firms, as lower entry barriers foster competition. Djankov, La Porta, Lopez-de-Silanes, and Shleifer (DLLS hereafter, 2002) examine entry barriers across 85 countries, and find that countries with heavier (lighter) regulation of entry have higher government corruption (more democratic and limited governments) and larger unofficial economies.[276] With much lower barriers to entry compared to other countries with similar (low) per capita GDP, China is once again an "outlier" in the DLLS sample given that China is one of the least democratic countries, and such countries tend to have high barriers to entry.[277] Survey evidence from AQQ (2005) reveals that there exist non-standard methods to remove entry barriers in China, which can reconcile these seemingly contradictory facts.[278]

Additional mechanisms of corporate governance are reputation, trust, and relationships.[279] Greif (1989, 1993) argues that certain traders' organizations in the 11th century were able to overcome problems of information asymmetry and the lack of legal and contract enforcement mechanisms, because they had developed institutions based on reputation, implicit contractual relations, and coalitions.[280] Certain aspects of the growth of these institutions resemble what worked to promote commerce and the financial system in China prior to 1949 (e.g., Kirby (1995)) and the operation of the shadow financial sector today (AQQ (2005)), in terms of how firms raise funds and contract with investors and business partners.

In addition, Greif (1993) and Stulz and Williamson (2003) point out the importance of cultural and religious beliefs for the development of institutions, legal origins, and investor protections.[281]

The above factors are of particular relevance and importance to China's development of institutions.[282] Without a dominant religion, some argue that the most important force in shaping China's social values and institutions is the set of beliefs first developed and formalized by *Kongzi* (Confucius).[283] This set of beliefs clearly defines family and social orders, which are very different from western beliefs on how legal codes are formulated.[284] Using the World Values Survey conducted in the early 1990s, LLSV (1997b) find that China has one of the highest levels of social trust among a group of 40 developed and developing countries.[285] We interpret high social trust in China as being influenced by Confucian beliefs. Throughout this paper and AQQ (2005; 2008) we have presented evidence that reputation and relationships make many financing channels and governance mechanisms work in China's Hybrid Sector.

There are other effective corporate governance mechanisms.[286] First, Burkart et al. (2003) link the degree of separation of ownership and control to different legal environments, and show that *family-run* firms will emerge as the dominant form of ownership structure in countries with weak minority shareholder protections, whereas professionally managed firms are the optimal form in countries with strong protection.[287] Survey evidence on the Hybrid Sector in AQQ and empirical results on the Listed Sector, along with evidence in Claessens et al. (2000, 2002) and ACDQQ (2008), suggests that family firms are a successful norm in China and other Asian countries.[288] Second, Allen and Gale (2000a) show that, if cooperation among different suppliers of inputs is necessary and all suppliers benefit from the firm doing well, then a good equilibrium with no external governance is possible, as internal, mutual monitoring can ensure the optimal outcome.[289] AQQ (2005) and ACDQQ (2008) present evidence on the importance of trade credits as a form of financing for firms in the Hybrid Sector.[290] Cooperation and mutual monitoring can ensure payments (as long as funds are available) among business partners despite the lack of external monitoring and contract enforcement.[291] The importance of trade credits is also found in other emerging economies (e.g., ACDQQ (2012) on India) as well as in developed countries (Burkart et el. (2011) on the U.S.).[292]

It is worth mentioning how entrepreneurs and investors alleviate and overcome problems associated with government corruption.[293] According to proponents of institutional development (e.g., Rajan and Zingales 2003b; Acemoglu and Johnson 2005), poor institutions, weak government, and powerful elites can severely hinder China's long-run economic growth.[294] However, our evidence shows that corruption has not prevented a high rate of growth for China's firms, even in Hybrid Sector firms, where legal protection is perhaps weaker and problems of corruption worse compared to firms in the State and Listed sectors.[295]

A potentially effective solution for corruption is competition among local governments/bureaucrats from different regions within the same country.[296]

Entrepreneurs can move from region to region to find the most supportive government officials for their private firms, which in turn motivates officials to lend "helping hands" rather than "grabbing hands" in the provision of public goods or services (e.g., granting of licenses to start-up firms); otherwise, there would be an outflow of profitable private businesses from the region (Allen and Qian 20 09).[297] This remedy is typically available in a large country with diverse regions like China.[298] Complementing this view, Xu (2011) reviews China's unique institutional foundation of a "regionally decentralized authoritarian system," in which the subnational governments have considerable autonomous power over regional economic decisions while simultaneously remaining under the control of the central government.[299] Under this structure, local governments play a major role in supporting TVEs, allocating bank credits to firms, and choosing good firms to get listed.[300] This system alleviates the information problem that regulators face, and creates incentives for sub-national governors though personnel control and regional competition.[301] Xu argues that this governance structure is responsible for the spectacular economic growth of China, despite weak enforcement of formal laws.[302]

To summarize, the extraordinary economic performance of China in recent decades, especially that of the Hybrid Sector, raises questions about the conventional wisdom of using the legal system as the basis of commerce.[303] Given the importance of legal systems to many economic systems, "Most observers would characterize the economic performance in China and India as 'successful *despite* the lack of western-style institutions,'" and the failure to adopt western institutions will be one of the main factors to halt the long-run economic growth.[304] By contrast, Allen and Qian (2010) argue that China's economy has been successful *because of* this lack of western-style institutions, in that conducting business outside the legal system in fast-growing economies such as China can actually be superior to using the law as the basis for finance and commerce.[305]

Focusing on dispute resolution and contract enforcement mechanisms based on the law and courts vs. alternative mechanisms operating outside the legal system, Allen and Qian (2010) argue that despite many well-known advantages, there are disadvantages in using legal institutions.[306] First, recent research on political economy factors, and in particular, work by Rajan and Zingales (2003a,b), shows that rent-seeking behaviors by vested interest groups can turn legal institutions into barriers to changes.[307] We expect these problems to be much more severe in developing countries and the costs of building good institutions can be enormous.[308] One way to solve this problem is *not* to use the law as the basis for commerce, but instead to use alternative mechanisms *outside* the legal system.[309] Evidence presented in this paper and other related work on China and other emerging economies (e.g., ACDQQ (2012) on India) suggests that these alternative mechanisms can be quite effective.

Second, in democracies there can be a lengthy political process before significant changes can be approved (by the majority of the population and/or legislature), and the people in charge of revising the law (e.g., politicians and judges) may lack the expertise of business transactions and have limited capacity (time and effort) to examine the proposed changes.[310] In the context of a fast-growing and frequently changing economy such as China, Allen and Qian (2010) show that there is an additional advantage of using alternative institutions because this type of system can adapt and change much more quickly than when the law is used.[311] In particular, competition can ensure the most efficient mechanism prevails, avoiding a political process that requires persuading the legislature and the electorate to revise the law when circumstances change.[312]

To conclude, we argue that while legal institutions along with formal financing channels are an integral part of developed economies' institutions, alternative mechanisms and financing channels play a much more prominent role in emerging economies. These alternative mechanisms can be superior to legal mechanisms in supporting business transactions in certain industries or entire economies.[313] Therefore, the development of alternative dispute resolution and contract enforcement mechanisms alongside the development of legal and other formal institutions can promote a broader base of economic growth that is also more sustainable in emerging economies.[314] The coexistence of and competition between alternative and legal mechanisms can also exert positive impact on the development of legal institutions by promoting adaptation and preventing disproportionate influence from interest groups.[315]

Summary and concluding remarks

One of the most frequently asked questions about China's financial system is whether it will stimulate or hamper its economic growth. Our answer to this question, based on examining the history and current status of the financial system and comparing our findings to the financial systems of other countries, is in three parts. First, the large banking sector dominated by state-owned banks has played a much more important role in funding the growth of many types of firms than the financial markets.[316] Second, the stock market has been growing fast since 1990, but has played a relatively limited role in supporting the growth of the economy[317] However, the role of the financial markets in the economy will become increasingly more significant.[318]

If we can show that the banking sector and financial markets have not impeded the growth of the economy, our third conclusion is that alternative financing channels have had great success in supporting the growth of the Hybrid Sector – the sector which contributes most of the economic growth, compared to the State and Listed Sectors. The shadow financial sector relies on alternative financing channels, including internal finance, and on alternative governance mechanisms, such as those based on trust, reputation and relationships, and competition in output and input markets to support the growth of the Hybrid Sector.[319] It is possible that these alternative institutions are superior to western-style legal institutions in supporting a fast-growing economy such as China's.[320]

We believe the formal financial sector of banks and financial markets will continue to develop; an ever-improving legal structure is desirable to facilitate this continued development. However, the informal and shadow banking sectors also have a great deal to contribute on an ongoing basis. These sectors do not rely on conventional legal underpinnings. The lack of conventional underpinning in the shadow banking sector should not be discouraged, as this structure can be an advantage in the growth of China's economy.

Notes

* Prepared for and presented at the Cornell International Law Symposium held on February 21, 2014. We are grateful to Robert C. Hockett and participants in the Symposium for their interesting and helpful comments. We also thank the editorial team for doing a very thorough check of the paper and sources.

1 Franklin Allen, Jun Qian & Meijun Qian, *Law, Finance, and Economic Growth in China,* 77 J. FIN. ECON. 57, 59 (2005) [hereinafter AQQ, *Law, Finance, and Economic Growth*].

2 *See China Overview*, THE WORLD BANK (Apr. 1, 2014), www.worldbank.org/en/country/china/overview.

3 Ann Williams, *Did China Just Overtake the US as World's Largest Economy? Well, Yes and No,* THE STRAITS TIMES (Oct. 9, 2014, 3:18 PM), www.straitstimes.com/news/business/economy/story/did-china-just-overtake-the-us-worlds-largest-economy-well-yes-and-no-20.

4 This paper draws heavily on our previous work, including AQQ, *Law, Finance, and Economic Growth-*, Franklin Allen, Jun Qian, & Meijun Qian, *China's Financial System: Past, Present, and Future, in* CHINA'S GREAT ECONOMIC TRANSFORMATION 506 (Loren Brandt & Thomas G. Rawski eds., 2008) [hereinafter AQQ, *Past, Present, and* Future]; Franklin Allen, Jun Qian, Chenying Zhang & Mengxin Zhao, *China's Financial System: Opportunities and Challenges, in* CAPITALIZING CHINA 46 (Joseph P.H. Fan & Randall Morck eds., 2013) [hereinafter AQZZ, *Opportunities and Challenges*], In particular, much of the data and many of the arguments made are from the latter paper.

5 *See* Franklin Allen & Douglas Gale, *A Welfare Comparison of Intermediaries and Financial Markets in Germany and the U.S.*, 39 EUR. ECON. R. 179, 180 (1995).

6 *See* AQZZ, *Opportunities and Challenges*, *supra* note 4.

7 *See infra* Table 4-B; AQZZ, *Opportunities and Challenges*, *supra* note 4, at 2.

8 Michael Wines, *China Bank I.P.P. Raises $19 Billion,* N.Y. TIMES (July 6, 2010), www.nytimes.com/2010/07/07/business/global/07ipo.html?_r=0.

9 *See* Tarhan Feyzioglu, *Does Good Financial Performance Mean Good Financial Intermediation in China?* 4–5 (Int'l Monetary Fund, Working Paper No. 170, 2009), *available at* www.imf.org/extemal/pubs/ft/wp/2009/wp09170.pdf.

10 *See* AQQ, *Past, Present, and Future*, *supra* note 4, at 2.

11 SHELDON GAO, DOW JONES INDEXES, CHINA STOCK MARKET IN A GLOBAL PERSPECTIVE 1 (2002), *available at* http://people.stern.nyu.edu/jmei/b40/ChinaIndexCom.pdf.

12 Allen Berger et al., *Bank Ownership and Efficiency in China: What Will Happen in the World's Largest Nation, 33* J. BANKING & FIN. 113, 114 (2009) ("The banking industry is larger than the stock markets in China, and as shown below, is very inefficient-particularly the Big Four banks."); Michael Pettis, *Why China's Financial Markets Are Inefficient,* CHINA SPECTATOR (Nov. 28, 2013, 7:05 AM), www.businessspectator.com.au/article/2013/11/28/china/why-chinas-financial-markets-are-inefficient.

13 Jennifer N. Carpenter et al., *The Real Value of China's Stock Market* 1 (2014), *available at* http://people.stem.nyu.edu/jcarpen0/pdfs/Carpenter%20Lu%20Whitelaw%20 2014%20-%20The%20Real%20Value%20of%20China's%20Stock%20Market.pdf.
14 *Id.* at 21.
15 AQZZ, *Opportunities and Challenges*, *supra* note 4, at 96.
16 Jing Jiang, *Shadow Banking in China: Battling the Darkness,* THE ECONOMIST (May 10, 2014), www.economist.com/news/finance-and-economics/21601872-every-time -regulators-curb-one-form-non-bank-lending-another-begins.
17 AQZZ, *Opportunities and Challenges*, *supra* note 4, at 96.
18 AQQ, *Past, Present, and Future*, *supra* note 4, at 506.
19 *Id.* at 507. We include firms partially owned by local governments in the Hybrid Sector for two reasons. First, despite the ownership stake of local governments and the sometimes ambiguous ownership structure and property rights, the operation of these firms resembles more closely that of a for-profit, privately-owned firm than that of a state-owned firm. Second, the ownership stake of local governments in many of these firms has been privatized.
20 *Id.* at 507–08.
21 *Id.* at 508.
22 *Id.*
23 For more descriptions of the pre-1949 history of China's financial system, *see* AQQ, *Past, Present, and Future*, *supra* note 4. For more anecdotal evidence on China's financial system in the same period, *see, e.g.*, William C. Kirby, *China Unincorporated: Company Law and Business Enterprise in Twentieth-Century China*, 54 J. ASIAN STUD. 43 (1995).
24 *See* AQQ, *Past, Present, and Future*, *supra* note 4, at 509.
25 *See* Kirby, *supra* note 23, at 45. For descriptions of family- and community-based mechanisms for contract enforcement, *see, e.g.,* Stephanie P. Chung, *Changes and Continuities: Evolution of a Chinese Family Business (1876–2004),* 3 ASIA EUR. J. 259, 260 (2005). When examining how disputes were resolved both in and outside of court, Goetzmann and Koll concluded that the passing of China's first Company law in 1904, which was intended to provide a better legal environment for business and commerce, did not lead to actual changes in corporate governance or the better protection of minority shareholder rights. *See* William Goetzman & Elisabeth Köll, *The History of Corporate Ownership in China: State Patronage, Company Legislation, and the Issue of Control, in* A HISTORY OF CORPORATE GOVERNANCE AROUND THE WORLD: FAMILY BUSINESS GROUPS TO PROFESSIONAL MANAGERS 150–51 (Nat'l Bureau of Econ. Research ed., 2005).
26 *See* Kirby, *supra* note 23, at 56.
27 *See* AQQ, *Past, Present, and Future*, *supra* note 4, at 509.
28 *See* id.
29 *See* id.
30 BOC, which is among the oldest banks currently in operation, was originally established in 1912 as a private bank and specialized in foreign currency related transactions. *Id.*
31 *Id.* at 509–10.
32 *Id.* at 510.
33 *Id.*
34 *Id.*
35 *Id.*
36 *Id.*
37 *Id.*
38 *See* Daniel Chow, *China's Response to the Global Financial Crisis: Implications for U.S.-China Economic Relations*, 1 Global Bus. L. Rev. 47, 65 (2011); Jing Leng, *The Interaction Between Domestic and Overseas Capital Markets and Corporate Governance of Chinese Listed Companies*, 7 STUD. INT'L FIN. ECON. & TECH L. 273, 284 (2005).

39 *See* AQQ, *Past, Present, and Future*, supra *note 4, at 510.*
40 *See id.*
41 *See id.* For more details on this law and its scope, *see* CHINA SEC. REGULATORY COMM'N (CSRC), www.csrc.gov.cn/pub/csrc_en (last visited June 6, 2014).
42 *See AQQ,* Past, Present, and Future, supra *note 4, at 510.*
43 *See id.* The China Banking Regulation Committee (CBRC) was also established to oversee the banking industry.
44 *See id.*
45 *See* AQQ, *Past, Present, and Future, supra* note 4, at 511.
46 *See id.*
47 *List of Fund Management Companies (November 2013),* CHINA SEC. REGULATORY COMM'N, www.csrc.gov.cn/pub/csrc_en/participants/FundsRelatedList/Fund Management Companies/201401/t20140110_242346.html (last visited Oct. 7, 2014).
48 Franklin Allen et al., *A Review of China's Financial System and Initiatives for the Future, in* CHINA'S EMERGING FINANCIAL MARKETS: CHALLENGES AND OPPORTUNITIES 8 (James R. Barth, John A. Tatom & Glenn Yago eds., 2009) [hereinafter, Allen et al., A *Review of China's Financial* System].
49 AQQ, *Past, Present, and Future*, supra *note 4, at 511.*
50 YONG ZHEN, CHINA'S CAPITAL MARKETS 250 (2013).
51 Allen et al., *A Review of China's Financial System, supra* note 48, at 49.
52 *Fund Profile: China Investment Corporation (CIC)*, THE SOVEREIGN WEALTH FUND INITIATIVE (Feb. 2012), http://fletcher.tufts.edU/SWFI-OLD/-/media/Fletcher/Microsites/swfi/pdfs/2012/profiles/CIC%20Fund%20Profile_Final.pdf (last visited Oct. *7,* 2014).
53 Michael H. Cognato, *China Investment Corporation: Threat or Opportunity?, in* 19 NBR ANALYSIS: UNDERSTANDING CHINA'S NEW SOVEREIGN WEALTH FUND 21 (July 2008).
54 *Id.* at 21–22.
55 AQQ, *Past, Present, and Future, supra* note 4, at 511.
56 *Id.*
57 Due to space limitations, we do not cover China's "foreign sectors" in this paper. For discussions on the history and the role of these sectors in supporting the growth of the economy, *see, e.g.,* Eswar Prasad & Shang-Jin Wei, *The Chinese Approach to Capital Inflows: Patterns and Possible Explanations, in* CAPITAL CONTROLS AND CAPITAL FLOWS IN EMERGING ECONOMIES: POLICIES, PRACTICES, AND CONSEQUENCES (Sebastian Edwards, ed., 2007) for a review.
58 *See infra* Table 1.
59 Allen et al., *A Review of China's Financial System*, *supra* note 48, at 11.
60 AQZZ, *Opportunities and Challenges*, *supra* note 4, at 77.
61 *See supra* Table 1; *see also id.* at 72. Levine (2002) uses bank overhead cost/total assets to measure banking sector efficiency, and used this measure to construct the "Structure Efficiency" and "Finance Efficiency" measures. However, the World Bank Financial Database no longer reports the overhead cost/assets ratio. We replace the overhead costs/assets ratio with the NPLs/loans ratio as an alternative measure of efficiency and use this variable to define other efficiency measures in Table 1.
62 AQZZ, *Opportunities and Challenges*, *supra* note 4, at 72.
63 AQQ, *Past, Present, and Future, supra* note 4, at 514.
64 Allen et al., *A Review of China's Financial System*, *supra* note 48, at 11.
65 *Id.* at 14.
66 *Id.*
67 *Id.*
68 AQZZ, *Opportunities and Challenges*, *supra* note 4, at 73.
69 *Id.*
70 *Id.*

71 *Id.*
72 *Id.*
73 *Id.* at 73–74.
74 *Id.* at 74.
75 *Id.*
76 *Id.*
77 *Id.*
78 *Id.*
79 *Id.*
80 We have not been able to obtain the continuous data under the old classification since 2010 because the PBOC changed the breakdown method of bank loans in terms of loan purposes and borrower types at that time.
81 *Id.*
82 *Id.*
83 *Id.* at 76–77.
84 *See generally* International Bank for Reconstruction and Development, China: *Financial Sector Assessment,* WORLD BANK 6 (2011).
85 *See* Allen et al., *supra* note 4, at 3–4.
86 *See* Kate Mackenzie, *Deflating Shadow Credit in China,* FIN. TIMES (Feb. 27, 2013), http://ftalphaville.ft.com/2013/02/27/1397152/deflating-shadow-credit-in-china.
87 *Id.*
88 Jamil Anderlini, *Into The Shadows: Risky Business, Global Threat,* FIN. TIMES (June 15, 2014), www.ft.cOm/intl/cms/s/2/al23375a-d774-lle3-a47c-00144feabdc0, html#axzz3 Ffw4w9Vp.
89 *See* COUNTRY REPORT NO. 14/235: PEOPLE'S REPUBLIC OF CHINA, INTERNATIONAL MONETARY FUND 42 (2014).
90 The term Total Social Financing (TSF), is defined by the PBOC as the total funds that the real economy obtained from the financial system over a certain period of time. It measures money offered by domestic suppliers, including financial institutions, Chinese households and non-financial entities. Thus, it offers a view of both borrowers and lenders. It also excludes proceeds from government bonds, which are used for government spending and deficit coverage, as well as all foreign-related items, such as foreign direct investment (FD1) and overseas debt. *See* Bob Davis, *Slower China Credit Is a Risk to Growth,* WALL St. J. (June 9, 2013), http://online.wsj.com/news/articles/SB10001424 127887324299104578534340906234614.
91 *See generally* Zhou Xiaochuan et al., THE PEOPLE'S BANK OF CHINA ANNUAL REPORT 2010 (2011), *available at* www.pbc.gov.cn/image_public/UserFiles/english/up load/File/Annual%20Report%202010.pdf.
92 *See* MONETARY POLICY ANALYSIS GROUP OF THE PEOPLE'S BANK OF CHINA, CHINA MONETARY POLICY REPORT, QUARTER FOUR, 2012, THE PEOPLE'S BANK OF CHINA 5–6 (2013), *available at* www.pbc.gov.cn/image_public/UserFiles/english/upload/File/%E8%B4%A7%E5%B8%81%E6%94%BF%E7%AD%96%E6%8A%A5%E5%91%8 A(l).pdf.
93 *Id.*
94 *Id.*
95 *Id.*
96 *Id.* at 5–7.
97 Due to the fast growth of small-scale lending companies, the PBOC started to release the quarterly report on small-scale lending companies since the fourth quarter of 2010. *See generally* MICRO CREDIT COMPANY STATISTICS BY PROVINCES (MUNICIPALITIES) (2013), THE PEOPLE'S BANK OF CHINA, *available at* www.pbc.gov.cn/publish/english/955/2013/20131030084112766413637/20131030084112766413637.html [hereinafter MICRO CREDIT COMPANY STATISTICS].

98 *See China Microfinance, Micro-Credit Companies,* MICRO FINANCE CHINA, *available at* www.microfinancechina.org/micro-credit-companies.html; MICRO CREDIT COMPANY STATISTICS, *supra* note 97.
99 *See generally* Margaret K. Lewis, *Criminal Law Pays: Penal Law's Contribution to China's Economic Development*, 47 VAND. J. TRANSNAT'L L. 371, 423–24 (2014).
100 *See id.*
101 *See* Jiang, *supra* note 16.
102 *See generally* CHINESE SHADOW BANKING: UNDERSTANDING KRIS AND RISK SCENARIOS, THOMSON REUTERS ACCELUS, *available at* http://accelus.thomsonreuters.com/whitepaper/chinese-shadow-banking-understanding-kris-and-risk-scenarios.
103 *See id.*
104 *See generally AQZZ,* Opportunities and Challenges, supra *note 4, at 63–138.*
105 *See generally Allen et al.,* The IPO of Industrial and Commercial Bank of China and the 'Chinese Model' 'of Privatizing Large Financial Institutions, *EUR. J. FIN. (2012).*
106 *See id.* at 93.
107 *See generally The People's Bank of China Annual Report 2012*, THE PEOPLE'S BANK OF CHINA (2013), *available at* www.pbc.gov.cn/publish/english/4133/2013/20130829090453489508948/20130829090453489508948.html.
108 AQZZ, *Opportunities and Challenges*, supra *note 4, at 64.*
109 *See generally* AQZZ, *Opportunities and Challenges, supra* note 4.
110 Postal savings, which are deposit-taking institutions affiliated with local post offices, constitute another form of non-bank intermediation that is not repotted in Table 3-B due to a lack of time series data. However, at the end of 2008, total deposits within the postal savings system exceeded RMB 2079 billion, or 9.5% of all deposits in China. *See* MICHAEL MARTIN, CONG. RESEARCH SERV., R42380, CHINESE BANKING SYSTEM: ISSUES FOR CONGRESS 5 (2012).
111 *See* Grant Turner, Nicholas Tan & Dena Sadeghian, *The Chinese Banking System,* RESERVE BANK OF AUSTRALIA BULLETIN 57–58 (Sept. 2012).
112 *Id. at* 58–60.
113 *Id.*
114 *See* John Howkins, *Guest Post: The Third Plenum and Cultural Industries,* FIN. TIMES (Nov. 26, 2013, 4:30 AM), http://blogs.ft.com/beyond-brics/2013/ll/26/guest-post-the-third-plenum-and-cultural-industries.
115 *See* Sonia L. Wong, *China's Stock Market: A Marriage of Capitalism and Socialism*, 26 CATO J. 389, 389 (2006), *available at* http://object.cato.org/sites/cato.org/files/serials/files/cato-journal/2006/ll/cj26n3-l.pdf.
116 *See generally* Gao, *supra* note 11.
117 This is the gross return at December 2013 from 1 unit of currency invested in each of the valued-weighted stock indexes at the beginning of 1992.
118 *See* Carpenter et al., *supra* note 13.
119 *See* Lily Fang, Jun Qian & Huiping Zhang, Out of the Limelight but in Play: Trading and Liquidity of Media and Off-media Stocks 21–22 (Jan. 28, 2012) (unpublished) (on file with Social Science Research Network), *available at* http://papers.ssrn.com/sol3/papers.cfm?abstract_id=1964440.
120 *See* Robert Cookson, *Chinese IPOs: Bumper Year Raises Expectation for 2010,* FIN. TIMES (Feb. 2, 2010, 4:05 PM), www.ft.com/intl/cms/s/0/30665c74-0edl-lldf-bd79–00144feabdc0.html#axzz3Fae9rlpd.
121 *See* Alexandra Harney & Richard McGregor, *Fish Eyes and Pearls in China,* FIN. TIMES (July 5, 2004, 5:00 AM), www.ft.eom/intl/cms/s/0/e6bd76ca-ce21-lld8–95cb-00000e251 lc8.html#axzz3Fae9rlpd.
122 *Id.*

123 *See* Jamil Anderlini, *On Asia: Renaissance Gives Shenzhen Added Stature,* FIN. TIMES (Aug. 3, 2007, 4:57 PM), www.ft.eom/intl/cms/s/l/a09c3ada-41d9-l ldc-8328 -0000779fd2ac.html#axzz3Fae9rlpd.

124 *See No Flash Boys in China's Sleepy Over-the-Counter Markets,* BLOOMBERG NEWS (Apr. 14, 2014, 6:08 AM), www.bloomberg.com/news/2014-04-14/no-flash-boys-in -china-s-sleepy-over-the-counter-markets.html.

125 *See, e.g.,* Lydia Guo, *China Cosco: More Fire Sales Ahead,* FIN. TIMES (May 27, 2013, 8:55 AM), http://blogs.ft.com/beyond-brics/2013/05/27/china-cosco-more-fire-sales -ahead/ ("Cosco has fallen into this special treatment category, with its trading name changed to 'ST Cosco.' The 'ST' is a warning of delisting risk, a severe embarrassment to the state-controlled company.")

126 *See* Winnie Liu, *China's OTC Market: The Shortcut,* ASIAN VENTURE CAPITAL J. (May 28, 2014, 1:33 PM), www.avcj.com/avcj/analysis/2346915/chinas-otc-market -the-shortcut.

127 *Id.*

128 *See* Robert Cookson, *Demand Swamps New Chinese Exchange,* FIN. TIMES (Oct. 30, 2009, 4:21 PM), www.ft.eom/intl/cms/s/0/4calac3c-c56f-llde-8193-00144feab49a. html#axzz3Fae9rlpd. Note that GEM is also commonly referred to as "ChiNext." *See* Emma Saunders, *Economic News Digest,* FIN. TIMES (Nov. 2, 2009, 1:20 PM), http:// blogs.ft.com/money-supply/2009/ll/02/economic-news-digest-16/.

129 *See* Cookson, *supra* note 128.

130 *See* Saunders, *supra* note 128.

131 Wei Shen, *Face Off: Is China a Preferred Regime for International Private Equity Investments – Decoding a China Myth from the Chinese Company Law Perspective,* 26 CONN. J. INT'L L. 89, 145 (2011).

132 *See* generally Josh Noble, *China's Shenzhen index outshines Shanghai,* FIN. TIMES, Aug. 12, 2013, www.ft.cOm/intl/cms/s/0/3df78366-0317-lle3-9a46-00144feab7de. html#axzz3Fae9rlpd.

133 Lan Xinzhen, *Expansion of the new third hoard will ease financing woes,* CHINA (Jan. 3, 2014) www.china.org.cn/opinion/2014-01/03/content_31079761.htm.

134 *CSRC Implements the State Council Decisions on Relevant Matters Concerning National SUE Share Transfer System, Marking Major Progress in the Development of Multitiered Capital Markets*, CHINA SEC. REGULATORY COMM'N (Dec. 14, 2013), available at www.csrc.gov.cn/pub/csrc_en/newsfacts/release/201401/t20140126_243284. html.

135 *CSRC Implements the State Council's Guiding Opinions on Launching the Pilot Program for Preferred Shares,* CHINA SEC. REGULATORY COMM'N (Nov. 30, 2013), www.csrc.gov.cn/pub/csrc_en/newsfacts/release/201402/t20140211_243686.html; *CSRC Releases Opinions on Further Promoting the IPO System Reform,* CHINA SEC. REGULATORY COMM'N (Nov. 13, 2014), www.csrc.gov.cn/pub/csrc_en/newsfacts/ release/201402A20140214_243817.html.

136 *CSRC Implements the State Council's Guiding Opinions on Launching the Pilot Program for Preferred Shares*, *supra* note 135

137 Cai Xiao, *CSRC announces rules for preferred company shares,* CHINA DAILY, Mar. 22, 2014, www.chinadailyasia.com/business/2014-03/22/content_15126525.html.

138 *CSRC Implements the State Council's Guiding Opinions on Launching the Pilot Program for Preferred Shares*, *supra* note 135.

139 *Id.*

140 Q&A *by CSRC Spokesperson on the Opinions on Further Promoting the IPO System Reform,* CHINA SEC. REGULATORY COMM'N (Nov. 30, 2013), www.csrc.gov.cn/pub/ csrc_en/newsfacts/release/20140 l/t20140108_242271 .html.

141 Shen Hong et al., *Reforms Could Put China's IPO Market Back in Business* (Nov. 15, 2013), http://blogs.wsj.com/chinarealtime/2013/ll/15/reforms-could-put-chinas-ipo-market-back-in-business/.
142 Franklin Allen et al., *Law, Institutions and Finance in China and India, in* EMERGING GIANTS 137 (Barry Eichengree et al. eds, Oxford University Press, 2010).
143 Randall Morck et al., *The Information Content of Stock Markets: Why Do Emerging Markets Have Synchronous Stock Price Movements?*, THE NAT'L BUREAU OF ECON. RESEARCH, www.nber.org/china/shangmorck.pdf (last visited Oct 8, 2014).
144 *Id.* at 2.
145 Franklin Allen, Jun Qian, Meijun Qian & Mengxin Zhao, *Review of China's Financial System and Initiatives for the* Future 21 (Wharton Fin. Inst. Ctr., Working Paper No. 08–28, 2008), *available at* http://ssrn.com/abstract=l *185877.*
146 *Id.* at 21.
147 *Id.* at 22.
148 *See infra* Table 4-B.
149 *See Allen, supra* note 145, at 22.
150 *Id.*; *see also* Michelle Leung, *The Rise of China's Corporate Bond Market*, S&P DOW JONES INDICES, MCGRAW HILL FINANCIAL INDEXOLOGY BLOG 1 (June 18, 2014, 10:30 PM), www.spindices.com/documents/education/practice-essentials-rise-of-chinas-corporate-bond-market.pdf.
151 Franklin Allen et al., *China's Financial System: Opportunities and Challenges*, 70 tbl.5-B (Nat'l Bureau of Int'l Research, Working Paper No. 17828, 2012), *available at* www.nber.org/papers/w17828.
152 As the IPO was suspended from October 2012 to December 2013, the total amount of the enterprise bonds issued (RMB 649.9 billion) in 2012 surpassed the total amount of capital raised in the domestic stock market (RMB 585.0 billion) for the first time in recent years. *Id.; see also* Allen, *supra* note 145, at 56 tbl.l.
153 Allen et al., *supra* note 145, at 56 tbl. 1.
154 *Id.* at 56, 58 tbls. l & 3-A pnls.A & B.
155 *Id.* at 56, 58, 61, 67 tbls. l, 3-A & 5-A figs. 4-A, 4-B, 4-C & 4-D.
156 *Id.* at 62 tbl.5-B.
157 Youxian Zeren Gongsi Shell Dengji Tijiao Cailiao Guifan (有限责任公司设立登记提交材料规范), [The Establishment of a Limited Liability Company Registered to Submit Material Specification] (promulgated SAIC Enterprise Registration Bureau) (SAIC)(China), *available at* www.saic.gov.cn/ywbl/bszn/nzdjzn/ gsdjtjclgf/201402/t20140228_142367.html.
158 AQZZ, *Opportunities and Challenges, supra* note 4, at 81, 111 tbl.8-A pnl.B.
159 Xinhua, *China's Nasdaq-style GEM starts trading,* SINA ENGLISH (Oct. 30, 2009), http://english.sina.eom/business/p/2009/1029/281487.html; Wang Xtn (王鑫)，*Chudngye Ban Zhdngyu Zdi Shenzhen Shan Liang Kdibdn (*倏业板终于在深圳闪_幵板*)* [*GEM has finally opened in Shenzhen, shiny plate]* SHENZHEN SPECIAL ZONE DAILY (Oct. 24, 2009), www.szse.cn/main/aboutus/bsyw/39740769.shtml; *see also* Cookson, *supra* note 128.
160 Andrea Beltratti, Bernardo Bortolotti & Marianna Caccavaio, *The Stock Market Reaction to the 2005 Non-Tradable Share Reform in China* 7–8 (ECB Working Paper Series, Working Paper No. 1339, May 2011), *available at* www.ecb.europa.eu/pub/pdf/scpwps/ecbwp1339.pdf.
161 *Id.* at 8.
162 *See infra* Table 5-B.
163 *Id.*
164 Beltratti et al., *supra* note 160, at 10; *see also* Jianping Mei, Jose A. Scheinkman & Wei Xiong, *Speculative Trading and Stock Prices: Evidence from Chinese A-B Share Premia,* 10–2 ANNALS OF ECONOMICS AND FINANCE 225, 234–36 (2009).

165 Mei, Scheinkman & Xiong, *supra* note 164, 234–236 & tbl.l. Explanations of the B share discount include: 1) Foreign investors face higher information asymmetry than domestic investors, 2) lower B share prices compensate for the lack of liquidity (due to low trading volume), and 3) the A share premium reflects a speculative bubble component among domestic investors.
166 *See id.*
167 Dennis Hudachek, *The Complete Guide To Chinese Share Classes,* ETF.com: White Papers (Nov. 12, 2012), www.etf.com/sections/white-papers/15113-the-complete-guide-to-chinese-share-classes.html?showall=&fullart=l&start=5.
168 *Id.; see also* Yap Lian Seng & Qiu Yang, *Making SGX Attractive to S-Chips,* LEXOLOGY STAMFORD LAW CORPORATION (Aug. 18, 2014), www.lexology.com/library/detail.aspx?g=0db983fc-6c21–4e52-blc3–9e3c7c08266a.
169 Gongsi Fa (中华人民共和国公司法) [Companies Law of the People's Republic of China] (promulgated by the Standing Committee of the Tenth National People's Congress of the People's Republic of China, Oct. 27, 2005, effective Jan. 1, 2006) Ch. IV §§ 3,4 Arts. 109, 118 (China) *available at* www.china.org.cn/china/Legislations Form2001–2010/2011–02/ll/content_21898292.htm.
170 *See id.* at Chs. II, IV §§ 2,4 Arts. 54, 118–19.
171 *See id.* at Ch. IV §§ 3,4 Arts. 109, 118.
172 *See id.* at Arts. 47, 109.
173 *See id.* at Arts. 104, 106, 130.
174 *See id.* at Art. 110.
175 Guidelines for Introducing Independent Directors to the Board of Directors of Listed Companies (Zhengjianfa [2001] No. 102) (promulgated by the China Securities Regulatory Commission, Aug. 16, 2001), www.csrc.gov.cn/pub/csrcen/newsfacts/release/200708/t20070810_69191.html (China).
176 STOYAN TENEV, CHUNLIN ZHANG & LOUP BREFORT, WORLD BANK AND INT'L FIN. CORP., CORPORATE GOVERNANCE AND ENTERPRISE REFORM IN CHINA: BUILDING THE INSTITUTIONS OF MODERN MARKETS 91 (2002).
177 *See* ALEX BRYSON, JOHN FORTH & MINGHAI ZHOU, CTR. FOR ECON. PERFORMANCE, WHAT DO WE KNOW ABOUT CHINA'S CEOS? EVIDENCE FROM ACROSS THE WHOLE ECONOMY 2 (2012).
178 Takao Kato & Cheryl Long, *Executive Compensation, Firm Performance, and Corporate Governance in China: Evidence from Firms Listed in the Shanghai and Shenzen Stock Exchanges* 17 (Inst, for the Study of Labor, Discussion Paper No. 1767, 2005).
179 *See generally* Wen Xiu & Ming Shuliang, *China's Execs Sweating Over Stock Options,* CAIJING.COM.CN (June 27, 2008, 4:35 PM), http://english.caijing.com.cn/2008–06–27/100071919.html.
180 *See* Kato & Long, *supra* note 178 at 16, 18.
181 Seejulan Du, Oliver M. Rui & Sonia M.L. Wong, *Financing-Motivated Mergers and Acquisitions: Evidence from Corporate China* 2–3 (Chinese Univ. of Hong Kong, Working Paper, 2008).
182 *Id.* at 7–8.
183 *See* Tenev et. al., *supra* note 176, at 81, 111, 113.
184 *See* Joseph D. Piotroski & T.J. Wong, *Institution and Information Environment of Chinese Listed Firms, in* CAPITALIZING CHINA 201 (Joseph P.H. Fan & Randall Morck, eds., 2013).
185 *Yi Zhang,* Law, Corporate Governance, and Corporate Scandal in an Emerging Economy: Insights from China *9–11 (Peking Univ., Working Paper, 2006),* available at http://papers.ssrn.com/sol3/papers.cfm?abstract_id=957549.
186 Katharina Pistor, The *Governance of China's Finance, in* Capitalizing China 35, 37–38 (Joseph P.H. Fan & Randall Morck, eds., 2013).

187 *About CSRC,* China Sec. Regulatory Comm'n (Oct. 10, 2014), www.csrc.gov.cn/pub/csrc_en/about.

188 *Main Functions and Responsibilities of SASAC,* State-owned Assets Supervision and Administration Commission (SASAC) (Oct. 11, 2014), www.sasac.gov.cn/n2963340/n2963393/2965120.html.

189 *See* Pistor, *supra* note 186, at 41, for a description of the complicated relationships among various regulatory agencies and the central government branches, and how these relationships affect the decision-making process of regulations and enforcement.

190 Joseph P.H. Fan & T.J. Wong, *Politically-connected CEOs, Corporate Governance and Post-IPO Performance of China's Newly Partially Privatized Firms*, 4, 33 (Chinese Univ. of Hong Kong, Working Paper, 2004).

191 *Id.* at 24.

192 *See* Franklin Allen & Douglas Gale, *Diversity of Opinion and Financing of New Technologies,* 8 J. Fin. Intermediation 68, 68–70 (1999) [hereinafter *New Technologies*]; Franklin Allen & Douglas Gale, *Diversity of Opinion and Resource Allocation,* in Comparing Financial Systems 403, 406 (2000) [hereinafter *Resource Allocation*],

193 *Id.*

194 *Id.*

195 *Id.*

196 *See, e.g.,* Samuel Kortum & Josh Lerner, *Assessing the Contribution of Venture Capital on Innovation,* 31 RAND J. Econ. 674, 674–75 (2000) (analyzing venture capital funding's positive affect on patenting industry); *see also* Leslie A. Jeng & Philippe C. Wells, *The Determinants of Venture Capital Funding: Evidence Across Countries,* 6 J. Corp. Fin. 241, 242 (2000).

197 *See* Jeng & Wells, *supra* note 196, at 242; *see abo* Bernard S. Black & Ronald J. Gibson, *Venture Capital and the Structure of Capital Markets: Bank versus Stock Markets,* 47 J. F. Econ. 243, 245 (1998).

198 *See* Jeng & Wells, *supra* note 196, at 241.

199 *See* Black & Gibson, *supra* notel97, at 245–46.

200 *See* Jeng & Wells, supra note 196, at 245 ("The past performance of venture capital-backed companies shows that venture capital has been very successful at backing companies with innovative technologies and tremendous growth potential.")

201 *See* Allen et al., *supra* note 145, at 34.

202 *Id.*

203 That is advanced relative to domestic companies but not the most advanced technologies.

204 *Id.*

205 *See New Technologies*, *supra* note 192, at 68–70; *Resource Allocation*, *supra* note 192, at 405.

206 *Id.*

207 *Id.*

208 *See* Allen et al., *supra* note 145.

209 *Id.*

210 *Id.*

211 *Id.*

212 *Id.*

213 Allen et al., *supra* note 145, at 7.

214 *Id.* at 35.

215 *Id.*

216 Allen et al., *supra* note 145, at 35.

217 *Id.*

218 *Id.*

219 *Id.*
220 *Id.*
221 *See* Keith Robinson et al., *The Qualified Foreign Institutional Investor Program in China-Recent Developments, New Opportunities and Ongoing Challenges*, 20 THE INVESTMENT LAWYER 1 (2013).
222 *Id.* at 2.
223 *Id.*
224 Allen et al., *supra* note 145, at 35.
225 *Id.*
226 *See* Y. Nancy Yi, *China's Capital Flow Regulation: The Qualified Foreign Investor and the Qualified Domestic Institutional Investor Programs*, 28 Rev. Banking & Fin. 299, 300 (2009).
227 *See generally id.*
228 *See* Robinson et al., *supra* note 221, at 2.
229 Allen et al., *supra* note 145, at 35.
230 *Id.* at 35–36.
231 Allen et al., *supra* note 145, at 36.
232 Report, *List of QFIIs (Until November 2013)*, CHINA SEC. REGULATORY COMM'N (Jan. 20, 2014), www.csrc.gov.cn/pub/csrc_en/OpeningUp/RelatedLists/QFIIs/201401A2014 0120_242787.htm.
233 *China Expands RQFII, QFII Investment Quota,* China Daily USA (Apr. 3, 2012), http://usa.chinadaily.com.cn/business/2012-04/03/content_14976215.htm; *China's Renminbi Qualified Foreign Institutional Investors (RQFII) Pilot Scheme Expanded,* ALLEN & OVERY (May 10, 2013), www.allenovery.com/publications/en-gb/Pages/ China%E2%80°/o99s-Renminbi-qualified-foreign-institutional.aspx.; YONG ZHEN, *supra* note 50, at 250.
234 *China Expands RQFII,* QFII *Investment Quota,* supra note 260; RICHARD MAZZONCHI ET AL., KWM CONNECT: QFII And RQFII- A PRACTICAL INSIGHT TO RECENT DEVELOPMENTS 2 (2013); Xie Yu, *Investors Brace for Bullish Market,* CHINA DAILY USA, (Dec. 10, 2013), http://usa.chinadaily.com.cn/business/2013–12/ 10/content_1 7164724.htm; YONG ZHEN, *supra* note 50, at 250.
235 JANIES R. BARTH ET AL., CHINA'S EMERGING FINANCIAL MARKETS: CHALLENGES AND OPPORTUNITIES 49 (2009).
236 *Id.*
237 *Id.*
238 *Id.*
239 Allen et al., AQZZ, *Opportunities and Challenges, supra* note 4, at 117.
240 Aidan Yao & Honglin Wang, *What are the Challenges and Problems Facing China's Outward Portfolio Investment: Evidence from the Qualified Domestic Institutional Investor Scheme* 1 (Hong Kong Inst, for Monetary Research, Working Paper No. 31/2012, 2012).
241 *See id.* at 5.
242 All firms including Hybrid Sector firms must disclose accounting and financial information to the local Bureau of Commerce and Industry that audits most reports. However, these data are then aggregated into the Statistical Yearbook without any firm-level publications. *See* AQZZ, *Opportunities and Challenges, supra* note 4, at 122.
243 China's National Bureau of Statistics (NBS) revised its total industrial output statistics in the 2000 Yearbook without any explicit explanations. The NBS significantly revised down outputs in previous years (i.e. 1997) compared to the 1998 Yearbook. To be consistent and avoid confusion, we only use data from NBS after 1998.

244 Due to data limitations, our calculations underestimate the State and Listed Sectors' output. For these sectors, we used as the total output the SOE's output and that of listed firms for which the State has at least a fifty percent ownership stake. However, this calculation excludes output from listed firms that are *not* majority owned by the State. The output for the Hybrid Sector is the difference between the total output and the total for the other two sectors. However, as mentioned above, only about 20%of listed firms do not have the State as the largest owner. Therefore, the total output for these firms is unlikely to change our overall conclusion about the Hybrid Sector's dominance over the other two sectors.

245 There is an ongoing process of privatizing SOEs. Potentially, this may bias the growth rate in favor of the Hybrid Sector as there are firms shifting from the State Sector to the Hybrid Sector. Yet the overwhelming majority of SOEs became Listed Sector firms (the main channel through which SOEs were partially privatized prior to 2004). Thus, this process is unlikely to change the validity of the results.

246 *See* Allen et al., *supra* note 48, at 123–24.

247 *Id.* at 124.

248 *Id.*

249 *Id.*

250 *Id.*

251 *Id.* at 124.

252 Franklin Allen, Jun Qian & Meijun Qian, *Will China's Financial System Stimulate or Impede the Growth of Its Economy, in* 129 Asia Program Special Report, China's Economy: Retrospect and Prospect 34, 39 (Loren Brandt et al. eds., 2005), www2. bc .edu/-qianju/Wilson-ChinaReport-072005.pdf.

253 Allen et al., *supra* note 145, at 42.

254 Our calculations of the total number of workers employed by the Hybrid Sector actually underestimate the actual work force in the sector, because the *Chinese Statistics Yearbooks* do not provide employment data for all types of firms (by ownership structure), especially small firms, in the Hybrid Sector. *Id.* at 36.

255 Nat'l Bureau of Statistics of China, *Employment and Wages: 4–1 Employment,* China Statistical Yearbook 2013, www.stats.gov.cn/tjsj/ndsj/2013/indexeh .htm.

256 *See, e.g.,* Nat'l Bureau of Statistics of China, *Employment and Wages: Brief Introduction,* China Statistical Yearbook 2013, www.stats.gov.cn/tjsj/ndsj/ 2013/indexeh.htm.

257 AQQ, *Law, Finance, and Economic Growth, supra* note 1, at 60.

258 *Id.*

259 Takeshi Jingu, Nomura Research Inst., *Risks and Opportunities in China's Growing P2P Lending Market,* 202 Iakyara 1 (2014), www.nri.eom/-/media/PDF/ global/opinion/lakyara/2014/lkr2014202.pdf. Since the peer-to-peer lending is still beyond the scope of regulators, there are no official statistics on this. According to Xinhua News, one of China's official websites, by the end of 2012, outstanding loans on domestic online P2P platforms stood at RMB 10 billion ($ 1.6 billion) and there were about 200 lending platforms at that point, with about 50,000 investors. Gao Changxin, *PBOC to Set Up P2P Custodians to Prevent Fraud,* Xinhuanet (Nov. 27, 2013, 1:22:44 PM), http://news.xinhuanet.com/english/business/2013-ll/27/c_132922240.htm. Since P2P online lenders have met the market's demand for fast mini-loans, the businesses are mainly facing to those start-ups. *Id.* However, due to the absence of regulations and entrance requirements, the sector is so chaotic that some local media reported in October 2013 that at least one P2P lending company went bankrupt every day. *Id.* After the Third Plenum Session of the 18th CPC Central Committee, it is reported that the PBOC is planning to introduce third-party custodians into P2P lending, after the numerous cases of fraud emerged from 2012 to 2013. *Id.*

260 AQQ, *Law, Finance, and Economic Growth, supra* note 1, at 94.

261 *Id.* at 94–95.
262 Kelly S. TSAI, BACK-ALLEY BANKING: PRIVATE ENTERPRISE IN CHINA 37, 39 (2002).
263 AQQ, *Law, Finance, and Economic Growth*, *supra* note 1, at 96.
264 *Id.* at 97.
265 Robert Cull & Lixin Colin Xu, *Institutions, Ownership and Finance: The Determinants of Profit Reinvestment Among Chinese Firms*, 77 J. FIN. ECON. 117, 126 (2005).
266 Donald Clarke, Peter Murrell & Susan Whiting, *The Role of Law in China's Economic Development, in* CHINA'S GREAT ECONOMIC TRANSFORMATION 375, 414 (Loren Brandt & Thomas G. Rawski eds., 2008).
267 Allen et al., *supra* note 252.
268 *Id.*
269 *Id.*
270 *Id.*
271 *Id.*
272 *Id.*
273 *Id.; see also TSAI,* supra *note 289.*
274 Allen et al., *supra* note 252.
275 Chong-En Bai et al., *Corporate Governance and Market Valuation in China 9* (The Williamson Davidson Inst., Working Paper No. 564, 2003); Franklin Allen & Douglas Gale, *Corporate Governance and Competition, in* CORPORATE GOVERNANCE: THEORETICAL AND EMPIRICAL PERSPECTIVES 23, 56–60, 61–62 (Xavier Vives ed., Cambridge Univ. Press 2000); John McMillan, *China's Nonconformist Reforms,* 11 INST. ON GLOBAL CONFLICT AND COOPERATION 3, 4, 6, 8 (1994); John McMillan, *Markets in Transition, in* 2 ADVANCES IN ECONOMICS AND ECONOMETRICS (David M. Kreps & Kenneth F. Wallis eds., Cambridge Univ. Press 1997).
276 Simeon Djankov et al., *The Regulation of Entry,* 117 Q. J. ECON. 1, 1 (2002)
277 *Id.* at 26–27, 35; *see also* AQQ, *Law, Finance, and Economic Growth*, *supra* note 1, at 97.
278 AQQ, *Law, Finance, and Economic Growth*, supra *note 1, at 97–99.*
279 Avner Greif, *Reputation and Coalitions in Medieval Trade: Evidence on the Maghribi Traders*, 49 J. ECON. HIST. 857, 859, 865, 881 (1989) [hereinafter Greif, *Reputation and Coalitions*]; Avner Greif, *Contract Enforceability Institutions in Early Trade: The Maghribi Traders' Coalition*, 83 AM. ECON. REV. 525, 526, 530, 531, 544 (1993) [hereinafter Greif, *Contract Enforceability Institutions*].
280 Greif, *Reputation and Coalitions, supra* note 306, at 859, 865, 881; Greif, *Contract Enforceability Institutions, supra* note 306, at 526, 530, 531, 544.
281 Greif, *Contract Enforceability* Institutions, supra note 306, at 525; Rene Stulz & Rohan Williamson, *Culture, Openness, and Finance,* 70 J. FIN. ECON. 313, 316–17, 346 (2003).
282 Martin King Whyte, *The Chinese Family and Economic Development: Obstacle or Engine?*, 45 ECON. DEV. & CULTURAL CHANGE 1, 6–7, 8, 13, 14, 20 (1996); Geert Hofstede & Michael Harris Bond, *The Confucius Connection: From Cultural Roots to Economic Growth,* 16 ORGANIZATIONAL DYNAMICS 5 (1988).
283 King Whyte, *supra* note 309, at 6–7, 8, 13, 14, 20; Hofstede & Harris Bond, *supra* note 309, at 5; AQQ, *Law, Finance, and Economic Growth, supra* note 1, at 60, 97.
284 King Whyte, *supra* note 309, at 6–7, 8, 13, 14, 20; Hofstede & Harris Bond, *supra* note 309, at 5; AQQ, *Law, Finance, and Economic Growth, supra* note 1, at 60, 97.
285 Interestingly, the same survey, used in LLSV (1997b), finds that Chinese citizens have a low tendency to participate in civil activities. However, our evidence shows that with effective alternative mechanisms in place, citizens in the developed regions of China have a strong incentive to participate in business and economic activities. AQQ, *Law, Finance, and Economic Growth, supra* note 1, at 97; Rafael La Porta et al., *Trust in Large Organizations,* 87 AM. ECON. REV. 310, 318 (1997).

286 Oliver Hart, *Corporate Governance: Some Theory and Implications,* 105 Econ. J. 678 (1995). Mike Burkart, Fausto Panunzi & Andrei Shleifer, *Family Firms* 3–4, 6, 21, 22, 37 (Nat'l Bureau of Econ. Research, Working Paper No. 8776, 2002).
287 Burkart et al., *supra* note 313, at 3–4, 6, 21, 22, 37.
288 *See,* e.g., AQQ, *Law, Finance, and Economic Growth, supra* note 1, at 89, 98; Stijn Claessens et al., *Disentangling the Incentive and Entrenchment Effects of Large Shareholdings,* 57 J. Fin. 2741, 2743, 2750, 2769–70 (2002); Stijn Claessens, Simeon Djankov & Larry H.P. Lang, *The Separation of Ownership and Control in East Asian Corporations,* 58 J. Fin. Econ. 81, 82, 103, 110 (2000). Franklin Allen et al., *The Financial System Capacities of China and India* 22–23, 22 n.12 (2008) (unpublished working paper) (on file with author).
289 FRANKLIN ALLEN & DOUGLAS GALE, COMPARING FINANCIAL INSTITUTIONS 16–17, 375–98 (MIT Press 2000).
290 *Id.* at 3, 20, 21; AQQ, Law, *Finance, and Economic Growth, supra* note 1, at 60, 95, 98.
291 ALLEN & GALE, *supra* note 289, at 316–17, 375–98.
292 Franklin Allen et al., *Financing Firms in India,* 21 J. FIN. INTERMED. 409, 410,422, 424, 441 (2012). Mariassunta Giannetti, Mike Burkart & Tore Ellingsen, *What You Sell is What You Lend? Explaining Trade Credit Contracts,* 24 REV. FIN. STUD. 1261, 1261–62 (2011).
293 *See generally* ADB/OECD Anti-Corruption Initiative for Asia and the Pacific, *Strategies for Business, Government, & Civil Society to Fight Corruption in Asia and the Pacific* (2009).
294 Gregory C. Chow, *Challenges of China's Economic System for Economic Theory,* 87 AM. ECON. REV. 321 (1997); Udo C. Braendle, Tanja Gasser & Juergen Noll, *Corporate Governance in China-Is Economic Growth Potential Hindered by Guanxi?,* 110 BUS. & SOC'Y REV. 389, 400–01, 402 (2005); Daron Acemoglu & Simon Johnson, *Unbundling Institutions,* 113 J. POL. ECON. 949 (2005); RAJAN RAGHURAM & LUIGI ZINGALES, SAVING CAPITALISM FROM THE CAPITALISTS: UNLEASHING THE POWER OF FINANCIAL MARKETS TO CREATE WEALTH AND SPREAD OPPORTUNITY (Random House 2003).
295 AQZZ, *Opportunities and Challenges,* supra *note 4, at 77–78.*
296 Franklin Allen & Jun Qian, *Corruption and Competition* 19, 20, 21, 23 (2007) (unpublished working paper) (on file with authors).
297 *Id.*
298 Franklin Allen, Jun Qian, Chenying Zhang & Mengxin Zhao, *China's Financial System: Opportunities and Challenges, in* CAPITALIZING CHINA 46 (Joseph P.H. Fan & Randall Morck eds., 2013).
299 *See* Chenggang Xu, *The Fundamental Institutions of China's Reforms and Development,* 49 J. ECON. LITERATURE 1076, 1078 (2011).
300 *See id.* At 1079.
301 *See id.* At 1116–17.
302 *See id.* At 1077.
303 Allen et al., *supra* note 48, at 46.
304 *See* Franklin Allen & Jun Qian, *Comparing Legal and Alternative Institutions in Finance and Commerce, in* GLOBAL PERSPECTIVES ON THE RULE OF LAW 1 (James Heckman & Robert Nelson, Routledge eds., 2010).
305 *Id.*
306 *Id.* at 4–5.
307 *Id.*
308 *Id. A* frequently discussed and controversial topic concerns intellectual property rights including patents and copyrights. The practice of enforcing intellectual property rights by courts is much more vigilant and prevalent in developed countries than in

developing countries such as China. An extensive literature in economics has found mixed evidence on the relationship between patent/copyright protection and the pace of innovations. While exclusive property rights provide strong incentives for innovations and do lead to more innovations in a few industries such as chemicals and pharmaceuticals, excessive protection deters competition, which is another important factor in spurring innovations. *Id.* at 3.

309 *Id.* at 5.

310 *Id.* at 28. A good example is the U.S. payment system. At the beginning of the 21st century the U.S. had a 19th century system: Checks had to be physically transported from where they were deposited to a central operations center, then to the clearer, and then back to the banks they were drawn on. Despite repeated calls for changes from the banks and businesses, the U.S Congress did not act on this simple yet costly problem until after September 11, 2001. All commercial flights were grounded for several days, completely halting the check clearing process. The Check Clearing for the 21st Century Act was signed in October 2003, allowing electronic images to be a substitute for the original checks, and thus the clearing process is no longer dependent on the mail and transportation system. *See id.* at 24–26.

311 *Id.* at 5.

312 *Id.* at 5–6.

313 *Id.* at 6.

314 *See id.* at 6.

315 *Id.*

316 Allen et al., *supra* note 48, at 54.

317 *Id.* at 54–55.

318 *Id.* at 55.

319 *Id.* at 55.

320 *Id.*

8

AN UPDATE ON FISCAL REFORM

Christine Wong

Source: In Ross Garnaut, Ligang Song and Cai Fang (eds.), *China's 40 Years of Reform and Development 1978–2018* (ANU Press, 2018).

In my chapter for the 2013 volume of the *China Update*, I described the evolution of China's system of public finance from the start of market transition, summarising progress to date and pointing to some of the remaining problems (Wong 2013b). It seems appropriate and timely for my chapter in this volume to focus on changes over the past five years – a period neatly bookended by the extensive reform package announced at the third plenum of the eighteenth Communist Party Congress in November 2013, and the latest reforms announced by the just-concluded nineteenth party congress. As it happens, these five years have been highly consequential in the reform of China's fiscal system and, although it is much too soon to know how the latest changes will play out, the direction of reform points to even more significant changes ahead, especially in central-local government relations.

One year after assuming the top leadership post in November 2012, Chinese President Xi Jinping rolled out a sweeping program of reform that was endorsed by the third plenum of the eighteenth party congress. The 60-point 'Decision on Several Major Questions about Deepening Reform' (Xi 2013) spells out an ambitious, comprehensive agenda of more than 300 reform initiatives that cover virtually every facet of China's economy, society and government, including reforms of the fiscal and financial sectors, state-owned enterprises (SOEs), land and property rights, liberalisation of factor prices, household registration, family planning and judicial and administrative reforms. In his 'explanatory notes' on these decisions, President Xi identified the reform of public finance as among the top three key issues to be addressed, noting that '[p]ublic finance is the foundation and important pillar of state governance' (Xi 2013).

Fiscal reforms were off to a rapid start under the energetic direction of then finance minister Lou Jiwei, who announced a comprehensive program that was to proceed in three phases. The first phase – to begin immediately – would focus on budget and public financial management reforms; phase two would begin in 2015 with a focus on reforms of the tax system; and phase three would begin in 2016 and focus on intergovernmental fiscal reform (Han et al. 2014).

Writing in the Communist Party journal *Qiushi*, Lou explained that China's fiscal system has not kept pace with the needs of its growing and increasingly complex economy:

> [T]he defects have become increasingly apparent: the budget management system is not standardized, transparent, or suited to the requirements of modern governance; the tax system . . . is not conducive to supporting the shift to the new development paradigm,[1] social fairness, or market integration. The division of responsibilities between the central and local governments is unclear and unreasonable . . . These problems . . . affect not only the stability and sustainability of the fiscal system itself, they also [adversely] affect the national development strategy and the effectiveness of macroeconomic policy.
>
> (Lou 2014)

Lou (2014) argued that, 'in this round of reform, small patches and fixes will no longer suffice', and fundamental reform of the fiscal system was needed to build the foundation to support the modernisation of governance called for by the decisions of the third plenum.

Party and legislative support came swiftly. In June 2014, the Politburo approved the program for comprehensive deepening reform of the fiscal system. In August 2014, the Standing Committee of the National People's Congress approved the revised Budget Law, which mandates numerous changes and, for the first time, authorises local governments to borrow money for capital investments (NPC Standing Committee 2014). These were followed with numerous State Council directives providing detailed guidelines for implementation – for example, both Document 43 on local government debt issuance and Document 45 on deepening budget reform and shifting to medium-term budgets came in September 2014, and Document 63 on building an accrual-based financial management system and Document 71 on improving the structure of expenditures and cleaning up transfers came in December 2014.

After 2014, the momentum of reform appears to have slowed significantly, with few legislative achievements. Little progress was made in tax reform. Of the three areas identified by Lou Jiwei, only the replacement of the business tax with the value-added tax (VAT) was completed; few changes have been made to resource taxes, and the much-discussed property tax is still awaiting submission to the National People's Congress. As for intergovernmental reform, although preparatory work began in early 2014, when provinces were asked to prepare proposals for the revision of expenditure assignments,[2] no concrete measures had been put forward before Lou retired as finance minister in November 2016. With the loss of its most forceful and vocal advocate, the fate of deep fiscal reform appeared more tenuous as Xi Jinping's first term drew to a close.

In this chapter, I trace the progress of reforms introduced since the third plenum (hereinafter referred to as the third plenum reforms) and argue that substantial progress has been made in building a framework for budget and public financial management that will provide strong support for the next phase, especially for intergovernmental reform. More importantly, the reforms have changed some incentives for local governments that have set in motion a new dynamic that should gradually clarify the boundary between the state and the market. However, some key aspects of the reform have to date been subverted – most notably, the effort to contain and manage local government debt, which was thwarted by a combination of political, institutional and economic factors.

Section two of this chapter provides a brief background of fiscal reforms over the past four decades and the problems leading up to the third plenum. Section three sets out the key measures of fiscal reform introduced since 2013, while section four assesses their implementation progress to date, focusing on changes in government financial reporting and transparency. Section five summarises and offers some concluding remarks on the prospects for fiscal reforms overall and on intergovernmental fiscal reform during Xi Jinping's second term.

Background to the third plenum fiscal reforms

In the course of transition over the past 40 years, China has had to completely rebuild the system of public finance and associated institutions – from the tax system to tax administration and budget management (Wong and Bird 2008; Wong 2013b). To date, the process has been incremental and reactive, aimed principally at 'putting out fires'. To stem the sharp fiscal decline caused by the dismantling of planning mechanisms that eroded state-owned enterprise profits – a primary source of government revenues in the old system – reforms focused first on rebuilding the government's revenue mechanism.[3] In 1994, a new system of taxes was put in place under the Tax Sharing System reform, which installed VAT, a business tax, a corporate income tax, a personal income tax and several taxes on the transactions of property and land. Though far from ideal, the tax system provides broad-based taxes and is highly income-elastic, and has produced buoyant revenues that grew at almost 1.5 times the rate of GDP through the first decade of this century.

With revenues recovering, the government turned in the late 1990s to financial management reform. A broad package was introduced that included new procedures for budget preparation and approval, and strengthened budget reporting to the National People's Congress. A new budget classification system was rolled out in 2006 to improve the tracking of expenditure by functional categories. Departmental budgets were introduced to clearly identify all resources and expenditures for each government department; the first step toward holding spending units accountable for the public monies they receive. Standardised procedures for government procurement were introduced, and a treasury single account was created to manage the government's cash receipts and payments. With these reforms,

China had begun to put in place the basic infrastructure for a modern system of budget management.

A glaring omission in the reforms was the neglect of changes needed to repair intergovernmental fiscal relations, which had been eroded through the fiscal decline of the 1980s and decisively broken in 1994, when the Tax Sharing System abruptly recentralised the share of revenues without adjusting expenditure assignments. Since 1994, expenditure shares have continued to shift downward to local governments, who account for more than 85 per cent of total budget expenditures today while collecting only half the revenues, and are thus heavily dependent on central government transfers to finance the huge fiscal gap. The distortions created by this dysfunctional intergovernmental system have long been considered key sources of inefficiency in the Chinese economy (World Bank 2002, 2007; Wong passim).

Despite the urgency of intergovernmental fiscal reform though, its prerequisite is the completion of reform of public financial management begun in the late 1990s. This is highlighted by a brief review of the decade preceding the third plenum decisions. Hitting its stride after joining the World Trade Organization (WTO) and riding the wave of an exceptionally buoyant global economy up to the Great Crash of 2008, the Chinese economy grew at double-digit annual rates during the period 2000–12. Government revenues grew even faster, at an annual rate of 22 per cent, and growing revenues allowed for a robust expansion of government. Under the banner of creating a 'harmonious society', many new programs were introduced aimed at improving public services and expanding the social safety net to include rural citizens (Wong 2010, 2016). Many of these programs are huge: the move to provide free rural education covered some 150 million students at the outset in 2006, although the number had fallen steeply to fewer than 100 million by 2013 (MOE 2016). The rural cooperative medical scheme is even bigger – covering more than 830 million participants at its peak – and the basic pension scheme covers more than 500 million people. These programs have added enormous costs to the budgets of the counties and districts – the administrative level responsible for the provision of these services. As a result, the county-level (tier four) share of national budget expenditures jumped from 26 per cent in 2000 to 46 per cent in 2013.[4]

Because these huge programs were rolled out without any significant adjustment to intergovernmental revenue-sharing arrangements, the added expenditure had to be met largely with transfers to county governments. Central government transfers to local governments grew from RMB246 billion in 2000 to RMB4.3 trillion in 2013. Of these, 74 per cent went to the county level, whose fiscal gap had grown to an aggregated total of RMB3.16 trillion![5]

This created several problems: first, the proliferation of programs led to an even greater proliferation of transfer programs, many of them earmarked. For example, there are at least half a dozen earmarked transfers for rural basic education, along with four to five categories of general transfers designed to support salary payments for teachers, calculated on various bases – and this is just at the central government level.[6] In China's fiscal system, these transfers have to be passed down through the administrative hierarchy level by level – from Beijing to the provinces, from the provinces to the municipalities and from the municipalities to the counties and districts. As they moved down through the hierarchy, earmarked grants were often divided further into finer categories as each administrative layer tried to target funds to where they were needed. By the time the funds reached the county level, there had sometimes been more than a dozen transfers just for basic education.[7] The earmarking was often ineffective (Liu et al. 2009), and the administrative burden of managing them created an extraordinary strain on the bureaucracy, far outstripping the capacities of the monitoring and supervisory systems (World Bank 2007).[8] While the new programs have expanded public services and brought many benefits, they have been marred by pervasive wastefulness, program capture, cost inflation and even the appearance of 'ghost teachers' and 'ghost schools'.[9]

The neglect of institutional reform was even more problematic in the cities, with the urban population growing from 191 million in 1980 to 731 million in 2013 (Wong 2013a, 2013b). Amid the steep fiscal decline in the 1980s through to the mid-1990s, the government had few resources to devote to urbanisation. To avoid hindering growth, political leaders tolerated and tacitly encouraged the use of informal, backdoor practices that enabled cities to obtain the resources needed for investment in infrastructure; China's municipalities grew and prospered by relying overwhelmingly on extra-budgetary resources – mainly land sales and off-budget borrowing (Wong 2009, 2013a). Even through the recent fiscal expansion, these practices continued and ratcheted up in intensity, operating largely beyond government financial oversight.[10] The easy access to money from land and borrowing, in an economy that was expanding at double-digit rates, led inexorably to excessive land takings, overdevelopment, urban sprawl and the creation of excess capacity in industry as cities competed for job-creating investment to raise land values. These activities also brought graft and corruption on an unprecedented scale, and left many cities with unsustainable levels of debt.

Many of the provisions in the fiscal reform package laid out in 2014 were aimed at correcting the problems just described: to build a more efficient framework for service delivery in a multilevel system and to rein in local government debt and extra-budgetary revenues and regain macroeconomic oversight over fiscal activities. Great emphasis was put on improving budget transparency and accountability by strengthening the legal foundations and giving the national and subnational people's congresses greater oversight authority. Intergovernmental reform aimed to clarify and realign revenue and expenditure assignments to reduce reliance on transfers, and tax reform aimed to reduce allocative distortions and make tax a more effective tool for supporting structural reforms of the economy and improving distributional outcomes.

Given the severity of the problems of local government debt and the extent of extra-budgetary financing, all efforts during the early phase of reform were focused on public financial management (PFM) reforms and regaining control over the budget and allocative processes, to establish the accountability mechanisms needed to support an improved intergovernmental fiscal system that would come later.

The Third Plenum reforms

By far the most important step in the fiscal reform package was the rollout of the revised Budget Law in August 2014, which laid the legal foundation for improving the budget process, codifying many aspects of central-local government responsibilities and building a robust system of PFM. Among its key provisions are stipulations for shifting to a medium-term budget framework to focus on expenditure planning and multiyear budget balancing, away from the rigidity of annual budget balancing and the associated pro-cyclical bias.

The law calls for budget reporting to be comprehensive, going beyond the traditional reporting of on-budget revenue and expenditure to include three additional components: the 'government fund budget', comprising the extra-budgetary and earmarked levies that were formerly called 'extra-budgetary revenues', the biggest piece of which is revenue from land sales; the 'state capital budget', comprising remittances from SOEs; and the 'social security fund budget', comprising receipts and expenditures for pension and social insurance schemes. While the Budget Law requires the joint reporting of the four budgets, it stops short of calling for their consolidated management and allocation.

In a press conference held just after the Budget Law's passage, then finance minister Lou explained that budget transparency is paramount for combating corruption and stemming it at the source. The new Budget Law sets disclosure requirements for the scope, timing and content of comprehensive government financial reporting, not only for the four budgets, but also for selected key items, including transfer payments, government debt and departmental budgets for spending units. It also specifies legal liabilities for the breach of these budget disclosure norms (Article 92).

To ensure the accuracy and comprehensiveness of the information provided, the law specifies that budget reporting be based on accrual accounting to reflect the true operations, financial status and financial sustainability of government in the medium and long terms (Article 79). This mandate to adopt accrual accounting was endorsed by the State Council four months later, when it issued its 'Reform plan for building the comprehensive financial reporting system using accrual accounting' (Document 63) (State Council 2014b). Together, the Budget Law and Document 63 essentially committed the government to creating a new system of financial reporting. Indeed, Document 63 was ambitious in calling for the establishment by 2020 of the four systems: the government accounting system, the government financial reporting system, the system of auditing and disclosure mechanisms for government financial reports and the system for analysing and applying the information from government financial reporting to improve budget outcomes.

Another critical change under the Budget Law is the authorisation given to provincial governments to borrow through the issuance of provincial government bonds, with tight supervision by central and provincial people's congresses. Under the call to 'open the front door, lock the back door', the Budget Law stipulates that local governments must report on the amount and mode of debt and its purpose, as well as specifying the repayment sources, mechanisms of supervision and legal liabilities (Articles 35 and 94). Detailed guidelines for a debt management system are laid out in State Council Document 43, which ordered local governments to classify and report all outstanding debt by the end of 2014, and assigned to provinces the key role of registering and monitoring this debt (State Council 2014a). It prohibited local governments from borrowing through enterprises or local government financial vehicles (LGFVs) and required that existing LGFVs be separated from local government finance. In addition, the document laid out an ambitious plan to tackle the stock of existing debt by swapping existing bank loans with provincial government bonds.

Progress in implementation

It is not possible in this short chapter to provide a comprehensive review of implementation progress for the third plenum reforms. In this section, I will focus on three key areas: the process and pace of introducing the new system of government financial reporting, progress in increasing the transparency of reporting of government accounts and progress in building a system for managing and containing local government debt.

Government financial reporting

The purpose of accrual accounting is to provide more accurate and comprehensive information on government financial outcomes, including government assets, liabilities, revenue, expenses and cash flows. The new government financial reporting system (GFRS)[11] is expected to form an important part of the foundation for building a modern system of fiscal management that will promote sustainability and good governance. From the start, the Ministry of Finance (MOF) made clear that the new GFRS would be built on international standards modified to fit China's conditions.

Because the new GFRS will be so different from previous financial reporting practices, building this new system will be a complex project with many steps – from extending the scope of reporting to adopting accrual accounting standards, developing standardised accounting rules, building a balance sheet that includes all entities with claims on public resources and establishing an integrated information system linking all reporting entities. In many countries that have adopted accrual accounting, the process of building the system took up to a decade of sustained effort (Liu et al. 2015). In China, the size and difficulty of the project are magnified many times by the large size of the country and the highly decentralised fiscal system, where the GFRS has to be adopted by subnational governments down to the county and district levels – a group that includes more than 3,200 budgeting authorities with widely varying capacities.[12]

Identifying the reporting entities is among the first critical tasks in building the GFRS. According to the principle that government financial reporting must include all entities that have a material impact on the government's fiscal position, international standards call for the inclusion of all SOEs as well as LGFVs that meet the control criteria.[13] Given the large number and size of SOEs in China, including their impact on government finances will be an important corrective to what has long been a blind spot in budget reporting.

There are different ways of including the enterprises depending on the nature of their interaction with the budget. SOEs that are strictly market-oriented and have only an arm's-length relationship with government can be included as commercial enterprises. They must file an annual report with the government disclosing their operations and financial status, but their assets and liabilities need not be included in the government balance sheet. Enterprises that have close, recurrent financial interaction with government would be classified as government business corporations, and their accounts must be fully consolidated in the government financial statement. The differing reporting requirements for the two types of enterprises are briefly summarised in Table 8.1.

The first big challenge for the GFRS reform is to collect financial information from SOEs as the basis for their classification as well as for recording. This is not as straightforward as it seems. Until now, enterprise information has been collected not by budget departments but by the State-owned Assets Supervision and Administration Commission (SASAC) and other supervisory agencies, with each agency using a different methodology for counting; there seems to be no agreed set of numbers. This is illustrated by the situation in Beijing Municipality. As shown in Table 8.2, data from four authoritative sources give significantly different statistics on the number of enterprises and their financial statistics.

Table 8.1 Classification of SOEs and their reporting in the GFRS

SOEs	
Government business corporations ('Public benefit' SOEs)	*Commercial SOEs*
• Full disclosure. • Fully consolidated in government financial statements. • Included in government's statements of operations, cash flow and balance sheets.	• Full disclosure in a separate schedule in government financial report. • Assets and liabilities are not included in government balance sheet. • Net assets are recognised as government investment in government balance sheets.

Table 8.2 Differing counts of SOEs in Beijing Municipality, 2013 (RMB billion)

	Number of enterprises	*Total assets*	*Total debt*	*Equity*	*Operating revenue*	*Profits*
A	790	2,333.5	1,202.1	1,131.4	1,068.0	70.9
B	549	573.3	458.6	395.7	436.2	33.1
C	–	2,520.9	1,724.5	796.4	949.9	47.2
D	7,040	3,513.5	–	1,098.6	1,106.6	65.3

Sources: Row A from NBS (2014: Table 13.4); B: BMBS (2014: Table 11.8); C: Beijing Municipal SASAC (2015); D: MOF (2014: 605–6).

– no data

One reason for the differences may be that some of the data refer to all SOEs, while others refer only to SOEs above a specified minimum size; however, a more significant reason for the conflicting numbers may be the complex ownership and control structures that characterise many SOEs. To illustrate, in 2015, there were 46 SOEs that reported directly to the Beijing Municipal SASAC, but most of these were actually enterprise 'groups' comprising many subsidiary companies, so that the number of municipal-owned SOEs was many multiples of 46. For example, the Beijing Municipal Drainage Group (one of the 46) had 28 subsidiaries that engaged in different parts of the water business, from supplying fresh water to disposal of waste water and pipeline management – many of them independent legal entities.[14] For complex enterprises like this, the classification exercise will likely have to go to the subsidiary level.

To complicate matters further, many SOEs engage in some public goods provision alongside their market activities. For example, the Beijing Municipal Infrastructure Investment Corporation is responsible for the financing and construction of subways – a task that has clear characteristics of being a public good – but it also owns 11 subsidiary companies that engage in for-profit land and real estate development, and the extent to which these activities cross-subsidise one another is unrecorded.

Given the pervasive lack of a clear boundary between the public and the market, financial interactions between governments and SOEs are often fuzzy and complex. In these circumstances, a strict application of the International Public Sector Accounting Standards (IPSAS) and Government Financial Statistics (GFS) rules might require the full inclusion (with line-by-line consolidation of their financial status) of a huge portion of SOEs in the GFRS, which would impose an impossible task for quick adoption. In addition, there are some 660,000 public institutions, such as hospitals, universities, research institutes and so on, that provide public services at the behest of government but also have business incomes, and whose financial relationship with government will require sorting through. To keep the task to manageable proportions, the interim solution – at least until 2015 – has been for many local governments to classify all SOEs as commercial and focus on classifying their LGFVs.[15] In some localities the exercise morphed to simply classifying profitable enterprises as 'commercial' and unprofitable ones as 'public benefit' and putting the latter on the budget.[16]

Unresolved issues in classification notwithstanding, other preparatory work has been proceeding on the GFRS. In November 2015, the MOF issued a document on government financial reporting methodology that laid out plans for determining the scope of the trial effort. The plans called for the development of government financial information systems and training to be conducted in 2016, and, beginning in 2017, compilation of the pilot GFRS (MOF 2015b). In March 2018, the MOF officially launched a pilot program for compiling government financial reports for the 2017 fiscal year using accrual accounting. In this phase, the pilot involves 20 central government agencies and 20 provinces or line item cities, and focuses only on the budgets of the pilot agencies, rather than the whole government (MOF 2018b). Those involved in the pilot are to follow the 140-page trial 'Guidelines for the Preparation of Financial Reports for Government Departments' (MOF 2018a).

The work on construction of a government balance sheet also appears to be progressing. Led by the National Bureau of Statistics (NBS), working with 10 other agencies including the National Development and Reform Commission (NDRC), pilot work was conducted from May 2015 to the end of 2016 in 11 provinces. A draft 'Work Program for National and Local Balance Sheet Preparation' was circulated for comment and was signed off in April 2017 by 13 ministries and sent to the State Council. In June of that year, it was approved at the thirty-sixth meeting of the Central Leading Group for Deepening Reform, and formally issued by the State Council on 6 August 2017, launching the next phase of the work (Xinhua 2017a). However, this document has not been made publicly available. It has been widely reported that a trial national balance sheet was constructed for 2013 but has also not been published (see, for example, 21st Century Economic Herald 2017).

Budget transparency

While the progress of building the GFRS has been largely invisible to the general public, the remarkable progress in budget transparency has been much more visible and quantifiable. In just three years since the Budget Law laid down a mandate to release government financial reports to the public, every subnational government down to the county level has set up a website from which a trove of fiscal information can be harvested by anyone with access to a computer or smartphone. This is in marked contrast with previous attempts to promote budget transparency – most notably in the earlier rounds of PFM reform in the late 1990s and mid-2000s, when there was little follow through and virtually no penetration to the subnational levels (Wong 2005; Liu 2017). Disclosure requirements are now codified and written into the Budget Law. Article 14 stipulates that governments at all levels must disclose their budgets to the public within 20 days of approval by the people's congress, and the disclosure 'shall explain important matters such as the receipt and uses of transfer payments and debt issuance'. Disclosure requirements are also applied to the budgets of government departments as well as to government procurement. The law also calls for budgets to be audited and for the audit reports on budget execution to also be made public (Article 73). Finally, Article 92 stipulates that failure to meet transparency requirements will trigger corrective action and an investigation into the administrative responsibilities of managers.

Monitoring and enforcement have followed. The MOF's Supervision Department issued a notification on 20 October 2015 announcing the first inspection would take place between 28 October and 20 November 2015. The stated purpose was to check compliance with the Budget Law's requirements for timeliness, completeness, level of detail and information disclosure (MOF 2015a). The inspection covered 258,296 budget units at the provincial, municipal and county levels, achieving 100 per cent coverage. It found compliance rates of 100 per cent at the provincial and municipal levels and 99 per cent at the county level for disclosures of both the 2015 budgets and the 2014 final accounts, but somewhat lower rates for disclosure of departmental budgets and provision of the required content (MOF 2016a).

On the basis of these findings, the MOF issued two documents in 2016 to provide further guidance on the scope of public disclosure. Document 123 stipulated that all local governments set up a unified online platform to disclose their budgetary information, and to include budget disclosure as an additional indicator in the performance evaluation of staff in local finance departments (MOF 2016b). Document 143 ('Operating Procedures for Local Government Budget Disclosures') provides more specific requirements: disclosures must cover all four budgets, with a minimum of six tables for the general budget, four tables for government funds and two each for the state capital budget and the social security fund budget (MOF 2016c). In 2016, an additional criterion was added to check for honesty, with inspectors urged to randomly select units and figures for verification, and to include their findings in the overall scoring.

Three rounds of nationwide inspections have been undertaken, including the third one concluded in December 2017 (Liu 2017). This monitoring effort and the change of incentives are clearly producing results. My own casual perusal of local budget reporting on government websites reveals a growing wealth of fiscal information that is now available online.

Local budget disclosures tend to follow the pace set by the MOF with some lag. For example, in 2009 the MOF provided 61 lines of detail in the final account of budget expenditures. In 2010, it moved to providing 1,020 lines of detail, and the number has since crept up to close to 1,100 lines. Many, but not all, local budget reports follow this template in providing detailed breakdowns of public expenditures running up to 1,000 lines or more. As required, they all contain information on transfers, both inflows and outflows, and all four budgets are provided and comply with the stipulated numbers of tables for each.

To date, these budget reports are still constructed under the old accounting system and on a cash basis. Detailed budgeting is quite advanced on the public finance budget (which used to be called in-budget), but less so on the government fund budget, and even less so on the state capital budget and the social security budget. As expected, the quality of reporting differs across regions, and is higher in the richer, more developed provinces than in the poorer, inland ones. At present, while the budgets are all available publicly, finding them is not always straightforward due to a lack of uniformity in where the information is placed, with budgets sometimes scattered across different websites or in different places within websites. The reporting format and content continue to differ across regions and administrative levels. With the increasingly stringent reporting requirements being implemented, these differences can be expected to shrink over time.

Indeed, this may already be changing. On 6 November 2017, Jiangsu officially launched the 'Jiangsu Budget and Final Accounts Open Access Platform', becoming the first province in China to provide a province-wide platform that includes all local government budget reporting. Developed and built by the provincial finance department and the government service office, the platform aims to provide a centralised portal from which all provincial-, municipal- and county-level budgets and final accounts information can be accessed by the public, and where all reports will use the same templates and uniform standards (Xinhua 2017b).

Managing and containing debt

The thrust of the reform effort in managing local government debt was to ameliorate the default risks from the large existing stock while moving local government borrowing from hidden, off-budget channels into the open, nudging local governments towards a more fiscally sustainable path.

Key provisions of the Budget Law were designed to put in place mechanisms for preventing unsupervised borrowing by local governments. For the first time, they are explicitly permitted to borrow, but under tight control. Article 35 stipulates that local governments can borrow only under quotas from the cap set by the National People's Congress and allocated by the State Council, and only for capital spending, with the use, repayment and assignment of responsibilities supervised by the local people's congresses. The borrowing must be done through bond issuance by the provinces, which are assigned responsibility for allocating and monitoring the debt. Local governments are prohibited from borrowing through any other means or organisations, and from providing guarantees for borrowing by state entities. Article 94 stipulates that any diversion or misuse of funds is punishable by dismissal of those responsible.

Under State Council Document 43, a plan was laid out to tackle the stock of existing debt and create a structure for managing it (State Council 2014a). Along with the Budget Law, this document prohibited LGFVs borrowing on behalf of local governments and ordered them to delink their finances from local government. All existing debt was to be classified as 'general', 'project' or 'enterprise' debt. All general and project debt would be moved to the government's accounts, and many LGFVs would be converted to SOEs. A national registry and an early warning system for local government debt would be built. A program was introduced in 2015 to swap government bonds for local government bank debt. By the end of 2017, RMB10.5 trillion in bonds had been swapped, significantly improving the term structure of local debt and reducing its servicing costs (NAO 2017).

Judging by the outcome of curtailing local government borrowing and keeping it within legal channels, these reform efforts have been a dismal failure. First, rather than fading into history, LGFVs have continued to flourish. World Bank staff estimated the total liabilities of LGFVs (in both bank credit and bonds) grew at more than 20 per cent per annum in both 2015 and 2016, surpassing the growth of overall corporate debt to see their share of outstanding debt in the nonfinancial corporate sector rise from 25 per cent in 2013 to 30 per cent in 2016 (World Bank 2017). In part, this was because the government temporarily lifted the restraint on LGFV borrowing in mid-2015 when economic growth slowed drastically. Ironically, because the debt reclassification exercise had removed a good deal of debt from the balance sheets of LGFVs, many were now in an improved position to borrow, and were unconstrained by the cap on government borrowing as their debt was, under the new Budget Law, not counted as government debt. One estimate has LGFV bonds reaching RMB47 trillion in June 2017 – nearly three times the total local government debt recorded in the MOF monitoring system (Yu et al. 2018).

Second, local governments have continued to find hidden ways to borrow, including new ones such as public-private partnerships and service procurement contracts. Other methods are not so new: borrowing from SOEs, LGFVs and local banks and pushing fiscal expenditures on to them, non-payment of construction contracts, and so on (Yu et al. 2018). The numerous problems exposed by MOF inspections and by the National Audit Office (NAO) came to the top leadership's attention by mid-2016, culminating in the 'Plan for Emergency Response to Local Government Debt Risks', issued by the State Council in October 2016, which required all local governments to set up a Leading Group for Debt Management and assign responsibilities for strengthening monitoring and preparing emergency responses (State Council 2016). In April and May 2017, a package of decrees was issued jointly by the MOF, NDRC, People's Bank of China (PBC), China Banking Regulatory Commission (CBRC), China Securities Regulatory Commission (CSRC) and the Ministry of Justice, setting out further responsibilities of local governments for monitoring and assigning accountability not only for direct debt, but also for contingent debts, and again stressing that LGFVs must be delinked from government finances. The MOF issued several more directives in 2017 reiterating the prohibition of off-budget borrowing and the use of LGFVs for borrowing.

The one bright spot has been the growth and development of a market for government securities, including local government bonds. Over time, this may become a normal channel for local government borrowing. According to the MOF's accounts, 90 per cent of the local government debt currently reported is held in government bonds. While they are still not market-based, this may change over time.

Conclusion

The fiscal reforms initiated by then finance minister Lou Jiwei were comprehensive in scope and extremely far reaching. They set about building infrastructure for budget management that is better able to support the increasingly large and complex public sector in China, which rivals the size of the US Federal Government in annual spending. When completed, the new government financial reporting system will provide detailed information on the true size and operations of the public sector that will support more sophisticated whole-of-government analyses. Accompanied by stringent disclosure rules and improved accounting standards, the system will provide higher-level governments with the information base for designing improved intergovernmental arrangements – the ultimate goal of Lou's reform package.

In this review, I have identified significant progress towards installing the GFRS. More importantly, I believe the process of collecting and scrutinising the financial claims of all state-owned entities on the budget has also set in motion a new dynamic that will gradually lead to a clarification of the boundary between the state and the market, as local governments have greater incentive to loosen their ties to SOEs to reduce the administrative burden of reporting as well as to improve the government's balance sheet to make room for new debt. The remarkable increase in transparency in local government financial reporting will enhance the ability of higher levels to hold local governments accountable and reduce opportunities for the diversion of funds. Putting this information into the public sphere will also create greater potential for public participation in budgeting, whether intended or not.

These reforms are just starting, however, and their progress is fragile and could easily be reversed. The failure of debt containment provides a perfect illustration of the uselessness of building structures when rules can be circumvented or are not enforced. Even though a national registry of local government debt has been in operation since 2015 – along with an early warning system for fiscal risks – to date, they are but empty shells, as they are unable to track hidden debt and do not count the contingent liabilities of LGFVs.

The experience of the past five years has confirmed the enormous difficulty of, and the long road ahead for, fiscal reform, which must compete with other macroeconomic concerns (such as the rate of growth) and powerful vested interests. The recent appointment of Liu Kun as finance minister signals that fiscal reform will continue in Xi Jinping's second term. With the focus turning to intergovernmental reform and doubling down on efforts to contain local government debt, Liu's experience in Guangdong should prove particularly useful since the province has been a leader in performance management and debt resolution.[17] While hoping for a supportive policy environment for fiscal reform, Minister Liu would do well to fast-track a program of capacity-building in the MOF and subnational finance bureaus. This new system is administratively far more demanding than the one being replaced, and will require higher-level skills.

Notes

1 As early as 2002, the government announced its goal of shifting to a development paradigm that promotes services and consumption in place of industry and investment (Wong 2010).
2 Fieldwork information, June 2014.
3 On the eve of reform, nearly 80 per cent of government revenue came from state-owned enterprises in industry (Wong 1993).
4 Author's calculations from Ministry of Finance (MOF) statistics.
5 Equal to 20 per cent of total expenditure in 2013.
6 MOF and fieldwork information.
7 Fieldwork information, 2006–07.
8 For the history of how systems of accountability were weakened by the dismantling of the planned economy and the subsequent long fiscal decline, see Wong (2009). For weaknesses of the systems of monitoring and evaluation, see Wong (2012, 2013a).
9 See World Bank (2007) and Fock and Wong (2008) for problems of rural public finance and service delivery, and Lin and Wong (2012) for examples of problems in the design and distribution of rural subsidies.
10 For an early account of how the central government was kept largely in the dark on the development of local government financial vehicles (LGFVs) and the extent of local government borrowing, see Wong (2011).
11 To distinguish this new system in China from the Government Financial Statistics (GFS) system widely adopted internationally, this chapter will refer to the Chinese system of government finance reporting as the GFRS.
12 Budgeting authorities include 31 provincial governments and five cities with 'line item' status (Shenzhen, Dalian, Qingdao, Ningbo and Xiamen), more than 300 prefectural level governments, 2,850 counties and districts and, of course, the central government itself.
13 This is true for both the International Monetary Fund's (IMF) GFS and the International Public Sector Accounting Standards (IPSAS). IPSAS determines that a government controls an entity if it meets the three criteria: 1) power over the entity (such as voting rights, the right to appoint senior management and to approve or veto the entity's business decisions); 2) exposure, or rights, to variable benefits (financial or nonfinancial) from its involvement with the entity; and 3) the ability to use its power over the entity to affect the nature or amount of the benefits from its involvement with the other entity.
14 Fieldwork information, June 2015.
15 Fieldwork, June 2015.
16 Fieldwork, June 2016.
17 Liu headed the debt resolution in the bankruptcy of the Guangdong International Trust and Investment Corporation in the late 1990s (Times Weekly 2018).

References

21st Century Economic Herald (2017), The Central Leading Group for Comprehensively Deepening Reform approved the work plan to compile national and local balance sheets, [in Chinese], *21st Century Economic Herald*, 27 June. Available from: www.cb.com.cn/economy/2017_0627/1188687.html.

Beijing Municipal Bureau of Statistics (BMBS) (2014), *Beijing Statistical Yearbook 2014*, Beijing: China Statistics Press.

Beijing Municipal State-owned Assets Supervision and Administration Commission (SASAC) (2015), Website, [in Chinese]. Available from: www.bjgzw.gov.cn/qt/forepageview/gzhy/gzhy15.jsp.

Fock, A. and Wong, C. (2008), *Financing rural development for a harmonious society in China: Recent reforms in public finance and their prospects*, World Bank Policy Research Working Paper 4693, August, Washington, DC: The World Bank.

Han, J., Li, G. and Yuxin, H. (2014), Deep changes that affect the modernization of the nation's governance system: Minister of finance Lou Jiwei explains the overall program for deepening reform of the fiscal system, *Xinhua*, 4 July.

International Monetary Fund (IMF) (2015), *Government Finance Statistics Manual 2014*, Washington, DC: IMF.

Lin, W. and Wong, C. (2012), Are Beijing's equalization policies reaching the poor? An analysis of direct subsidies under the 'three rurals' (Sannong), *China Journal* 67(January). doi.org/10.1086/665738.

Liu, L., Pradelli, J. and Zhao, M. (2015), *International experience on subnational financial reporting for managing fiscal risks*, World Bank Policy Note (Draft), Washington, DC: The World Bank.

Liu, M. (2017), An important promoter of 'transparent government': A special inspection of local budgets and final accounts open a 'window' for the public, *China Finance and Economics News*, 1 March. Available from: www.mof.gov.cn/zhengwuxinxi/caijingshidian/zgcjb/201703/t20170301_2544207.html.

Liu, M., Wang, J., Tao, R. and Murphy, R. (2009), The political economy of earmarked transfers in a state-designated poor county in western China: Central policies and local responses, *The China Quarterly* 200(December): 973–94. doi.org/10.1017/S0305741009990580.

Lou, J. (2014), Deepening reform of the fiscal and tax system to build a modern system of public finance, [in Chinese], *Qiushi* 20(13 October).

Ministry of Education (MOE) (2016), *Chinese Education Statistical Yearbook*, Beijing: China Statistics Press.

Ministry of Finance (MOF) (2014), *China Accounting Yearbook 2014*, Beijing: MOF.

Ministry of Finance (MOF) (2015a), *Notification on launching a special inspection of the situation of local budget disclosures*, [in Chinese], Doc. 84, Supervision and Inspection Bureau, 20 October, Beijing: MOF.

Ministry of Finance (MOF) (2015b), *Notification on the issuance of government financial reporting methodology (trial)*, MOF Doc. 212, 16 November, Beijing: MOF.

Ministry of Finance (MOF) (2016a), *Bulletin on inspection of local budget and final accounts and NEV subsidies*, [in Chinese], 8 September, Beijing: MOF Press Office. Available from: www.mof.gov.cn/zhengwuxinxi/bulinggonggao/tongzhitonggao/201609/t20160908_2413434.htm.

Ministry of Finance (MOF) (2016b), *Notice on conscientiously doing a good job on local government budget disclosures*, [in Chinese], MOF Doc. 123, Beijing: MOF. Available from: yss.mof.gov.cn/zhengwuxinxi/zhengceguizhang/201609/t20160924_2426035.html.

Ministry of Finance (MOF) (2016c), *Operating procedures for local government budget disclosures*, [in Chinese], MOF Doc. 143, Beijing: MOF. Available from: www.mof.gov.cn/gp/xxgkml/yss/201611/t20161121_2510868.html.

Ministry of Finance (MOF) (2018a), *Circular of the Ministry of Finance on revising and printing the 'guidelines for the preparation of financial reports for government departments (trial)'*, [in Chinese], MOF Doc. 29, 1 March, Beijing: MOF. Available from: www.weichicaiwu.com/law/4258.html.

Ministry of Finance (MOF) (2018b), *Notice of the Ministry of Finance on launching the pilot work of 2017 government financial report compilation*, [in Chinese], MOF Doc. 34, 12 March, Beijing: MOF. Available from: www.waizi.org.cn/doc/31883.html.

National Audit Office of China (NAO) (2017), Report of the Ministry of Finance on resolutely stopping local governments illegally raising debt, [in Chinese], 12 December, *Wall Street News*. Available from: wallstreetcn.com/articles/3051249.

National Bureau of Statistics (NBS) (2014), *China Statistical Yearbook 2014*, Beijing: China Statistics Press.

National People's Congress (NPC) Standing Committee (2014), *Decision on revising the 'People's Republic of China Budget Law'*, [in Chinese], 31 August, Beijing: NPC of the People's Republic of China. Available from: www.npc.gov.cn/npc/xinwen/2014–09/01/content_1877061.htm.

State Council (2014a), *Opinion on strengthening management of local government debt*, Doc. 43, 21 September, Beijing: State Council.

State Council (2014b), *Reform plan for building the comprehensive financial reporting system using accrual accounting*, [in Chinese], Doc. 63, 12 December, Beijing: State Council.

State Council (2016), *Plan for emergency response to local government debt risks*, [in Chinese], Office of the State Council Letter No. 88, 27 October, Beijing: State Council.

Times Weekly (2018), Finance Minister Liu Kun's past in Guangdong, [in Chinese], *Times Weekly*, 27 March. Available from: news.sina.com.cn/c/2018–03–27/doc-ifysrpxk6278916.shtml.

Wong, C. (1993), Public Finance and Economic Decentralization, in W Galenson (ed.), *China's Economic Reform in the 1990s*, Ann Arbor: University of Michigan Press.

Wong, C. (2005), Public sector budgeting issues in China, in Organisation for Economic Co-operation and Development (OECD), *Governance in China*, Paris: OECD Publishing.

Wong, C. (2009), Rebuilding government for the 21st century: Can China incrementally reform the public sector?, *China Quarterly* 200(December). doi.org/10.1017/S0305741009990567.

Wong, C. (2010), Fiscal reform: Paying for the harmonious society, *China Economic Quarterly* 14(2): 22–7.

Wong, C. (2011), The fiscal stimulus program and problems of macroeconomic management in China, *OECD Journal on Budgeting* 11(3): 1–24. doi.org/10.1787/budget-11–5kg3nhljqrjl.

Wong, C. (2012), *Toward building performance-oriented management in China: The critical role of M&E and the long road ahead*, ECD Working Paper Series No. 27, September, Washington, DC: World Bank Independent Evaluation Group.

Wong, C. (2013a), Paying for urbanization: Challenges for China's municipal finance in the 21st century, in R. Bahl, J. Linn and D. Wetzel (eds), *Metropolitan Government Finances in Developing Countries*, Cambridge, MA: Lincoln Institute for Land Policy.

Wong, C. (2013b), Reforming China's public finances for long-term growth, in R. Garnaut, C. Fang and L. Song (eds), *China: A new model for growth and development*, Canberra: ANU E Press. doi.org/10.22459/CNMGD.07.2013.10.

Wong, C. (2016), Budget reform in China: Progress and prospects in the Xi Jinping era, *OECD Journal on Budgeting* 15(3): 27–36. doi.org/10.1787/budget-15–5jm0zbtm3pzn.

Wong, C. and Bird, R. (2008), China's Fiscal System: A Work in Progress, in L. Brandt and T. Rawski (eds), *China's Great Transformation: Origins, Mechanism and Consequences of the Post-Reform Economic Boom*, New York: Cambridge University Press.

World Bank (2002), *China: National Development and Sub-national Finance, a Review of Provincial Expenditures*, Report No. 22951-CHA, April, Washington, DC: World Bank.

World Bank (2007), *China: Public services for building the new socialist countryside*, Report No. 40221-CN, Washington, DC: The World Bank.

World Bank (2017), *China Economic Update – December 2017: Growth, resilience and reform momentum*, 19 December, Washington, DC: The World Bank.

Xi, J. (2013), An explanation of the Chinese Communist Party Central Committee decision on several major questions about deepening reform, [in Chinese], *Xinhua*, 15 November. Available from: news.xinhuanet.com/politics/2013-11/15/c_118164294.htm.

Xinhua (2017a), National Bureau of Statistics answers reporters' questions on the programme for national and local balance sheet preparation, [in Chinese], *Xinhua*, 31 October. Available from: www.xinhuanet.com/fortune/2017–10/31/c_129729861.htm.

Xinhua (2017b), Government finance reports can be checked and supervised in Jiangsu, *Xinhua Daily*, 11 November. Available from: news.sina.com.cn/o/2017–11–07/doc-ifynmnae2405315.shtml.

Yu, H., Wang, X. and Teng, J. X. (2018), China battles hidden local government debt, *Caixin Global*, 11 March. Available from: www.caixinglobal.com/2018–03–11/china-battles-hidden-local-government-debt-101219793.html.

Zhang, Y. S. and Barnett, S. (2014), *Fiscal vulnerabilities and risks from local government finance in China*, IMF Working Paper No. 14/4, January, Washington, DC: International Monetary Fund.

9

IMPLEMENTING CHINA'S WTO COMMITMENTS IN CHINESE FINANCIAL SERVICES LAW

Sanzhu Zhu

Source: China Review, 6, 2, 2006, pp. 3–33.

When China acceded to the World Trade Organization (WTO) in December 2001, China made a series of commitments to further open up its banking, insurance, securities and auto financing markets. The commitments were stated in detail in the section 7 of the Schedule of Specific Commitments on Services,[1] supplementary to China's general commitments stated in the Protocol on the Accession of the People's Republic of China[2] and the Report of the Working Party on the Accession of China.[3] Since then China has embarked upon a process of implementing these commitments and reforming China's financial services law and regulations. This article attempts to examine some of the issues and problems highlighted in the WTO annual transitional reviews of the implementation by China of its WTO commitments.[4] It then analyses the economic impacts that the changes of China's financial services law and regulations has brought about in implementing China's commitments. Finally it looks at the perspectives of future changes of China's financial services law and regulations.

Banking

China's WTO commitments on banking services covered a wide range of banking services, including deposit services, lending of all types, financial leasing, all payment and money transmission services, guarantees and commitments, foreign exchange trading for own account or for customers. In summary, China committed that foreign financial institutions would be permitted to provide foreign currency services without client or geographic restrictions upon accession; within two years after accession foreign financial institutions could provide local currency services to Chinese enterprises and within five years to all Chinese clients; geographic restrictions to local currency business would be phased out within five years; any existing non-prudential measures restricting ownership, operation, branching and licenses would be eliminated within five years after accession.[5]

After China's accession, China promulgated the Regulations on Administration of Foreign-invested Financial Institutions on 20 December 2001, effective as of February 1, 2002 (hereinafter as 2001 Regulations). On January 29, 2002, the Implementing Rules for the 2001 Regulations was issued by the People's Bank of China (PBOC) (hereinafter as 2002 Implementing Rules). This set of regulations and implementing rules became a direct source of implementation of China's commitment on banking services. The 2002 Implementing Rules was soon amended in July 2004 and new implementing rules came into effect on September 1, 2004 (hereinafter as 2004 Implementing Rules).

In April 2003, China Banking Regulatory Commission (CBRC) was set up to take up regulatory functions formerly exercised by the PBOC. In December of the same year the Law on the Regulation of Banking Industry was adopted, which set out general principles as well as specific regulatory requirements for the banking industry. It confers the CBRC with powers to issue rules and measures and to authorise establishments of domestic and foreign banking financial institutions.[6] Since its establishment, the CBRC has played an active role in day-to-day implementation of China's WTO commitments. The Announcement on Further Opening up Renminbi Business to Foreign-invested Financial Institutions, announced on October 24, 2003, was one of the WTO implementation documents from the CBRC, which added Jinan, Fuzhou, Chengdu and Chongqing as opening-up cities for local currency business effective as of December 1, 2003.

Requirements for foreign-invested financial institutions

The 2001 Regulations defines foreign-invested financial institutions as those financial institutions that have been authorised to establish and operate in China in accordance with Chinese law and regulations in one of the five forms, namely, a wholly foreign-owned bank the headquarter of which is in China, a branch of foreign banks, a joint venture bank established by foreign financial institutions and Chinese parties, a wholly foreign-owned finance company the headquarter of which is in China, and a joint venture finance company established by foreign financial institutions and Chinese parties.[7]

A key requirement complaint about by the WTO member states was so-called one-year-waiting rule for branching. According to Articles 14 and 15 of the 2002 Implementing Rules, if foreign banks, joint venture banks and wholly foreign-owned banks apply to increase their branches in China, they have to wait for one year to submit their applications to the PBOC from the date they received their last approval to open up a branch. This rule was criticised, first, as being inconsistent with China's commitment in the Schedule of Specific Commitments on Services to only retain prudential restrictions in its licensing regime for banking[8] and second, as constituting a very significant barrier to market access, which had not been scheduled by China in its WTO commitments.[9]

In response to the complaints of the WTO member states, China amended this one-year-waiting rule in the 2004 Implementing Rules. Articles 16 and 17 of the 2004 Implementing Rules have now replaced Articles 14 and 15 of the 2002 Implementing Rules, in which the one-year-waiting rule has been deleted. Foreign banks, joint venture banks and wholly foreign-owned banks can now submit applications for branching without waiting for one year. But there is one situation where the one-year-waiting rule still applies in the same way as before. That is when applicant banks fail to contact local department of the CBRC within 15 days after the CBRC has accepted their application and notified them.

There were debates among Chinese scholars about whether the market entry requirements set out by the 2001 Regulations and the 2002 Implementing Rules were consistent with China's WTO commitments. Some scholars compared requirements for domestic banks and foreign-invested banks and pointed out that there were restrictive requirements that were inconsistent with China's WTO commitments. One example cited was the requirement prescribed in Articles 4 and 5 of the 2002 Implementing Rules that the sole shareholder or the largest shareholder of a wholly foreign-owned bank or sole foreign shareholder or the largest foreign shareholder of a joint venture bank must be commercial banks.[10]

Other scholars analysed the restrictive requirements from a prudential point of view, arguing that some of the restrictive requirements were consistent with China's WTO commitments while others were not. The qualification for the sole or the largest shareholder for foreign-invested banks was also regarded by this group of scholars as being inconsistent with China's WTO commitments.[11] The 2004 Implementing Rules subsequently made some changes, like the one-year-waiting rule, but other restrictive requirements remained the same. It seems that if a restrictive requirement is absolutely necessary in accordance with prudential principle, it should not be argued as being inconsistent with China's WTO commitment. But as there is a degree of prudence, prudential principle could be used by China as an argument to justify unnecessary restrictive rules that constitute market barriers and thus inconsistent with China's commitment.

Economic impacts of the changes of banking law and regulations

Since 1979 when the first representative office of foreign banks was set up in China, China's banking services market has been gradually opened up to foreign financial institutions. The opening-up process has been from the cities of special economic zones and coastal regions to the big cities in other parts of China, and from foreign currency business to local currency business. China's WTO accession and subsequent changes to banking law and regulations have promoted this opening-up process to a new height. By the end of October 2004, 62 foreign banks from 19 countries and regions had established 204 businesses in China, among which 105 were permitted to provide local currency business; cities opened up for local currency business were increased to 18 and a total of 223 representative offices had been set up.[12]

Table 9.1 Foreign Bank Establishments in China by the End of October 2004

Business established by foreign banks	*Licences for local currency business*	*Cities opened up for local currency business*	*Representative offices*
204	105	18	223

Before China's WTO accession, the customers of foreign banks came mainly from multinational companies operating in China and Chinese-foreign equity and cooperative joint ventures. The banking law and regulations have now implemented China's WTO commitment to allow foreign banks to provide local currency business to Chinese enterprises, which has intensified competition between foreign banks and domestic banks. Consequent to the increased foreign participation and competition as a result of the relaxation of banking law and regulation, an urgent need to reform Chinese state-owned commercial banks has been highlighted.

Tang Shuangning, deputy chairman of the CBRC, said in a speech at the 2004 APEC Finance and Development Program Forum that without improving the competitiveness of Chinese commercial banks the gap between foreign banks and Chinese banks would increase when Chinese banking market fully opens up in 2006, and this would have a huge impact on banking sector and would also affect the sustainable development of national economy.[13] The decision China made at the end of 2003 to restructure Bank of China and China Construction Bank by injecting an unprecedented US$ 45 billion foreign exchange reserve reflected such an urgent need to reform Chinese state-owned commercial banks in the context of post-WTO.

By the end of 2004 the total asset of foreign banks in China reached US$ 65.9 billion, being a 1.8% of the total asset of all banking institutions in China.[14] Martin Fish, the head of China operation of Standard Chartered Bank commented in an interview that the market share of foreign banks in China was not big yet, but the role they played in moving the market forward was much greater than the market share.[15] As new measures and regulations are being adopted to further open up China's banking services market, there is no doubt that the market share of foreign banks and their impact on China's banking industry and national economy will increase.

Among the measures implemented by the CBRC at the end of 2004, a green channel was initiated to speed up approval process for foreign financial institutions to set up business in West and North-East regions. In addition, if they apply for local currency business in these regions, their applications would be favoured with a relaxed requirement for profits. Instead of taking into account only the profit of the applicant branch, all the profits the applicant bank made from all its branches in China would be taken into account when approving the application.[16] These measures will encourage foreign banks to move into West and North-East poorer regions, but on the other hand, such preferential policies designed to speed up economic development in certain regions will create unequal treatment among foreign banks as well as between Chinese domestic and foreign banks.

Future changes of banking law and regulations

In the process of gradually opening up China's banking services market in the past twenty years, China promulgated a series of administrative regulations. The first was the 1985 Regulations on the Administration of Foreign Banks and Chinese-foreign Joint Venture Banks in Special Economic Zones. This was followed by the 1990 Measures on the Administration of Foreign Financial Institutions and Chinese-foreign Joint Venture Financial Institutions in Shanghai, the 1991 Measures on the Administration of Representative Offices of Foreign Financial Institutions, the 1994 Regulations on the Administration of Foreign-Invested Financial Institutions, and the 1996 Provisional Measures on the Administration of Renminbi Business Trial by Foreign Financial Institutions in Shanghai Pudong.

It is clear that the pattern of these regulations and measures was closely associated with the economic reform and opening-up policy implemented in China since 1979. They reflected different stages of the economic reform and opening-up policy, starting first from special economic zones and then to the rest part of China. In line with the government's overall policy to attract foreign investments, a combination policy of restrictions and preferential treatments was implemented in banking regulations. On one hand, there were many restrictions for foreign banks ranging from entry requirements, business scope, locations and branching, on the other hand, preferential treatments were employed to attract foreign banking investment, such as preferential income tax rates implemented in special economic zones.

The evolution of banking law and regulations in the past twenty years indicates that the future changes of banking law and regulations will be guided by the economic reform and opening-up policy in the context of post-WTO. A central theme running through the reform of banking law and regulations at present is the implementation of China's WTO commitments. One can see that China is implementing its WTO commitments on banking services stage by stage and some positive reforms are taking place. But in the meantime, various restrictions are still in place, which need to be reviewed and changed in the future.

As banking law and regulations continue to implement China's commitments, it is anticipated that foreign participation in China's banking industry will be steadily increasing. It is natural for foreign banks to expand their business in China. They would like to have a more relaxed legal and regulatory environment and a wider scope of business, for example, local currency futures business.[17] On the other hand, national financial security is a paramount concern from China's point of view. Some scholars advocated an effective control of foreign financial institutions and their participation in China's banking industry through legislations on banking takeover activities in order to prevent Chinese banks from falling into the hands of foreign banks.[18] It seems that an appropriate approach is to strike a right balance between the need to further relax legal and regulatory environment for foreign participation in China's banking industry and the need to safeguard national financial security.

Insurance

China's WTO commitments on insurance services covered a wide range of insurance services including life insurance, health, pension and annuities insurance, nonlife insurance and reinsurance. A distinction was made between foreign non-life insurers and life insurers. In summary, non-life insurers were permitted to establish as a branch or as a joint venture with 51% foreign ownership and within two years after accession as a wholly owned subsidiary; life insurers were permitted upon accession 50% foreign ownership in a joint venture with the partners of their choice; non-life insurers were permitted to provide a full range of non-life insurance services to both foreign and domestic clients within two years after accession and within three years health insurance, group insurance and persons annuities insurance to foreigners and Chinese were allowed.[19]

Immediately after China's accession, China promulgated the Regulations on the Administration of Foreign-invested Insurance Companies on December 12, 2001 (hereinafter as 2001 Regulations) to implement China's commitments on insurance services. It set out the regulations for the establishment and operation of three types of foreign-invested insurance companies, namely, joint ventures with Chinese partners, wholly foreign-owned insurance companies, and foreign insurance branch companies. The Implementing Rules for the 2001 Regulations was promulgated by China Insurance Regulatory Commission (CIRC) two and half years later on March 15, effective as of June 15, 2004 (hereinafter as 2004 Implementing Rules). This set of regulations was a primary source of rules for the implementation of China's commitments on insurance services.

China's insurance law, the Insurance Law of the PRC was first enacted in 1995. It was amended in accordance with China's WTO commitment in October 2002, effective as of January 1, 2003. It applies equally to Chinese domestic and foreign-invested insurance companies. In accordance with the 2002 Insurance Law, the CIRC has also issued a number of implementing documents. The Procedures on the Establishment of Reinsurance Companies was one of them, which was issued on and effective as of September 17, 2002 and applicable to both domestic and foreign-invested reinsurance companies.

Requirements for foreign-invested insurance companies

Subject to the commitment China made, foreign insurers can choose to take the form of a joint venture insurance company with Chinese partners, a wholly foreign-owned insurance company, or a foreign insurance branch company.[20] The establishment of foreign-invested insurance companies are approved by the CIRC in accordance with the requirements and procedures prescribed in the 2001 Regulations and 2004 Implementing Rules.

A key requirement which was challenged by the WTO member states was capital requirements. 2001 Regulations required foreign-invested insurance companies to have an initial minimum paid-up capital 200 million (hereinafter "million" refers to RMB unless otherwise indicated) for the establishment of the company and an additional 50 million for per branch of the company to be established.[21] This requirement was challenged by the WTO member states, for example, Canada expressed serious concern at the first annual review in October 2002 arguing that the application of such capital requirements on a branch-by-branch basis was very high by international standards.[22] During the second annual review in December 2003, Canada voiced the same concern and requested China to ensure that the entry regime was efficient and not overly burdensome for foreign insurance firms.[23] China replied that these requirements applied equally to both domestic and foreign insurers and were an integral part of a prudential regulatory framework.[24]

Before the WTO accession, China promulgated the Regulations on the Administration of Insurance Companies in January 2000, which primarily applied to domestic Chinese insurance companies. A distinction was made between a national insurance company and a regional one. A minimum registered capital 500 million was required for national insurance companies and 200 million for regional companies. National companies could establish up to three and regional up to two branches without adding more registered capitals but for more branches an additional 50 million per branch was required. When the capital of a national insurance company reached 1.5 billion and regional companies 500 million, no further capital was required for establishing new branches.[25]

In response to the concerns of the WTO member states, the 2004 Implementing Rules has lowered the capital requirements substantially.[26] A joint venture insurance company or a wholly foreign-owned insurance company, having paid up a minimum capital 200 million for the initial establishment, shall add up an additional capital of no less than 20 million when applying for a branch at provincial level outside their residence. As the registered capital of the joint venture insurance company or wholly foreign-owned insurance company reaches 500 million, no further capital is required for establishing new branches. The amendment was welcomed by the WTO member states as a positive step.[27]

Economic impacts of the changes of insurance law and regulations

In early 1980s, foreign insurers began to establish representative offices in China. On September 11, 1992, the PBOC promulgated the Provisional Measures on the Administration of Shanghai Foreign-invested Insurance Institutions, which allowed foreign insurance companies to establish in Shanghai branch companies or joint ventures with Chinese insurance companies or other Chinese financial institutions. It required that foreign insurer applicants should have been in

Table 9.2 Foreign Insurance Establishments in China as in June 2005

Foreign-invested insurance companies	**41**	**Located in 9 cities: Beijing, Shanghai, Guangzhou, Tianjin, Dalian, Shenzhen, Chongqing, Suzhou and Haikou**
Foreign insurance representative offices	188 (representing 124 companies)	Located in 15 cities: Beijing, Shanghai, Guangzhou, Tianjin, Dalian, Shenzhen, Chongqing, Suzhou, Wuhan, Chengdu, Xiamen, Qingdao, Nanjing, Hangzhou and Fuzhou

insurance business for over 30 years; they should have a representative office in China for three consecutive years and they should have a total asset of more than US$ 5 billion at the end of the year prior to their application.[28] In September 1992, AIA Shanghai Branch, the first foreign insurance company in China since 1949, was established in Shanghai.

The implementation of China's commitment by the insurance law and regulations has moved China's insurance services market towards a full opening-up to foreign insurers, which has brought about a significant increase of foreign-invested insurance companies and representative offices. AIA, for example, now has five branches in Shanghai, Beijing, Guangzhou, Shenzhen and Suzhou. In June 2005, there were altogether 41 foreign-invested insurance companies and 188 representative offices located in 15 cities across China, as shown in the Table 9.2.[29]

China's insurance services industry is one of the fast growing industries in Chinese economy with a 30% average annual increase rate, yet it is at an early stage of development and much improvement is needed.[30] Fully opening up China's insurance services market would create more opportunities for foreign insurers to participate and contribute in this process of development and improvement. Most authors look at both positive and negative impacts on China's insurance market as a result of the changes of insurance law and regulations in accordance with China's commitments. On one hand, advanced management and quality services are brought into China, but on the other hand, competition becomes more intense for market shares and professionals.[31]

The development and improvement of China's insurance services industry will be important to the success of reforms in other areas as well. Reform on social security is one of these areas. Pension, annuities, medical and health insurances contribute to an important part of the social security system and as such would play an important role in the reform of China's social security system. In other areas, such as aviation and transportation insurance, the relaxation of insurance law and regulations according to China's WTO commitments would, on one hand, provide more opportunities for foreign insures to participate in the economic development of these industries, and on the other hand, help develop these particular insurance services to their full ranges and strength to serve these industries.

Future changes of insurance law and regulations

Wu Dingfu, Chairman of the CIRC, said at 2005 China Insurance International Forum that China would implement WTO commitments seriously, further open up China's insurance market and actively adopt advanced international insurance experiences and technologies. He also said that China's modern insurance regulatory system should be developed towards a rule-based, market-based and information-based regulatory system.[32] It seems that there is little doubt about China's seriousness that it will continue to implement its commitment on insurance services. The action that is needed to take at present is to review and change those unnecessary restrictive rules for the establishment and operation of foreign-invested insurance companies.

In accordance with Article 8 of 2001 Regulations, foreign insurers have to satisfy three key qualifications for foreign-invested insurance companies. First, they should have been in insurance business for over 30 years, second, they should have a representative office in China for two consecutive years, and third, they should have a total asset of more than US$ 5 billion at the end of the year prior to their application. These qualifications were first appeared in 1992 Provisional Measures on the Administration of Shanghai Foreign-invested Insurance Institutions. Later in 1995 the requirement for the establishment of representative office was reduced to two consecutive years. In the negotiation process with WTO member states these requirements became part of China's commitment. More than ten years on, China should go beyond its current WTO commitments to lower these qualification requirements for small and intermediate foreign insurers.

Similarly, current position of foreign life insurers needs to be reviewed. Article 3 of 2004 Implementing Rules implemented China's commitment that life insurers were permitted a 50% foreign ownership in a joint venture upon accession. No further commitment was made by China to allow life insurers to establish as a wholly owned subsidiary. Compared with non-life insurers who were permitted to establish as a branch or as a joint venture with 51% foreign ownership and within two years after accession as a wholly owned subsidiary with no further restrictions, life insurers are in a more restrictive position.

On a more general level, future changes to insurance law and regulations would depend upon changes in other areas of law. Tax law is an example. In order to attract foreign investments, Chinese tax law and regulations have been implementing a tax preferential policy for foreign investment for many years. Foreign-invested insurance companies, like other foreign investment enterprises have benefited from this tax preferential policy. Some authors argued that, on one had, Chinese domestic insurance companies were subject to a heavy tax which affected their development and competitiveness, but on the other, foreign-invested insurance companies were benefit from preferential tax rates, which should be changed in accordance with the principle of national treatment.[33]

Securities

According to Section 7 of China's Schedule of Specific Commitments on Services, China pledged that, first, foreign services suppliers, upon China's accession, will be permitted to establish joint ventures with foreign investment up to 33% to conduct domestic securities investment fund management business and within three years after China's accession, foreign investment shall be increased to 49%. Second, within three years after China's accession, foreign securities institutions will be permitted to establish joint ventures with a foreign minority ownership not exceeding one third of the equity to engage directly in underwriting A-shares and underwriting and trading B and H shares as well as government and corporate debts, and launching investment funds.[34]

To implement these commitments, China Securities Regulatory Commission (CSRC) in June 2002 promulgated the Rules on the Establishment of Fund Management Company with Foreign Equity Participation (hereinafter as 2002 JV Fund Company Rules) and the Rules on the Establishment of Securities Companies with Foreign Equity Participation (hereinafter as 2002 JV Securities Company Rules). The 2002 JV Fund Company Rules was later replaced by the 2004 Measures on Administration of Fund Management Company of Securities Investment (hereinafter as 2004 Measures on Fund Company). On 16 October 2002, Guo An Fund Management Co. Ltd, the first Chinese-foreign joint venture fund management company, was approved for its establishment, which marked an important step taken by China in implementing its commitments in the securities services sector.[35] At the end of 2004, there were 52 fund management companies in China, 14 of which were Chinese-foreign joint ventures, being one third of all the fund management companies in China.[36]

Another important development in opening up China's securities market in the context of China's WTO accession is the introduction of so-called QFII scheme (Qualified Foreign Institutional Investors scheme). In November 2002, the CSRC and PBOC jointly promulgated the Provisional Measures on Administration of Securities Investment in China by Qualified Foreign Institutional Investors (hereinafter as 2002 QFII Measures), which allow selected QFIIs to invest in China's securities market. By the end of March 2005, 26 foreign financial institutions had been approved as qualified QFIIs, for which a total of US$3,700 million foreign exchange quota had been allocated by the State Administration of Foreign Exchange, shown below in Table 9.3.[37]

Joint venture fund management company and joint venture securities company

The 2002 JV Fund Company Rules defines the "fund management company with foreign equity participation" as a fund management company that is transformed when foreign shareholders are assigned, or subscribe to, the equity in a domestic fund management company or a joint venture fund management company set up

Table 9.3 Approved QFIIs by the End of March 2005

No	*QFII*	*Custodian Bank*	*Investment quota*	*RMB special account*
1	UBS Limited	City group Shanghai branch	$ 800m	Opened
2	Nomura Securities Co., Ltd	City group Shanghai branch	$ 50m	Opened
3	Citigroup Global Markets Limited	Standard Chartered Shanghai branch	$ 400m	Opened
4	Morgan Stanley & International Limited	HSBC Shanghai branch	$ 400m	Opened
5	Goldman Sachs & Co.	HSBC Shanghai branch	$ 50m	Opened
6	The Hongkong and Shanghai Banking Corporation Limited	China construction bank	$ 200m	Opened
7	Deutsche Bank AG	City group Shanghai branch	$ 300m	Opened
8	ING Bank N.V.	Standard Chartered Shanghai branch	$ 50m	Opened
9	JPMorgan Chase Bank	HSBC Shanghai branch	$ 50m	Opened
10	Credit Suisse First Boston (Hong Kong) Limited	China industry and commerce bank	$ 150m	Opened
11	Nikko Asset Management Co., Ltd	Transportation bank	$ 250m	Opened
12	Standard Chartered Bank Hong Kong	Bank of China	$ 75m	Opened
13	Hang Seng Bank Limited	China construction bank	$ 50m	Opened
14	Daiwa Securities SMBC Co.,Ltd	China industry and commerce bank	$ 50m	Opened
15	Merrill Lynch International	HSBC Shanghai branch	$ 75m	Opened
16	Lehman Brithers International Europe	China agriculture bank	$ 75m	Opened
17	Bill & Melinda Gates Foundation	HSBC Shanghai branch	$ 100m	Opened
18	ABN AMRO Bank N.V.	HSBC Shanghai branch	$ 75m	Opened
19	Societe Generale	HSBC Shanghai branch	$ 50m	Opened
20	Barclays Bank PLC	Standard chartered Shanghai branch	$ 75m	Opened
21	BNP Parisbas	China agriculture bank	$ 75m	Opened
22	Dresdner Bank Aktiengesellschaft	China industry and commerce bank	$ 75m	Opened
23	Fortis Bank	Bank of China	$ 100m	Opened
24	Power Corporation of Canada	China construction bank	$ 50m	Opened
25	CALYON S.A.	HSBC Shanghai branch	$ 75m	Not yet opened
26	INVESCO Asset Management Limited	Bank of China	$ 50m	Not yet opened

by foreign and Chinese parties. The foreign equity in a fund management company was limited to 33% and within three years after China's accession, this limit would be increased to 49%.[38] There was no provision in the 2002 JV Fund Company Rules about what happened after three years. The 2004 Measures on Fund Company provides that the ratio of foreign equity shall not exceed the commitment made by the government on the opening-up of China's securities industry,[39] which makes this limit flexible in line with the government's future commitments and policy.

Under the 2002 JV Fund Company Rules, Chinese and foreign parties were required to have no less than 300 million or equivalent paid-up capitals to qualify for partners of a joint venture fund management companies.[40] This requirement effectively limited the number of Chinese companies who could be chosen by foreign partners to form a joint venture. Concerns were raised by the representatives of WTO member states, questioning whether this limitation was compatible with the commitment undertaken in paragraph 314 of the Report of Working Party on the Accession of China in which China promised for a free choice of Chinese joint-venture partners, subject to the prudential and specific sector requirements.[41]

In October 2003, the Law of the PRC on Securities Investment Fund was enacted. It provides that only main shareholders of fund management companies are required to have no less than 300 million registered capital.[42] Accordingly the 2004 Measures on Fund Company has lowed the 300 million requirement to 100 million except for the main Chinese partner who holds no less than 25% of the shareholding of the company.[43] Now foreign partners have a wider choice of Chinese partners except for the main Chinese shareholder. But, the 300 million has not been lowered for foreign partners. Any foreign partner has to have a paid-up capital of equivalent 300 million.[44] This unequal treatment of foreign and domestic partners limits the number of foreign financial institutions who could enter into Chinese market and who could be chosen by Chinese partners.

In accordance with the 2002 JV Securities Company Rules, a joint venture securities company can engage in a range of securities businesses including, first, underwriting A shares, B and H shares as well as government and corporate debts, second, brokerage for B shares and H shares, third, brokerage and self dealing of government and corporate bonds, and fourth, other businesses as approved by the CSRC.[45] Chinese and foreign parties can set up a joint venture securities company either by converting a Chinese domestic securities company when foreign parties accept or subscribe for the equity of the Chinese securities company, or by setting up a new joint venture.[46] Either way, as a key restriction in line with China's commitment, foreign shareholders were not allowed to exceed one third of the equity of the joint venture.[47] It is noticeable that the scope of business prescribed in the 2002 JV Securities Company Rules is narrower than what China committed to the WTO. The trading B and H shares and launching investment funds committed in the Section 7 of Schedule of Specific Commitments on Services were not expressly included.

Qualification requirements for QFII scheme

The 2002 QFII Measures defines qualified foreign institutional investors as those foreign institutions who have satisfied the requirements prescribed in the 2002 QFII Measures and who have been authorised by the CSRC to invest in China's securities market with allocated foreign exchange quotas from the State Administration of Foreign Exchange. They include fund management companies, insurance companies, securities companies, and other asset management companies.[48]

To qualify for the QFII scheme, foreign institutional investors have to satisfy a series of high requirements. Fund management companies have to be in fund business for over five years and the asset under management in the most recent financial year should be above US$ 1 billion; insurance companies have to be in insurance business for over thirty years with a registered capital of US$ 10 billion and the securities asset under management in the most recent financial year should be above US$ 1 billion; securities companies have to be in securities business for over thirty years with a registered capital of US$ 10 billion and the securities asset under management in the most recent financial year should be above US$ 1 billion; commercial banks should be among the 100 largest commercial banks around the world in terms of total assets in the most recent financial year and the securities asset under management should be above US$ 1 billion.[49]

The applicants have to go through a multi-tier and multi-stage approval process. They have to first designate a custodian bank to apply on their behalf. The custodian bank submits required documents to the CSRC and the SAFE and upon approval from the CSRC an investment licence is issued, with which the custodian bank can apply to the SAFE for foreign exchange quota. In order to act as a custodian bank for a QFII, banks have to satisfy the requirements prescribed by the 2002 QFII Measures and submit relevant documents to the CSRC, PBOC and SAFE for approval. Once being approved, QFIIs open a special RMB account with the custodian bank who within five wording days file the account information to the CSRC and the SAFE.[50] Through a designated local broker, QFIIs are allowed to invest in the shares, government bonds, convertible bonds and enterprise bonds listed on the stock exchange, and other financial products approved by the CSRC.[51] Each single QFII in a listed company can hold no more than 10% of the total shares of the company and the total QFIIS in the company can hold no more than 20% of the total shares of the company.[52]

China's QFII scheme is modelled on the QFII schemes of some other markets, in particular, Taiwan who introduced a QFII scheme in 1991. Professor Li Chong, the School of Economy of Beijing Normal University argued that China's current QFII scheme is a more restricted system than other countries in terms of qualifications, supervision, investment and administration of funds.[53] Taiwan's QFII scheme at its early stage, for example, required that commercial banks should be among the 500 largest commercial banks around the world. China currently requires for the 100 largest commercial banks. The combination of a multi-tier and multi-stage approval process and highly restrictive requirements means that only a selected group of large international fund management companies, insurance companies, securities companies, and commercial banks could qualify for the QFII scheme.

Economic impacts of the changes of securities law and regulations

In 1980s, foreign securities companies started to set up representative offices in China. In 1991 B-share was introduced and this was followed by H-share in Hong Kong. Since then foreign investors have been able to invest in China's B-share market and H-share market through a Chinese broker or a foreign broker. But the opening up of China's securities market has been limited. China's WTO commitment on securities market has opened up a new chapter in opening up China's securities market. The implementation of the commitment by the securities law and regulations on QFII scheme, joint venture fund management companies and joint venture securities companies will have an unprecedented impact on China's securities market and economy.

On July 9, 2003, UBS, through its QFII agent Shenyin & Wanguo Securities Co. Ltd, settled the first purchase of A-shares, which marked the official entry of QFII funds into China's A-share market.[54] As the Table 9.3 above shows, a total of US$3,700 million foreign exchange quota had been allocated to 26 qualified QFIIs by the end of March 2005. The investment of such a large amount of funds in shares and various government and enterprise bonds would increase the supply of capitals to the market. Two thirds of UBS's investments, for example, had been invested by the end of 2003 in 35 shares, 11 convertible bonds and 10 securities investment funds which covered over 10 industries ranging from electricity, steel, to transportation.[55]

China's securities market has been for a long time dominated by individual investors and speculative investments. Introduction of QFII scheme would improve current structure of institutional investors on China's securities market and help regulate investment behaviours. Antony Neil QC, chief advisor of the CSRC and former chairman of the Hong Kong Securities and Futures Authorities, believed that the introduction of QFII scheme would help change the market from being dominated by individual investors to being dominated by institutional investors.[56] Zhou Xiaochuan, former Chairman of the CSRC between February 2000 to December 2002 and current governor of the PBOC emphasised that at the heart of the introduction of QFII scheme was to promote medium and long term investments and to limit short term speculations.[57]

The establishment of joint venture fund management companies and joint venture securities companies between foreign and Chinese partners would help improve services standards and increase competitiveness of Chinese companies. Chen Xuerong, chairman of the board of directors of Xiangcai Securities, whose company formed the first joint venture securities company after the promulgation of the 2002 JV Securities Company Rules, commented that the main purpose of having foreign partners was to improve our current management standards, introduce matured management ideas and increase the competitiveness.[58]

Future changes of securities law and regulations

In January 2004, the State Council issued a so-called 9-point blueprint for the future development of China's capital market, which states: "strictly fulfil China's WTO commitments on opening up securities services sector, to encourage qualified foreign securities institutions to invest in securities companies and fund management companies, and to continue trials of the scheme of QFII."[59] It seems certain that the policy of opening up China's securities market would not be changed. The issue is when and to what extent the current restrictive law and regulations on the QFII scheme, the joint venture fund management companies and securities companies would be further relaxed.

Taiwan's QFII scheme which evolved in several stages over the years since 1991 is regarded by Chinese policymaker and scholars as a successful experience.[60] In 1991, for example, Taiwan restricted commercial banks to the 500 largest commercial banks around the world and this was relaxed to 1000 in 1993 and was completely lifted in 2000. As China's QFII is modelled on Taiwan's experience in many ways it is expected that China would follow a same approach to relax the control step by step.

But the future change to the current law and regulations on the QFII scheme is not isolated to the QFII scheme itself. On one hand, it relates to China's WTO commitments and on the other hand it depends upon the progress of some other important reforms, such as the reform on China's foreign exchange control which was started in 1994. Zou Lin, Director of the Capital Account Department of the State Administration of Foreign Exchange commented in an interview that the reform on the convertibility of capital account was gradually stepping up and once it is liberalised there will be no need for the QFII foreign exchange quota.[61]

A paramount concern about securities market is security and its impact on the national economy and the society. Zhao Xijun, deputy director of finance and securities research centre, People's University of China argued that because the QFII is currently based on a very strict regulatory policy the risk linking with the QFII is not apparent. But as the QFII is gradually relaxed and the reform of China's foreign exchange system deepens, the issue of how to effectively prevent the risk brought about by the QFII will be very much a concern.[62] Li Chong, Professor of the College of Economy, Beijing Normal University argued that there is a need to tighten the regulations in order to effectively control outflow of QFII capitals.[63] It was apparent that 1997 Asia financial crisis was a lesson for government policymakers and law drafters. Their concern drawn from this crisis would be reflected in the future changes of securities law and regulations.

Auto financing

According to the commitment China made in the Section 7 of the Schedule of Specific Commitments on Services, China should open up motor vehicle financing market to foreign non-bank financial institutions upon China's accession to the WTO. But because the regulation that was intended to implement this commitment was not put in place until October 2003, it was not possible in the first and second year after China's accession for foreign non-financial institutions to apply for the establishment of a commercial presence in China to engage in automotive financing business. The WTO member states complaint about this delay in the annual transitional reviews.[64]

The Measures on the Administration of Automotive Financing Companies and the Detailed Implementing Rules for the Measures on the Administration of Automotive Financing Companies were finally issued by the CBRC in October and November 2003 respectively (hereinafter as 2003 Measures on Auto Financing Company and the Implementing Rules). In August 2004, having obtained a final approval from the CBRC, GMAC-SAIC Automotive Finance Co. Ltd. became China's first non-bank joint venture financial institution to conduct automotive financing services.[65] By the end of May 2005, four foreign-invested automotive financing companies had been set up and one had been given an initial approval to start preparation, the details of which are shown in the Table 9.4.[66]

In August 2004, the People's Bank of China and CBRC jointly took a further step to promulgate the Measures on the Administration of Automotive Loans, effective as of October 1, 2004 (hereinafter as 2004 Measures on Auto Loans). Thus, together with the 2003 Measures on Auto Financing Company and the Implementing Rules, a regulatory framework has been established to regulate automotive financing services in the context of China's WTO accession.

Table 9.4 Foreign-invested Auto Financing Companies in China by the End of May 2005

Company	*Type*	*Business starting time*
GMAC-SAIC Auto Financing Co. Ltd	Joint venture	August 2004
Volkswagen Auto Financing (China) Co. Ltd	Wholly foreign owned	September 2004
Toyota Auto Financing (China) Co. Ltd	Wholly foreign owned	December 2004
Ford Automotive Finance China Ltd	Wholly foreign owned	Granted final approval in May 2005 and will start business at the beginning of the third quarter of 2005
DaimlerChrysler		Granted initial approval for preparation pending final approval from CBRC to start business

Requirements for establishment and operation of auto-finance companies

Although the WTO member states welcomed the 2003 Measures on Auto Financing Company as a step to implement China's commitment on automotive financing, they raised various questions about those provisions that set out restrictive conditions and high requirements.[67] These restrictive requirements include, first, that shareholders of an automotive financing company must have a total asset above 4 billion, annual business revenue above 2 billion, registered capital above 300 million and profitable for the last three years, second, the minimum registered capital of the automotive financing company must be 500 million, third, direct branching from abroad is not allowed and no automotive financing company can set up any branch or subsidiary, and fourth, operations of the company may be stopped if it makes loss in one year of more than 50% of the capital or the accumulated loss in three consecutive years representing more than 30% of the capital.[68]

China argued that the minimum capital requirements and other requirements imposed on automotive financing companies were of a prudential nature, based on the fact that the automotive financing market in China was just at an early stage and the regulatory body lacked risk control capacity and supervision experiences. Besides, all these requirements were non-discriminatory and applied to both foreign and domestic automotive financing companies.[69]

Some Chinese scholars argued in support of the complaint of the WTO member states. They submitted that there were rules in the 2003 Measures on Auto Financing Company and the Implementing Rules that created barriers for a large scale development of foreign invested automotive financing companies in China.[70] First, the scope of business was restricted. Hire-purchase, an important business of foreign automotive financing companies, was not included in the scope of business; second, the way in which foreign-invested automotive financing company could raise capital was restricted. They were only allowed to take deposits from shareholders in China, transfer and sell auto loan receivables, and borrow from financial institutions; third, loan rates were restricted. They could only be floated between 10–30% of the base rate set by the central bank; and fourth, branching was restricted. No branch or subsidiary was allowed. Others argued in favour of China's stand, taking into consideration of the position of domestic companies. Jia Xinguang, chief analyst of China Automobile Industry Consultant Development Company, submitted that few domestic companies could meet very high capital requirements at present, which would allow time for foreign investment to capture China's automotive financing market.[71]

Economic impacts of the auto financing regulations

Auto financing market is a newly emerged market in China. In September 1998, the PBOC promulgated the Measures on the Administration of Automotive Consumer Loans (hereinafter as 1998 Measures on Auto Consumer Loans), which formally marked the beginning of a consumer automotive financing market in China. The PBOC at that time limited the business of automotive consumer loans to only selected branches of four state-owned commercial banks and limited the loans only applicable to vehicles manufactured in China.[72] In the same period of time, foreign automotive financing companies started to show their interests in China's market. GMAC started a preparing work in 1998 with a view to provide auto financing services later in China.[73] As early as in December 1996, Ford Credit set up a representative office in Beijing and carried out certain activities, such as sponsoring an auto financing research project led by the State Planning Commission.[74]

China's young auto financing market is seen as a market with a huge potential. It is estimated by the General Motors that by 2010 China would become the third largest car market following U.S. and Japan.[75] At present, auto financing in China constitutes only about 20–30% of car sales, which is in a sharp contrast with about 70% globally and 80–85% in the U.S.[76] There is therefore a huge potential for China's auto financing market to develop. Some scholars regarded auto financing as a "golden key" to open up a sustainable consumer car market in China.[77]

To develop China's young auto financing market, China first has much to learn from the experience of those countries where auto financing has been around for many years. One of the important impacts of bringing in foreign automotive financing companies in China is that it can help China introduce new ideas and services. Dr Yang Zaiping, deputy director of the Research Bureau of the CBRC commented that the introduction of auto financing into China has actually introduced three new creations, that is, the creation of automotive financing companies, the creation of new products, and the creation of a new system.[78] The 2003 Measures on Auto Financing Companies and the Implementing Rules have provisions regarding secondhand vehicle financing and financing for vehicle parts, which are new services and products to China. By virtue of their experienced professional services achieved over many years in their home countries, the foreign automotive financing companies can play an important role to help China in this learning process.

Since 1998 China's auto financing market has been dominated by domestic commercial banks. The entry of foreign professional players into China following the 2003 Measures on Auto Financing Company and the Implementing Rules has changed the structure of this market. Foreign automotive financing companies are regarded as having several advantages over Chinese commercial banks. First, they have natural connections with car manufactures and the two forces could jointly provide preferential benefits to consumers. Second, unlike banks where auto credit business is only one of their businesses, foreign automotive financing companies carry out auto financing as their core business and thus have specialised experiences. Third, foreign automotive financing companies can provide customised loans and repayment plans according to the different needs of customers.[79] All of these advantages could contribute to the development of a diversified auto financing market in China. Ultimately, such a diversified development would bring more benefits to Chinese car consumers, which is a good thing.

Some scholars see the promulgation of 2003 Measures on Auto Financing Company and the Implementing Rules and subsequent entry of foreign automotive financing companies into China as a threat to domestic commercial banks and auto financing companies. They argued that once the market is opened up, any efforts made by Chinese financial institutions would fail, as foreign automotive financing companies such as GMAC could, for example, use the scope of price discount of their own brand cars to offer preferential loans, therefore it would be a win-win situation for both the sale of their cars and auto loans.[80] But what this view failed to see is that the competition as a result of the entry of foreign automotive financing companies is after all a good thing for domestic banks and auto financing companies. Such competition would put pressures on Chinese auto financing providers to improve their services. In fact, before the promulgation of 2003 Measure on Auto Financing Company and the Implementing Rules, Chinese auto financing providers had already started to improve their services to prepare for the forthcoming competition. In 2002, for example, Nanjin branch of Pudong development bank set up a one stop service centre for the convenience of customers in dealing with all the formalities involved in car purchase and financing.[81]

Future changes of auto financing regulations

As discussed above, the 2003 Measure on Auto Financing Company and the Implementing Rules are in many ways restrictive for the foreign-invested automotive financing companies. Liu Yingyi, the finance director of the GMAC-SAIC Auto Financing Co. Ltd. was quoted as commenting that "present auto financing law and regulations seriously restrict our development".[82] Such comments were echoed by Chinese policy makers and scholars. Xu Hongyuan, for example, the director of the development department of the State Information Centre commented that lack of operational capitals was the main reason why automotive financing companies were left without competitive advantages.[83] Although China generally implemented its WTO commitment to open up auto financing market to foreign automotive financing companies, restrictive requirements for their establishment and operation were making the operation of their business difficult.

To lift restrictive provisions in the 2003 Measures on Auto Financing Company and the Implementing Rules therefore will be the focal point for the future changes of auto financing regulations. When the 2003 Measures on Auto Financing Company and the Implementing Rules were promulgated, it was welcomed by foreign automotive financing companies who had been anxiously waiting for their promulgation. It was not surprise that GMAC and SAIC reacted immediately to submit their application to the CBRC in November 2003 to set up the joint venture GMAC-SAIC Automotive Finance Co. Ltd.[84] But because of the restrictive rules, coupled with other negative elements of the market, the reality for the GMAC-SAIC and other foreign providers was not so promising. It was reported that by the end of 2004, the total deals that had been done by the GMAC-SAIC and Volkswagen Auto Financing (China) Co. Ltd were less than a thousand.[85]

High entry requirements, restriction on the scope of business, particularly hire-purchase, and limited channels for capital were highlighted as several pressing issues that needed to be reviewed. There is clearly a substantial gap between what the 2003 Measures on Auto Financing Company and the Implementing Rules stipulated and the normal practice of those countries where auto financing has been around for many years. In May 2004, the State Commission for Development and Reform, upon an approval from the State Council, issued an important policy document, the Development Policy for Automobile Industry, which replaced the 1994 Development Policy for Automobile Industry. On one hand, the document generally states that the government encourages the adaptation of "international matured ideas and experiences" about auto sales, management, services by auto manufacturers, financial institutions and other services providers,[86] but on the other hand, a cautious and conservative tone appears when it comes to specific issues, like hire-purchase business.[87] Judging from this mixed signal from the Development Policy for Automobile Industry, it seems no radical changes could be expected in the near future for the 2003 Measures on Auto Financing Company and the Implementing Rules.

A positive note, however, was shown by the 2004 Measures on Auto Loans which amended the 1998 Measures on Auto Consumer Loans. Among other positive changes, new provisions were introduced to allow loans to be issued to secondhand car purchases.[88] Considering that the 1998 Measures on Auto Consumer Loans was on a trial basis and only selected branches of four state-owned commercial banks were allowed to carry out auto consumer loan business at that time, the 2004 Measures on Auto Loans was indeed a solid step moving forward. But in the meantime, contrary to the high expectations of commentators, certain crucial restrictive provisions remain the same as in the 1998 Measures on Auto Consumer Loans. Maximum term of loans, for example, remained unchanged at 5 years.[89]

The emergence of foreign automotive financing companies in China is a result of the implementation by auto financing regulations of China's WTO commitment, but also is because of a market force. It is estimated that during 2000 to 2005, the demand for cars in China has kept increasing at a rate of 20–25%.[90] It would be unhelpful if the auto financing regulations continue to create unnecessary barriers and restrictions to the participation of foreign auto financing companies in a fast growing automobile market in China. The 2004 Development Policy for Automobile Industry, a blueprint for China's automobile industry, clearly states that the government "support" the development of an auto credit consumer market,[91] but what is lacking in the current auto financing regulations is a more open and relaxed approach as opposed to a conservative and cautious approach. In addition, future changes of the regulations also depend upon the establishment of some other relevant systems, such as an effective and reliable credit information system in China.

Conclusion

In the past few years, China has promulgated and amended a series of laws, regulations and implementing rules in banking, insurance, securities and auto financing to implement its WTO commitment to further open up these financial services markets. The banking, insurance and securities regulators, CBRC, CIRC and CSRC, played an important day-to-day implementing role to issue detailed implementing rules and measures and to authorise foreign financial institutions. The legislative effort China made was impressive, so was the effort made by the financial regulators.

But on the other hand, questions and complaints were raised by the WTO member states in the process of annual transitional reviews about various restrictive rules and requirements, such as one-year-waiting rule in banking regulations, capital requirements in insurance regulations and branching restrictions in auto financing. Amendments have since been made to some of these restrictive rules and requirements, but others remained unchanged. China argued that these rules and requirements were made in accordance with prudential principles and were non-discriminatory and therefore were not inconsistent with China's WTO commitments. Different views were expressed by Chinese scholars and commentators on the implementation of China's WTO commitments in financial services law and regulations, some of which were liberal in support of further lifting restrictions while others protective in support of a cautious and restrictive approach.

Since 1979 China has opened up step by step banking, insurance and securities markets to foreign investments in line with China's overall economic reform and open-door policy. The implementation of China's WTO commitments on financial services and the reform of China's financial services law and regulations have brought this opening-up process into a new stage, which in turn has had significant impacts on each of these sectors and on the national economy as a whole. The establishment of foreign financial institutions has increased, more cities have been opened up for local currency business, new auto financing market has been promoted, new QFII scheme has been implemented, new management systems and quality services have been introduced which has intensified competitions and brought benefits to customers. Some see these developments positively for China's reform programmes while others see them as threats to the development of domestic financial industry.

Central to the current drafting of financial services laws and regulations is a cautious and step-by-step approach from the government and financial regulators as financial services market is viewed as being sensitive to national financial security and vulnerable to crisis. Some scholars and commentators call for changes to current high entry requirements and other restrictive barriers while others advocate a more strict control on some areas such as banking takeover activities and outflow of QFII funds to safeguard national financial interests and stability. It is necessary to strike a right balance between further opening up following market forces and safeguard of national financial security. Future changes of China's financial services law and regulations depend upon China's continuous implementation of its WTO commitments and further opening up of financial markets and also upon the progress of the reforms in some other areas, such as foreign exchange, taxation, social security system and personal credit information network.

Notes

1 WTO document series WT/ACC/CHN/49/Add.2.
2 WTO document series WT/L/432.
3 WTO document series WT/ACC/CHN/49.
4 The first annual review was carried out on 21 October 2002, the second on 1 December 2003 and the third on 23 November 2004.
5 See Section 7 of the Schedule of Specific Commitments on Services.
6 Articles 15 to 32.
7 Article 2.
8 See paragraph 5 of the Communication from Canada for the first annual review (S/FIN/W/20).
9 See paragraphs 15 and 16 of the Communication from the European Communities for the second annual review (S/FIN/W/32).
10 Guo Xiaoyong, "Xin waizi yinhang shichang zhunru biaozhun yu zhongguo rushi chengnuo de bijiao yanjiu" (A Comparative Study on New Market Entry Criteria for Foreign Banks and China's WTO Commitments), *Guoji shangwu yanjiu* (International Commerce Study), issue 5, 2004, p. 31.
11 Ibid., p. 34.
12 Liu Mingkang, "Xinwen fabuhui shang de jianghua" (Speech at the Press Conference), December 1, 2004, www.cbrc.gov.cn.
13 Tang Shuangning, "APEC Jinrong yu fazhan xiangmu luntan shang de fayan" (Speech at the APEC Finance and Development Programme Forum), November 28, 2004, www.cbrc.gov.cn.
14 Liu Mingkang, (Note 12).
15 See "Fang zhada yinhang zhongguo qu zongcai Mai Tianhui (Martin Fish)" (Interview Martin Fish, the Head of China Operation of Standard Chartered Bank), *Zhongguo waihui guanli* (China Foreign Exchange Administration), issue 1–2, 2004.
16 Liu Mingkang, (Note 12).
17 See the interview with Martin Fish (Note 15).
18 Meng Bin, Du Kuanqi, "Waizi jinhang yu woguo de jinrong anquan" (Foreign Banks and Financial Security of Our Country), *Shichang zhoukan* (Market Weekly), issue 9, 2004, p. 66.
19 See Section 7 of the Schedule of Specific Commitments on Services.
20 Article 2, 2001 Regulations.
21 Ibid., Article 7.
22 See paragraph 37 of the minutes of the review (S/FIN/M/37).
23 See paragraph 8 of the Communication from Canada for the second annual review (S/FIN/W/33).
24 See the statement made by China's WTO representative, paragraph 51 of the minutes of the first annual review (S/FIN/M/37) and paragraph 32 of the minutes of the second annual review (S/FIN/M/43).
25 Articles 7(1) and 13.
26 Article 28.
27 See, for example, paragraph 2 of the Communication from United States for the second annual review (S/FIN/W/35).
28 Articles 2 and 5.
29 The figure was published at the CIRC's website www.circ.gov.cn (last visited 24 June 2005).
30 Wu Dingfu, "Zhongguo baoxian guoji luntan shang de jianghua" (Speech at the China Insurance International Forum), May 23, 2005, www.circ.gov.cn.
31 See, for example, Xiong Zhengde, "Waizi baoxian gongsi dui woguo baoxianye de yingxiang jiqi duice" (The Impact of Foreign-invested Insurance Companies on

Insurance Industry of Our Country and Countermeasure), *Caijing lilun yu shijian* (Theory and Practice of Finance and Economics), issue 2, 1997, p. 57–58.

32 Wu Dingfu (Note 30).

33 See Peng Jinbin, Li Yujian, "Woguo yinjin waizi baoxian gongsi de guanli celue" (Tactics on the Administration of Introducing Foreign Insurance Companies to Our Country), *Fujian jinrong* (Fujian Finance), issue 12, 2000, p. 30.

34 See Section 7 of the Schedule of Specific Commitments on Services.

35 See "China Approves First Joint Venture Management Firm", *People's Daily Online* (English), October 18, 2002.

36 See Liu Hongru, "Zongjie guoqu kaichuang weilai: tuidong zhongguo jijin de jiankang fazhan" (Reflect on the Past and Create the Future: Promote a Healthy Development of China's Fund Industry), *Zhongguo jinrong* (China Finance), issue 1, 2005, p. 22.

37 The information was published at the State Administration of Foreign Exchange's website www.safe.gov.cn (last visited on 15 June 2005).

38 Articles 2 and 8.

39 Article 10.

40 Articles 6 and 7.

41 See paragraph 63 of the minutes of the second annual review (S/FIN/M/43).

42 Article 13 (iii).

43 Articles 7 and 9.

44 Article 9 (iii).

45 Article 5.

46 Article 2.

47 Article 10.

48 Article 2.

49 Article 7, 2002 QFII Measures.

50 Ibid., Articles 8, 9, 10, 12, 13, 14, and 23.

51 Ibid., Article 18.

52 Ibid., Article 20.

53 Li Chong, "QFII: woguo xian jieduan kaifang jinrong shichang de heshi moshi" (QFII: a Suitable Model for Opening up Financial Market at Current Stage of Our Country), *Huanan jinrong yanjiu* (South China Finance Study), issue 5, 2003, p. 37.

54 See the Annual Report 2003 of Shenyin & Wanguo Securities Co. Ltd., p. 28.

55 See Zhu Huacheng et al, "Shui shi QFII de xinchong" (Who is QFII's New Favourite), *Zhengquan Daokan* (Securities Weekly Guide), issue 14, 2004, p. 44.

56 See Zhang Quanru, "Zhou Xiaochuan: woguo jubei QFII tiaojian" (Zhou Xiaochuan: Our Country has QFII Conditions), *Zhengce yu guanli* (Policy and Management), issue 9, 2002, p. 57.

57 Ibid., p. 56.

58 See, "Quanshang jiakuai zujian waizi cangu zhengquan gongsi" (Securities Companies Step up Establishing Securities Companies with Foreign Participation), *Shanghai zhengquan bao* (Shanghai Securities News), June 11, 2002.

59 Point 9, *the Opinion on Promoting Reform, Opening up, and Stable Development of the Capital Market*, the State Council.

60 See, for example, Ba Shusong, "Lun zhongguo ziben shichang de kaifang lujing xuanzhe" (On the Choice of the Route for Opening up China's Capital Market), *Shijie jingji* (World Economy), issue 3, 2003, p. 69.

61 See "QFII zhengce yiru jiwang" (QFII Polity will be the Same as Before), *Zhongguo waihui guanli* (China Foreign Exchange Administration), issue 7, 2004, p. 16.

62 See Zhao Xijun, "QFII qidong zheng dangshi" (QFII Starts up Just at the Right Time), Zhongguo waihui guanlin (China Foreign Exchange Administration), issue 1–2, 2004.

63 See Li Chong, at p. 39 (Note 53).

64 See, for example, paragraph 10 of the Communication from Japan for the first annual review (S/FIN/W21).
65 See "GM Obtains Approval for Auto Finance", *People's Daily Online* (English), August 6, 2004.
66 See Yang Xiwei, Gu Qianjiang, "Waizi qiche jinrong gongsi: jinrong kaifang xinliangdian" (Foreign Auto Financing Company: New Light Spot for Financial Opening-up), www.people.com.cn, June 1, 2005.
67 See, for example, paragraph 21 and 22 of the Communication from European Communities for the second annual review (S/FIN/W/32).
68 Articles 5, 7, 14 and 29.
69 See the statement made by China's WTO representative, paragraph 35 of the minutes of the second annual review (S/FIN/M/43).
70 See Wang Ping, Cao Mengfei, "Woguo fazhan waizi qiche jinrong gongsi ruogan wenti tanxi" (An Inquiry on Several Issues Regarding the Development of Foreign-invested Auto Financing Company in China), *Fujian Jinrong* (Fujian Finance), issue 6, 2004, p. 20.
71 See Zhang Wenqiang, "Fute huozhun jinru, qiche jinrong waizi yongdong" (Ford Obtained Approval to Enter, Auto Finance Foreign Investment Surge), *Zhengquan shibao,* (Securities Times), August 6, 2004.
72 See the PBOC'notice attached to the 1998 Measures on Auto Consumer Loans.
73 See Si Wanfang, "Tongyong de xiayige zhanchang" (GM's Next Battleground), *Xin caijing* (New Finance and Economy), issue 12, 2003, p. 80 and 82.
74 Ibid.
75 See Yao Hui "Qiche xindai dazhan yichu jifa" (Auto Financing Battle could Break out at any Moment), *Guojijinrong bao* (International Finance News), June 28, 2002.
76 See Si Wanfang (Note 73).
77 See Cao Jianhai, "Zhongguo de qiche xiaofei shichang he xiaofei huanjing" (China Auo Consumer Market and Consumer Environment), *Shangye jingji yu guanli* (Commercial Economy and Management), issue 7, 2003, p. 12.
78 See Yang Xiwei, Gu Qianjiang (Note 66).
79 See Yao Hui (Note 75).
80 See Si Wanfang, at p. 81 (Note 73).
81 See Yao Hui (Note 75).
82 See "Qiche jinrong zai zhongguo kaiju bull" (Auto Financing's Start in China not Favourable), *Zhongguo qiche bao* (China Automobile News), January 3, 2005.
83 See "Rongzi qudao yu huoli shouduan kunrao qiche jinrong gongsi" (Channel for Raising Capital and Means to Make Profits Troubled Auto Financing Companies), *Zhongguo qiche bao* (China Automobile News), May 28, 2005.
84 See Si Wanfang, at p. 80.
85 See supra note 82.
86 Article 33.
87 Article 65 requires that foreign investments go through a verification process before they can engage in leasing business.
88 Articles 2, 4, 6, 22 and 26.
89 Article 6.
90 See Yao Hui (Note 75).
91 Art 65.

10

PEOPLE'S REPUBLIC OF CHINA FINANCIAL SECTOR ASSESSMENT PROGRAM TECHNICAL NOTE

Systemic Oversight of Financial Market Infrastructures

Monetary and Capital Markets Department, and Finance and Markets Global Practice, World Bank

Source: November 2017.

Executive Summary

China's landscape for Financial Market Infrastructures (FMIs) is one of the largest and most complex in the world. It consists of a range of payment, clearing and settlement systems, including several interbank payment systems, securities settlement systems and central counterparties (CCPs). Many of the systems have high volumes by international comparison and are systemically important at a national level. Disruptions, both operational and financial, in one of these FMIs may significantly impact the functioning of the Chinese economy. The landscape is subject to changes, following international developments, such as the establishment of a cross-border interbank payment system (CIPS) and a CCP for over-the-counter (OTC) derivatives. The development of new, innovative products, for example, in the area of internet payments, is changing the landscape further.

FMIs in China have been analyzed from a supervision, oversight, and systemic risk management perspective. The mission focused on overarching indicators of FMI's safety and resilience, i.e., i) supervision and oversight by the People's Bank of China (PBC) and the China Securities Regulatory Commission (CSRC); ii) system wide risks; and iii) risk management practices within systemically important FMIs. Such a system wide approach is appropriate, given China's highly interdependent and interconnected network of FMIs, banks, and other financial institutions.

Since the previous FSAP the supervision and oversight of FMIs has strengthened through the adoption of the CPSS-IOSCO Principles for FMIs (PFMI); the full implementation of the PFMI is the next step. The public adoption of the PFMI by the authorities in 2013, and the establishment of an interagency platform to assess FMIs (the 'PFMI office') are commendable and important achievements. Full implementation of the principles by FMIs is the next step and is expected to enhance the resilience and stability of the FMIs. The level of implementation of the requirements varies greatly among the different systems. FMIs, and their authorities, are encouraged to actively reform risk management practices where needed, notably, the China Securities Depository and Clearing Corporation Limited (CSDC) should improve its delivery versus payment arrangements and modernize its credit and liquidity risk management to limit potential significant credit and liquidity losses. The four futures exchanges should reorganize the risk management function over the full length of their organizations.

In order to achieve this, authorities should ensure that they get the appropriate staff levels in quantity and quality. Resources to fulfill the respective mandates are tight for the PBC and the CSRC. Despite increased responsibilities, the number of staff has not increased in line with new tasks under the PFMI and new market developments. Ensuring an appropriate level of human resources will allow adequate regulation and supervision of FMIs, which contributes to financial stability. Not only an increase in the absolute number of staff is needed, but also an increase in staff with good knowledge of international standards and risk management practices. This includes knowledge of (quantitative) risk models for CCPs, such as margin, credit and liquidity models.

The legal basis for FMI supervision should be strengthened and the mission welcomes the various legal initiatives in this regard. The current supervisory framework contains potential legal risks. A main vulnerability relates to the lack of a statutory framework for futures markets, which may potentially create legal uncertainty about the CSRC's powers to enforce change where needed. With a further growth and development of the market, for example, when new cross-sector products are developed, such as in the OTC derivatives markets, gaps or overlaps in regulation may appear with subsequent risks for financial stability. Authorities' initiatives, such as the development of the 'China Financial Infrastructure Supervisory Rules,' the drafting of a comprehensive futures market law, amendments to the securities law, and the drafting of a dedicated national payment system (NPS) law, are expected to strengthen the supervisory framework for FMIs and enhance clarity.

Furthermore, the mission found weaknesses in the legal framework for FMIs regarding finality and netting of transactions, which potentially expose FMIs and their participants to significant credit and liquidity risks. It is recommended to enact a comprehensive statute, or otherwise adopt statutory provisions, to provide a high degree of legal certainty for all relevant material aspects covering all FMIs. The legal basis should be strengthened among other things to provide for unambiguous recognition of settlement finality in the event of insolvency of a participant; protection of netting arrangements; provisions for bankruptcy remoteness of pledged collateral; close-out netting; and prescriptions to overcome any zero-hour rules.

Cyber risk has been identified by authorities as an important supervisory topic in relation to FMIs. Authorities may strengthen their joint efforts and address this issue explicitly under the PFMI office. A cyber security law was issued in 2016 and will come into effect as per June 2017. The 'Cyberspace at the Administration of China,' which is a body under the State Council, conducts cyber security tests at a national level. With the promulgation of the cyber security law, cooperation between the PBC, the CSRC and FMIs may further improve insights on cyber security and contribute to the awareness and assessments of cyber risks. Joint crisis coordination mechanisms and testing of crisis communication protocols can further improve the management and monitoring of these risks. Where weaknesses were identified, these should be addressed in the PBC's and the CSRC's supervisory activities as a priority.

Finally, resilience of FMIs can be strengthened through the provision of central bank services to all solvent, systemically important FMIs. The PBC currently provides settlement services to the China Central Depository & Clearing Corporation Limited (CCDC) and the Shanghai Clearing House (SHCH). It may consider extending these services to the CSDC and other CCPs, under the condition that the FMIs strengthen their risk management practices, and, in addition to the CSRC's supervision, are subject to macroprudential oversight of the PBC. Although private sector liquidity must constitute the first line of defense for FMIs against liquidity shortfalls, there could be extreme circumstances in which their liquid resources turn out to be insufficient or unavailable. Providing solvent FMIs with access to emergency central bank liquidity, against adequate collateral, ensures that they can continue to make payments to counterparties and would thereby maintain the stability of the market. Furthermore, the provision of central bank accounts will reduce FMIs' exposure to commercial banks and may also be used for settlement purposes, reducing credit and liquidity risks related to the use of settlement banks.

Introduction[1]

1 **FMIs are typically considered systemically important due to the central role they play in interbank, money and capital markets.**[2] FMIs provide the central infrastructure (comprised of institutions, rules, procedures, risk management frameworks, and technical platforms) to clear and settle payments, securities and derivatives transactions, and therefore, lay at the core of the functioning of a sound financial system. If FMIs are not properly managed they can be sources of financial shocks and may potentially have a negative impact on economic and financial stability. For example,

Table 10.1 China: Recommendations

	Timing	*Authorities*
Recommendations for the oversight of FMIs		
Strengthen legal framework for the regulation and supervision of FMIs, through the development of a dedicated law on the supervision of FMIs, the adoption of the Futures Market Law, changes to the Securities Market Law, and the drafting of a NPS Law.	ST-MT	PBC, CSRC
Ensure a sufficient number of staff with relevant expertise.	ST	PBC, CSRC
Strive for full and consistent implementation of the PFMI, in particular: • Update supervisory regulations and FMI rules to reflect the PFMI; • Improve DVP arrangements within the CSDC; • Implement a risk governance structure within the four futures exchanges.	ST-MT	PBC, CSRC
Explicitly evaluate risks related to links of the CSDC with other central securities depositories (CSDs).	MT	CSRC
Recommendations to manage system-wide risks		
Adopt finality and netting at a statutory level in line with international standards.	ST-MT	PBC, CSRC
Supervise cyber resilience of FMIs as part of the PFMI office.	ST	PBC, CSRC
Develop recovery and resolution planning in line with international guidance.	MT	PBC, CSRC
Adopt policy to provide central bank services to FMIs.	MT	PBC
Recommendations for the risk management of high-value payment system (HVPS) and SHCH		
HVPS: review fees and the timings of the intraday repo window.	ST	PBC
HVPS: review use of open market operations (OMO) for intraday liquidity requirements.	MT	PBC
HVPS: review collateral haircut methodology and ensure independent validation.	ST	PBC
HVPS: operationalize mark-to-market module.	ST	PBC
HVPS: revise priority levels of instant transfer transactions.	ST	PBC
HVPS: prescribe a cut-off time for withdrawal of transactions in queue.	MT	PBC
HVPS: examine introduction of time varying fees for payment instructions.	MT	PBC
HVPS: complete and disclose publicly CPSS-IOSCO Disclosure framework.	ST	PBC
SHCH: appoint independent chair at the Risk Management Committee (RMC).	ST-MT	PBC, SHCH
SHCH: ensure regular reporting of operational and IT risks to chief risk officer (CRO).	ST	PBC, SHCH

(*Continued*)

Table 10.1 (Continued)

	Timing	*Authorities*
SHCH: dispose of exposure thresholds per clearing member.	ST	PBC, SHCH
SHCH: apply haircuts to cash collateral.	MT	PBC, SHCH
SHCH: ensure independent validation of credit models at least annually.	ST	PBC, SHCH
SHCH: conduct liquidity stress tests on a daily basis.	ST	PBC, SHCH
SHCH: further develop business continuity plans by introducing a hot site.	MT	PBC, SHCH
SHCH: increase the number of liquidity providers and settlement banks.	MT	PBC, SHCH

1 MT: Medium-term; ST: Short-term.

the failure of one of the payment systems or securities settlement systems can result, not only in losses spreading through the system, but also in an ineffective implementation of monetary policy and a loss of confidence in the financial system. The failure of a CCP may result in unexpected losses for its participants, and in extreme circumstances, causing systemic disruptions.

2 **The main objective of this note is to analyze financial stability issues related to FMIs in China, using international standards and good practices. The analysis focuses on the capacity of the supervisory and oversight structure to identify and manage vulnerabilities related to FMIs, i.e.:**

   a the regulatory, supervisory and oversight framework, supervisory practices, available resources, transparency, adoption of international standards and domestic and cross-border cooperation and coordination;
   b identification and management of system wide risks or common issues of concern for all or the majority of FMIs, such as legal gaps, cyber risks, and recovery and resolution planning;
   c analyzing risks related to systemically important payment systems (SIPS) and CCPs, including HVPS and the SHCH for OTC derivatives.

3. **Recommendations in this note are based on the international agreed standards for FMIs, i.e., the CPSS-IOSCO Principles for Financial Market Infrastructures (PFMI).** The analysis of the supervision of FMIs takes the five responsibilities for authorities of the PFMI as reference (Box 6.1). The note also considers guidance prepared by the Financial Stability Board (FSB), and the Committee on Payments and Markets Infrastructures-International Organization of Securities Commission (CPMI-IOSCO) on resolution and recovery of FMIs, respectively, as well as CPMI-IOSCO guidance on cyber resilience for FMIs.

4. **The analysis builds on findings of earlier assessments.** The analysis takes into account the recommendations made during the 2011 China FSAP as well as the findings of the CPMI-IOSCO implementation monitoring assessments. The main findings of the 2011 FSAP and CPMI-IOSCO assessments are summarized in Appendix I.

Box 6.1 The Five Responsibilities of the PFMI

Responsibility A: Regulation, Supervision, and Oversight of FMIs
FMIs should be subject to appropriate and effective regulation, supervision, and oversight by a central bank, market regulator, or other relevant authority.

Responsibility B: Regulatory, Supervisory, and Oversight Powers and Resources
Central banks, market regulators, and other relevant authorities should have the powers and resources to carry out effectively their responsibilities in regulating, supervising, and overseeing FMIs.

Responsibility C: Disclosure of Policies with Respect to FMIs
Central banks, market regulators, and other relevant authorities should clearly define and disclose their regulatory, supervisory, and oversight policies with respect to FMIs.

Responsibility D: Application of the Principles for FMIs
Central banks, market regulators, and other relevant authorities should adopt the CPSS-IOSCO Principles for financial market infrastructures and apply them consistently.

Responsibility E: Cooperation with Other Authorities
Central banks, market regulators, and other relevant authorities should cooperate with each other, both domestically and internationally, as appropriate, in promoting the safety and efficiency of FMIs.

Source: CPSS IOSCO Principles for Financial Market Infrastructures, April 2012.

Description of FMIs in China

A. Overview of FMIs

5. **China's landscape for FMIs is one of the largest and most complex in the world.** It consists of a range of payment, clearing and settlement systems,

including several interbank payment systems, settlement systems and CCPs for securities, exchange-traded derivatives OTC derivatives. The different systems are interlinked and settle all directly or indirectly (through their settlement banks) in the real-time gross settlement system, which is the HVPS, operated by the PBC, as illustrated in Figure 10.1. Many of the systems have high volumes by international comparison. For example, HVPS is the fourth largest payment system in the world, the China Securities Depository and Clearing Corporation (CSDC) ranks as the sixth largest securities CCP and the China Futures Exchange (CFFEX) ranked number five in 2015. Appendix II provides for a description of the main FMIs. Appendix III contains key statistics per FMI.

6 **In China, many domestic FMIs can be considered systemically important.** The HVPS can be considered systemically important given its huge settlement volumes, clearing approximately s16 percent of the annual GDP on a daily basis, and its direct and indirect links to all other FMIs. The three CSDs can be considered systemically important, due to their central role in the interbank bond and securities markets and their role as custodian for CCP collateral. Also, all CCPs are systemically important as risk concentrators in various financial markets. The bulk electronic payment system (BEPS) could also be considered a SIPS, due to the high volumes and critical role for retail and corporate payments. Appendix IV contains an overview of systemic indicators for the main FMIs (size, interconnectedness, substitutability and unique functions, such as facilitating monetary operations and collateral management).

7 **All FMIs are state-owned.** The main payment systems are owned and operated by the PBC, whereas the PBC and/or the state have ownership, directly or indirectly, in the CCDC, CIPS and SHCH. The securities and futures market CCPs and CSDC are either owned by their members or shareholders, many of which are partly or fully state-owned institutions.

B. Overview of the supervisory and oversight framework

8 **Authorities responsible for the supervision and oversight of FMIs are the PBC and the CSRC.** The PBC is the main supervisor of payment systems and FMIs for the interbank bond, foreign exchange (FX) and OTC derivatives markets. The payment and settlement department (PSD) of the PBC is responsible for the regulation and supervision of the payment systems, whereas the financial market department is responsible for the regulation and supervision of the CCDC, SHCH and the foreign currency payment system (FCPS). The CSRC is responsible for clearing and settlement systems for corporate securities and derivatives. Its market supervision department regulates and supervises the CSDC, whereas the futures supervision department regulates and supervises the four exchange-traded derivatives CCPs. Table 10.2 summarizes the regulatory and supervisory structure for FMIs in China.

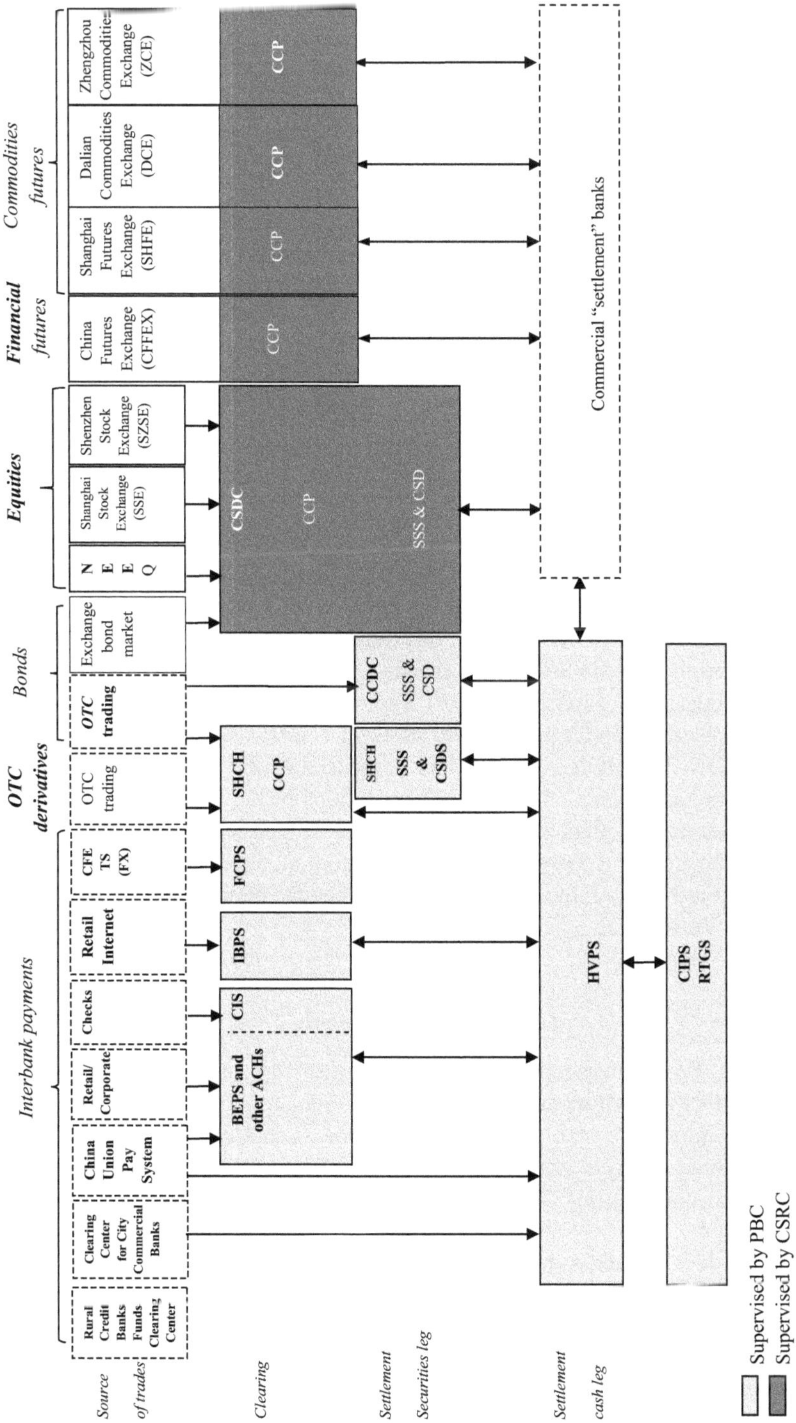

Figure 10.1 China: FMI Landscape

Source: IMF Staff.

Table 10.2 China: Overview of Authorities Responsible for FMIs

Supervisory authority	*Department*	*FMI*	*Main Law*
PBC	Payment and Settlement department	HVPS, BEPS, internet banking payment system (IBPS), CIS, CIPS, FCPS, China Union Pay, Clearing Center for City Commercial Banks, and the Rural Credit Banks Funds Clearing Center.	PBC Law
	Financial Market department	CCDC, SHCH	PBC Law
CSRC	Market Supervision department	CSDC	Securities Law
	Futures Supervision department	CFFEX, Dalian Commodities Exchange (DCE), Shanghai Futures Exchange (SHFE), Zhengzhou Commodities Exchange (ZCE).	No law, but futures regulation

9 **The State Administration of Foreign Exchange (SAFE) is involved in the supervision of the SHCH.** SAFE is a subsidiary of the PBC and is responsible for policy matters related to FX markets and products. In that regard, SAFE is involved in the approval of products to be cleared by the SHCH in coordination with the PBC as supervisor of SHCH.

10 **The Ministry of Finance (MOF) and the China Banking Regulatory Commission (CBRC) are stakeholders in relation to the supervision of the CCDC.** The MOF as shareholder of the CCDC and issuer of government securities has an interest in the safe operations of the CCDC and regulates debt issuance, payment and custody matters, which relate to CCDC's operations. The CBRC is responsible for the appointment of the chairman of the CCDC. Furthermore, the CBRC has outsourced the maintenance of three registers to the CCDC.

C. Recent developments

11 **China's FMI landscape is changing following reforms initiated by authorities as well as private initiatives.** Changes result from regulatory reforms adopted by China as a G20 member, and China's policy to open up financial markets gradually to foreign investors and cross-border trading. Also, the ongoing development and growth of markets trigger private initiatives.

12 **Recent developments include:**

- In January 2014, the SHCH started the clearing of OTC derivatives, i.e., Chinese Yuan (CNY) interest rate swaps (IRS). China is keen to comply with the commitment laid out at the G20 Pittsburgh summit in 2009 to clear all standardized derivatives through CCPs. In July 2014, clearing of CNY IRS became mandatory onshore in China for dealers and clients.

- In October 2015, the China's CIPS was launched to facilitate the clearing and settlement of cross-border renminbi payments and to support the renminbi in becoming a major global currency. CIPS is a real time gross settlement (RTGS) system that provides both onshore and offshore banks a central location for clearing renminbi payments and is directly linked to the HVPS. These features reduce the need for banks to navigate payment pathways via offshore clearing hubs or through correspondent banks.
- Finally, the use of e-money instruments offered by nonbank payment providers in China has grown exponentially. Amongst the nonbank payment providers are Alipay, and Tenpay, which are some of the biggest players, with Alipay having the biggest market share. Nonbank payment service providers and the products offered by them are regulated by the PBC in terms of administrative measures for payment services provided by nonfinancial institutions of 2010, and Administrative measures on online payment by nonbank payment institutions of 2015. The details of the volume and value of e-money instruments from 2013 to 2015 are given in Table 10.6 in Appendix III. In the coming years, these retail payments could become systemically important and any failure could impact public confidence in non-cash retail payments.

Analysis of selected issues

A. Oversight and supervision of FMIs

13. **This section analyzes to what extent the supervisory frameworks for FMIs are in line with the five responsibilities of the PFMI.** The objective is to benchmark China's regulatory, supervisory and oversight framework against international standards and analyze whether there are any gaps or issues of concern that enable the buildup of systemic risk. Recommendations are made to further mitigate risks to financial stability and align the framework with international standards.

Regulation, supervision and oversight of FMIs (responsibility A)

14. **The legal framework for the regulation, supervision and oversight FMIs in China consists of several 'segments', along the lines of different financial markets and laws.** The availability of a statutory supervisory framework differs per segment, as well as the availability of clearly defined criteria for the identification of FMIs that should be subject to regulation, supervision and oversight.

15. **Payment systems for interbank transactions are subject to regulation and supervision of the PBC based on the PBC law.** The PBC Law prescribes that the PBC maintain the normal operation of the payment, clearing and settlement systems (Article 4(9)) and shall organize, or assist in organizing, a clearing system for banking financial institutions (Article 27). The PBC Law does not include explicit criteria for FMIs to be subject to regulation, supervision and oversight of the PBC.
16. **The PBC's role as regulator, supervisor and overseer is clear from regulations and public statements.** In 2011, the PBC published the Notice of Business Supervision and Management Rules of the China Foreign Exchange Trade System. In 2016, the PBC issued the Notice on Amending the Related Management System of the Payment System, amending six regulations on HVPS and identifying "Settlement finality" in HVPS and BEPS. Furthermore, the PBC has publicly declared that it will apply the PFMI to the China National Clearing Center (CNCC),[3] CIPS, China Union Pay, the Clearing Center for City Commercial Banks, and the Rural Credit Banks Funds Clearing Center.
17. **Similarly, securities settlement systems, CSDs and CCPs for interbank bond and FX markets are regulated and supervised by the PBC based on the PBC Law and subsequent regulations and notices.** In 2011, the PBC published the Notice of Business Supervision and Management Rules of SHCH, and the Notice of Business Supervision and Management Rules of CCDC. In 2014, the PBC published a notice related to the establishment of a CCP for OTC derivatives, effectively mandating the central clearing for certain CNY IRS contracts. Furthermore, the PBC has publicly declared that it will apply the PFMI to CCDC and SHCH.
18. **Securities settlement systems, CSDs and CCPs for securities markets are regulated and supervised by the CSRC based on a statutory framework.** The securities law (Articles 155 and 157) specifies that CCPs and CSDs for the securities market are subject to the supervision of the CSRC. The CSRC has identified the CSDC as a CSD and CCP that falls under its regulation and supervision, and publicly declared that the PFMI apply to the CSCD. OTC transactions in the securities market are regulated through the Regulation for the National Equities Exchange and Quotations (NEEQ) system.
19. **CCPs in the futures market are regulated and supervised by the CSRC based on a dedicated regulation and underlying measures.** There is no specific law covering futures markets; the futures markets are regulated based on the Regulations on Administration of Futures Trading (2017 revision), issued by the State Council, and the Measures for the Administration of Futures Exchanges (2007), issued by the CSRC. The CSRC has identified the SHFE, DCE, ZCE, CFFEX, and CSDC as CCPs that fall under its regulation and supervision, and publicly declared that it will apply the PFMI to these exchanges. Futures transactions in OTC markets are not covered by the existing regulations.

20. **The current supervisory framework contains potential legal risks.** A main vulnerability relates to the lack of a statutory framework for futures markets. Rights and obligations defined in other laws might not be (fully) consistent with the CSRC's measures, potentially creating potential legal uncertainty about the CSRC's powers to enforce changes, where needed, as its powers are based on secondary legislation. The statutory basis of the PBC's regulation and supervision does not contain clear criteria for FMIs that are subject to its oversight. This may create confusion about the scope and powers of the PBC's responsibilities in relation to the responsibilities of other authorities. With a further growth and development of the market, for example, when new cross-sector products are developed, such as in the OTC derivatives markets, gaps or overlaps in regulation may appear with subsequent risks for financial stability.

21. **The mission encourages strengthening of the legal framework for the regulation and supervision of FMIs, and welcomes in that regard the following ongoing legal initiatives:**

- Authorities have started developing the 'China Financial Infrastructure Supervisory Rules' with the intention to further develop these into a law, outlining the regulatory, supervisory and oversight responsibilities for the all relevant authorities for FMIs in China, and reflecting the principles and concepts of the PFMI.
- The securities market Law is currently being revised, seeking to add new requirements for the risk management frameworks of securities CCPs and CSDs.
- The CSRC drafted a comprehensive futures market law, which will provide the CSRC with a legal basis to regulate and supervise futures markets, including CCPs. The draft law may include requirements for CCPs, based on the PFMI, including finality and netting. The draft law has been send to the National People's Congress of the People's Republic of China. No timeline has been set yet for its promulgation.
- The drafting of a national payments law to provide a clear legal basis for the regulation and supervision of payment systems and payment instruments, and subsequent requirements.

22. **Authorities may benchmark their proposed national model for the supervision of FMIs against jurisdictions with comparable markets in size and complexity.** For example, the approach taken in the United States can be considered. Similar to China, the U.S. FMI landscape consists of a relatively high number of FMIs, which are supervised by various authorities. The Dodd-Frank Act, Title VIII, identifies supervisory agencies (i.e. the Federal Reserve, Securities Commission and Commodity Futures Trading Commission) that have a primary jurisdiction over a designated FMI, which, in case an FMI is regulated by multiple regulators, have the primary responsibility for prescribing and implementing risk management standards. In addition to the identification of primary regulators, the Act expands the

Federal Reserve's role in the supervision, examination, and rule enforcement of all systemically important FMIs. For example, a primary regulator should conduct its annual examinations in consultation with the Federal Reserve as to the scope and methodology of the examination. The Federal Reserve may also participate, at its discretion, in such examinations. This approach allows the Federal Reserve, in cooperation with the other agencies, and complementary to existing supervisory and regulatory provisions, to address systemic risks consistently and strengthens its authority to induce change where necessary from a macroprudential perspective.[4]

Powers and resources (responsibility B)

23. **The PBC has sufficient powers to obtain information and induce change or enforce corrective action if needed.** Formal powers are vested with the PBC under the PBC law and various Administrative Measures. The PBC draws its powers from Articles 4 (9), 27, 32 and 46 of the PBC law. These are supplemented by administrative measures such as: (i) Measures for the administration of the entry and exit payment system of banking financial institutions; (ii) Administrative measures of PBC payment system participants; (iii) Business approach of HVPS; (iv) Operational management approach of payment system of PBC; and (v) Crisis management plan for payment and settlement systems.
24. **The CNCC, the operator of the main payment systems, is a public entity within the PBC, and the CCDC and SHCH are supervised by the PBC, allowing the PBC to obtain information of the payment system's functions, activities and overall financial condition, risk management, and whatever information it deems necessary.** The information enables the PBC to assess adherence to the relevant regulations and policies, as well as the risks of the payment systems on its members and the broader economy. The PBC also approves the risk management measures of the FMIs before they are published. Its powers reach as far as critical service providers (CSPs).
25. **The legal and regulatory framework provides the CSRC with sufficient powers to supervise and oversee the CSDC and the four futures CCPs, however, the futures market should be supervised based on a law, as mentioned under Responsibility A.** According to the provisions of the securities law, the regulation on the administration of futures trading, and other relevant laws and regulations, as well as the authorization of the State Council, the CSRC has the following powers:

- Request information where needed.
- Approval of the articles of association and business operational rules and review and approval of the appointment or removal of the general manager.

- Approval of the business implementation rules, relevant systems, new products and business models. Major incidents need to be reported.
- Evaluation of the annual performance of the CSDC and the four CCPs, including their board of directors and management.
- Use of enforcement tools, if needed, which include penalties, the issuance of warnings or orders to correct, confiscation of illegal gains and issuing orders to close down in severe cases. The CSRC may also use its powers towards responsible staff through warnings or eventually a disqualification.

Nevertheless, as mentioned under Responsibility A, the lack of a dedicated futures law may create legal uncertainty about the CSRC's enforcement powers.

26. **The CSRC has the ability to supervise CSPs.** The CSRC published several normative documents including the Information System Audit Standards for Securities and Futures Industries, which provide the CSRC with the possibility to conduct a comprehensive assessment and on-site inspection of the IT management, server room management, network management, and key information systems used by the CSDC and four CCPs.

27. **Resources to fulfill the respective mandates are tight for the PBC and the CSRC.** Despite increased responsibilities the number of staff has not increased in line with the new responsibilities under the PFMI and new market developments. The PSD and the financial markets department have 32 and 36 staff members respectively, which is tight given that these departments are responsible for many other issues in addition to regulation and oversight of FMIs. The number of staff involved in PFMI assessments is relatively small. The PBC currently draws resources from other departments and locations. With regard to the CSRC, the CSDC is mainly regulated and supervised by the market supervision department with a staff of approximately 40 members to cover all equity exchanges as well as the CSDC, of which 3 staff members are engaged in the CCP and CSD. The four futures exchanges, including the CCPs, are supervised by the futures supervision department with 27 full time staff resources, of which one staff member is involved in the supervision of the CCPs. Other departments within the CSRC may assist as needed, such as the fund and intermediary supervision department, bond market supervision department, international affairs department, enforcement bureau, and the legal affairs department.

28. **Authorities should ensure that they get the appropriate staff levels, both in quantity and quality.** Ensuring an appropriate level of human resources, both in quantity and quality, will allow adequate regulation and supervision of the FMIs in line with the PFMI, and contributes to financial stability. Not only an increase in the absolute number of staff is needed, but also an increase in staff with good knowledge of international standards and risk management practices. This includes knowledge of quantitative risk models for CCPs, such as margin, credit and liquidity models.

Transparency (responsibility C)

29. **The PBC discloses its policies and regulations related to payment systems.** The basic policy objective of the PBC on HVPS is to "maintain normal operation of payment system and clearing systems" as stated in the PBC Law. The PBC discloses the regulations and any revisions to the regulations to the public through its annual report, website, and press announcements.
30. **The PBC discloses its policies and regulations on the securities depository and the CCP for the OTC interbank derivatives bond market.** The basic policy objective of the PBC for the CCDC and SHCH is "ensure efficiency, security and protection of investors' legitimate rights". The PBC law, administrative measures on bond register and custody in the inter-bank bond market and regulations on SHCH have defined the roles and the basic institutional arrangements of SHCH and CCDC.
31. **The CSRC discloses its policies and regulations on securities depositories, clearing institutions, securities and derivatives FMIs.** The basic policy objective of the CSRC on these FMIs is "ensuring safety and high efficiency." The securities law, regulations on the administration of futures trading, measures for the administration of securities registration and clearing, measures for the administration of futures exchange and other relevant laws and regulations have defined the roles and the basic institutional arrangements of for these FMIs.

Implementation of the PFMI (responsibility D)

32. **The authorities have publicly stated that they adopt the PFMI.** According to the Circular on Implementation of Principles for Financial Mark Infrastructures (Yin Ban Fa [2013] No.187 and Zheng Jian Fa [2013] No.42) and the Circular on Conducting Assessment on Financial Market Infrastructures (Document Yin Ban Fa [2013] No.239) jointly issued by the CSRC and the PBC, the PBC and the CSRC fully adopt the FMI principles.
33. **The PBC and CSRC have established a Steering Group on FMIs.** The PBC and the CSRC jointly released the Notice on Establishment of Steering Group and its secretariat on Financial Market Infrastructures (Document Yin Ban Fa [2014] No.106). According to the Notice, the steering group is responsible for guiding the development and reform of FMIs, coordinating on major issues pertaining to development and reform, and jointly promoting the implementation of the PFMI. In addition to the steering group, as mentioned before, a PFMI office has also been established by both regulators. The establishment of the steering group and the PFMI office underline the authorities' commitment towards the adoption and consistent application of the PFMI in China.
34. **As requested by the authorities, all relevant FMIs have carried out a self-assessment.** The self-assessment was followed by an external assessment by

a joint team of experts from the PBC and the CSRC under the umbrella of the steering group and PFMI office. The set timelines for the self-assessment and external assessment were January and March 2014 respectively. The PBC is currently deciding what the next step should be.

35. **The implementation of the PFMI should be strengthened by reviewing and where necessary strengthening the regulations and measures of the authorities, as well as the rules of the FMIs.** The CSRC is referencing the PFMI to review its regulations and measures for possible improvements. Also, the rules of the CSDC and four futures CCPs could be further updated to reflect the practices in line with the PFMI. This exercise may be accomplished by taking into account the results of the self-assessment and the external assessment. Such an approach would result in mitigating the identified risks and contribute to systemic and financial stability.

36. **The team found that the compliance with the PFMI varies among FMIs.** Where some FMIs seem to have adopted the PFMI largely in their rules and daily operations, i.e., the CCDC and SHCH, other FMIs would need further implementation of the requirements in their organization and daily processes.

37. **Illustratively, the CSDC should be advised to improve its delivery-versus-payment (DVP) arrangements in the settlement of the exchange traded securities and strengthen the validation of its existing margin methodology:**

- Although DVP is addressed in the legal framework, the actual DVP arrangements do not sufficiently protect counterparts against the loss of the full principal value of transactions. DVP should be implemented by linking the final settlement of securities to the final settlement of the funds leg. The current practice of final settlement of securities taking place on T+0 and final funds settlement on T+1 exposes CSDC to both principal and replacement cost risks. Though Article 49 in Chapter 4 of the Regulations on Securities Registration and Settlement states that settlement should take place in a DVP mode, it is possible for the buyer of the securities to sell the securities, before making the payment for the securities and the settlement of the funds leg. Though it is understood that there is a provision of claw-back of the securities from the buyer, this is an ex-post measure which does not mitigate the principal risk. In order to mitigate credit risk and achieve greater safety and efficiency, the authorities could introduce ex-ante measures such as: (i) blocking the delivered securities in the buyer's account till the settlement of the funds leg is completed with CSDC enjoying a lien on the blocked securities in the account of the buyer; or (ii) alternately, create a special securities account of CSDC where the securities are lodged, till the completion of the settlement of the funds leg and transferring the securities to the buyer's account thereafter. Adoption of such measures would result in mitigating credit risk and result in DVP.

- The valuation models used for calculation of initial margin should be independently validated by a qualified external expert on an annual basis, to mitigate model risk. At a minimum, the validation should be carried out by staff with sufficient expertise who are independent of the developers and the users of the margin model. Additionally, margin calculation and back-testing should be carried out on a daily basis, the latter to evaluate whether there are any exceptions to the initial margin coverage. The model used to determine the adequacy of the default waterfall financial resources should also be subjected to validation.

38. **In addition, the futures exchanges should further enhance the quality of their risk management framework by establishing a dedicated risk management department, in line with international best practices.** The risk management department should have an independent reporting line to the Council (equivalent to the Board of directors). This arrangement provides the advantage to the Council to get to weigh risk (as provided by the risk management department) and business potential (as reported by the business departments) and take appropriate decisions based on the risk appetite and the type of products. In the existing arrangements, the risk management is often divided between business departments (the settlement department being responsible for stress testing) and the market supervision department for other areas of risk management.
39. **The risk management governance structure of the futures exchanges should be aligned to make the risk management department responsible for managing the enterprise wide risk management**, rather than the RMC, which is an executive level body, comprising heads of departments and the CEO. The risk management department should lay down a clear and documented enterprise wide risk management strategy, which should be approved by the RMC and endorsed by the Council. In addition, the RMC should be chaired by a sufficiently knowledgeable individual who is independent of the executive management and it should have an independent reporting line to the Council, to which it reports on a regular basis on all matters pertaining to risk management.
40. **Closer scrutiny on the composition of the components of the default waterfall and its use for taking care of the default of a participant should be carried out.** The waterfall composition for instance also includes resources used for overcoming liquidity shortfalls. The financial resources in the revised waterfall composition should be subjected to the ongoing regular stress tests by the individual exchanges as also by the China futures monitoring center (responsible for stress tests across all futures exchanges). The results of such examination by the China futures monitoring center should be shared with the CSRC, if not already being done so. This would enable the

regulator to get an overarching view on the safe and efficient functioning of the futures exchanges and would be another enabling tool in its supervision and oversight kit.

41. **In line with transparency norms as outlined in Principle 23, the regulatory authorities should advise all FMIs under their respective regulatory jurisdictions, to complete and publicly disclose their responses to the CPMI-IOSCO *Disclosure framework for financial market infrastructures.*** It is noted that the SHCH and CCDC have publicly disclosed their responses to the disclosure framework in English and Chinese.
42. **The existing governance and oversight arrangements over CCDC should be recalibrated to clearly distinguish the roles of the PBC, MOF, and CBRC.** The recalibration should establish the PBC as the authority responsible for overseeing the functioning of the CCDC as an FMI. The respective roles of the MOF and the CBRC should be reset taking into account the above approach. Such a measure would provide clear reporting lines to CCDC as also help in avoiding any conflicts of interest and minimize regulatory arbitrage, if any.
43. **To facilitate greater understanding of the PFMI, the CSRC may hold dedicated workshops on the PFMI for the staff of FMIs on a periodical basis.** This would facilitate capacity building and contribute to the ongoing implementation process of the PFMI. It is understood that the PBC already provides such workshops.
44. **In line with international best practices, the operator and overseer roles of the PBC with regard to the HVPS and other payment systems are distinct.** The HVPS is operated by the CNCC, a separate public entity in the PBC, while the PSD is responsible for the oversight and regulation of all payment systems including the HVPS. The CNCC and the PSD are staffed by different personnel of the PBC.

Cooperation among authorities (responsibility E)

45. **Cooperation between the PBC and the CSRC is well established with regard to the implementation of the PFMI, through the Steering Group for FMIs and the PFMI office. This cooperation could be further strengthened in the law.** The PBC is responsible for the overall planning and coordination of the implementation of PFMI, and takes the lead to report the progress to the State Council and the international organizations. This is supplemented by the establishment of the PFMI office in the PBC, consisting of technical staff of both regulators. The PBC and the CSRC invite each other into their respective assessment teams, officially exchange the self-assessment reports of the relevant FMIs, and jointly facilitate the implementation of the PFMI. To ensure the efficiency and effectiveness of their regulatory cooperation, the CSRC and the PBC hold periodical meetings with the deliberations being recorded in minutes to facilitate coordination. The reviews of

the legal framework, as discussed under Responsibility A, could reflect these cooperation practices to further strengthen and formalize them.

46. **Domestic cooperation between the PBC, the CBRC, the CSRC, and the CIRC (China Insurance Regulatory Commission) is multi-tiered.** These are: (i) coordinating and cooperating through the State Council which is responsible for overall financial stability and crisis management; cooperating through the existing financial regulation and coordination mechanism, i.e., the Financial Regulatory Coordination Joint Ministerial Committee (JMC); and (iii) others. In case of a crisis event related to FMIs, the authorities will coordinate under the leadership of the State Council to jointly establish an interim work team to facilitate communication, consultation and coordination. The JMC is tasked with a coordination role in maintaining financial stability and mitigating regional and systemic risks. The JMC reports to the State Council.

47. **CSDC and SHCH have multiple roles as a CCP, CSD, and SSS. CSDC, CCDC, and SHCH are FMIs that have cross-border links**. The CSDC has link arrangements with the Hong Kong Stock Exchange under the Shanghai-Hong Kong and Shenzhen-Hong Kong Stock Connect programs. The CSDC also has a link arrangement with the CSD in Singapore to support transfer of share stocks, which however is limited to the shares of one listed company and the volume and value of trades is insignificant. CCDC and SHCH linked to the central money-markets Unit after the launch of the Bond Connect pilot program on July 3, 2017.

48. **As for cross-border cooperation, the CSRC and Hong Kong Securities and Futures Commission (HKSFC) have a memorandum of understanding (MOU) on strengthening of regulatory and enforcement cooperation under Shanghai-Hong Kong Stock Connect and Shenzhen-Hong Kong Stock Connect.** In terms of regulation of the above inter-jurisdictional business, the CSRC has established a periodical coordination and supervisory cooperation mechanism with HKSFC for ensuring the safe and efficient functioning of the FMIs involved.

49. **Link related risks should be evaluated by the CSRC.** Evidence of the exchange of information between authorities concerning PFMI assessments of the involved FMIs, was not available in English to the assessment team. The cross-border link arrangements covered by the Stock Connect programs should be evaluated to identify, monitor and manage legal, credit, and liquidity risks, including a high level of protection of investor for the rights of the investor CSD participants.

50. **The FCPS provides multicurrency services.** Before adding a new currency, the PBC consults with relevant central banks of issue for their comments and suggestions. The PBC does not designate FCPS as a SIPS, as its turnover is not very significant. Notwithstanding this, the PBC notifies the volume and value of the foreign currency transaction to the relevant authorities on a quarterly basis.

B. System-wide risks

51. **This section discusses common risks to which the system as a whole is exposed.** The section starts with an analysis of interdependencies between FMIs and financial institutions, which shows the existence of several significant interconnections and underpins the need for resilient FMIs. The section then discusses the need for finality and netting at a statutory level and cyber security measures for FMIs. Recovery and resolution arrangements for FMIs are discussed as relatively new measures to manage extreme, but plausible circumstances. The section concludes with recommendations regarding central bank services and emergency liquidity assistance by the PBC.

Interdependencies Between FMIs and Financial Institutions

52. **China's landscape for FMIs is an interconnected network of financial institutions, with a significant overlap of members between multiple FMIs.** Figure 10.2 displays the network for the main FMIs in China and 609 members, consisting of 318 banks, 239 brokers, 2 insurers, and 50 other.[5] The large majority of members are Chinese entities.
53. **The network graph shows that the largest FMI node in the network is clearly HVPS,** followed by CCDC, as these systems have the largest settlement values and the highest number of members. CSDC is the third largest FMI in turnover, and SHFE the third largest FMI in number of members. The importance of HVPS is further emphasized by direct links to other FMIs (CCDC, SHCH, and CIPS) and indirect links to the remaining FMIs (Figure 10.1).

Table 10.3 China: Overlapping Members between FMIs (At a consolidated level)[1]

	HVPS	*CCDC*	*SHCH*	*CSDC*	*CFFEX*	*SHFE*	*ZCE*	*DCE*
HVPS	100%							
CCDC	39%	100%						
SHCH	21%	28%	100%					
CSDC	13%	30%	53%	100%				
CFFEX	5%	12%	24%	38%	100%			
SHFE	8%	17%	36%	40%	82%	100%		
ZCE	5%	12%	23%	38%	83%	61%	100%	
DCE	5%	13%	25%	39%	86%	63%	91%	100%

Sources: PBC, CSRC, and IMF staff estimates.

[1] Numbers are for September 30, 2016, except for HVPS and SHCH, for which the dates are December 31, 2016 and November 24, 2016, respectively. The sample of participants contain 609 members, which is a consolidated membership set, based on the top 200 members of the CCDC and all members of the other FMIs. The different members were consolidated at the highest level possible.

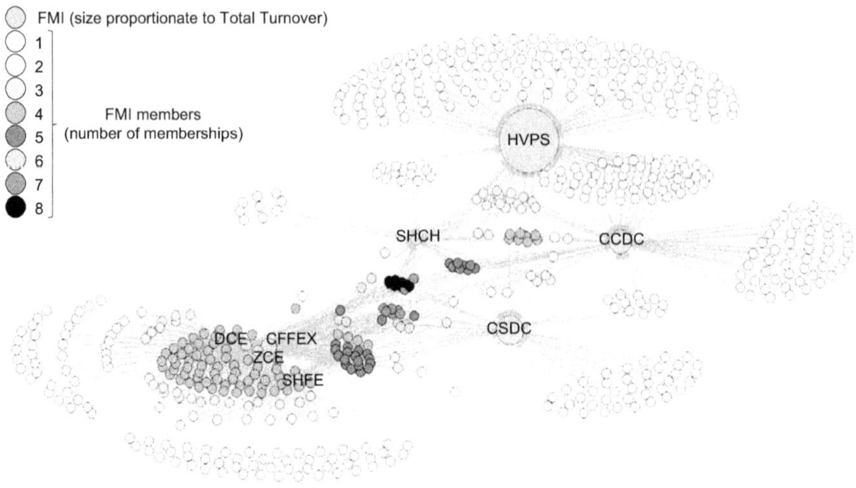

Figure 10.2 China: Network Graph for the Main FMIs in China and Their Members
Sources: PBC, CSR, and IMF staff estimates.

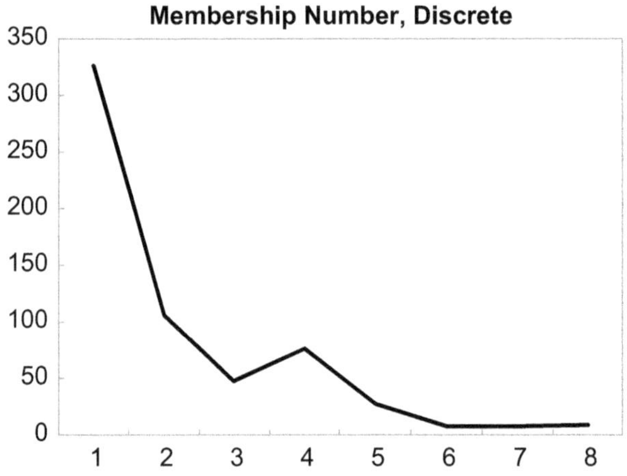

Figure 10.3 China: Number of Members (Y axis) and their Number of Memberships in FMIs (X axis)
Source: IMF Staff estimates.

54. There are nine banks that have a membership in all FMIs, of which eight are Chinese banks and one is a U.S. bank. The Chinese banks are all among the largest banks in the country. Another eight banks have a membership in seven FMIs, and 76 banks have a membership in four FMIs (Figure 10.3).

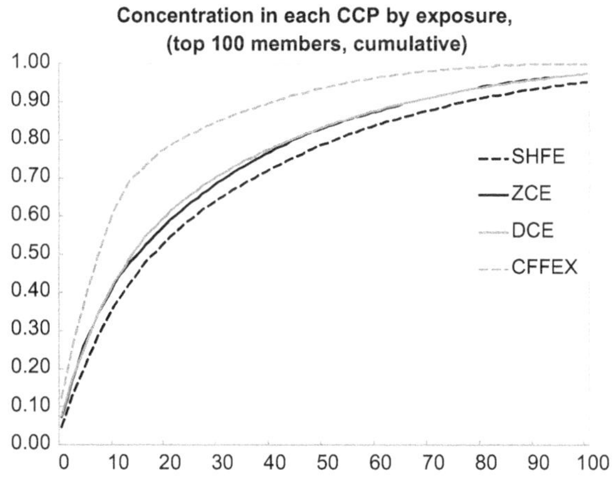

Figure 10.4 China: Percentage of Members Responsible for Exposure in Each CCP
Source: IMF Staff estimates.

55. The network graph further shows the existence of several clusters:

- The four futures CCPs have a highly overlapping member base. ZCE and DCE's overlap for more than 90 percent, whereas CFFEX's member base overlaps with the other three futures exchanges for more than 80 percent (Table 10.3). Turnover and exposures (measured in margin) are somewhat concentrated with approximately a quarter to a third of the member based responsible for 80 percent of turnover and exposure (Figure 10.4).
- CSDC also highly overlaps with the four futures CCPs, with around 40 percent of CSDC's members also being member of these CCPs.
- The overlap between members of CCDC and SHCH is more than 50 percent, which may relate to the fact that both FMIs are active in the interbank bond market.
- The member base of HVPS is more related to those of CCDC and SHCH, illustrating also that CCDC and SHCH settle their cash payments directly in the HVPS.

56. This high interconnectivity suggests that contagion from a financial or operational failure of a FMI or critical member could quickly spread through the financial system if proper safeguards are not in place. Data for CSDC and CCDC show that the default of the two participants, and their affiliates with the largest losses, not only affects these FMIs, but also other FMIs, due to the multiple memberships of these participants. For example, a default of the two participants with the largest exposures in CSDC coincides with the default of these participants in another 5–12 FMIs, including several CCPs. For CCDC, the default of the two largest participants (measured in turnover) would coincide with the default of these entities in 4–8 other FMIs.

57. **This analysis emphasizes the need for**: i) resilient FMIs that are able to stop a contagion of losses and act as firewalls following the default of one or more participants. This requires full implementation of the PFMI for each FMI and a strengthening of the legal framework through the adoption of finality and netting; ii) the need for recovery and resolution planning to ensure the provision of critical operations and services as a going concern, also during extreme circumstances; and iii) crisis preparedness and an ex-ante understanding of how, potentially, losses may spread through the financial system. This underlines the need for cooperation among authorities at a domestic level and an international level as well as joint crisis exercises that simulate the default of operational disruptions at members and FMIs. It also requires an ex-ante policy of the PBC with regard to the provision of central bank services, including liquidity support.

Finality and netting

58. **Finality and netting are addressed in China at the level of regulations, measures and rules.** Since the FSAP in 2011, the PBC, CSRC, and individual FMIs have taken measures to define finality and netting in their regulations, notices and rules. Although this is an improvement to the regulatory framework it does not provide watertight protection against a potential revocation of transactions or collateral payments, or an unwinding of netted positions, following the bankruptcy of a bank, as the concepts of finality and netting are not unambiguously included in the Securities Law, as required by international standards.[6] Finality and enforceability of netting and collateral arrangements should be at the level of the law, because they derogate from the Insolvency statute (a formal law in its own right). A lower level of regulatory norm (or FMI self-regulation) cannot validly and with legal certainty do it. Revocation of transactions, collateral payments or unwinding of positions may result in large liquidity and credit losses and represent systemic risk for FMIs and their members.

59. **It is recommended to unambiguously include these concepts in statutory law to provide a high degree of legal certainty for all relevant material aspects covering all FMIs.** The legal basis should be strengthened among other things to provide for recognition of settlement finality in the event of insolvency of a participant; recognition of multi-lateral netting; provisions for bankruptcy remoteness of pledged collateral; close out netting; and prescriptions to overcome any zero-hour rules. The drafting of new laws, or reviews of existing laws, as discussed under Responsibility A, create a good opportunity to introduce these concepts at a statutory level. Alternatively, authorities may enact a comprehensive statute on finality and netting. This will improve the consistency with the Bankruptcy Law, among others, and also facilitate the determination of Chinese CCPs as qualifying CCPs, or QCCPs, by foreign authorities or banks.[7]

Cyber resilience of FMIs

60. **Authorities have identified cyber risk as an important supervisory topic in relation to financial institutions, including FMIs.** A cyber security law was issued in 2016 and will come into effect as per June 2017. The law applies to all critical institutions in China and identifies key institutions in different sectors that are required to take specific measures to protect IT systems and enhance their security level. Within the financial sector the law specifically identifies FMIs as critical institutions for financial stability. In 2016, the CSRC organized an industry-wide contingency test on information security. More than 10 institutions participated in the test, including securities exchanges, futures exchanges, CSDC and market institutions. The test was jointly planned with the Ministry of Industry and Information Technology and the National Energy Administration, and was observed by the Cyberspace Administration of China and the PBC. The exercise tested the emergency response capabilities of the FMIs supervised by the CSRC. The PBC and CSRC have both issued information security requirements, and focus on strengthening the autonomous control of information systems for the FMIs under their respective responsibility.
61. **Authorities may strengthen their joint efforts and address cyber resilience explicitly under the PFMI office.** With the promulgation of the cyber security law, cooperation between the PBC, the CSRC and FMIs may further improve insights on cyber security and contribute to the awareness and assessments of cyber risks. The CPMI-IOSCO guidance on cyber resilience for FMIs may be used as a benchmark.[8] Joint crisis coordination mechanisms and testing of crisis communication protocols can further improve the management and monitoring of these risks. Where weaknesses were identified, these should be addressed in the PBC's and the CSRC's supervisory activities as a priority.

Recovery, resolution and liquidity support

62. **FMIs have developed recovery plans.** Where some FMIs have developed recovery plans in line with international standards, recovery plans of other FMIs need further development, beyond business continuity planning (BCP) and default management.
63. **Resolution planning is at an early stage.** Resolution planning has the objective to sustain critical operations and services if an FMI potentially becomes non-viable as a going concern, while avoiding a bail out at the expense of taxpayers' money. The PBC is studying the features of these arrangements in the Chinese context. So far, no legal framework has been developed, or a resolution authority been appointed.
64. **Resilience of FMIs can be strengthened through the provision of central bank services to solvent, systemically important FMIs.** The PBC currently

provides settlement services to CCDC and SHCH. It may consider extending these services to the CSDC and other CCPs, under the condition that the FMIs strengthen their risk management practices, and, in addition to the CSRC's supervision, are subject to macroprudential oversight of the PBC. Although private sector liquidity must constitute the first line of defense for FMIs against liquidity shortfalls, there could be extreme circumstances in which their liquid resources turn out to be insufficient or unavailable. Special financing arrangements could be made by the central bank for the above circumstances to ensure that they can continue to make payments to counterparties and would thereby maintain the stability of the market. Furthermore, the provision of central bank accounts will reduce FMIs' dependence on collateral services provided by commercial banks and may also be used for settlement purposes, significantly reducing credit and liquidity risks related to the use of settlement banks.

C. Analysis of HVPS and SHCH

65. **This section analyzes the risk management practices of two main FMIs in China, the HVPS and SHCH.** Findings and recommendations are based on discussions with the authorities and the two FMIs, as well as the public disclosure document of the SHCH. The HVPS is the RTGS system owned and operated by the PBC, and the SHCH operates a CCP and CSD. It offers CCP services for bonds, OTC traded interest rate derivatives, FX spot and FX derivatives, and freight and commodity derivatives. Appendix II and III provide more details on the two FMIs.

Analysis of HVPS

66. **The HVPS is generally a robust, safe and efficient system with a "V" topology.** The HVPS system was upgraded in 2013, with several advanced features. HVPS version 2 features include: (i) liquidity saving offsetting mechanism; (ii) single point access to the participants; (iii) ISO 20022 message formats; and (iv) an increase in operating hours which is 8:30 am to 5:00 pm for normal settlement and 5:00 pm to 8:30 pm for specific business. Further, business continuity and disaster recovery is being enhanced with three operating centers in two locations (with the third operating center becoming functional this autumn).
67. **The PBC Law provides the legal basis for the PBC to operate the HVPS.** Article 27 of the PBC Law prescribes that the PBC shall organize, or assist in organizing, a clearing system for banking financial institutions and provide clearing services and in conjunction with the banking regulatory authority under the State Council, formulate rules for payments and settlements. Further, as part of its functions and responsibilities, the PBC under Article 4 (9) is enjoined to maintain the normal operation of the payment, clearing and settlement systems.

68. **A dedicated RMC for the HVPS, chaired by the Deputy Governor, is tasked with the responsibility for the overall risk management framework for the HVPS.** The heads of relevant departments of the PBC such as the PSD, CNCC, and IT are members of the RMC. Select participants are also invited for the meetings of the RMC, which is held every quarter. All risk related measures pertaining to credit, liquidity and operational risks are discussed during these meetings and action plans for further improvements to the system are drawn up for implementation.
69. **Participants in HVPS are divided into direct and indirect participants.** There are 305 direct participants and 141,023 indirect participants by the end of 2016. Most of direct participants are commercial banks with RMB reserve accounts at PBC, and the others are PBC's Accounting Department, Treasury Department and FMIs, having direct participant interfaces with HVPS. Indirect participants are other smaller commercial banks (mainly rural) which route their transactions through direct participants for making and receiving payments in the HVPS.
70. **Credit risk is largely mitigated in HVPS.** Transactions are settled in real time on a gross basis based on availability of funds in the sending participant's account. Secondly, the PBC provides intraday liquidity support to participants on a fully collateralized basis in the form of intraday repos with a fee, thereby mitigating its own credit risk exposure. The intraday liquidity funds have to be repaid by the participant by the end of the day, failing which it is converted into an overnight facility at a penal rate of interest. Participants tend to use the OMO facility or borrow in the interbank market, for their liquidity needs as these are cheaper sources of liquidity compared to the fee based intraday repo facility.
71. **The PBC should review the existing practices related to the fees and the timings of the intraday repo window, and the use of OMO facility.** The fee for the intraday repo facility, acts as a disincentive and limits the use of intraday repo by the participants, as it is in addition to the opportunity costs borne by them. Secondly, intraday repo is available only till 5:00 pm, though the operating hours of the system continue till 8:30 pm. The non-availability of the intraday repo facility beyond 5:00 pm could impose liquidity pressures on the participants especially, in times of stressed market conditions.
72. **The use of OMO (which is primarily a monetary policy tool), by participants for their intraday liquidity needs in the HVPS, would need to be reviewed and examined by the PBC.** Participants either use the OMO facility or borrow in the interbank market, as these are cheaper sources of liquidity compared to the intraday repo facility. Participants could be exposed to liquidity risk pressures if either the OMO is not available on a daily basis or if the interbank market timings do not match with the operating hours of the HVPS.
73. **Collateral management practices should be reviewed by the PBC and brought in line with the PFMI.** A uniform haircut ratio of 10 percent is

imposed on all collateral, which, set in 2004 has not been changed till now. The mark to market module for valuing the collateral on a daily basis, though developed, has not been made operational. In order to mitigate residual credit risk, the PBC should review its haircut methodology and mark to market the collateral on a daily basis. In addition, the haircut methodology and procedures should be subject to an independent validation at least once a year.

74. **Enhanced liquidity risk management tools under HVPS version 2, comprise:** (i) queuing and settlement of transactions on a first-in-first-out (FIFO) basis; (ii) priority levels for transactions; use of automated bilateral and operator initiated multilateral offsetting mechanisms; (iv) online queue monitoring by participants and the system operator; and (v) online verification of clearing account balances by participants. Transactions are settled in HVPS using a combination of FIFO and priority levels. Transactions with the same priority level will be taken up for settlement based on the time at which the transaction has been received. The PBC will alert the participants on a queue build-up, but by itself does not change the priority levels; only the participants have the ability to change the priorities of their own transactions.

75. **Given the systemic nature of the instant transfers (which are DVP transactions and net clearing settlement files from FMIs), these should be assigned a higher priority in order to mitigate liquidity risk.** In the extant framework, instant transfers have the lowest level of priority at priority 7. A rejection of an instant transfer transaction could have unintended liquidity and systemwide risks on participants and other FMIs, given the system-wide dependencies, especially if it were to take place at the end of the day when funding markets may not be in operation and the intraday repo window is closed. Though the rules specify that the FMI originating the instant transfer is responsible for its settlement, as the system operator, the PBC should take measures to mitigate liquidity and credit risks. Accordingly, these instant transfer transactions should be assigned a higher priority to bring them on par with either priority level 3 or 4 transactions.

76. **The PBC should deploy other liquidity risk mitigation tools such as:**

    a. **prescribing a cut-off time in the rules of the system,** beyond which a participant cannot withdraw a transaction pending in the queue for settlement, to avoid creating liquidity risks. Currently, participants can withdraw pending transactions at any time during the operating hours, which may cause liquidity pressures for other participants. The rules should accordingly be revised to clearly define the point in time after which unsettled payments may not be revoked by a participant.

    b. **introducing a time varying fee structure.** Participants currently pay a flat fee per payment transfer irrespective of the time at which the payment transfer is sent. Under a time varying fee scheme, participants would pay a lower fee for those payment transfers sent earlier to the system for settlement, while those sent towards the end of the operating hours would attract a higher fee. Such a measure would aid in improving liquidity flows in the HVPS system, and also act as an incentive to participants to submit their payment transfers earlier into the system.

77. **The RMC is responsible for the operational risk management strategy of the HVPS which is divided into managing internal and external operational risks.** HVPS has a main operating center and a backup center located 300 kilometers away from the main center. A third operating center is coming up in a different location and would start functioning this autumn. The HVPS system functions with a high level of reliability, operational capacity and adheres to the recovery point objective (RPO) and recovery time objective (RTO). HVPS has a holistic BCP involving the central system and all the participants including the other FMIs with a crisis and event management component. Apart from the FMIs, around 70 key direct participants (with significant volumes and value of transactions) also have backup centers.
78. **A consultative approach is followed by the PBC before effecting any changes to the HVPS rules and regulations.** The proposed changes are circulated to the participants and their feedback is elicited and taken into consideration, before the changes are implemented. In addition, HVPS user group meetings are held every six months.
79. **HVPS as an FMI, should complete and disclose publicly responses to the CPSS-IOSCO Disclosure framework for financial market infrastructures on a regular basis.** The responses to the Disclosure framework should be publicly disclosed both in Chinese and English. It is understood that a self-assessment of HVPS has been carried out, but it should be noted that the self-assessment and the public disclosure of responses to the Disclosure framework are distinct and serve different purposes with different objectives.

Analysis of SHCH

Generally, risk management practices of the SHCH are well designed, and in line with the PFMI. Nevertheless, the mission found several issues of concern that would benefit from further development to align SHCH fully with the PFMI. The SHCH has modern risk management systems, a risk management department, a RMC, and a set of responsibilities, rules, procedures and practices to manage both operational and financial risks. Several issues for improvement, identified by the mission, are described in the following paragraphs.

80. **The risk-management governance should be further strengthened by appointing an independent chair for the RMC**. Currently, the Chairman of the Board of Directors also chairs the RMC, which does not support an independent analysis of risks within the RMC. The Chairman of the Board of Directors may include 'business' considerations in the risk assessment of the RMC. It is therefore recommended to appoint a sufficiently knowledgeable person as chair of the RMC, who is independent of the SHCH's executive management, and who leads independent risk analysis and subsequent report-

ing to the Board of Directors. This construction allows the Board to receive complete and unbiased information about the risks faced by the SHCH and the management of those risks and balance these against business considerations. Independent reporting enables board members to exercise objective judgment after fair consideration of all information and views.

81. **Operational and IT risks should be regularly reported to the CRO.** Currently, the risk management department is the only department within SHCH that reports to the CRO. As the risk management department 'only' covers the management of credit, liquidity and market risks, other risks, such as operational and IT risks, are not regularly reported to the CRO. It is recommended to address this, preferably by having the risk management department also cover operational and information technology (IT) risks. Alternatively, staff of the Operational and IT Departments that are responsible for risk management should have a direct reporting line to the CRO. The CRO reports all types of risks to the RMC through his/her direct reporting line.

82. **SHCH has defined exposure thresholds per clearing member, which may result in uncovered exposures for the CCP and can therefore not be part of SHCH's risk management approach.** SHCH monitors its exposures towards clearing members during the day. If, due to new positions or market volatility, a clearing member's exposures are not fully covered by collateral, SHCH does not necessarily call for intraday margin. Instead, it has defined thresholds per clearing member, and will only call for intraday margin if these thresholds are reached. This means that, during the day, the CCP may be exposed to credit risks. The requirement of Principle 4 that 'current and potential future exposures to each participant should be fully met' is not fully implemented by SHCH. SHCH's initial margin calculation should be further developed to ensure that its potential future exposures are covered with a single-tailed confidence level of 99 percent.

83. **SHCH does currently not apply a haircut to cash collateral.** Only the CCP service for FX spot and derivatives transactions accepts foreign currency, i.e., USD. USD collateral currently comprises only a small part of all margins. Nevertheless, it is recommended to adopt haircuts for cash collateral in line with the PFMI and international practices to protect the CCP against potential fluctuations in the exchange rate.

84. **SHCH's margin and collateral models should be subject to independent validation. The** credit risk models, including the margin and haircut models, are not validated by reviewers that are sufficiently independent. Validation of the models should be performed by personnel with sufficient expertise, who are independent of the personnel that created and use the models. These experts could be drawn from within SHCH. However, review by external experts, such as academics or consultants, is also possible. Independent validations should take place at least annually.

85. **Liquidity stress testing needs to take place daily.** Currently, SHCH conducts liquidity stress tests on a quarterly basis. In line with Principle 7, SHCH

must be able to effect intraday and multiday settlement and meet other payment obligations on time under a wide range of potential stress scenarios. To that purpose the FMIs should be able to conduct liquidity stress testing on a daily basis.

86. **BCP is well-developed; however, it is recommended to deploy a hot backup site and continue developing BCP arrangements.** Apart from the main operational center in Shanghai, SHCH has a disaster recovery site in Shanghai and in Beijing. BCP plans are developed and regularly tested. While the backup sites can take over the IT operations, operational staff needs to be transported from the primary to the secondary site. Also, testing does not necessarily test the full load of operations at the backup site. It is recommended to further strengthen the BCP, for example, through full and regular switching of all operations between the primary and secondary sites and the establishment of a hot backup site.

87. **Finally, SHCH may increase the number of liquidity providers and settlement banks for foreign currencies to reduce potential disruptions in case one of these supporting banks fails.** SHCH has contracted 2 banks as liquidity provider for USD liquidity needs and 2 banks for credit lines in other currencies. Furthermore, SHCH has selected 2 settlement banks for USD settlements and 1 for other currencies. It is recommended to increase the number of liquidity providers and settlement banks for non-RMB to mitigate concentration risks and interdependencies. This is important as the default of one of these banks may significantly impact SHCH, and its ability to fulfil its obligations as a CCP. For example, in times of stress, one of SHCH's liquidity providers may default, resulting in no or reduced access to credit lines, causing potentially significant liquidity risk to SHCH. The loss of a settlement bank exposes SHCH to operational problems.

APPENDIX I

2011 FSAP and CPMI-IOSCO implementation monitoring assessment results

2011 FSAP summary of main recommendations

- Complete the legal and regulatory framework through: (i) enactment of a payment system law to give full protection to settlement finality and netting arrangements; (ii) interpretation of the "Enterprise Bankruptcy Law" to avoid a "zero-hour rule"; (iii) upgrade of payment systems rules and procedures to the level of PBC regulation.
- For derivatives clearing and settlement, develop a statutory law containing provisions on derivative trading including among other issue, the enforceability of trades, finality, netting, novation, investor protection and collateral protection.
- The PBC should clarify in detail its policy stance in payment system oversight in a publicly available document, which would expand on the scope of its actions and its plans to achieve its public policy objectives in payment system matters.
- Although a high-level cooperation framework among relevant authorities does exist, structure cooperation for CCPs and CSDs at the technical level more formally. Authorities should also further foster cooperation between them and the private sector and other relevant stakeholders by creating an appropriate forum to discuss payment and settlement matters.
- For CCDC, separate clearly the oversight function of the PBC, the other supervisory tasks of CBRC and MOF, and the operational responsibility of the PBC.
- Upgrade links between CCDC and CSDC to enhance connectivity among Interbank Bond Market, Shanghai Stock Exchange (SSE), and Shenzhen Stock Exchange (SZSE), support further development, and contribute to efficiency in all three markets.

CPMI-IOSCO implementation monitoring results

CPMI-IOSCO Implementation Monitoring Level	*Assessment results for China*	*Publication*
Level 1. Assess whether a jurisdiction has completed the process of adopting the legislation and other policies that will enable it to implement the principles and responsibilities;	The Chinese jurisdiction has the highest ratings in all categories, meaning that final implementation measures are in force for all types of FMIs, both for the Principles as well as the Responsibilities.	CPMI-IOSCO 'Implementation monitoring of PFMI: Third update to Level 1 assessment report', June 2016
Level 2. Assess whether the content of new legislation and policies is complete and consistent with the principles and responsibilities;	Not available for China.	
Level 2/3. Assess whether the content of new legislation and policies are complete and consistent with the responsibilities and implemented by the authorities;	The Chinese jurisdiction is found to observe all responsibilities.	Draft CPMI-IOSCO 'Assessment and review of application of Responsibilities for authorities', November 2015

APPENDIX II

Description of FMI landscape[9]

Payment systems

The PBC has developed several interbank payment systems, which include:

- The HVPS: Established in 2005, the HVPS mainly handles inter-city and local credit transfers above a given value as well as urgent low-value transfers electronically. Payment instructions are sent in real time and cleared transaction by transaction. The payments system backbone currently operates in a decentralized way (multi-entry point) with access points in each of the 32 provinces, autonomous regions and cities having province-level status. The HVPS system is interconnected to many trading, payments and securities settlement systems to allow for central bank money settlement.
- The BEPS: deals mainly with local and non-local paper-based debit payments as well as low-value credit transfers below a given value. In June 2006, BEPS was put into operation nationwide. The system sends payment instructions in bulk, nets in real time and settles at regular times.
- The check imaging system (CIS): a check truncation system supporting the use of checks nationwide. The CIS enables electronic exchange of check images, automated clearing of the exchange "paper" instruments and multilateral net settlement of the exchange instruments at the HVPS. The system was launched in June 2007 and is available nation-wide.
- The IBPS: handles mainly interbank retail payment transactions via the internet, enabling customers to submit online payments and obtain results in real time. IBPS has been put into operation nationwide since August 2010.
- The China domestic FCPS: this is an RTGS system developed by the PBC for the foreign currency payments incurred by domestic purchases of goods and services. It was put into operation at the end of April 2008. FCPS can process payments in eight currencies: USD, HKD, GBP, EUR, JPY, CAD, CHF, and AUD. It does not involve FX transactions.
- The China's CIPS: a RTGS systems that provides both onshore and offshore banks a central location for clearing renminbi payments and is directly linked to China National Advanced Payment System (CNAPS).

All these payment systems are owned by the PBC. HVPS, BEPS, and IBPS are the three primary application systems of the CNAPS. In addition, there are numerous check clearing houses around the country administered by the PBC local offices or delegated to banks when the locality has not a PBC branch. China Union Pay handles the clearance of cards transactions whose balances are settled in the HVPS. Two other automated clearing houses (ACHs) are: i) the Clearing Center for City Commercial Banks, owned by City Commercial Banks; and ii) the Rural Credit Banks Funds Clearing Center, owned by 30 Rural Credit Banks.

CCPs

- The CSDC provides stock exchange markets with such services as centralized registration, custody, clearing and settlement. It delivers multilateral netting services as a CCP, as well as securities and funds settlement services as an operator of the securities clearing and settlement system. The CSDC is owned by the SSE (50 percent) and the SZSE (50 percent). Both stock exchanges are member owned entities.
- The SHCH is the CCP for bonds, OTC traded interest rate derivatives, FX spot and FX derivatives, and freight, and commodity derivatives. SHCH provides netting and centralized clearing services in RMB and foreign currencies as well as for cross-border transactions in RMB approved by the PBC. SHCH is owned by the China Foreign Exchange Trade System (46.67 percent), CCDC (33.33 percent), the China Banknote Printing and Minting Corporation (10 percent), and the China Gold Coin Incorporation (10 percent). These four entities are, on their turn, all owned by the PBC and/or the State.
- In addition, there are four main futures exchanges, which all have their own in-house clearing and settlement arrangements, including CCP services. The three commodities exchanges are the SHFE (copper, aluminum, zinc, steel wire rod, rebar, natural rubber, fuel oil, and gold), the DCE (soybean, corn, polyethylene, palm oil, and PVC) and the Zhengzhou Commodities Exchange (ZCE) (wheat, cotton, sugar, rapeseed oil, and rice). The CFFEX clears financial derivatives traded on its exchange platform. All futures exchanges are member owned entities.

Securities settlement systems (SSS) and central securities depositories (CSDs)

- The CCDC provides services such as issuance, registration, custody, settlement, redemption and information products for the bond market. It is the only institution entrusted by the MOF to be the depository for Government securities and has linkages with the OMO System of the PBC. The CCDC is fully owned by the MOF.
- SHCH registration and settlement system SHCH provides participants in the interbank bond market with registration and settlement services for warrants

and commercial paper subject to the regulation of the PBC. SHCH is owned by the China Foreign Exchange System (46.67 percent), CCDC (33.33 percent), the China Banknote Printing and Minting Corporation (10 percent), and the China Gold Coin Incorporation (10 percent). These four entities are, on their turn, all owned by the PBC and/or the state.

- The SSS of the CSDC provides settlement services for transactions in securities listed on the Shanghai and Shenzhen stock exchanges, concerning stocks, funds, warrants, treasury bonds, local government bonds, corporate bonds and convertible bonds, etc., as well as for the exchange bond market. Government securities can also be traded in the stock exchanges. For this purpose, the CSDC holds an omnibus account at the CCDC and beneficial owner securities settlement for stock exchange transactions is done through CSDC's books (Figure 10.1).

APPENDIX III

Statistics of FMIs

Table 10.1 China: Key Statistics FMIs (2014)

	(millions, total for the year)	*(CNY billions, total for the year)*	*(end of year)*	*(measured for value of trades)*
	Number of trades	*Value of trades*	*Number of participants*	*Their rank worldwide*
Payment Systems				
HVPS	712	2,346,893	131,653	#4 out of 65
BEPS	1,435	22,075	131,522	#37 out of 65
Exchanges				
Shanghai SE	1,742	128,149	258	#5 out of 39
Shenzhen SE	1,851	44,470	120	#11 out of 39
CCPs (data for 2010)				
CSDC	3,106	63,937	220	#6 out of 38
CSDs				
CSDC	3,890	251,625	nap	NA
CCDC	1.13	244,541	6,681	NA

Source: CPMI, Statistics on payment, clearing and settlement systems in the CPMI countries.

Table 10.2 China: Trading Volumes and Global Rank for Chinese Derivatives Exchanges (2015)

Exchange	*Title*	*Value (USD millions)*	*Value (CNY millions)*	*Exchange Total Value (USD millions)*	*Exchange Total Value (CNY millions)*	*Worldwide Exchange Rank (2015)*
CFFEX	Treasury bond futures	950,709	6,010,675	67,587,209	417,760,470	#5
	Interest rate options					
	Stock index futures	66,636,500	411,749,795			

(*Continued*)

Table 10.2 (Continued)

Exchange	*Title*	*Value (USD millions)*	*Value (CNY millions)*	*Exchange Total Value (USD millions)*	*Exchange Total Value (CNY millions)*	*Worldwide Exchange Rank (2015)*
	Single stock index options					
DCE	Commodities options			6,698,390	41,935,973	#19
	Commodities futures	6,698,390	41,935,973			
SHFE	Commodities futures	10,148,100	63,555,263	10,148,100	63,555,263	#15
	Commodities options					
	Value of share trading					
ZCE	Commodities futures	4,944,870	30,805,485	4,944,870	30,805,485	#22
	Commodities options					

Source: World Federation of Exchanges, CSRC.

Table 10.3 China: E-money Instruments

		2013	*2014*	*2015*
E-money instruments	volume (10 thousand)	2,578,316.77	3,333,286.81	10,523,315.16
	value (100 million Yuan)	10,751,606.11	14,046,457.77	25,062,261.90
Internet	volume (10 thousand)	2,367,418.50	2,857,446.97	3,637,133.31
	value (100 million Yuan)	10,607,832.04	13,760,202.94	20,182,100.53
Phone	volume (10 thousand)	43,466.39	23,444.10	29,841.89
	value (100 million Yuan)	47,394.04	60,391.12	149,891.54
Mobile	volume (10 thousand)	167,431.88	452,395.74	1,383,635.13
	value (100 million Yuan)	96,380.04	225,863.70	1,082,161.85
Others	volume (10 thousand)			1,082,085.56
	value (100 million Yuan)			2,376,390.46

Source: People's Bank of China.

Key Payment Systems, Number and Value of Transactions, 2010-2014

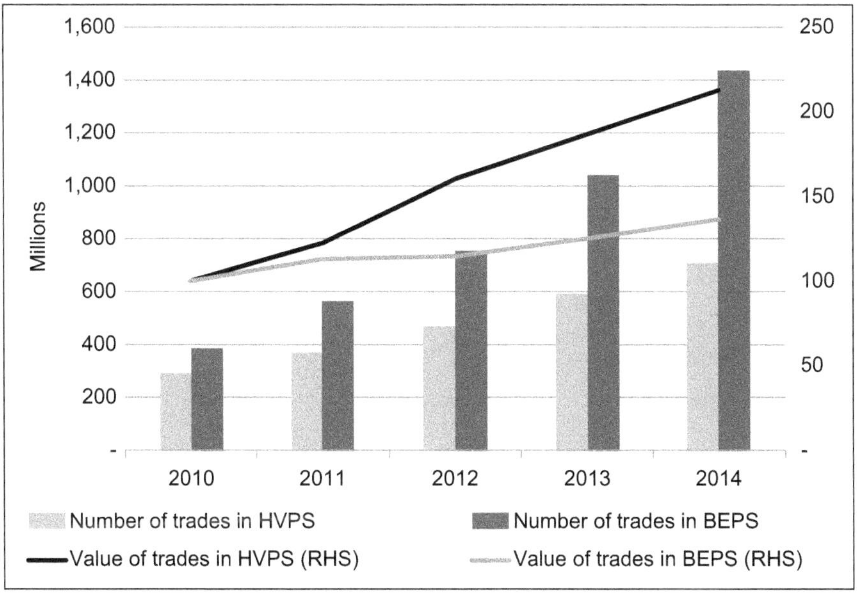

Key Stock Exchanges, Number and Value of Transactions, 2010-2014

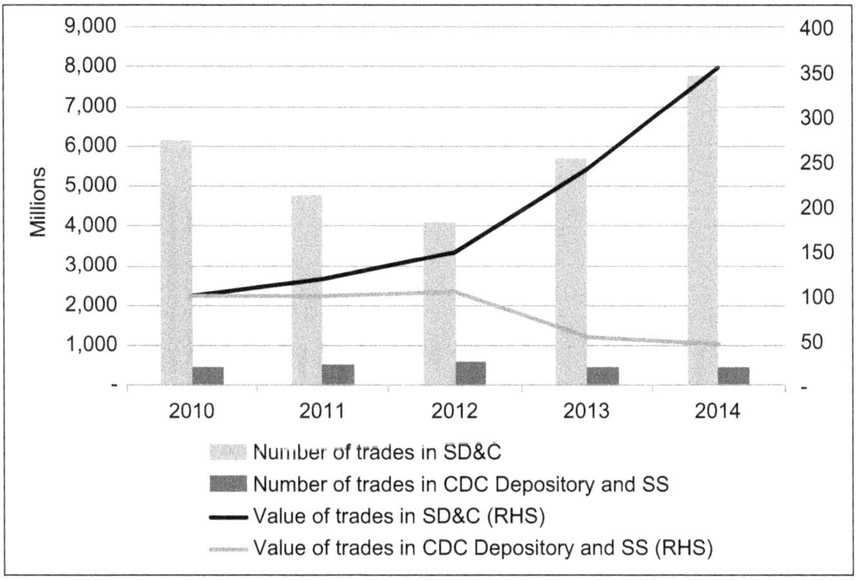

Figure 10.A1 Key Transactions Indicators

Source: CPMI, Statistics on payment, clearing and settlement systems in the CPMI countries, CSRC, People's Bank of China.

Key Stock Exchanges, Number and Value of Transactions, 2010-2014

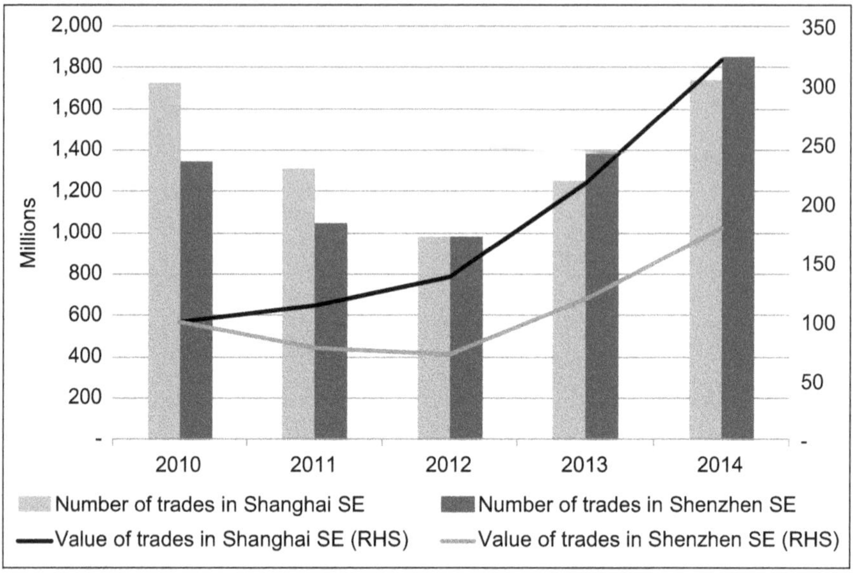

Turnover Derivatives Exchanges, Value of Transactions, 2013-2015

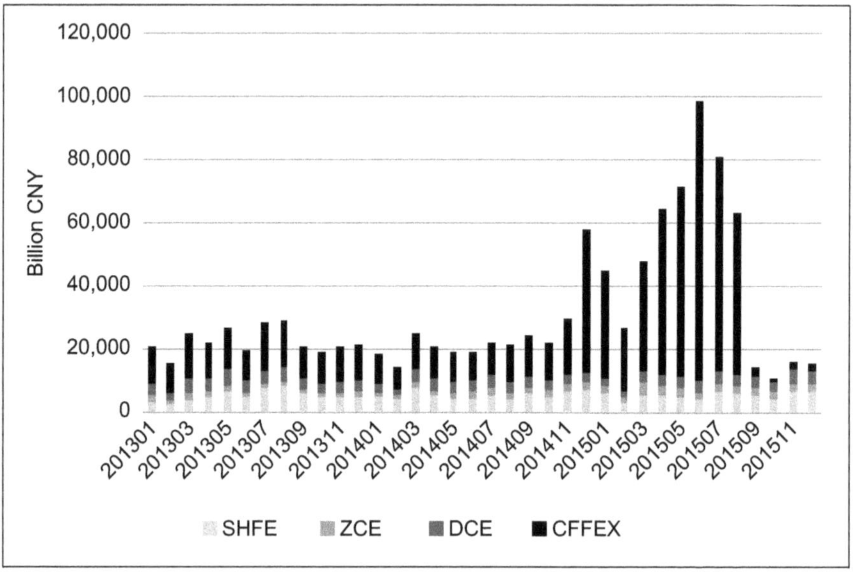

Figure 10.A1 (Continued)

APPENDIX IV

Systemic risk indicators domestic FMIs

	Daily settlement value 2015, billion RMB (percent of GDP)	*Nr. of members (November 2016)*	*Critical for other FMIs*	*Potential substitute*	*Type of markets served*	*Other critical functions*
			Main payment systems			
HVPS	11,761 (16 %)	305	CCDC, CSDC, CIS (indirect other FMIs)	One or more commercial banks	All interbank transactions	Monetary policy operations
CIPS	0.0 (0.0%)	28		One or more commercial banks	Interbank retail trades	
BEPS	68.67 (0.1%)	305	–	HVPS	Interbank retail trades	
CIS	1236.74 (1.6%)	2,170	–	BEPS	Interbank retail trades	
IBPS	76.57 (0.1%)	174	–	HVPS	Interbank retail trades	
FCPS	Few millions	51		One or more commercial banks	FX interbank trades	
China union Pay	136.13 (0.2%)	1639		One or more commercial banks	Card payments	
Clearing Center for City Commercial Banks	1.49 (0.0%)	100		One or more commercial banks	Corporate and retail transactions	

(*Continued*)

(Continued)

	Daily settlement value 2015, billion RMB (percent of GDP)	*Nr. of members (November 2016)*	*Critical for other FMIs*	*Potential substitute*	*Type of markets served*	*Other critical functions*
Rural Credit Banks Funds Clearing Center	9.94 (0.0%)	67		One or more commercial banks	Corporate and retail transactions	
			CSDs			
CCDC	3,509 (5.1%)	2,812	Collateral management for CCPs	SHCH	Interbank bond market	Monetary policy operations; collateral management
SHCH	326.06 (0.4%)	86	Same as CCDC	CCDC	Interbank bond market	Collateral management
CSDC	2067.65 (2.7%)	142	Same as CCDC	CCDC/ SHCH	Equity market	Collateral management
			CCPs			
CSDC	2067.65 (2.7%)	142	–	One of the other CCPs	Equity market	–
SHCH	167.41 (0.2%)	86			OTC derivatives, bond and FX markets.	
ZCE	122.71 (0.2%)	151	–	One of the other CCPs	Commodity derivatives	–
DCE	166.53 (0.2%)	164	–	One of the other CCPs	Commodity derivatives	–
SHFE	253.31 (0.3%)	202		One of the other CCPs	Financial and commodity derivatives	
CFFEX	1664.46 (2.2%)	147	–	One of the other CCPs	Financial derivatives	–

GLOSSARY

BEPS	Bulk Electronic Payment System
BCP	Business Continuity Planning
CBRC	China Banking Regulatory Commission
CCDC	China Central Depository & Clearing Corporation Limited
CCP	Central Counterparty
CFFEX	China Futures Exchange
CIPS	Cross-border Interbank Payment System
CIRC	China Insurance Regulatory Commission
CIS	Check Imaging System
CLS	Continuous Linked Settlement
CMG	Crisis Management Group
CNAPS	China National Advanced Payment System
CNCC	China National Clearing Centre
CNY	Chinese Yuan
CPMI	Committee on Payments and Market Infrastructures
CPSS	Committee on Payment and Settlement Systems
CRO	Chief Risk Officer
CSD	Central Securities Depository
CSDC	China Securities Depository and Clearing Corporation Limited
CSP	Critical Service Provider
CSRC	China Securities Regulatory Commission
DCE	Dalian Commodities Exchange
DVP	Delivery-versus-Payment
FCPS	Foreign Currency Payment System
FIFO	First-in-First-out
FMI	Financial Market Infrastructure
FSB	Financial Stability Board
FX	Foreign Exchange
HKSFC	Hong Kong Securities and Futures Commission
HVPS	High-Value Payment System
IBPS	Internet Banking Payment System
IOSCO	International Organization of Securities Commissions

IRS	Interest Rate Swap
IT	Information Technology
JMC	Joint Ministerial Committee for Financial Regulatory Coordination
LCH	London Clearing House
MOF	Ministry of Finance
MOU	Memorandum of Understanding
NPS	National Payment System
OMO	Open Market Operations
PBC	People's Bank of China
PFMI	CPSS-IOSCO Principles for Financial Market Infrastructures
PSD	Payment and Settlement Department
OTC	Over-the-Counter
RMC	Risk Management Committee
RTGS	Real Time Gross Settlement
SAFE	State Administration of Foreign Exchange
SHFE	Shanghai Futures Exchange
SHCH	Shanghai Clearing House
SIPS	Systemically Important Payment System
SSE	Shanghai Stock Exchange
SSS	Securities Settlement System
SZSE	Shenzhen Stock Exchange
ZCE	Zhengzhou Commodities Exchange

Notes

1 The Technical Note was prepared by Gynedi Srinivas, Senior Financial Sector Expert of the World Bank and Froukelien Wendt, Senior Financial Sector Expert from the IMF, for the 2017 China FSAP. Their analysis was based on information provided by the authorities, publicly available information, as well as discussions with the PBC, CSRC, CBRC, CCDC, CSDC, SHCH, SHFE, banks, and other financial institutions. Excellent research assistance was provided by David Jutrsa and Shaoyu Guo from the IMF Monetary and Capital Markets Department.

2 See Introduction to the CPSS-IOSCO Principles for Financial Market Infrastructures, April 2012. FMIs cover payment systems, securities settlement systems (SSS), central securities depositories (CSDs), central counterparties (CCPs) and trade repositories.

3 CNCC is a public entity in the PBC that operates the HVPS, IBPS, BEPS, FCPS, and the CIS.

4 See, for example, the US FSAP 2015, https://www.imf.org/external/pubs/cat/longres.aspx?sk=43057.0.

5 The number of 609 is a consolidated cleaned membership set, based on the top 200 members of the CCDC and all members of the other FMIs. The different members were consolidated at the highest level possible. Data is of September 30, 2016, except for HVPS and SHCH, for which the dates are December 31, 2016 and November 24, 2016, respectively.

6 The Securities Law Articles 120 requires that transactions conducted in line with the trading rules cannot be altered and Article 167 mentions netting. The drafting does not specify that this is unambiguously the case when a member defaults, not does it specify

the point after which a trade is final or irrevocable. There is no mentioning of the protection of netted positions against unwinding, following a member default.

7 A qualifying CCP is an entity that is licensed to operate as a CCP, and is permitted by the appropriate regulator/overseer to operate as such with respect to the products offered. This is subject to the provision that the CCP is based and prudentially supervised in a jurisdiction where the relevant regulator/overseer has established, and publicly indicated that it applies to the CCP on an ongoing basis, domestic rules and regulations that are consistent with the PFMI. As is the case more generally, banking supervisors still reserve the right to require banks in their jurisdictions to hold additional capital against their exposures to such CCPs via Pillar 2 (Basel Committee on Banking Supervision, Capital requirements for bank exposures to central counterparties, April 2014).

8 Issued in June 2016, http://www.bis.org/cpmi/publ/d146.htm.

9 Based on the CPSS Redbook China, 2012, and discussions held during the mission.

Lightning Source UK Ltd.
Milton Keynes UK
UKHW051812300922
409682UK00009B/12

9 781138 845367